Colloquial
Amharic

THE COLLOQUIAL SERIES
Series Adviser: Gary King

The following languages are available in the Colloquial series:

Afrikaans
Albanian
Amharic
Arabic (Levantine)
Arabic of Egypt
Arabic of the Gulf and
  Saudi Arabia
Basque
Breton
Bulgarian
Cambodian
Cantonese
Catalan
Chinese
Croatian
Czech
Danish
Dutch
English
Estonian
Filipino
Finnish

French
German
Greek
Gujarati
Hebrew
Hindi
Hungarian
Icelandic
Indonesian
Irish (forthcoming)
Italian
Japanese
Korean
Latvian
Lithuanian
Malay
Mongolian
Norwegian
Panjabi
Persian
Polish
Portuguese

Portuguese of Brazil
Romanian
Russian
Scottish Gaelic
Serbian
Slovak
Slovene
Somali
Spanish
Spanish of Latin
  America
Swahili
Swedish
Tamil
Thai
Turkish
Ukrainian
Urdu
Vietnamese
Welsh
Yoruba (forthcoming)

COLLOQUIAL 2s series: *The Next Step in Language Learning*

Chinese
Dutch
French

German (forthcoming)
Italian
Russian

Spanish
Spanish of Latin
  America

All these Colloquials are available in book & CD packs, or separately. You can order them through your bookseller or via our website www.routledge.com.

Colloquial
Amharic

The Complete Course for Beginners

David Appleyard

Routledge
Taylor & Francis Group

LONDON AND NEW YORK

First published in 1995 by Routledge
2 Park Square, Milton Park, Abingdon, Oxon, OX14 4RN

Simultaneously published in the USA and Canada
by Routledge
270 Madison Ave, New York, NY 10016

Reprinted 2000, 2001, 2003 (twice), 2006 (twice), 2007, 2008

*Routledge is an imprint of the Taylor & Francis Group,
an informa business*

Typeset in Times Ten by Florence Production Ltd, Stoodleigh, Devon

Printed and bound in Great Britain by
TJ International Ltd, Padstow, Cornwall

British Library Cataloguing in Publication Data
A catalogue record for this book is available from the
British Library

Library of Congress Cataloging in Publication Data
A catalog record for this book has been requested

ISBN 978-0-415-10003-8 (book)
ISBN 978-0-415-30134-3 (CD)
ISBN 978-0-415-44599-3 (pack)

Contents

Introduction

The aims and scope of this book

This book will provide you with an introduction to modern, colloquial Amharic. By the end of the course you should be able to carry on a reasonable conversation on most everyday topics, express yourself in writing and read simple Amharic. Amharic is a rich and often complex language, and to be able to pick up a novel, or even a magazine or newspaper article and read it without difficulty does take several years of intensive practice. After working through this book, though, you should have much of the necessary groundwork to make your way in the language. I should like to express my gratitude to Yalew Kebede for checking the Amharic dialogue and passages in this course and for his assistance in the recording of the accompanying cassettes.

In the last twenty years more and more foreigners have begun to learn Amharic. Nonetheless, Ethiopians are still enchanted when foreigners can speak even a little of their language. Amharas are intensely proud of their linguistic heritage, and rightly so. To these people to 'know Amharic' means far more than just being able to speak the language. In Addis Ababa you will find that many educated Ethiopians can speak some English, but an ability to speak even a modest amount of Amharic will open many doors to you amongst this courteous and hospitable people.

Each lesson contains one or more dialogues or texts for reading which are designed to introduce new grammar, new vocabulary and a new situation or context of language use. The accompanying exercises are intended for the practice of each of these aspects of the language-learning process. You should do all the exercises thoroughly and be confident that you have mastered the content of each lesson before you move on to the next one.

The Amharic language

Amharic is the official language of Ethiopia, spoken by 17.5 million people as a first language, and by 5 million more as a second language. Thanks to urbanization, the development of mass communications and a national education system, Amharic is understood almost throughout the whole country. There are, however, somewhere between seventy and ninety languages spoken within the political boundaries of Ethiopia and Eritrea, the greater number of which are spoken by only a few thousand people. Amharic may or may not have the largest number of speakers – the question is disputed and Ethiopian statistics are not always the most reliable. The fact remains, however, that Amharic has been the language of government and the ruling group in Ethiopia since the end of the thirteenth century. Only after the fall of Mengistu Haile Maryam's Marxist régime in May 1991 was the position of Amharic questioned. To date, however, no other Ethiopian language has been able to offer a serious challenge to the supremacy of Amharic, if only because no other language has had the experience of being used as the language of a modern state with all that that entails. Apart from Amharic, only Tigrinya has had any extensive history of being a language of literacy prior to the 1974 revolution. The process of bringing other Ethiopian languages into full literacy was begun under the Marxist government and will inevitably increase pace in years to come.

Despite its long history, Amharic really only became the written language of Ethiopia from the second half of the nineteenth century onwards, when Emperor Theodore [Tewodros] II actively encouraged its use in the government bureaucracy. Prior to that, though, there are some examples of written Amharic going back some six hundred years. The language of literacy in Ethiopia was Classical Ethiopic – also called Ge'ez – which remains the language of the Ethiopian Orthodox liturgy today, in much the same way as Latin was used until recently in the Roman Catholic Church. Since the end of the last century, Amharic has developed an extensive and sophisticated written literature, making it one of the largest, if not the largest vernacular literature in Sub-Saharan Africa.

Amharic belongs to the Semitic family of languages, the most well-known members of which are Arabic and Hebrew. Amharic is, however, very different from either of these and together with the other Semitic languages of Ethiopia, such as Tigrinya, forms a quite distinct branch within the family. Semitic languages have been spoken in Ethiopia for more than two thousand years and during that time have been much influenced by the other languages of the region with which they have come into contact.

The sounds of Amharic

The pronunciation of a language cannot really be satisfactorily described for the non-specialist learner in an introduction of this kind, other than to give the briefest of indications. In order to learn how Amharic is pronounced you need to hear it and practice speaking it as much as possible. For the student working on his or her own this can usually be best attained through the use of the accompanying cassettes. Listen to the language as much as possible, and do not be afraid of speaking it out aloud to yourself.

The following descriptions of the sounds of Amharic are only guidelines and should be read in accompaniment with the cassettes.

The vowels ◘◘

Amharic has seven vowels. In the transcription used in this book these are represented as follows: **ä, a, e, ï, i, o, u**. (To see how these are indicated in the Ethiopian script, see 'Script' below.)

ä is like the sound of the first 'a' in English 'again', or 'er' in 'bigger', or the sound of hesitation often written 'uh'. The sound of **ä** is very susceptible to the surrounding consonants. If it either follows or is followed by a **w** it has a slightly rounder sound, something like the sound of 'a' in English 'what'. Similarly, if it either follows or is followed by a **y** or follows any other of the so-called palatal consonants – **š, č, č', ž, j, ñ** – it sounds something like the 'e' in English 'yet'. If you have the cassettes listen to hear precisely how **ä** sounds in these different positions:

däm	blood	**t'äjj**	honey wine
nägä	tomorrow	**šäššä**	he ran away
wänd	male, man	**täwä**	he left
näw	he is	**yät**	where?

a is quite a different sound, like the English exclamation 'ah!', or the 'a' in 'father':

abbat	father	**laba**	feather

e is like the vowel in English 'gate' or 'way', but without the final 'y' sound. In fact, it often has a slight 'y' sound in front of it. Listen to the sound of the Amharic word **bet**, if you can. Some people pronounce this as if it were **byet**:

bet	house	**resa**	dead body

ï is a difficult sound to master at first as it has no exact English equivalent. It is sometimes like the 'y' in English 'pretty', or the second vowel in 'horses', but most of the time it is rather in between this and the sound of **ä**, described above.

Like **ä**, it is very susceptible to the consonants around it. When following or followed by a **w** it sounds more like 'u' in English 'put', or 'oo' in 'good'. Similarly, when following or followed by **y**, or following a palatal consonant it sounds more like the vowel 'i' in English 'pin'.

Again, if you have the cassettes listen to hear how **ï** sounds in different positions:

sïm	name	**bïrd**	cold
lïjj	child	**šïfta**	bandit
č'ïs	smoke	**wïč'č'**	outside
wïha	water	**yïlal**	he says

i is like the vowel 'ee' in English 'feet':

bič'č'a	yellow	**riz**	beard

o is rather like the vowel in English 'shore' or 'war', but often has a slight 'w' sound in front of it. Listen to the sound of the Amharic word **bota**, which some people pronounce as if it were **bwota**:

bota	place	**tolo**	quickly

u is like the vowel 'oo' in English 'moon':

ruz	rice	**hullu**	all

The consonants

Amharic has twenty-eight consonants, or rather twenty-seven full consonants plus one 'non-consonant'. In the transcription used in this book the following consonants have much the same sound as in English: **b, p, d, j, t, m, n, f, w, s** (as in 'sing'), **z, y** (as in 'yes'), **g** (as in 'go'), **k, h, l** (as in 'light'), **r** and **v** (this last sound occurs only in words borrowed from English, like **yunivärsiti**).

b is like English 'b' at the beginning of a word, or when following **m, n, r** or **l**, or when doubled, but elsewhere it has a softer sound that may sound a little like English 'v':

bal	husband	**abba**	daddy
arba	forty	**zïmb**	fly
rob	Wednesday	**abäba**	flower

h is like English 'h' except at the end of a word where some people pronounce it more strongly, like 'ch' in Scots 'loch':

hod	belly	**wïha**	water
yïh	this	**alläh**	you have

r is always sounded, as a flap or when doubled as a trill as in Scots English:

ruz	rice	**zär**	seed
bärr	door	**karra**	knife

A number of special letters are used in the transcription, but the sounds they represent are similar to English:

č is like 'ch' in English 'church'	**čalä**	he could	**mäče**	when?
š is like 'sh' in English 'shoe'	**šum**	chief	**wïšša**	dog
ž is like 's' in English 'leisure'	**žïrat**	tail	**gäži**	governor
ñ is like 'n' in English 'news',				
or 'gn' in 'cognac'	**näñ**	I am	**ïñña**	we

There is a set of sounds in Amharic which have no correspondents in English. These are the so-called 'glottalized', 'ejective' or 'explosive' consonants, each of which has a non-glottalized counterpart from amongst the consonants we have already looked at. These glottalized consonants cannot be easily or usefully described within the scope of this book, but suffice it to say they have a sharper, more 'explosive' sound than their non-glottalized pairs. You really need, however, to hear them spoken by a native speaker to be able to reproduce them accurately. It is important to distinguish between glottalized and non-glottalized sounds as there are many pairs of words that are differentiated in this way:

t – t'	**tära**	turn, queue	**t'ärra**	he called
	mätta	he hit	**mät't'a**	he came
č – č'	**näčč**	she is	**näč'č'**	white
k – k'	**käbbärä**	he got rich	**k'äbbärä**	he buried
	näkka	he touched	**näk'k'a**	he woke up

In the transcription used in this book the glottalized sounds are all written with an apostrophe:

t' a glottalized t	t'ïru	good	t'ot'a	monkey
k' a glottalized k	k'än	day	k'wank'wa	language
p' a glottalized p	p'ap'p'as	bishop	ityop'p'ïya	Ethiopia
č' a glottalized č	č'äw	salt	bič'č'a	yellow
s' a glottalized s	s'afä	he wrote	gäs'	page

The remaining member of the inventory of consonants in Amharic is not really a consonant at all, but marks a syllable which begins with a vowel without a preceding consonant. We need to regard this as a sort of consonant because it is indicated in the script as such, where it actually has two different symbols. Some speakers may pronounce a full break or 'glottal stop' between two vowels separated in this way, though others slide from one vowel to the other without a noticeable pause.

säat	hour, watch	bïïr	pen
ïgziabïher	God	t'aot	idol
aïmïro	intelligence, conscience	lik'ä mälaïkt	archangel

Double consonants

Double or long consonants (also called 'geminate' consonants) are clearly pronounced: the ll in allä 'there is' is distinctly longer than the l in alä 'he said'. It is vitally important to distinguish single from double consonants in pronunciation as the length of a consonant may often affect the meaning of a word, as in the above example. Compare also the following pairs of words:

wana	swimming	wanna	main, principal
gäna	yet	gänna	Christmas
bälu!	say!	bällu	they ate
abay	liar	abbay	Blue Nile

Script

Amharic is written in a script of its own which is used only in Ethiopia. The same script is also used for writing both Classical Ethiopic (also called Ge'ez), the language of Ancient Ethiopia, still used today in the liturgy of the Ethiopian Orthodox Church, and

Tigrinya, a language closely related to Amharic, spoken in Eritrea and northern Ethiopia. Under the previous regime, there was an initiative to write other Ethiopian languages, too, in the same script. At present, however, there is a move to develop orthographies based on the Roman alphabet for some of the other major Ethiopian languages, such as Oromo.

The Ethiopian script is called in Amharic **fidäl**, which is also the word for 'letter'. It may look at first sight a very complex system, but with practice you will soon get used to it. If you want to read anything in Amharic, as well as write the language yourself, you will need to know it. Read through the following pages first but do not try and learn everything about the script before you start the first lesson. All dialogues are transcribed in the first five lessons, as are all new vocabulary and grammatical forms throughout the book. You should practise writing and reading in Amharic right from the start, but it should become fun trying to recognize familiar words written in **fidäl**. Amharas and Tigreans are very proud of their script as an expression of the historical and cultural independence of Ethiopian civilization.

The Ethiopian script is not strictly speaking an alphabet, but what is called a syllabary. This means that each letter or symbol usually represents a whole syllable like **da** or **du, ki** or **no**. So, if you want to write the Amharic word **bota**, which means 'place', you will need only two letters **bo + ta** and not four as in the English transcription: so ቦታ. In current use there are 276 such letters. But don't let this put you off. There are regular patterns in the system and you won't have to learn 276 completely different shapes.

There are thirty-three basic shapes. These generally represent the consonants followed by the vowel **ä**; so taking the word **bota** ቦታ again, in its basic shape the first letter becomes በ with the sound **bä**, and the second letter becomes ተ with the sound **tä**. These basic shapes are altered in various ways, for example, by the addition of small lines or circles, or by the shortening or lengthening of a stroke, to indicate a different vowel following the base consonant. To make **bo** the right-hand vertical is shortened: ቦ; but to make **ba**, the left-hand vertical is shortened: ባ; and to make **bi** a short line is added to the foot of the right-hand vertical: ቢ, and so on. Similarly, to turn ተ **tä** into **ta**, a leftward curve is added to the base of the letter: ታ; but to make **to** a small circle is added at the top: ቶ, and so on. As there are seven vowels in Amharic, so there are six modifications of the basic shape making what are called the seven 'orders' of the Ethiopian syllabary which are in the traditional sequence, **bä, bu, bi, ba, be, bï** and **bo**.

Not all Amharic words, however, are made of open syllables like **bota**. There are words with closed syllables, ending in a consonant or sometimes two, like **bet, k'än, hod, arb** and **mändär**. How do we write these? The sixth order, the one which indicates the vowel ï, also indicates a consonant without a vowel: so ብ, for example, is both **bï** and **b**, as in **bïrr** ብር 'Birr (Ethiopia dollar)' and **arb** ኣርብ 'Friday'. We shall look in more detail at the sixth order in the first lesson.

You will remember that we have already said that there are twenty-seven consonants in Amharic, but thirty-three consonant baseshapes in the syllabary. This is because some consonants can be represented by more than one letter: so, **s** has two representations, as do **s'** and the non-consonant base, whilst **h** has as many as four possibilities. The reasons for this are historical and whilst some people, for instance, may write **s** in one word with one letter and **s** in another word with a different letter, it cannot be said that there are exact spelling rules as in English, there are merely preferences. When you meet a new word see how it is spelled and you won't go wrong if you keep to that spelling.

The first order

Let's have a look now at the first order, the basic shapes of the letters which indicate a consonant followed by the vowel ä. We can divide the first order letters into five groups according to shape.

(a) letters with one vertical or 'leg':

k'ä	tä	čä	pä	gä	nä
ቀ	ተ	ቸ	ፐ	ገ	ነ

ñä	yä	ha
ኘ	የ	ኀ

(b) letters with two verticals or 'legs':

bä	vä	sä	šä	kä	hä	zä	žä
በ	ቨ	ሰ	ሸ	ከ	ኸ	ዘ	ዠ

s'ä	p'ä	dä	jä	lä	a
ጸ	ጰ	ደ	ጀ	ለ	አ

(c) letters with three verticals or 'legs':

t'ä	č'ä	ha
ጠ	ጨ	ሐ

(d) letters with a rounded bottom:

s'ä	mä	sä	wä	ha	a
θ	መ	ሡ	ወ	ሀ	ዐ

(e) letters with a level bottom:

rä	fä
ረ	ፈ

There are a couple of things you may notice here. First, you can see that both ሠ and ወ are pronounced the same, i.e. sä, and both ዐ and θ are pronounced as s'ä. Similarly, both ሀ and ዐ have the sound a, the 'non-consonant' plus the vowel a, whilst ሀ, ሐ and ኀ are all three pronounced as ha; ኸ, on the other hand, is pronounced hä. Second, these last six letters also illustrate another point that you may have noticed. The first-order letters ሀ, ዐ, ሀ, ሐ and ኀ are all read as if they had fourth a, not first ä order vowels, whilst ኸ is the only way of writing the sound hä. If you want to write the sound ä alone there is a special letter ኸ, but this occurs in only one word in Amharic: ärä ኸረ, which means 'Oh dear!'.

The second order

The formation of the second order, which indicates the base consonant followed by the vowel u, is very simple. You simply add a short horizontal line to the middle of the right-hand side of the basic letter shape, except for ru and fu which add a short vertical line beneath the base line:

k'u	tu	ču	pu	gu	nu	ñu	yu	hu
ቁ	ቱ	ጙ	ፓ	ጉ	ኑ	ኙ	ዩ	ኁ

bu	vu	su	šu	ku	zu	žu	s'u	p'u	du
ቡ	ቩ	ሱ	ሹ	ኩ	ዙ	ዡ	ጹ	ጱ	ዱ

ju	lu	u	hu
ጁ	ሉ	ኡ	ኍ

t'u	č'u	hu
ጡ	ጩ	ሑ

s'u	mu	su	wu	hu	u
ፁ	ሙ	ሡ	ዉ	ሁ	ዑ

ru	fu
ሩ	ፉ

The third order

The third order, which indicates the base consonant followed by the vowel **i** is mostly formed by adding a short horizontal line to the bottom of the right-hand side of the letter. If the basic first order shape is one of those with one, two or three 'legs' then the sign for the third order is added directly. If, however, the basic shape has a rounded bottom then an extra 'leg' is added to the letter to carry the sign of the third order. Notice that **ri** and **fi** are formed differently, as is **yi** which doesn't follow the expected pattern!

k'i	ti	či	pi	gi	ni	ñi	hi
ቂ	ቲ	ቼ	ፒ	ጊ	ኒ	ኚ	ሒ

bi	vi	si	ši	ki	zi	ži	s'i	p'i	di
ቢ	ቪ	ሲ	ሺ	ኪ	ዚ	ዢ	ጺ	ጲ	ዲ

ji	li	i	hi
ጂ	ሊ	እ	ኺ

t'i	č'i	hi
ጢ	ጪ	ሕ

s'i	mi	si	wi	hi	i
ጼ	ሚ	ሢ	ዊ	ሂ	ኢ

ri	fi
ሪ	ፊ

yi
ዪ

The fourth order

The fourth order, which indicates the base consonant followed by the vowel **a**, is formed in a number of ways depending on the shape of the basic first order letter.

Most of the letters with one 'leg' make the fourth order by adding a leftwards curving line to the bottom of the single 'leg'. Notice, though, that **na** and **ña** are different.

k'a	ta	ča	pa	ga	ya	ha
ቃ	ታ	ቻ	ፓ	ጋ	ያ	ሃ

na	ña
ና	ኛ

The letters with two and three 'legs' shorten the left-hand 'leg' or 'legs':

ba	va	sa	ša	ka	za	ža	s'a	p'a	da
ጠ	ቨ	ሰ	ሸ	ከ	ዘ	ዠ	ጸ	ጰ	ዳ

ja	la	a	ha
ጀ	ለ	ኀ	ኸ

t'a	č'a	ha
ጠ	ጨ	ሐ

The letters with rounded bottoms add an extra 'leg', as they do to form the third order, but without adding the short horizontal line, and **ra** and **fa** are different as usual:

s'a	ma	sa	wa	ha	a
ፀ	ማ	ሠ	ዋ	ሃ	ዓ

ra	fa
ራ	ፋ

The fifth order

The fifth order, which indicates the base consonant followed by the vowel **e**, is also easily formed. It is marked by a small loop or semicircle attached to the bottom of the base shape in the same way as the short horizontal line is added to form the third order. This means that letters with rounded bottoms will need to add an extra 'leg' to carry the sign. Be careful, though, to note that **č'e** and **ye**, though indicated by a small loop, differ in how the loop is attached!

k'e	te	če	pe	ge	ne	ñe	he
ቄ	ቴ	ቼ	ቴ	ጌ	ኔ	ኜ	ኄ

be	ve	se	še	ke	ze	že	s'e	p'e	de
ቤ	ቬ	ሴ	ሼ	ኬ	ዜ	ዤ	ጼ	ጴ	ዴ

je	le	e	he
ጄ	ሌ	ኤ	ኼ

t'e	he
ጤ	ሔ

s'e	me	se	we	he	e
ፄ	ሜ	ሤ	ዌ	ሄ	ዔ

re	fe
ሬ	ፈ

č'e	ye
ጬ	ዬ

The sixth order

The sixth order, indicating both the consonant plus the vowel ï and the consonant alone, is very diverse in the way it is formed. Have a look at the forms of the sixth order in the chart at the end of the introduction and see how many different patterns of formation you can identify. Because of the complexity of these patterns, however, we shall leave a fuller analysis until the first lesson.

The seventh order

The seventh order, which indicates the consonant followed by the vowel **o**, has three different characteristic patterns of formation and a small number of isolated forms. Most of the letters with a single 'leg' add a small circle at the top of the letter, but note that **yo**, **go** and **po** are formed quite differently:

k'o	to	čo	no	ño	ho
ቆ	ቶ	ፎ	ኖ	ኞ	ሖ

yo	go	po
ዮ	ጎ	ፖ

The letters with two and three 'legs' mostly shorten the right-hand 'leg' or 'legs' to form the seventh order, i.e. making a mirror image of the fourth order. Note, however, that **lo** is formed by adding a small circle to the right-hand side of the base shape.

bo	vo	so	šo	ko	zo	žo	s'o	p'o	do
ቦ	ቮ	ሶ	ሾ	ኮ	ዞ	ዦ	ጾ	ጶ	ዶ

jo	o	ho	t'o	č'o	ho
ጆ	ኦ	ሆ	ጦ	ጮ	ሖ

lo
ሎ

Of the letters with rounded bottoms four form the seventh order by adding a short leftward curving line to the centre of the bottom of the base shape. Note that **ho** and **mo** are formed differently:

s'o   so   wo   o
ይ   ሦ   ሞ   የ

ho   mo
ሆ   ሞ

Lastly, **ro** and **fo** form their seventh orders by adding a small circle to the top right-hand corner of the letter:

ro   fo
ሮ   ፎ

1 Now see how much of the following you can read (there are answers given in the key to the exercises)

ገም ጋም ማሞ ሚደ ሚጻ ሙይ መራ ማሩ ራራ ሃር ሠራ
ሲሶ ሃራ ሠዋ ዋዌ ጨዋ ጋሪ ጋራ ጋር ፉር ፉራ ገታ
ጌታ ጋት ነገ ነጋ ጤና ወኚ ዋሻ ጌጠ ተኛ ተራ ቱታ
ዋዜማ ዓላማ ዓሳማ ሙክራ ቢላዋ ጉማሪ ሠላሳ ሒሳቡ
ሑጻዴ አበሹ ጉጻዮ

Further vowel signs

In addition to the seven vowel orders, there are special symbols to represent the combination of certain consonants followed by **wa**, as for example in the word **k'wank'wa** 'language' which is usually written as ቋንቋ, i.e. **k'wa + n + k'wa**. The **wa** letters are formed by the addition of a horizontal bar added either to the top or the bottom of the consonant base, which is often in a shape similar to the fourth order. The letters that occur are as follows. Note that there are some variants:

k'wa	twa	čwa	gwa	nwa	ñwa	hwa	bwa	swa	šwa	kwa
ቋ	ቷ	ቿ	ጓ	ኗ/ኗ	ኟ/ኟ	ኋ	ቧ	ሷ	ሿ	ኳ

zwa	žwa	s'wa	dwa	jwa	lwa	t'wa	č'wa	mwa	rwa	fwa
ዟ	ዧ	ጿ	ዷ	ጇ	ሏ	ጧ	ጯ	ሟ	ሯ/ሯ	ፏ

In addition to these the four letters **k'**, **k**, **g** and **h** also have special symbols for combinations with **w** and other vowels:

k'wä	k'wi	k'we	k'wï		kwä	kwi	kwe	kwï
ቈ	ቊ	ቌ	ቍ		ኰ	ኲ	ኴ	ኵ

gwä	gwi	gwe	gwï		hwä	hwi	hwe	hwï
ጐ	ጒ	ጔ	ጕ		ኈ	ኊ	ኌ	ኍ

All but the wä and wï forms are not really used in Amharic.

Numerical signs

Amharic also has its own symbols for numbers. You will meet these again in the book when we look at counting in Amharic. Nowadays European numerical signs, the so-called 'Arabic' numerals such as we use in English, are also used, but you will still need to learn the indigenous Ethiopian system as well.

There are separate symbols for each of the units, each of the tens, '100' and '10,000':

1 ፩ 2 ፪ 3 ፫ 4 ፬ 5 ፭ 6 ፮ 7 ፯ 8 ፰ 9 ፱ 10 ፲ 20 ፳ 30 ፴
40 ፵ 50 ፶ 60 ፷ 70 ፸ 80 ፹ 90 ፺ 100 ፻ 10,000 ፼

Fidäl ፊደል 🔲

The Amharic syllabary is usually presented as a grid with the vowel orders as the horizontal and the consonants as the vertical axis. There are two traditional sequences, one called **ha-hu** ሀሁ, and the other **abugida** አቡጊዳ, following the sounds of the first letters reading along the horizontal axis. Both of these are used in dictionaries published in Ethiopia, though the first one, the ሀሁ, is the most common. It is also the sequence that is used, with some adaptation, in dictionaries published abroad.

1st order		2nd order		3rd order		4th order		5th order		6th order		7th order	
υ	ha	ሁ	hu	ሂ	hi	ሃ	hə	ሄ	he	υ	hï	ሆ	ho
ለ	lä	ሉ	lu	ሊ	li	ላ	la	ሌ	le	ል	lï	ሎ	lo
ሐ	ha	ሑ	hu	ሒ	hi	ሓ	ha	ሔ	he	ሕ	hï	ሖ	ho
መ	mä	ሙ	mu	ሚ	mi	ማ	ma	ሜ	me	ም	mï	ሞ	mo
ሠ	sä	ሡ	su	ሢ	si	ሣ	sa	ሤ	se	ሥ	sï	ሦ	so
ረ	rä	ሩ	ru	ሪ	ri	ራ	ra	ሬ	re	ር	rï	ሮ	ro
ሰ	sä	ሱ	su	ሲ	si	ሳ	sa	ሴ	se	ስ	sï	ሶ	so
ሸ	šä	ሹ	šu	ሺ	ši	ሻ	ša	ሼ	še	ሽ	ši	ሾ	šo
ቀ	k'ä	ቁ	k'u	ቂ	k'i	ቃ	k'a	ቄ	k'e	ቅ	k'ï	ቆ	k'o
በ	bä	ቡ	bu	ቢ	bi	ባ	ba	ቤ	be	ብ	bï	ቦ	bo
ተ	tä	ቱ	tu	ቲ	ti	ታ	ta	ቴ	te	ት	tï	ቶ	to
ቸ	čä	ቹ	ču	ቺ	či	ቻ	ča	ቼ	če	ች	či	ቾ	čo
ኀ	ha	ኁ	hu	ኂ	hi	ኃ	ha	ኄ	he	ኅ	hï	ኆ	ho

1st order		2nd order		3rd order		4th order		5th order		6th order		7th order	
ነ	nä	ኑ	nu	ኒ	ni	ና	na	ን	ne	ን	nï	ኖ	no
ኘ	ñä	ኙ	ñu	ኚ	ñi	ኛ	ña	ኜ	ñe	ኝ	ñï	ኞ	ño
አ	a	ኡ	u	ኢ	i	ኣ	a	ኤ	e	እ	ï	ኦ	o
ከ	kä	ኩ	ku	ኪ	ki	ካ	ka	ኬ	ke	ክ	kï	ኮ	ko
ኸ	hä	ኹ	hu	ኺ	hi	ኻ	ha	ኼ	he	ኽ	hï	ኾ	ho
ወ	wä	ዉ	wu	ዊ	wi	ዋ	wa	ዌ	we	ው	wï	ዎ	wo
ዐ	a	ዑ	u	ዒ	i	ዓ	a	ዔ	e	ዕ	ï	ዖ	o
ዘ	zä	ዙ	zu	ዚ	zi	ዛ	za	ዜ	ze	ዝ	zï	ዞ	zo
ዠ	žä	ዡ	žu	ዢ	ži	ዣ	ža	ዤ	že	ዥ	žï	ዦ	žo
የ	yä	ዩ	yu	ዪ	yi	ያ	ya	ዬ	ye	ይ	yï	ዮ	yo
ደ	dä	ዱ	du	ዲ	di	ዳ	da	ዴ	de	ድ	dï	ዶ	do
ጀ	jä	ጁ	ju	ጂ	ji	ጃ	ja	ጄ	je	ጅ	jï	ጆ	jo
ገ	gä	ጉ	gu	ጊ	gi	ጋ	ga	ጌ	ge	ግ	gï	ጎ	go
ጠ	t'ä	ጡ	t'u	ጢ	t'i	ጣ	t'a	ጤ	t'e	ጥ	t'ï	ጦ	t'o
ጨ	č'ä	ጩ	č'u	ጪ	č'i	ጫ	č'a	ጬ	č'e	ጭ	č'ï	ጮ	č'o
ጰ	p'ä	ጱ	p'u	ጲ	p'i	ጳ	p'a	ጴ	p'e	ጵ	p'ï	ጶ	p'o
ጸ	s'ä	ጹ	s'u	ጺ	s'i	ጻ	s'a	ጼ	s'e	ጽ	s'ï	ጾ	s'o
ፀ	s'ä	ፁ	s'u	ፂ	s'i	ፃ	s'a	ፄ	s'e	ፅ	s'ï	ፆ	s'o
ፈ	fä	ፉ	fu	ፊ	fi	ፋ	fa	ፌ	fe	ፍ	fï	ፎ	fo
ፐ	pä	ፑ	pu	ፒ	pi	ፓ	pa	ፔ	pe	ፕ	pï	ፖ	po

The wa letters

k'wa twa čwa gwa nwa ñwa hwa bwa swa šwa kwa
ቈ ቷ ጯ ጓ ኋ/ኗ ኟ/ኟ ኋ ቧ ሷ ሿ ኳ

zwa žwa s'wa dwa jwa lwa t'wa č'wa mwa rwa fwa
ዟ ዧ ጿ ዷ ጇ ሏ ጧ ጯ ሟ ሯ/ፚ ፏ

The other w letters or 'labiovelars'

1st order		3rd order		5th order		6th order	
ቈ	k'wä	ቊ	k'wi	ቌ	k'we	ቅ	k'wï
ኰ	kwä	ኲ	kwi	ኴ	kwe	ኵ	kwï
ጐ	gwä	ጒ	gwi	ጔ	gwe	ጕ	gwï
ኈ	hwä	ኊ	hwi	ኌ	hwe	ኍ	hwï

1 ሰላምታ sälamta

Greetings

By the end of this lesson you should be able to:

- use some personal pronouns (I, you, etc.)
- form the present tense of the verb 'be'(I am, you are, etc.)
- form some simple possessive phrases (my, your, etc.)
- use some simple formal and informal greetings

An informal meeting

Hirut and Kebbede are old friends who meet by chance in the street

ከበደ   ጤና ይስጥልኝ ሂሩት። እንደምን ነሽ? ደኅና ነሽ?
ሂሩት   ጤና ይስጥልኝ ከበደ። አዎ ደኅና ነኝ። አንተስ እንደምን ነህ?
ከበደ   እኔም ደኅና ነኝ እግዚር ይመስገን።
ሂሩት   ኃይሉ ደኅና ነው?
ከበደ   አዎ እሱም ደኅና ነው።
ሂሩት   አባትና እናትህ ደኅና ናቸው?
ከበደ   አዎ ደኅና ናቸው።
ሂሩት   በል አሁን መሄድ አለብኝ። ደኅና ሁን።
ከበደ   ደኅና ሁኚ ሂሩት።

KÄBBÄDÄ: t'ena yïst'ïllïñ Hirut. ïndämïn näš? dähna näš?
HIRUT: t'ena yïst'ïllïñ Käbbädä. awo, dähna näñ. antäss, ïndämïn näh?
KÄBBÄDÄ: ïnem dähna näñ, ïgzer yïmmäsgän.
HIRUT: Haylu dähna näw?
KÄBBÄDÄ: awo, ïssum dähna näw.
HIRUT: abbatïnna ïnnatïh dähna naččäw?
KÄBBÄDÄ: awo, dähna naččäw.
HIRUT: bäl ahun mähed alläbbïñ. dähna hun.
KÄBBÄDÄ: dähna huñi, Hirut.

KEBBEDE:	*Hello, Hirut. How are you? Are you well?*
HIRUT:	*Hello, Käbbädä. Yes, I'm well. And you, are you well?*
KEBBEDE:	*I'm fine, too, thanks.*
HIRUT:	*Is Haylu well?*
KEBBEDE:	*Yes, he's fine, too.*
HIRUT:	*Are your father and mother well?*
KEBBEDE:	*Yes, they're well.*
HIRUT:	*Well, I've got to go. Goodbye.*
KEBBEDE:	*Goodbye, Hirut.*

Vocabulary

ጤና ይስጥልኝ	t'ena yïst'ïlliñ	hello! (*lit.* 'may he [God] give [you] good health for my sake!')
እንዴምን	ïndämïn	how
ደኅና	dähna	well, fine
አዎ	awo	yes
-ስ	-(ï)ss	how about . . . (*added to the end of the word*)
-ም	-(ï)mm	also, too (*added to the end of the word*)
አግዚር ይመስገን	ïgzer yïmmäsgän	thank you (*lit.* 'may God be praised!')
አባት	abbat	father
እናት	ïnnat	mother
-ና	-(ï)nna	and . . . (*added to the end of the first word:* አባትና እናት *abbatïnna ïnnat* father and mother)
አባትና እናትህ	abbatïnna ïnnatïh	your father and mother
በል አሁን	bäl ahun	well then, well now
መሄድ አለብኝ	mähed alläbbiñ	I have to go (*lit.* 'it is on me to go')

Some personal pronouns

እኔ	ïne	I
አንተ	antä	you (masculine and informal)
እሱ	ïssu	he

The verb 'to be'

The present tense

ነኝ	näñ	I am
ነህ	näh	you are (masculine and informal)
ነሽ	näš	you are (feminine and informal)
ነው·	näw	he is
ናቸው·	naččäw	they are

The imperative

ሁን	hun	be! (masculine and informal)
ሁኝ/ሁኚ	huñ/huñi	be! (feminine and informal)

A formal meeting 📼

Mr Mulugeta and Mrs Hiywet meet. They do not know one another very well

ወይዘር ሕይወት:	ጤና ይስጥልኝ አቶ ሙሉጌታ። እንደምን አደሩ? ደኅና ነዎት?
አቶ ሙሉጌታ:	ደኅና ነኝ። ወይዘር ሕይወት። እግዚር ይመስገን። እርስዎስ እንደምን ነዎት? ደኅና ነዎት?
ወይዘር ሕይወት:	አዎ ደኅና ነኝ። የርስዎ ሚስት እንደምን ናቸው?
አቶ ሙሉጌታ:	የኔ ሚስት ደኅና ነች። እግዚር ይመስገን። እኛ ሁላታችንም ደኅና ነን።
ወይዘር ሕይወት:	እሺ፡ ደኅና ይዋሉ።
አቶ ሙሉጌታ:	ደኅና ይዋሉ።

Wäyzäro Hïywät:	t'ena yïst'ïllïñ Ato Mulugeta. ïndämïn addäru? dähna näwot?
Ato Mulugeta:	dähna näñ, Wäyzäro Hïywät. ïgzer yïmmäsgän. ïrswoss, ïndämïn näwot? dähna näwot?
Wäyzäro Hïywät:	awo dähna näñ. yärswo mist ïndämïn näččäw?
Ato Mulugeta:	yäne mist dähna näčč. ïgzer yïmmäsgän. ïñña hulättaččïnïm dähna nän.
Wäyzäro Hïywät:	ïšši, dähna yïwalu.
Ato Mulugeta:	dähna yïwalu.

Mrs Hiywet:	*Hello, Mr Mulugeta! How are you?*
Mr Mulugeta:	*I am well, thank you. And you, Mrs Hiywet,*
	how are you? Are you well?
Mrs Hiywet:	*Yes, I am well. How is your wife?*
Mr Mulugeta:	*My wife is well, thank you. We are both well.*
Mrs Hiywet:	*Goodbye.*
Mr Mulugeta:	*Goodbye.*

Vocabulary

አቶ	ato	Mr
ወይዘር	wäyzäro	Mrs
እንደምን አደሩ	indämin addäru	good morning (*lit.* how did you spend the night?)
ሚስት	mist	wife
ሁለታችንም	hulättaččïnïm	both of us (*lit.* our two)
እሺ	iśśi	OK, alright
ደኅና ይዋሉ	dähna yïwalu	goodbye (*lit.* spend the day well!)

More parts of the verb 'to be'

ነዎት	näwot	you are (formal or polite)
ናቸው	naččäw	he/she is, they are (formal or polite)
ነች	näčč	she is
ነን	nän	we are

More personal pronouns

እርስዎ	ïrswo	you (formal or polite)
የርስዎ	yärswo	your (formal and polite)
የኔ	yäne	my
እኛ	ïñña	we

Grammar

'You', 'he', 'she' and 'they': informal v. formal

From the dialogues you can see that there are various ways of expressing 'you' and 'he' or 'she', and the accompanying verb, according to whether you are being informal or formal. This is what is known as the register of the language used.

In the informal register, which you use when talking to someone whom you either know well and are close to, or with someone of lower status than yourself such as a child or a servant, you also have to distinguish whether the person(s) you are talking to is (are) a man, ነህ näh 'you are' (masculine and informal), a woman, ነሽ näš 'you are' (feminine and informal), or several people, men or women, ናችሁ naččuh 'you are' (plural and informal).

> Note that ናችሁ, though written as **'naččihu'** is pronounced as **naččuh**. This goes for the ending **-aččihu** at the ends of other words too. See if you can find any more in this lesson.

In the formal or polite register, which you use when talking to someone you are not familiar with or who is of higher status than yourself, you do not need to make any further distinction, ነዎት näwot 'you are' (formal or polite). In Amharic, you also need to distinguish informal from formal when you are talking about someone, ነው näw 'he is' (general or informal), ነች näčč 'she is' (general or informal), ናቸው naččäw 'they are' (general or informal), but note ናቸው naččäw which is also 'he is, she is, they are' (formal or polite).

Greetings

In the first two dialogues you have encountered various kinds of greetings: ጤና ይስጥልኝ t'ena yïst'ïllïñ 'hello!', and also እንዳምን ነህ/ነሽ/ነዎት indämïn näh/näš/näwot, as well as እንዳምን አደሩ indämïn addäru.

The first and second set can be used on all occasions. The second kind of expression relates to the time of day when the greeting is expressed: እንዳምን አደሩ indämïn addäru implies meeting in the daytime after at least one night's absence.

If you meet someone in the evening you would say እንዳምን ዋሉ indämïn walu, *lit.* 'How have you spent the day?' The phrase ደህና ይዋሉ dähna yïwalu, which you met in the second dialogue, contains a different part of the same verb.

Both of the expressions እንዳምን አደሩ indämïn addäru and እንዳምን ዋሉ indämïn walu are in the formal or polite register; for the equivalent informal versions you would have to substitute the following: አደርክ addärk (masculine), አደርሽ addärš (feminine), አደራችሁ addäraččuh (plural), or ዋልክ walk (masculine), ዋልሽ walš (feminine), ዋላችሁ walaččuh (plural). Note the pronunciation of አደራችሁ and ዋላችሁ!, if you have the cassettes.

	Daytime greeting		Evening greeting	
እንደምን... indämin ...				
masc. familiar	አደርክ	...addärk	ዋልክ	...walk
fem. familiar	አደርሽ	...addärš	ዋልሽ	...walš
pl. familiar	አደራችሁ	...addäraččuh	ዋላችሁ	...walaččuh
pol.	አደሩ	...addäru	ዋሉ	...walu

We will look at the forms of these verbs in more detail in the third lesson.

Personal pronouns and 'to be'

In the dialogues, then, you have met the following forms of the verb 'to be': ነኝ näñ 'I am', ነህ näh 'you are (masculine and informal)', ነሽ näš 'you are (feminine and informal)', ነው näw 'he is', ነች näčč 'she is', ነን nän 'we are', ነዎት näwot 'you are (formal or polite) and ናቸው naččäw 'they are'.

In Amharic, verbs are traditionally cited in the 'he...' (third person masculine) form. The full set of forms of ነው 'to be', which occurs only in the present tense, is therefore as follows:

ነኝ		näñ	I am
ነህ		näh	you are (masc. and informal)
ነሽ		näš	you are (fem. and informal)
ነው		näw	he is
ነች	or ናት	näčč or nat	she is
ነን		nän	we are
ናችሁ		naččuh	you are (pl. and inf.)
ናቸው		naččäw	they are
ነዎ	or ነዎት	näwo or näwot	you are (for. or pol.)
ናቸው		naččäw	he/she is, they are (for. or pol.)

The base is **ነ-** nä- to which are added the following endings marking the person of the subject. Remember these endings because you will encounter them later, though used in a different way, for instance, recall the phrases **ጤና ይስጥልኝ** t'ena yïst'ïllïñ 'hello!' (*lit.* 'may God give you health for me') and **መሄድ አለብኝ** mähed alläbbïñ 'I have to go' (*lit.* 'it is on me to go') from the first dialogue where **-ኝ** -ñ is equivalent to 'me'.

singular		*plural*	
-ñ	I	-n	we
-h	you (masc. and inf.)	-ačč̣uh	you (pl. and inf.)
-š	you (fem. and inf.)		
-w	he	-ač̣čäw	they
-äčč̣ or -at	she		
formal			
-wo or -wot	you (for. or pol.)		
-ač̣čäw	he, she (for. or pol.)		

Remember that the ending -ač̣čäw is both general plural 'they' and polite 'he, she or they'. Also, don't forget that the ending that is spelled -ač̣čïhu (as for example on **ናችሁ**) for 'you' (plural) is pronounced as -ač̣čuh.

The corresponding personal pronouns, some of which you have already met in the dialogues, are as follows. These are called the 'independent pronouns' because they are whole words, unlike the suffixes just described. Normally, the independent pronouns are only used for emphasis, but you will need to know them, for instance, if someone asks 'Who is it?' and you want to say 'It's me', **እኔ ነኝ** ïne näñ (lit. 'I am').

singular		
እኔ	ïne	I
አንተ	antä	you (masc. and inf.)
አንቺ	anči	you (fem. and inf.)
እሱ or እርሱ	ïssu or ïrsu	he
እሷ or እርሷ	ïsswa or ïrswa	she

(this can also be written using the wa- letter: **እሷ** or **እርሷ**)

plural		
አኛ	ïñña	we
እናንተ	ïnnäntä	you (pl. and inf.)
እነሱ or እነርሱ	ïnnässu *or* ïnnärsu	they
formal		
አስዎ or አርስዎ	ïsswo or ïrswo	you (pol. or for.)
አሳቸው or አርሳቸው	ïssaččäw or ïrsaččäw	he, she (pol. or for.)

'My', 'your', 'his', etc. and possessive phrases

In the second dialogue you met the forms የርስዎ ሚስት yärswo mist 'your wife' and የኔ ሚስት yäne mist 'my wife'. You may recognize the pronouns አርስዎ and እኔ inside the words meaning 'your' and 'my', and from this you can see that possessives may be formed by prefixing የ - yä-. This may be added to nouns as well as pronouns.

Consider the phrases የኃይሉ ሚስት yäHaylu mist 'Haylu's wife', or የተማሪ መጽሐፍ yätämari mäs'haf 'a student's book' (ተማሪ, student, መጽሐፍ - book). Note the order of words; the possessor always precedes the person or thing possessed, just as in the English pattern 'a student's book'.

Spoken Amharic does not normally like two vowels to stand next to one another in the same word. So, when the word to which የ - yä- is added begins in a vowel, like አርስዎ ïrswo or እኔ ïne or አንተ antä, then either of two things happens: one of the vowels is dropped, or a supporting sound or 'glide' is inserted between the vowels.

In order to discover which vowel is dropped we can represent the 'hierarchy' of vowels as follows (the 'weakest' and most susceptible to being dropped are at the bottom):

```
a, e, i, o, u
      ä
      ï
```

So, ï gives way to all other vowels: yä- + ïne > የኔ yäne; ä gives way to the vowels of the top row only: yä- + abbat > የአባት yabbat.

When two vowels of the top row come into contact usually a supporting sound or 'glide' (**w** or **y**) is inserted between them: **tämari + -očč > ተማሪዎች tämariwočč, gwaddäñña + -e > ጓደኛዬ gwaddäññaye**. You'll find these last two words in the dialogue in the next lesson. Note, however, that when two **a**s come together they merge into a single **a**: **gwaddäñña + -aččäw > ጓደኛቸው gwaddäññaččäw**. Look out for some more possessive phrases also in the next lesson.

There is another way of indicating possession in Amharic when the possessor is a pronoun. Again, you will encounter an example in the next lesson, but full discussion of the grammar will be left until a later lesson.

Exercises

1 Look at the following sentences and mark whether they are in the informal (I) or formal and polite (P) mode

1 እንደምን ነህ? ደኅና ነህ?
2 ጺሩት ደኅና ነች ።
3 ያንተ አባት ደኅና ናቸው?
4 እርስዎ እንደምን ነዎት?
5 አባትና እናትህ እንደምን ናቸው?
6 ደኅና ናችሁ?
7 ደኅና ሁን ፡ በበዪ ።

2 Complete the following sentences with the correct form of the verb ነው

1 ያንተ አባት እንደምን _____ ?
2 ጺሩት ፡ ደኅና _____ ?
3 እኔ በጣም ጥሩ _____ ።
4 እርሳቸው የኔ አባት _____ ።
5 ወይዘር ሕይወት የርሳቸው ሚስት _____ ።
6 እንተስ ፡ ደኅና _____ ? አዎ ፡ ደኅና _____ ።

3 Fill in the correct personal pronoun(s) in the following sentences

1 _____ እንደምን ነች?
2 እግዚር ይስጥልኝ _____ ደኅና ነኝ ።

3 አጎትና እናት ደጎና ናቸው? እም ፡ _____ ደጎና ናቸው ።
4 ሕይወት ፡ _____ እንደምን ነሽ?
5 እኔ ደጎና ነኝ ። _____ ፡ እንደምን ናችሁ?

4 Combine pairs of the following words to make possessive phrases. If there are some words you don't know, look them up in the glossary at the end of the book

እኔ መጽሐፍ ዮርባ አጎት ጋዴሉ እናት ገንዘብ ጌሩት ሰዓት ምላ ልጃገረድ ልብስ ሚስት ሁለታችን

Script

The sixth order: form and value

Look through the dialogues in this lesson and see how many sixth-order letters you can find. The word ትምሕርት tïmhïrt 'lesson' is itself made up entirely of sixth-order letters, as is ይስጥልኝ yïst'illiñ in the expressions ጤና ይስጥልኝ t'ena yïst'illiñ and እግዜር ይስጥልኝ ïgzer yïst'illiñ. From these and other words that you can find, you can see that there is no single way of forming the sixth-order from the basic first-order letter. There are in fact as many as twelve different devices involved, which means you will probably find it easier to learn the sixth-order of each letter separately rather than trying to guess it.

(a) central hook at the top:

hï	k'ï	tï	čï	ï
ሕ	ቀ	ት	ች	እ

(b) vertical line on top:

ï	s'ï
ዕ	ፀ

(c) horizontal line mid right:

dï	jï	s'ï	p'ï	wï
ድ	ጅ	ጽ	ጵ	ው

(d) horizontal line mid left:

bï
ብ

(e) curve right at top:

   rï   fï

   ሪ   ፊ

(f) hook left at top:

   nï   ñï   zï   žï

   ኀ   ኘ   ዘ   ዠ

(g) slanting line at top:

   sï   šï

   ስ   ሽ

(h) curve left midway:

   hï

   ኀ

(i) curve left at bottom:

   mï   sï

   ም   ሥ

(j) central kink:

   pï   hï   kï   hï   t'ï   č'ï

   ፕ   ህ   ክ   ኽ   ጥ   ጭ

(k) circle left:

   lï   gï

   ል   ግ

(l) irregular:

   yï

   ይ

The sixth-order also needs special attention because, unlike the other orders, it has two values: consonant + vowel ï and consonant without a vowel. You can see this from the word ትምህርት **tïmhïrt** where only the first ት and ህ are pronounced with ï. There are rules which tell you whether a sixth-order is to be read with or without a vowel, but they are complicated and it would not be helpful to list them here in detail.

One point that is useful to remember, though, is that at the end of a word the sixth-order is practically always without a vowel. Only if a word which ends in two consonants is closely followed by another which begins in a consonant in a phrase is a short ï vowel pronounced at the end of the first word: አንድ ተማሪ andï tämari 'a student' but አንድ አስተማሪ and astämari 'a teacher'.

Conversely, at the beginning of a word the sixth-order is almost always pronounced with the vowel – so, from words you have met in this lesson ጥሩ t'ïru 'good', ስም sïm 'name', እናት ïnnat 'mother', ምሳ mïsa 'lunch', and so on. Look at the transcriptions of words containing sixth-order letters in this and the following lessons to see how this operates.

Exercises

5 Here are some words and names that may be familiar to you which are written in the Ethiopian script. See how far you can identify them

አዲስ አበባ፡ ኢትዮጵያ፡ ጋሌ ሥላሴ፡ ፕሮግራም፡ ሚይ ዴይ፡ ሎጃክ፡ ፖስታ፡ ቲያትር፡ ፓስታ፡ ሬፕብሊክ፡ ኢኮኖሚክስ፡ ቢሲክሌት

6 Practise writing out the dialogues you have met in this lesson

2 በትምህርት ቤት
bätimhirt bet
At school

By the end of this lesson you should be able to:

- ask simple questions
- form the plural of nouns – *house, houses*, etc.
- use the demonstratives – *this, that, these, those*
- say where things are

Asking questions 🔲

Melaku meets Hiywet and Almaz who are new arrivals at school;
Hiywet asks a lot of questions

መላኩ:	ጤና ይስጥልኝ። ስሜ መላኩ ነው። የናንተስ?
ሕይወት:	የኔ ስም ሕይወት ነው። የጓ የጓደኛዬ ስም አልማዝ ነው። እኔ ተማሪ ነኝ። አንተስ: ተማሪ ነህ?
መላኩ:	አዎ: እኔም ተማሪ ነኝ። እናንተ አዲስ ተማሪዎች ናችሁ?
ሕይወት:	አዎ: አዲስ ተማሪዎች ነን። ያ ሰው ማን ነው? ተማሪ ነው?
መላኩ:	ኧሽ – አሳቸው አቶ ከበደ ናቸው። የኛ አስተማሪ ናቸው።
ሕይወት:	ጥሩ አስተማሪ ናቸው?
መላኩ:	አዎ: በጣም ጥሩ አስተማሪ ናቸው።
ሕይወት:	አሳቸው ምን ያስተምራሉ?
መላኩ:	የንግሊዝኛ ቋንቋ አስተማሪ ናቸው። የንግሊዝኛ ቋንቋ በጣም አስቸጋሪ ነው።
ሕይወት:	ያችስ ቤት? ማን ናት? አስዋም አስተማሪ ናት?
መላኩ:	አይደሉም እንዴ! ወይዘሮ ፀሐይ ናቸው: የትምሕርት ቤቱ ጸሐፊ ናቸው።
ሕይወት:	አሁን የክፍል ጊዜ ነው?
መላኩ:	አይደለም: የምሳ ሰዓት ነው!

MÄLAKU: t'ena yïst'ïlliñ. sïme Mälaku näw. yännantäss?
HIYWÄT: yäne sïm Hïywät näw, yässwa yägwaddäññaye sïm Almaz
näw. ïne tämari näñ. antäss, tämari näh?
MÄLAKU: awo, ïnem tämari näñ. ïnnantä addis tämariwočč naččuh?
HIYWÄT: awo, addis tämariwoč nän. ya säw man näw? tämari näw?
MÄLAKU: ä-ä - ïssaččäw ato Käbbädä naččäw. yäñña astämari naččäw.
HIYWÄT: t'ïru astämari naččäw?
MÄLAKU: awo, bät'am t'ïru astämari naččäw.
HIYWÄT: ïssaččäw mïn yastämïrallu?
MÄLAKU: yängïlizïñña k'wank'wa astämari naččäw. yängïlizïñña
k'wank'wa bät'am asčäggari näw.
HIYWÄT: yaččïss set? man nat? ïsswamm astämari nat?
MÄLAKU: aydällum ïnde! Wäyzäro S'ähay naččäw. yätïmhïrt betu
s'ähafi naččäw.
HIYWÄT: ahun yäkïfïl gize näw?
MÄLAKU: aydälläm, yämïsa säat näw!

MELAKU: *Hello! My name is Melaku. What are yours?*
HIYWET: *My name is Hiywet and my friend's name is Almaz. I'm a*
student. And you, are you a student?
MELAKU: *Yes, I'm a student, too. Are you new students?*
HIYWET: *Yes, we're new students. Who is that man? Is he a*
student?
MELAKU: *Ha-ha, he's Mr. Kebbede. He's our teacher.*
HIYWET: *Is he a good teacher?*
MELAKU: *Yes, he's a very good teacher.*
HIYWET: *What subject does he teach?*
MELAKU: *He's an English language teacher. English language is*
very difficult!
HIYWET: *And what about that woman? Who is she? Is she a*
teacher, too?
MELAKU: *No, she's Mrs. Tsehay. She's a school secretary.*
HIYWET: *Is it class time now?*
MELAKU: *No, it's lunch time!*

Vocabulary

ስሜ   sïme my name (ስም sïm name) : a*nother way of saying*
የኔ ስም.
ጓደኛ   gwaddäñña friend, companion (ጓደኛዬ gwaddäññaye
my companion)

ተማሪ	tämari student (ተማሪዎች tämariwočč students)	
አስተማሪ	astämari	teacher
ትምሕርት ቤት	tïmhïrtï bet school (lit. 'study house'). ትምሕርት study, lesson, class; also sometimes pronounced as tïmïrt, dropping the 'h'. ትምሕረት ቤቱ tïmhïrtï betu 'the school'	
አዲስ	addis	new
ጥሩ	t'ïru	good
አስቸጋሪ	asčäggari	difficult
በጣም	bät'am	very
ሰው	säw	man
ቤት	set	woman
ያስተምራሉ	yastämirallu he teaches (for.)	
እንግሊዝኛ	ïngïliziñña English (language). እንግሊዝ ïngïliz English, እንግሊዛዊ ïngïlizawi Englishman, እንግሊዛዊት ïngïlizawit Englishwoman, እንግሊዝ አገር ïngïliz agär England	
ቋንቋ	k'wank'wa	language
እንዴ	ïnde (expression of surprised contradiction) አይደሉም እንዴ aydällum ïnde she certainly is not (for.)	
ጸሐፊ	s'ähafi	secretary
ሰዓት	säat	hour, time, noon, watch, clock
ምሳ	mïsa	lunch
አሁን	ahun	now
ክፍል	kïfïl	class
ጊዜ	gize	time

Some more pronouns

ያ	ya	that (masc.)
ያች or ያቺ	yačč or yačči	that (fem.)
ማን	man	who?
ምን	mïn	what?

Some more parts of the verb 'to be'

አይደለም	aydälläm	he is not, it is not
አይደሉም	aydällum	she is not (for.)

Grammar
Word order

From a simple Amharic sentence, such as አቶ ከበደ የኛ አስተማሪ ናቸው ato Käbbädä yäñña astämari naččäw 'Mr. Kebede is our teacher', you can see that the order of words in Amharic is different from the English equivalent. The most important feature in the Amharic is that the verb (here ናቸው) comes last. You will find that this rule is usually strictly applied in Amharic, even when the sentence is very long. Look at the other sentences in the dialogue and see where the verbs come: you will see that almost every sentence ends with a verb.

Forming questions

Questions can be of two types: the first anticipates the answer 'yes' or 'no'. In Amharic this kind of question is usually formed simply by using the question intonation, raising the pitch of your voice at the end of the sentence. This is in contrast to the simple statement intonation where the pitch drops towards the end of the sentence: ተማሪ ነው? – ተማሪ ነው። 'Is he a student?' – 'He is a student'. Note that the order of words is not altered in Amharic. Another way of forming this kind of question is to add ወይ wäy after the verb at the end and to use the usual question intonation: ጥሩ ነው ወይ? t'ïru näw wäy 'Is it good?'. A third method is to add the suffix -ን -nï (note the final vowel is pronounced) to the end of the verb; this is however more common in written than spoken Amharic.

The second kind of question asks for specific information and uses a question word like 'who', 'what', 'when'. In the dialogue you met two such question words in Amharic: ማን 'who' and ምን 'what'. From the dialogue you can see that in Amharic these words usually come before the verb: ያ ሰው ማን ነው? ya säw man näw? 'who is that man?' (lit. 'that man is who?'). In combination with the verb ነው 'to be' these are often written as a single word: ማንነው mannäw 'who is it?' and ምንነው mïnnäw 'what is it?' (the latter also means 'what's the matter?' and sometimes 'why is it?'). Another way of saying 'what is it?' is ምንድን ነው, ምንድነው or ምንድር ነው mïndïnnäw or mïndïrnäw.

Note that when you write these as a single word you do not need to repeat the 'n': ነ alone reads as -nnä-.

Other question words

Some other useful question words include: ይት yet *or* የት yät 'where?': ከይት käyet 'from where?'; ወዴት wädet 'to where?'; መቼ mäče 'when?'; ለምን lämïn or ስለምን sïlämïn 'why?'; እንደምን ïndämïn *or* እንዴት ïndet 'how?'; ስንት sïnt 'how much?' *or* 'how many?'. Look at the following examples:

ትምህርት ቤቱ ይት ነው?	tïmhïrtï betu yet näw?	where is the school?
መቼ መጣህ?	mäče mät't'ah?	when did you come?
እንደምን አደርክ?	ïndämïn addärk?	how did you pass the night?
ከበደ ስለምን አልመጣም?	Käbbädä sïlämïn almät't'am?	why didn't Kebede come?
ወዴት ትሄዳ ኳ ለህ?	wädet tïhedalläh?	where are you going (to)?
ዋጋው ስንት ነው?	wagaw sïntï näw?	how much is the price?

Plurals of nouns

Forming the plural of nouns in Amharic is very simple: in the dialogue you met the form ተማሪዎች tämariwočč 'students' alongside ተማሪ tämari 'student'. From this you can see that the plural here is formed by adding the suffix -wočč to the singular form. Other examples from the vocabulary might include: አስተማሪዎች astämariwočč 'teachers'; ጸሐፊዎች s'ähafiwočč 'secretaries'; ቋንቋዎች k'wank'wawočč 'languages'; ጓደኛዎች gwaddäññawočč 'companions'. All of these nouns end in a vowel in the singular. If, however, the noun ends in a consonant, like ቤት bet 'house', ሰው säw 'man', ሴት set 'woman', ሚስት mist 'wife', አባት abbat 'father', etc., then the form of the plural suffix is -očč: ቤቶች betočč, ሰዎች säwočč, ሴቶች setočč, ሚስቶች mistočč, አባቶች abbatočč.

You can also add -očč to nouns ending in a vowel by dropping the final vowel of the singular form: ተማሮች tämaročč, ጓደኞች gwaddäññočč.

Note, however, that nouns ending in -awi forming the names of nationals, like እንግሊዛዊ ïngilizawi 'Englishman' or ኢትዮጵያዊ ityop'p'ïyawi 'Ethiopian', form their plurals by changing the ending -awi to -awïyan. So:

የኛ አስተማሪዎች ኢትዮጵያውያን ናቸው
yäñña astämariwočč ityop'p'ïyawïyan naččäw
our teachers are Ethiopians

እኛ እንግሊዛውያን ነን ::
iñña ingïlizawïyan nän
we are English

More will be said about some irregular plural forms and the use of the plural in later lessons.

Gender agreement: masculine and feminine

As you can see from the personal pronouns, for example, Amharic has two genders in the singular, እሱ 'he', እስዋ 'she' and only one in the plural እነርሱ 'they'. Most nouns follow natural gender: those denoting females are feminine, ያቺ ሴት yačči set 'that woman', and those denoting males as well as inanimate objects are generally masculine, ያ ሰው ya säw 'that man', ያ መጽሐፍ ya mäs'haf 'that book'. Some nouns that denote inanimates, such as ፀሐይ s'ähay 'sun', አገር agär 'country', ከተማ kätäma 'town', መኪና mäkina 'car' are often formulated as feminines, but not always. So ይቺ መኪና የኔ ናት yïčči mäkina yäne nat 'this car is mine', ይች አገር ቆንጆ ነች yïčč agär k'onjo näčč 'this country is beautiful'.

Expressing 'this' and 'that'

In the dialogue you met two demonstratives ያ 'that' (masc.) and ያች 'that' (fem.). Unlike adjectives, which do not change for gender, demonstratives have separate masculine and feminine as well as plural forms.

ያ	ya	that (masc.)
ያች or ያቺ	yačč or yačči	that (fem.)
እነዚያ	innäzziya	those

ይህ	yïh	this (masc.)
ይች or ይቺ	yïčč or yïčči	this (fem.)
እነዚህ	innäzzih	these

So, using words that you know already, you can say: ይህ ቤት yïh bet 'this house', ይቺ አስተማሪ yïčči astämari 'this (woman) teacher', እነዚህ ተማሪዎች innäzzih tämariwočč 'these students'; ይህ ጥሩ ሰው yïh t'iru säw 'this good man'; ይቺ ጥሩ ሴት yïčči t'iru set 'this good woman'; እነዚህ ጥሩዎች ሰዎች innäzzih t'iru-wočč säwočč 'these good people'; እነዚህ ቆንጆዎች ሴቶች innäzzih k'onjowočč setočč 'these beautiful women'.

When a preposition, like **ñ**, **bä** 'in, at', or **h** **kä** 'from', or **ωደ** **wädä** 'to, towards' etc., comes before a demonstrative, the demonstratives are changed as follows:

ይህ	becomes	ዚህ	zzih
ይቺ/ይች	become	ዚቺ/ዚች	zziččï/zzič
ያ	becomes	ዚያ	zziya
ያቺ/ያች	become	ዚያቺ/ዚያች	zziyaččï/zziyač
እነዚህ	and እነዚያ	remain unchanged.	

Therefore: በዚህ ቤት **bäzzih bet** 'in this house'; ከዚያች ቆንጆ ሴት **käzziyačč k'onjo set** 'from that beautiful woman'; በ(እ)ነዚህ ትምሕርት ቤቶች **bännäzzih timhirti betočč** 'in these schools'.

Agreement of plural adjectives

The phrase እነዚህ ጥሩዎች ሰዎች 'these good people' shows that when an adjective describes a noun in the plural it, too, may appear as a plural with the suffix -(w)očč. So አስቸጋሪዎች ቋንቋዎች **asčäggariwočč k'wank'wawočč** 'difficult languages', ቆንጆች ሴቶች **k'onjočč setočč** 'beautiful women', ብርቱዎች ተማሪዎች **birtuwočč tämariwočč** 'hard-working students'. The adjective, though, does not have to agree; you can also say ብርቱ ተማሪዎች **birtu tämariwočč**, and so on. Similarly, you can say either እነዚህ ተማሪዎች ብርቱ ናቸው **innäzzih tämariwočč birtu naččäw** or እነዚህ ተማሪዎች ብርቱዎች ናቸው **innäzzih tämariwočč birtuwočč naččäw** 'these students are hard-working'.

Expression of 'no'

In the first lesson you learned the word አዎ **awo** 'yes'. Unfortunately, the expression of 'no' in Amharic is not quite so simple. To say 'no' in Amharic you, in effect, have to say '. . . is not', which means that you must form the verb in accordance with its logical subject. This is why Melaku's answer to Hiywet's question about Mrs. Tsehay begins አይደለም. . . **aydällum** *lit.* 'she is not', but equivalent to the English 'no', and yet later he says አይደለም **aydälläm** lit. 'he/it is not', i.e. 'it is not (study time, but) it is lunch time'. The verb አይደለም is the negative form of ነው **näw**. All verbs in Amharic have a special negative form, but fortunately they are not all as irregular as this. You will meet the full set of forms of አይደለም later in this lesson.

Exercises

1 Rewrite the following sentences using plural forms

> *Example* ይህ ቤት ትልቅ ነው → እነዚህ ቤቶች ትልቅ ናቸው

1 ደች ቤት የኔ እንት ናት።
2 እኔ ተማሪ ነኝ።
3 እሱ አስተማሪ ነው።
4 እርስዋ አስተማሪ ናች።
5 አንቺ ቆንጆ ልጃገረድ ነሽ።
6 የኔ አስተማሪ ኢትዮጵያዊ ናቸው።

2 Answer the following questions about the dialogue in Amharic

1 መላኩ ተማሪ ነው?
2 የንግሊዝኛ ቋንቋ ቀላል ነው ወይስ አስቸጋሪ?
3 ወይዘር ፀሐይ አስተማሪ ናት?
4 አሁን የምሳ ሰዓት ነው?
5 ሕይወት የአልማዝ ጓደኛ ናት?
6 አቶ ከበደ ጸሐፊ ናቸው?

3 Fill in the correct form of the demonstrative in the blanks

1 አቶ ከበደ በ _____ ትምሕርት ቤት አስተማሪ ናቸው።
2 _____ ቤት የኔ ሚስት ነች።
3 ይት ነው? እ _____ ነው።
4 _____ ሰዎች ጥሩዎች ናቸው።
5 ከ _____ ብርቱ ተማሪ ጋር ይሂዱ!

Going to a restaurant 🔲

Almaz and Hiywet decide to go for lunch by themselves, but don't know the way

ሕይወት: እኔ ራበኝ። እኔ ጠማኝ። ወደ ምግብ ቤት እንሂድ!
አልማዝ: ምግብ ቤት እዚህ አለ? ወዲስ ወደ ከተማ እንሂድ?
ሕይወት: በዚች ከተማ ብዙ ምግብ ቤቶች አሉ።

አልማዝ: አሺ: ወይ ከተማ እንሂድ - ጊዜ አለን? ከምሳ
በኋላ ትምሕርት በስንት ሰዓት ነው?
ሕይወት: ትምሕርት የለም:: ስለዚህ ብዙ ጊዜ አለን!
አልማዝ: ጥሩ ነው - ከተማውስ ወዴት በኩል ነው? እኔ
አላውቅም::
ሕይወት: እዚያ ላይ አንድ ልጅ አለ:: እንጠይቀው! ወንድም:
ከተማው በዬት በኩል ነው? ሩቅ ነው? ጥሩ ምግብ
ቤት ዬት አለ?
ልጅ: እዚያ ታች ፖስታ ቤት አጠገብ ጥሩ ምግብ ቤት
አለ:: ሩቅ አይደለም: በጣም ቅርብ ነው:: መጀመሪያ
በስተቀኝ ከዚያም ወደ ግራ ይሂዱ::
ሕይወት: እግዚር ይስጥልኝ::

....

አልማዝ: ይኸው! ምግብ ቤቱ እዚህ ነው... አረ! እምግብ
ቤቱ ውስጥ ብዙ ሰው አለ:: ቦታ የለም:: ወደ ሌላ
ምግብ ቤት እንሂድ!
ሕይወት: አሺ: ይኸው: አሳላፊ እዚህ አለ:: እንጠይቀው::
ጋሼ ሌላ ምግብ ቤት በዚህ አካባቢ አለ?
አሳላፊ: አለ:: አዲስ ዓለም ምግብ ቤት ከቢኒማ ቤት
በስተጀርባ ማዘጋጃ ቤት ፊት ለፊት አለ::
አልማዝ: አሁንስ እኔንም ራበኝ: ጠማኝም እንዲሁም ደከመኝ::
ቶሎ ቶሎ እንሂድ!

HIYWÄT: ïne rabäñ. ïne t'ämmañ. wädä mïgïb bet ïnnïhid!
ALMAZ: mïgïb bet ïzzih allä? wäyïss wädä kätäma ïnnïhid?
HIYWÄT: bäzzičč kätäma bïzu mïgïb betočč allu.
ALMAZ: ïšši, wädä kätäma ïnnïhid – gize allän? kämïsa
bähwala tïmhïrt bäsïntï säat näw?
HIYWÄT: tïmhïrt yälläm. sïläzzih bïzu gize allän!
ALMAZ: t'ïru näw – kätämawïss wädet bäkkul näw? ïne alawk'ïm.
HIYWÄT: ïzziya lay andï lïjj allä. ïnnït'äyyïk'äw! wändïmm, kätämaw
bäyet bäkkul näw? ruk' näw? t'ïru mïgïb bet yet allä?
LIJJ: ïzziya tač posta bet at'ägäb t'ïru mïgïb bet allä. ruk'
aydälläm, bät'am k'ïrbï näw. mäjämmäriya bästäk'äñ,
kässiyamm wädä gra yïhidu.
HIYWÄT: ïgzer yïst'ïlliñ.

....

ALMAZ: yïhäw! mïgïb betu ïzzih näw . . . ärä, ïmïgïb betu wïst' bïzu
säw allä. bota yälläm. wädä lela mïgïb bet ïnnïhid!
HIYWÄT: ïšši. yïhäw, asallafi ïzzih allä. ïnnït'äyyïk'äw! gašše, lela
mïgïb bet bäzzih akkababi allä?

ASALLAFI: allä. "Addis Aläm" mïgïb bet käsinima bet bästäjärba mazzägaja bet fit läfit allä.
ALMAZ: ahunïss ïnenïm rabäñ, t'ämmañïmm ïndihum däkkämäñ. tolo tolo ïnnïhid!

HIYWET: *I'm hungry. I'm thirsty. Let's go to the restaurant!*
ALMAZ: *Is there a restaurant here? Or, should we go into town?*
HIYWET: *There are lots of restaurants in this town.*
ALMAZ: *OK, let's go into town. Do we have time? When are there classes after lunch?*
HIYWET: *There aren't any classes. So we have lots of time!*
ALMAZ: *Good – but which way is the town. I don't know.*
HIYWET: *There's a boy over there. Let's ask him! . . . Hey, which way is the town? Is it far? Whereabouts is there a good restaurant?*
BOY: *There's a good restaurant down there, near the post office. It's not far, it's very near. First go right and then to the left.*
HIYWET: *Thanks.*

•••••••••••

ALMAZ: *Here's the restaurant . . . Oh, there are a lot of people in the restaurant; there's no room. Let's go to another restaurant.*
HIYWET: *OK. Here's a waiter. Let's ask him. Waiter, is there another restaurant in this area?*
WAITER: *Yes. The 'New World' restaurant is behind the cinema, opposite the town hall.*
ALMAZ: *I'm hungry and I'm thirsty and tired now, too. Let's hurry up!*

Vocabulary

ምግብ ቤት	mïgïb bet	restaurant, canteen
ምግብ ቤቱ	mïgïb betu	the restaurant
ፖስታ ቤት	posta bet	post office
ማዘጋጃ ቤት	mazzägaja bet	town hall
ሲነማ ቤት	sinima bet	cinema
ወይስ	wäyïss	or (*marking an alternative or additional question*)
ብዙ	bïzu	much, many
እሺ	ïšši	OK, alright!

ከተማ	kätäma	town, city
ከተማው	kätämaw	the town
ልጅ	lïjj	child, boy, girl, son, daughter
ሩቅ	ruk'	far, distant
ቅርብ	k'ïrb	near, close
መጀመሪያ	mäjämmäriya	first
ቀኝ	k'äñ	right
ግራ	gïra/gra	left
ይኸው	yïhäw	here it is!
ሌላ	lela	other
እሬ	ärä	why! oh! (*an exclamation of surprise or dismay said when something unexpected happens. Also occurs as* ኢሬ *ïrä or* ኤሬ *erä. Note the special letter* ኧ *for the sound* ä *at the beginning of the word*)
አሳላፊ	asallafi	waiter
ጋሼ	gašše	(*familiar term of address to a man older than oneself; lit.* 'my shield')
ወንድም	wändïmm	(*familiar term of address to a man the same age as or a little younger than oneself; lit.* 'brother')
አካባቢ	akkababi	vicinity, nearby area
ዓለም	aläm	world
እንዲሁም	ïndihum	and likewise, and also
ቶሎ ቶሎ	tolo tolo	(very) quickly
እዚህ	ïzzih	here
እዚያ	ïzziya	there

Some verb forms

ራበኝ	rabäñ	I'm hungry (*lit.* 'it hungers me')
ጠማኝ	t'ämmañ	I'm thirsty (*lit.* 'it thirsts me')
ደከመኝ	däkkämäñ	I'm tired (*lit.* 'it tires me')
እንሂድ	ïnnïhid	let's go!
እንጠይቀው	ïnnït'äyyïk'äw	let's ask him!
አላውቅም	alawk'ïm	I don't know
ይሂዱ	yïhidu	go (*pol.*)

Some prepositions

በ	bä-	in, at, by
ከ	kä-	from
እ	ï-	in, at, to

ወደ	wädä	towards
ስለ	sïlä	about, because of
ስለዚሀ	sïläzzih	so, therefore (*lit.* 'because of this')
በስተ	bästä	in the direction of. *Occurring in the following:*
በስተጀርባ	bästäjärba	to the rear
በስተቀኝ	bästäk'äñ	to the right
በስተግራ	bästägra	to the left

Some postpositions

በኩል	bäkkul	in respect of, in the direction of
በኋላ	bähwala	after
ታች	tač	down
ላይ	lay	up
አጠገብ	at'ägäb	next to
ውስጥ	wïst'	inside
ፊት ለፊት	fit läfit	opposite (*lit.* 'face to face')

More verbs which express 'to be'

አለ	allä	there is
አሉ	allu	there are
የለም	yälläm	there isn't
የሉም	yällum	there aren't

Note also

አለን	allän	we have

Grammar

Prepositions and postpositions

You can see from the dialogue that in Amharic the equivalents of English prepositions, such as **'in, behind, opposite, from'**, etc:, are of two kinds: like the English prepositions they either come in front of the noun, or conversely they follow it. The latter kind are called 'postpositions'. Often you will find postpositions combined with prepositions, as in the phrase አምገብ ቤቱ ውስጥ **ïmïgïb betu wïst'** 'in(side) the restaurant'. Particularly in the spoken language, though, the prepositional element may be dropped, as in ፖስታ ቤት አጠገብ **posta bet at'ägäb** 'near the post office'.

With place names, like አዲስ አበባ or ሎንደን, you do not need to add any preposition to say 'to . . .' or 'in . . .': ሎንደን እኖራለሁ **London ïnorallähw** 'I live in London'; አዲስ አበባ እንሂድ **Addis Abäba ïnnïhid** 'Let's go to Addis Ababa'.

Prepositions in Amharic are also of two kinds: a small number consist of one syllable only and these are always written joined on to the front of the word they go with: ከትምሕርት ቤት **kätïmhïrtï bet** 'from school', አቤት **ïbet** 'at home'; other prepositions contain more than one syllable and these may be written either joined on to or separate from the following word: ወደ ሲኒማ ቤት/ወደሲኒማ ቤት **wädä sinima bet** 'to the cinema'.

The single-syllable prepositions in Amharic are very few in number, but some of them have a very wide range of meanings. Rather than give exhaustive lists of meanings here, it is better if you learn how to use these by observing them as they are used in the dialogues. You can also see that there is some degree of overlap in meaning between some of the prepositions. The following meanings can therefore only be a general indication:

በ	bä	in, at (*place or time*); with, by (*instrument*)
ከ	kä	from; to (*direction*); with, by (*instrument*); than
ለ	lä	to, for (*recipient or beneficiary*)
እ	ï	to (*direction*), at (*place*)

Here are some more useful two-syllable prepositions:

ወደ	wädä	to, towards (*direction*)
እስከ	ïskä	as far as, up to, until (*place or time*)
እንደ	ïndä	like, as (*comparison*)
ስለ	sïlä	about, because of, according to (*subject or cause*)
ያለ	yalä	without

The preposition በስተ **bästä** is used in some useful words denoting direction:

በስተቀኝ	bästäk'äñ	to the right
በስተግራ	bästägra	to the left
በስተኋላ	bästähwala	to the rear
በስተጀርባ	bästäjärba	to the back of
በስተዚህ	bästäzzih	this way, in this direction
በስተዚያ	bästäzziya	that way, in that direction

Remember that either the final vowel of the preposition or the first vowel of a following noun which begins with a vowel may be dropped in accordance with the 'hierarchy' of vowels: ከኔ **käne** 'from me' (ከ + እኔ), ወደ አዲስ አበባ/ወ ዳዲስ አበባ **wädä Addis Abäba / wäd Addis Abäba** 'to Addis Ababa'; ለአልማዝ/ላልማዝ **lä Almaz / lAlmaz** 'for Almaz'.

The postpositions combine most frequently with the prepositions በ -, ከ - or እ -, and sometimes with ወደ. Remember that the preposition can sometimes be left out.

በቤት ውስጥ	bäbet wïst'	inside the house, in the house
በጠረጴዛ ላይ	bät'äräp'eza lay	on the table
ከቤት ውስጥ	käbet wïst'	from inside the house
ከጠረጴዛ ላይ	kät'äräp'eza lay	from on the table
እቤት ውስጥ	ïbet wïst'	inside, into the house
ከተማሮች ጋር	kätämaročč gar	with the students
አልማዝ ጋር	Almaz gar	with Almaz

Here, then, are some useful postpositions:

ውስጥ	wïst'	inside
ውጭ	wič'č'	outside
ላይ	lay	on top
ታች	tač	beneath
ጋር	gar	with (*accompaniment*); *combines with* ከ -
ዘንድ	zänd	at the house of
በኋላ	bähwala	behind, after
በፊት	bäfit	in front of, before

The verb 'to be' in relation to place

In the first lesson you learned the verb ነው **'is'**, but in the last dialogue you met another verb, አለ, which also translates as 'is' or 'there is'. The verb አለ is used to point out the existence of something, as in በቤት ውስጥ ብዙ ሰው አለ **bäbet wïst' bïzu säw allä** 'there are a lot of people in the house', i.e. equivalent to the English 'there is' and 'there are'. It is also used in the sense of 'to be (in a place)', as in አልማዝ እቤት አለች **Almaz ïbet alläčč** 'Almaz is at home', ተማሮቹ እሲኒማ ቤት አሉ **tämaročču ïsinima bet allu** 'the students are at the cinema'.

The verb ነው can also be used in the sense of 'to be in a place' when the place is overtly mentioned. So the last two sentences could also be expressed by አልማዝ እቤት ነች Almaz ïbet näč and ተማሮቿ እሲኒማ ቤት ናቸው tämaročču ïsinima bet naččäw.

The inflected form of the verb አለ is given below. You should make a special note of the endings. You will meet them again in the negative forms of both አለ and ነው, and also in the simple past tense of all other verbs.

አለሁ	allähw *(but written as* **allähu)**	I am
አለህ	alläh	you are (masc. & inf.)
አለሽ	alläš	you are (fem. & inf.)
አለ	allä	he is; there is (masc.)
አለች	alläčč	she is; there is (fem.)
አለን	allän	we are
አላችሁ	allaččuh *(but written as* **allaččïhu)**	you are (pl. & inf.)
አሉ	allu	they are; there are; he/she is (pol.); there is (pol.); you are (pol.)

The base is አለ - allä- and the endings are:

		singular		plural	
1st person	-hw	I		-n	we
2nd person	-h	you (masc. & inf.)		-aččuh	you (inf.)
	-š	you (fem. & inf.)			
3rd person	-ä	he		-u	they;
	-äčč	she			
				formal	
				-u	he, she, they, you

There are a number of things to note about this inflexion:

(a) the endings of the first person singular ('I') and the second person plural ('you' plural and inf.) are pronounced slightly differently from how they are written. However this is true only when the endings come at the very end of the word and there is no further suffix added;

(b) the endings in the verb አለ are added to the base allä- which itself ends in a vowel; so when the endings -ä and -äčč of the third person masculine ('he') and third person feminine ('she') are added, one of the äs is dropped; also the ending **-u** of the third person plural ('they', etc.) replaces the final ä of the verb stem;

(c) unlike the verb ነው, there is no special second person ('you') polite form to go with the pronoun እርስዎ; instead the third person plural is used. You will find that this is true of all verbs except ነው.

In the last dialogue you saw that the negative of አለ is የለም 'there is not', and earlier you met the negative of ነው, which is አይደለም 'he is not'. Both of these inflect with the same endings as አለ preceding the final – ም. So:

base የለ + ending + ም   base አይደለ + ending + ም

የለሁም	yällä*hu*m	አይደለሁም	aydällä*hu*m
	I am not, *etc.*		I am not, *etc.*
የለህም	yällä*h*im	አይደለህም	aydällä*h*im
የለሽም	yällä*š*im	አይደለሽም	aydällä*š*im
የለም	yäll*ä*m	አይደለም	aydäll*ä*m
የለችም	yällä*čč*im	አይደለችም	aydällä*čč*im
የለንም	yällä*n*im	አይደለንም	aydällä*n*im
የላችሁም	yäll*aččihu*m	አይደላችሁም	aydäll*aččihu*m
የሉም	yäll*u*m	አይደሉም	aydäll*u*m

Exercises

4 Turn the following sentences into negatives

Example አልማዝ እቤት አለች። ➔ አልማዝ እቤት የለችም።

1 ያቸ ቤት ወደሔር ሕይወት ናት?
2 እነዚህ ተማሪዎች እንግሊዛውያን ናቸው።
3 ወንድሜ እትምህርት ቤት አለ።
4 እሱ የተረፈ እንጀት ነው?
5 አሁን ጊዜ አለ።
6 እሲኔማ ቤት አለን።

5 Rewrite the following sentences so that the verb in brackets agrees with the noun or pronoun subject

1 እነዚህ መጽሐፍች (አይደለም)።
2 ብዙዎች ሰዎች አዚህ (አለ)።
3 እናንተ ጥሩዎች ልጆች (ነው)።
4 አልማዝና ሕይወት ተማሪዎች (አይደለም)።
5 አቶ መላኩ፡ እንደምን (አለ)?
6 ከሲኒማ ቤት በስተኋላ ብዙዎች ቤቶች (አለ)።
7 አንቺ ደህና (ነው)? እም፡ እግዚር ይመስገን ደህና (ነው)።
8 እኔና ውንድሜ ተማርኝ (አይደለም)።
9 ልጆች አዚህ (የለም)።
10 አንተ ጥሩ ልጅ (አይደለም)።

6 In the left-hand column are some adjectives from the dialogues in this lesson. Pair them up correctly with their opposites in the righthand column

ጥሩ	ቀላል
ትልቅ	መጥፎ
አዲስ	ሩቅ
አስቸጋሪ	አርጌ
ቅርብ	ትንሽ

7 Answer the following questions using the words and phrases relating to place, set out below

እቤት፡ ከከተማ ሩቅ፡ ከማዘጋጃ ቤት በስተቀኝ፡ አዚህ ታች፡ በጠረጴዛ ላይ፡ እትምህርት ቤት፡ ከቲያትር ፊት ለፊት፡ እቤት ውስጥ፡

Example ተማርች ዬት ናቸው? → እትምህርት ቤት ናቸው።

---

1 የኔ መጽሐፍ ዬት ነው?
2 እንድ ጥሩ ምግብ ቤት ዬት አለ?
3 ያንቺ ቤት ቅርብ ነው? አይደለም፡ _____
4 ፖስታ ቤት በስተገራ ነው? አይደለም፡ _____
5 በዚህ ከተማ ባንክ አለ?
6 አልማዝና መላኩ ዬት ናቸው?
7 ጠረጴዛ ዬት ነው?
8 አልማዝና ከበደ ዬት ናቸው?

Script

Writing double or 'geminate' consonants

Have a look at the transcribed versions of the dialogues you have met so far and you will see many instances of Amharic words which contain double consonants: innäzzih; innantä; mazzägaja; aydälläm; yist'illiñ; abbat; yimmäsgän, and so on. These double consonants, which are also sometimes called 'geminate', are not, however, represented in the script: እነዚህ innäzzih is written with only one ነ and only one ዚ, isswa እስዋ with only one ስ, abbat አባት with only one ባ, and so on. Both nä and nnä are represented by the single letter ነ, both si (and s) and ssi (and ss) by ስ, both ba and bba by ባ. In a word where two identical consonants are written next to one another, the first in the sixth order, such as ትልልቅ tilillik' or አባርረ abbarirre there has to be the vowel i to separate them.

Double consonants are very important in Amharic and must always be carefully pronounced. They often make all the difference in meaning:

		Both written
alä he said	allä there is	አለ
gäna yet	gänna Christmas	ገና
wana swimming	wanna important	ዋና
yigäbal he enters	yiggäbbal it's right	ይገባል
mäfälläg to want	mäffäläg to be wanted	መፈለግ
bälu say!	bällu they ate	በሉ
abay liar	abbay Blue Nile	አባይ

When learning a new item of vocabulary, or a new grammatical form (where double consonants are usually predictable) you will need to pay special attention.

Exercises

8 Rewrite the following transcribed Amharic words in Ethiopian script, and then check your answers in the key

wäddo	säñño	hizb	azzo	assab	mälliso	k'ät't'ilo	k'ut't'a
bärr	zär	gimmaš	wanna	agäññä	isat	gazet'a	mäto

gänna	gäna	duda	rädda	s'ät't'ïta	ïttïm	ayyale	tïnnïš
t'ïnt	tïrf	tärräfä	gabïčča	t'äk'lalla	lela	hïggu	tïgu

9 Practise writing out the dialogues in this lesson

3 ድንገተኛ ግንኙነት
dïngätäñña
giniññunnät

A chance meeting

By the end of this lesson you should be able to:

- express possession using the verb 'to have'
- form the simple past tense (I came, he gave, etc.)
- use the definite article (the)

Asking questions ▢▢

Almaz and Hiywet meet Mr Mulugeta

አልማዝ ፦ እንግዲህ አሁን ምግብ ቤቱ ደረስን።

ሕይወት ፦ አዎ፤ መልካም ነው። እዚህ ቦታ አለ።

አልማዝ ፦ ኧረ! አቶ ሙሉጌታ አሉ። እሳቸው ካባቴ ጓደኞች
እንዱ ናቸው። እንደምን ዋሉ አቶ ሙሉጌታ?
ደህና ነዎት?

አቶ ሙሉጌታ ፦ ጤና ይስጥልኝ አልማዝ። ደህና ነኝ። እግዜር
ይመስገን። እንደምን ዋልሽ? አንቺ ዛሬ ትምሕርት
የለሽም እንዴ?

አልማዝ ፦ ደህና ነኝ እግዚር ይመስገን። አይ፤ ዛሬ ከሰዓት
በኋላ ከፍል የለንም። ሕይወት ጓደኛዬ ናት።
አሁም እንደኔ ተማሪ ናት። እኔና ሕይወት ወደ
አንድ ሌላ ምግብ ቤት ሂድን ነገር ጋን ቦታ
አላገኘንም። ምሳ መብላት ፈለገን።

አቶ ሙሉጌታ ፦ እባካችሁ፤ ኞር! እኔም ከናንተ ትምሕርት ቤት
ከብዙ ዓመት በፊት ነበርኩ። እኔና ያልማዝ አባት
አብረን ተማርን። አገርሽ ዬት ነው ሕይወት?
አዲስ አበባ?

ሕይወት ፦ አይደለም። አገሬ ጂማ ነው። የዛሬ ሁለት ሳምንት
አዲስ አበባ ገባሁ። አባቴ በጂማ የመንግሥት
ሠራተኛ ናቸው፤ ነገር ግን እዚህ አዲስ አበባ

ተወለዱ። ወደዚህ ከተማ መምጣት አልፈለጉም።
አሁን ገን ካልማዝ ጋር ተዋወቁና የከተማውን
ኑር በጣም ለመድኩት። ትምሕርቴንም ስጨርስ
እዚህ ለመኖር እፈልጋለሁ።

ALMAZ:	ïngïdih, ahun mïgïb betu därräsïn.
HIYWÄT:	awo, mälkam näw. ïzzih bota allä.
ALMAZ:	ärä! ato Mulugeta allu. ïssaččäw kabbate gwaddäññočč andu naččäw . . . ïndämïn walu ato Mulugeta? dähna näwot?
ATO MULUGETA:	t'ena yïst'ïllïñ Almaz. dähna näñ, ïgzer yïmmäsgän. ïndämïn walš? anči zare tïmhïrt yälläšïm ïnde?
ALMAZ:	dähna näñ, ïgzer yïmmäsgän. ay, zare käsäat bähwala kïfïl yällänïm. Hïywät gwaddäññaye nat. ïsswamm ïndäne tämari nat. ïnenna Hïywät wäd andï lela mïgïb bet hedïn, nägär gïn bota alagäññänïmm. mïsa mäblat fällägïn.
ATO MULUGETA:	ïbakkaččuh, nor! . . . ïnemm kännantä tïmhïrtï bet käbïzu amät bäfit näbbärkw. ïnenna y Almaz abbat abrän tämarn. agärïš yet näw Hïywät? Addis Abäba?
HIYWÄT:	aydälläm, agäre Jimma näw. yäzare hulätt sammïnt Addis Abäba gäbbahw. abbate bäJimma yämängïst särratäñña naččäw, nägär gïn ïzzih Addis Abäba täwällädu. wädäzzih kätäma mämt'at alfälläghum. ahun gïn k Almaz gar täwawwäk'ïnïnna yäkätämawn nuro bät'am lämmädkut.. tïmhïrtenïm sïč'ärrïs ïzzih lämänor ïfällïgallähw.

ALMAZ:	*Well, we're here now.*
HIYWET:	*Yes, that's fine. There's room here.*
ALMAZ:	*Oh, Mr Mulugeta's here. He's one of my father's friends . . . How are you, Mr Mulugeta?*
MR MULUGETA:	*Hello Almaz. I'm well, thank you. How are you? Don't you have school today, eh?*
ALMAZ:	*I'm fine, thanks. No, this afternoon we don't have any classes. Hiywet is my friend. We're both students. Hiywet and I went to another restaurant, but we couldn't find any room. We wanted to eat lunch.*
MR MULUGETA:	*Please, join me! . . . I went to the same school many years ago. Almaz's father and I studied together. Where do you come from, Hiywet, from Addis Ababa?*

HIYWET: *No, I come from Jimma. I arrived in Addis Ababa two weeks ago. My father is a government official in Jimma, but he was born here in Addis Ababa. At first I didn't want to come to the city. But now I've got to know Almaz and I've got quite used to city life. When I've finished my studies I want to live here.*

Vocabulary

እንግዲህ	ïngïdih	well then, well now
መልካም	mälkam	excellent, fine
አንዱ	andu	one of (*used with the preposition* ከ; *here meaning* 'from, out of')
እንዴ	ïnde	what! (*a particle indicating surprise;* እንዴ *may be used alone, or may be put at the end of a statement or question, as in* አይደለም እንዴ aydällum ïnde! *in the first dialogue in lesson two*)
ዛሬ	zare	today
ክፍል	kifïl	class, section, room
ነገር ግን	nägär gïn	but, however
ግን	gïn	but, however (*usually placed after the first word or phrase in the sentence*)
እባካችሁ	ïbakkaččuh	please (pl. & inf.)
እባክህ	ïbakkïh	(masc. & inf.)
እባክሽ	ïbakkïš	(fem. & inf.)
እባክዎ	ïbakkïwo	(for.)
ያው	yaw	the same; demonstrative ያ + -w, *so* ወዲያው *is* ወዲያ + ያው.
አገር	agär	country, land
ሳምንት	sammïnt	week
የዛሬ ሁለት ሳምንት	yäzare hulätt sammïnt	two weeks ago (*lit.* 'today two weeks')
መንግሥት	mängïst	government, state
ሠራተኛ	särratäñña	worker
ኑሮ	nuro	life, lifestyle

Some verb forms

ደረስን	därräsïn	we arrived
ደረስኩ	därräskw	I arrived (*note that the pronunciation differs slightly from the spelling;*

– the ending -ኩ is sounded as -kw as long as no further suffix is added to the word)

ገባሁ	gäbbahw	I entered, I arrived
ሄድን	hedïn	we went
ሄድኩ	hedkw	I went
ነበርኩ	näbbärkw	I was
ፈለግን	fällägïn	we wanted
መብላት ፈለግን	mäblat fällägïn	we wanted to eat
አልፈለግሁም	alfälläghum	I didn't want
መምጣት	mämt'at	I didn't want to come
አልፈለግሁም	alfälläghum	
አላገኘንም	alagäññänïm	we didn't find
ተማርን	tämarn	we studied
አብረን ተማርን	abrän tämarn	we studied together (*lit.* 'we being together, we studied')
ተወለዱ	täwällädu	he was born (for.)
ተዋወቅን	täwawwäk'ïn	we got to know one another
ለመድኩ	lämmädkw	I got used to, became familiar with
ለመድኩት	lämmädkut	I got used to it
ስጨርስ	sïč'ärrïs	when I finish
መቀመጥ	mäk'k'ämät'	to live, settle
የለሽም	yälläšim	you don't have (fem. & inf.)
የለንም	yällänïm	we don't have
ኖር	nor	welcome! (*a fixed greeting said to welcome a new arrival*)

Notes on the dialogue

1 ከባቴ ጓደኞች አንዱ **kabbate gwaddäññočč andu** 'one of my father's friends', *lit.* 'the one out of my father's friends'. Whenever another preposition, such as ከ- here, is added to the front of a possessive phrase beginning with የ- 'of', the የ- is dropped: የባቴ ጓደኞች **yabbate gwaddäññočč** 'my father's friends' but ከባቴ ጓደኞች **kabbate gwaddäññočč** 'out of my father's friends'.

2 The greeting ኖር **nor** 'welcome!' is said when one or more guests or newcomers arrive to join a group or party. Anyone seated normally rises when saying this. In some areas people say ኑሩ **nuru** or ይኑሩ **yïnuru** (*for.*) instead. These are all connected with the verb ኖረ **norä** 'stay'. The response may be simply በግዜር **bägzer** or በግዜር አይገባም **bägzer ayïggäbbam** lit. 'by God, it's

not right!'. To say 'welcome!' in more general terms, and somewhat more formally, you can say እንኳን ደኅና መጡ inkwan dähna mät't'u, lit. 'how nice you've come safely'. The verb, in this case, መጡ, has to have the appropriate form for the status etc., of the person addressed: መጣህ mät't'ah (*male and inf.*), መጣሽ mät't'aš (*female and inf.*), መጣችሁ mät't'ačcuh (*plural*), መጡ mät't'u (*for.*).

3 ከአልማዝ ጋር ተዋወቅን kä'Almaz gar täwawwäk'in 'I got to know Almaz' lit. 'we knew one another with Almaz'. Although Hiywet is speaking only about herself, because 'getting to know one another' (ተዋወቅ) involves both her and Almaz the verb is put into the first person plural, the 'we' form. Some other verbs which denote an action done by more than one person to one another (i.e. what is traditionally called the 'reciprocal') operate in the same way, as for example ተገናኘ tägänaññä 'meet' lit. 'find one another'; አንተ ጋር ተገናኘን kantä gar tägänaññän 'we met with you', i.e. 'I met you'.

Grammar

Expressing 'to have'

In the dialogue you met two different verb forms denoting possession, 'to have': የለሽም 'you don't have' and የለንም 'we don't have'. You may recognize that these are expansions of the verb የለም 'there isn't', and indeed they literally mean 'there isn't to you' and 'there isn't to us', respectively. In other words, Amharic does not have a separate verb meaning 'to have', but uses the verb of existence አለ (and as here its negative የለም) combined with a pronoun suffix which indicates the possessor, the person who 'has' something. This also means to say that the thing which is possessed, the thing which someone 'has', becomes in Amharic the subject and the verb አለ, etc., has therefore to agree with this. Accordingly, there are different forms of the verb according to whether the object or thing possessed is masculine, feminine or plural.

Consider how you might say 'I have one son' and 'I have two sons' in Amharic. Literally, this would be 'one son he is to me' and 'two sons they are to me'; አንድ ልጅ አለኝ andi lijj allän but ሁለት ልጆች አሉኝ hulätt lijjočč alluñ; or 'I have one daughter' – lit. 'one daughter she is to me' : አንዲት ልጅ አለችኝ andit lijj alläččiñ.

You can see from these last examples that the marker of 'to me' (i.e. 'I' as possessor) is the consonant **ን** added to the end of the verb. In the examples in the dialogue, however, the marker of the possessor, **ሽ** 'to you' and **ን** 'to us' occurred before the final **ም** of **የለ-ም**; compare **መጽሐፍ አለኝ** mäs'haf alläñ 'I have a book' and **መጽሐፍ የለኝም** mäs'haf yälläñïm 'I don't have a book'. As you will see, many negative verbs end in **ም** and whenever a further pronoun suffix is added, it is placed before this final **ም**. For instance, the past tense of **አለ** is **ነበረ** näbbärä 'there was', and the past of **የለም** is **አልነበረም** alnäbbäräm 'there wasn't'. So, 'I had a son' is **ልጅ ነበረኝ** lïjj näbbäräñ (*lit.* 'a son he was to me'), but 'I didn't have a son' is **ልጅ አልነበረኝም** lïjj alnäbbäräñïm (*lit.* 'a son he was not to me').

The endings of the persons 'to me', 'to you', 'to him' . . . etc., are as follows. You will find that they are almost identical to the endings of the verb **ነው** 'to be'.

Singular		
1st per.	to me	-ñ, -ïñ
2nd per. masc.	to you	-h, -ïh
2nd per. fem.	to you	-š, -ïš
3rd per. masc.	to him	-w (on **አለ**, **የለ-**, **ነበረ**, **አልነበረ-**)
		-ïw (on **አለች**, **የለች-**, **ነበረች**, **አልነበረች-**)
		-t (on **አሉ**, **የሉ-**, **ነበሩ**, **አለነበሩ-**)
3rd per. fem.	to her	-at

Plural		
1st per.	to us	-n, -ïn
2nd per.	to you	-aččuh
3rd per.	to them	-aččäw

Formal		
2nd per.	to you	-wo/-wot
3rd per.	to him, her	-aččäw

Note that the endings -**h**, -**š** and -**n** are pronounced as -**ïh**, -**ïš** and -**ïn**, respectively when added to the feminine forms አለች and የለች-, ነበረች and አልነበረች-.

The verb 'to have' forms the following patterns:

	With masc. object		with fem. object		with pl. object	
I have	አለኝ	alläñ	አለችኝ	alläččïñ	አሉኝ	alluñ
you have	አለህ	alläh	አለችህ	alläččïh	አሉህ	alluh
you have	አለሽ	alläš	አለችሽ	alläččïš	አሉሽ	alluš
he has	አለው	alläw	አለችው	alläččïw	አሉት	allut
she has	አላት	allat	አለቻት	alläččat	አሉዋት	alluwat
we have	አለን	allän	አለችን	alläččïn	አሉን	allun
you have	አላችሁ	allaččuh	አለቻችሁ	alläččaččuh	አሉዋችሁ	alluwaččuh
they have	አላቸው	allaččäw	አለቻቸው	alläččaččäw	አሉዋቸው	alluwaččäw
you have	አላዎ	alläwo	አለችዎ	alläččwo	አሉዎ	alluwo

You may notice that four of the above words are ambiguous: አለህ can mean 'you are' or 'you have'; similarly አለሽ, አላችሁ and አለን 'we are' or 'we have'.

The verb 'to not have' forms the following pattern:

	With masc. object		with fem. object		with pl. object	
I don't have	የለኝም	yälläñim	የለችኝም	yälläččïñim	የሉኝም	yälluñim
you...	የለህም	yällähim	የለችህም	yälläččïhim	የሉህም	yälluhim
you...	የለሽም	yälläšim	የለችሽም	yälläččïšim	የሉሽም	yällušim
he...	የለውም	yälläwm	የለችውም	yälläččïwm	የሉትም	yällutim
she...	የላትም	yällatim	የለቻትም	yälläččatim	የሉዋትም	yälluwatim
we...	የለንም	yällänim	የለችንም	yälläččïnim	የሉንም	yällunim
you...	የላችሁም	yällaččïhum	የለቻችሁም	yälläččaččïhum	የሉዋችሁም	yälluwaččïhum
they...	የላቸውም	yällaččäwm	የለቻቸውም	yälläččaččäwm	የሉዋቸውም	yälluwaččäwm
you...	የላዎትም	yälläwotim	የለችዎትም	yälläččwotim	የሉዎትም	yälluwotim

Similarly, possession in the past is expressed by replacing አለ, አለች, አሉ by ነበረ, ነበረች, ነበሩ, näbbärä, näbbäräčč, näbbäru respectively, and in the negative by substituting አልነበረ-, አልነበረች-, አልነበሩ- alnäbbärä-, alnäbbäräčč-, alnäbbäru- for የለ-, የለች-, የሉ-, with the final -ም added after the pronoun suffixes.

Exercises

1 Complete the following sentences, supplying the correct form of 'have'

1 እኔ ወንድም _____.
2 እኛ ዛሬ ትምሕርት _____.
3 አልማዝ ትንሽ እነት _____.
4 ተረፈ ስንት መጽሐፍ _____?
5 አንተ ሁለት መኪናዎች _____?
6 ወይዘር ፀሐይ ሁለት ልጆች _____.
7 እንቺ ብዙ ገንዘብ _____? አዎ፣ ብዙ ገንዘብ _____.

2 Turn the above sentences (a) into negatives, and (b) into the past tense

3 How would you say the following in Amharic

1 Asäffa and Hirut have four children.
2 We don't have a lot of money.
3 Mr Mulugeta's wife has a red car.
4 I had a lot of classes yesterday.
5 Mrs Tsehay had a beautiful restaurant.
6 The teacher didn't have any books.
7 Do you have many brothers? No, I don't have a brother.

4 How would you say in Amharic (a) that you have the following items, and (b) that you don't have them?

አዲስ መኪና
ሦስት ሚስቶች
ሁለት ወንድሞችና እንዲት እህት
ጥሩ መንገሥት
ብዙ ኢትዮጵያውያን አስተማሪዎች

Grammar

The simple past tense

In the dialogue you met a number of verbs in the past tense: **ደረስኩ**, **ደረስን**, **ፈለግን**, **ሄድኩ**, **ሄድን**, and so on. Like **ነበረ**, which forms the past of **አለ** 'to be', these are all in the simple past, sometimes also called the simple perfect form. As its name suggests, this is the simplest of the main verb tenses in Amharic and as such we shall begin our examination of the verb with this tense. The third person masculine of the simple past, the 'he-form', is also the shape in which verbs are cited in Amharic dictionaries. So, in order to find the meaning of **ሄድኩ**, for example, you would have to look the word up under its third person masculine form **ሄደ**, where you will find the meaning 'go'. This is also the practice followed in the glossary at the end of this book. The same form, the third person masculine of the simple past, also provides the clues to identifying the class to which a verb is assigned, which you will need to know in order to form correctly the other tenses and parts of the verb.

Verbs in Amharic are in the first instance classified according to the number of consonant letters in the basic stem of the simple past. So, **ደረሰ**, **ፈለገ**, **ለመደ**, **አደረ** all have three consonant-letters and as such are called 'triconsonantal' or 'triliteral'. On the other hand, **ሄደ**, **ጻፈ**, **መጣ**, **ሰጠ**, **ሆነ**, etc., have only two consonant letters and are therefore called 'biconsonantal' or 'biliteral'.

The triconsonantal verbs all have the same shape in the simple past: three first-order letters. The biconsonantal verbs, however, have different shapes and this distinction becomes especially important in the formation of other tenses. It will therefore be as well to learn the classification of a verb right from the start. For the moment, here are the six commonest classes of verbs:

Class			*Sample*	*Simple past stem*
Triliteral		[3-lit]	**ደረሰ**, **ፈለገ**, etc.	**därräs-**, **fälläg-** etc.
Biliteral	Type 1	[2-lit^1]	**መጣ** (1st + 4th order)	**mät't'a-**
	Type 2	[2-lit^2]	**ሰጠ** (1st + 1st order)	**sät't'ä-**
	Type 3	[2-lit^3]	**ጻፈ** (4th + 1st order)	**s'af-**
	Type 4	[2-lit^4]	**ሄደ** (5th + 1st order)	**hed-**
	Type 5	[2-lit^5]	**ሆነ** (7th + 1st order)	**hon-**

There are some verbs in the dialogues that you have already met which look as if they are triliteral such as አገኘ (አላገኘንም), ተማረ (ተማርን), or which seem to have more than three consonants, such as ተፈወቀ (ተፈወቀን) or ተወለደ (ተወለዳ). These, however, are not simple or basic stem-types as in the above classification, but are what are called derived stems. Their simple stems, on the basis by which their classification is made, are in fact biliteral of type 2-lit² *ገኝ, biliteral of type 2-lit³ *ማረ, or triliteral ለወቀ and ወለደ, respectively. Do not worry about this for the moment! There are some very useful and important verbs, however, which are in fact derived stems of this sort and these will therefore be introduced into the vocabulary before full discussion of their grammatical patterns.

You have already met the endings of the simple past in the verb አለ; it is one of the irregularities of Amharic that this verb looks like a simple past but in fact has a present meaning. The stem of አለ, that is the form to which the endings are added is, you will recall, **allä-**, which ends in a vowel and belongs to the 2-lit² type like ሰጠ 'give', or አየ 'see' (stems **sät't'ä-, ayyä-**).

Biliteral stems of the 2-lit¹ type also end in a vowel, such as መጣ 'come', or ሰማ 'hear' (stems **mät't'a-, sämma-**). The other biliteral and triliteral stems end in a consonant: ደረሰ 'arrive' (stem **därräs-**), ጻፈ 'write' (stem **s'af-**), ሄደ 'go' (stem **hed-**), ሆነ 'become' (stem **hon-**). This distinction is important because it affects the choice of some of the personal endings in the simple past. The personal endings of the simple past are set out below.

Singular			
1st per.	I ...	-hw, -kw	(-kw after a consonant only)
2nd per. masc.	you ...	-h, -k	(-k after a consonant only)
2nd per. fem.	you ...	-š	
3rd per. masc.	he ...	-ä	
3rd per. fem.	she ...	-äčč	

Plural		
1st per.	we ...	-n, -ïn
2nd per.	you ...	-aččuh
3rd per.	they ...	-u	(replacing the final vowel of the stem)

<table>
<tr><td colspan="4">*Formal*</td></tr>
<tr><td>2nd per.</td><td>you . . .</td><td>-u</td><td>(i.e. the 3rd plural form)</td></tr>
<tr><td>3rd per.</td><td>he, she . . .</td><td>-u</td><td>"</td></tr>
</table>

Notes

1 Remember the effects of the hierarchy of vowels. The ending of the first person plural is pronounced with the sixth-order vowel ï only on consonant stems to avoid an awkward resulting cluster of two consonants: so, ነገርን näggärn 'we spoke' but ደረስን därräsïn 'we arrived'.

2 Remember that only the verb ነው has a special second-person formal form; all other verbs use the third person plural for the second and third persons of the formal.

Here are samples of all six different verb classes:

3-lit

ደረስኩ/ደረስሁ	därräskw, därräshw	I arrived
ደረስክ/ደረስሁ	därräsk, därräsh	you arrived [masc. and inf.]
ደረስሽ	därräsš	you arrived [fem. and inf.]
ደረሰ	därräsä	he arrived
ደረሰች	därräsäčč	she arrived
ደረስን	därräsïn	we arrived
ደረሳችሁ	därräsaččuh	you arrived [pl.]
ደረሱ	därräsu	they arrived
		you arrived, he/she arrived [for.]

2-lit¹			*2-lit²*		
መጣሁ	mät't'ahw	I came	ሰጠሁ	sät't'ähw	I gave
መጣህ	mät't'ah	you came	ሰጠህ	sät't'äh	you gave
መጣሽ	mät't'aš	you came	ሰጠሽ	sät't'äš	you gave
መጣ	mät't'a	he came	ሰጠ	sät't'ä	he gave
መጣች	mät't'ačč	she came	ሰጠች	sät't'äčč	she gave

2-lit¹			2-lit²		
መጣን	mät't'an	we came	ሰጠን	sät't'än	we gave
መጣችሁ	mät't'aččuh	you came	ሰጣችሁ	sät't'aččuh	you gave
መጡ	mät't'u	they came, *etc.*	ሰጡ	sät't'u	they gave, *etc.*

2-lit-³			2-lit-⁴		
ጻፍኩ/ጻፍሁ	s'afkw, s'afhw	I wrote	ሄድኩ/ሄድሁ	hedkw, hedhw	I went
ጻፍክ/ጻፍህ	s'afk, s'afh	you wrote	ሄድክ/ሄድህ	hedk, hedh	you went
ጻፍሽ	s'afš	you wrote	ሄድሽ	hedš	you went
ጻፈ	s'afä	he wrote	ሄደ	hedä	he went
ጻፈች	s'afäčč	she wrote	ሄደች	hedäčč	she went
ጻፍን	s'afin	we wrote	ሄድን	hedin	we went
ጻፋችሁ	s'afaččuh	you wrote	ሄዳችሁ	hedaččuh	you went
ጻፉ	s'afu	they wrote, etc.	ሄዱ	hedu	they went, etc.

2-lit⁵		
ሆንኩ/ሆንሁ	honkw, honhw	I became
ሆንክ/ሆንህ	honk, honh	you became
ሆንሽ	honš	you became
ሆነ	honä	he became
ሆነች	honäčč	she became
ሆንን/ሆን	honïn, honn	we became
ሆናችሁ	honaččuh	you became
ሆኑ	honu	they became, etc.

Here are some more useful verbs to add to your vocabulary. From now onwards all new verbs in the vocabulary will be cited in the third person masculine of the simple past. Please be careful to note to which class they belong.

ነገረ	näggärä	speak, talk	አወቀ	awwäk'ä	know
ወሰደ	wässädä	take, take away	ወጣ	wät't'a	go up, go out
በላ	bälla	eat	ጠጣ	t'ät't'a	drink
ገዛ	gäzza	buy	ሸጠ	šet'ä	sell
ጀመረ	jämmärä	begin	ጨረሰ	č'ärräsä	finish
ሰማ	sämma	hear	አየ	ayyä	see
ከፈተ	käffätä	open	ዘጋ	zägga	close
ሠራ	särra	make, work	ቆየ	k'oyyä	wait, stay put
ጻፈ	s'afä	write	ላከ	lakä	send

The negative of the simple past is formed by prefixing አል - and suffixing - ም, as with አልነበረም alnäbbäräm 'he was not', the negative of ነበረ näbbärä 'he was'. If the verb begins in l, like ለመደ lämmädä 'he got used to' or ላከ lakä 'he sent', the አል - is prefixed as normal but the resulting double l may be written either in full or as any other double consonant: alämmädäm 'he did not get used to' አልለመደም or አለመደም; allakäm 'he did not send' – አልላከም or አላከም.

Be careful to note how the negative of a verb beginning in a is written, such as, for example, አወቀ awwäk'ä 'he knew': አላወቀም alawwäk'äm 'he did not know'. An example is set out for you below in the box.

Singular			
1st per.	አልፈለግሁም	alfälläghum	I did not want
2nd per. masc.	አልፈለግህም	alfälläghim	you did not want
2nd per. fem.	አልፈለግሽም	alfällägšim	you did not want
3rd per. masc.	አልፈለገም	alfällägäm	he did not want
3rd per. fem.	አልፈለገችም	alfällägäččim	she did not want

Plural			
1st per.	አልፈለግንም	alfällägnim	we did not want
2nd per.	አልፈለጋችሁም	alfällägaččihum	you did not want
3rd per.	አልፈለጉም	alfällägum	they did not want; he, she, you did not want (for.)

Note that with the addition of the negative ending ም, the personal endings of the first person singular and the second person plural are pronounced as they are written: ከፈልኩ käffälkw 'I paid' but አልከፈልኩም alkäffälkum 'I did not pay'; ከፈላችሁ käffälaččuh 'you paid' but አልከፈላችሁም alkäffälaččïhum 'you did not pay'.

Exercises

5 Rewrite the following sentences so that the verb in brackets appears in the correct form (you might need to look some words up in the glossary)

1 ሕይወት ምሳ (አልፈለገም)።
2 እኔና ተረፈ ወደ ፖስታ ቤት (ሄደ)።
3 አቶ ሙሉጌታ ስንት ገንዘብ (አለው)? ብዙ ገንዘብ (የለውም)።
4 አንተ ምሳ መቼ (በላ)? ከሁለት ሰዓት በፊት (በላ)።
5 እነዚህ ተማሪዎች ጻፎ (በላ)ና ቡና (ጠጣ)።
6 እናቴ ቡናና ስኳር (ገዛ)።
7 እናንተ ከቶት (ደረስ)? ከአሥመራ (ደረስ)።
8 አቶ ከበደ ነጋዴ ነበሩ፤ ሻይና ቡና (ሸጠ)።

6 How would you say the following in Amharic?

1 I didn't want to eat lunch.
2 Almaz and Kebede bought a new car.
3 Mrs Tsehay went to the post office.
4 Did you have some coffee?
5 Where did the students go?
6 Mr Mohammed didn't pay the bill.
7 Almaz, when did you see the film?
8 My mother opened the door.

Grammar

The definite article

The forms ምግብ ቤቱ, ከተማው, and ወደዚያው, which occur in this and previous lessons all contain the definite article which corresponds to English 'the'. The Amharic definite article is not used in quite the same way as English 'the', for one thing it is used less frequently than we use 'the'. It is always used to refer to something that has already been mentioned and which is therefore known to the speaker and the listener.

The Amharic definite article is suffixed to the end of the noun (or pronoun) and has two basic forms: one for masculine and plural nouns and one for feminine nouns. The masculine article has two shapes, **-u** if the noun ends in a consonant, and **-w** if it ends in a vowel.

If the noun is:	Add:		Examples:	
masc. and pl. and ends in a consonant	-u	ቤቱ	betu	the house
		ልጁ	lïjju	the child, the boy
		ቤቶቹ	betočču	the houses
		ከተማዎቹ	kätämawočču	the cities
and ends in a vowel	-w	ተማሪው	tämariw	the student
		ምሳው	mïsaw	the lunch
		ኑሮው	nurow	the life
fem.	-wa	ከተማዋ	kätämawa	the city
		ልጅዋ	lïjjwa	the girl

An alternative form of the feminine article is the suffix **-itu** or **-itwa** (**-yitu** or **-yitwa** after a noun ending in a vowel), so you can also say ልጂቱ **lïjjitu** or ልጂቷ **lïjjitwa** 'the girl' and ከተማይቱ or ከተማይቷ **kätämayitu** or **kätämayitwa** 'the city'.

The nouns ሰው **säw** 'man' and ሴት **set** 'woman' do not usually add the definite article suffix directly, but have a special, extended definite suffix in **-ïyye-** or **-ïyyo-**. So:

masc.	-ïyye + -w	ሰውየው	säwïyyew	the man
fem.	-ïyyo + wa	ሴትዮዋ	setïyyowa	the woman

A small number of other nouns, too, follow this pattern, such as አባት **abbat** 'father' and እናት **ïnnat** 'mother': አባትየው **abbatïyyew** 'the father' and እናትዮዋ **ïnnatïyyowa** 'the mother'.

Whenever an adjective is used to describe a noun with the definite article 'the', for example in a phrase like 'the big house', the article suffix in Amharic is placed on the adjective and not on the noun. In other words, the article suffix travels backwards on to the adjective. Thus: ቤቱ **betu** 'the house' but ትልቁ ቤት **tïllïk'u bet** 'the big house'; ልጂቱ **lïjjitu** 'the girl' but ትንሿ ልጅ **tïnnïšwa lïjj** 'the little girl'.

Possessive pronoun suffixes

In lesson one you learned how to express 'my, your, his', etc., by using the possessive preposition የ - followed by the independent pronoun, as in የኔ ስም **yäne sïm** 'my name', *lit.* 'name of me'. In lesson two, however, you saw that the same could be expressed by one word, adding a suffix to the noun, as ስሜ **sïme** 'my name'. This second method is in fact the more usual way of expressing a pronoun possessor in Amharic. Have another look at the dialogue where you will find some other nouns with possessive pronoun suffixes: አባቴ 'my father'; አገሬ 'my home region', አገርሽ 'your home region', ሁለታችን 'the two of us' (*lit.* 'our two').

The possessive pronoun suffixes are as follows. Note that some of the suffixes have different forms according to whether the noun to which they are added ends in a consonant or a vowel: 'my' is -e after a consonant, ቤቴ **bete** 'my house', but -ye after a vowel ጓደኛዬ **gwaddäññaye** 'my friend'; 'his' is -u after a consonant – ቤቱ **betu** 'his house', but -w after a vowel ጓደኛው **gwaddäññaw** 'his friend'. Also, the three suffixes 'our' -aččïn, 'your' -aččuh, and 'their' -aččäw follow the rules of vowel hierarchy when added to a noun ending in a vowel, inserting a 'glide' w if the noun ends in -o or -u, a 'glide' y if it ends in -i or -e, and dropping the a vowel if it ends in -a.

noun ends in:	cons.	vowel	examples	
my	-e	-ye	ቤቴ, ተማሪዬ	bete, tämariye
your (masc.)	-ïh	-h	ቤትህ, ተማሪህ	betïh, tämarih
your (fem.)	-ïš	-š	ቤትሽ, ተማሪሽ	betïš, tämariš
his	-u	-w	ቤቱ, ተማሪው	betu, tämariw
her	-wa	-wa	ቤትዋ, ተማሪዋ	betwa, tämariwa
his, her (form.)	-aččäw	-aččäw,	ቤታቸው,	betaččäw
		-yaččäw,	ተማሪያቸው,	tämariyaččäw,
		-waččäw	ዳቦዋቸው	dabbowaččäw
our	-aččïn	-aččïn,	ቤታችን,	betaččïn
		-yaččïn,	ተማሪያችን,	tämariyaččïn,
		-waččïn	ዳቦዋችን	dabbowaččïn

noun ends in:	cons.	vowel	examples	
your (plural)	-aččuh	-aččuh,	ቤታችሁ,	betaččuh
		-yaččuh,	ተማሪያችሁ,	tämariyaččuh,
		-waččuh	ዳ በዋችሁ	dabbowaččuh
their	-aččäw	-aččäw,	ቤታቸው,	betaččäw
		-yaččäw,	ተማሪያቸው,	tämariyaččäw,
		-waččäw	ዳ በዋቸው	dabbowaččäw
your (for.)	-wo	-wo	ቤትዎ, ተማሪዎ	betwo, tämariwo

The possessive suffixes of the third person masculine, 'his . . .' and the third person feminine, 'her . . .', have the same shape as the masculine/plural and feminine definite articles. This means that a word such as ተማሪው tämariw is ambiguous, and can mean both 'the student' and 'his student'; similarly መኪናው mäkinawa is both 'the car' (cars are usually thought of as feminine) and 'her car', and ልጆቹ lijjočču is both 'the children' and 'his children'.

A noun with a possessive suffix added to it is counted as a definite noun, which means that an accompanying adjective has to have the definite article added to it. You will see later that there are other ways in which nouns with possessive suffixes behave like definite nouns. Examples are set out below:

ቤቴ bete ትልቁ ቤት tillik'u bet the big house
my house ትልቁ ቤቴ tilik'u bete my big house

እህትህ ihitih ትንሿ እህት tinnišwa ihit the little sister
your sister ትንሿ እህትህ tinnišwa ihitih your little sister

ተማሪዎቻችን tämariwoččaččin ትጉዎቹ ተማሪዎች tiguwočču
our students tämariwočč
the hard-working students

ትጉዎቹ ተማሪዎቻችን tiguwočču
tämariwoččaččin
our hard-working students

Exercises

7 Convert the pronoun possessives in የ- in the following sentences into possessive suffixes, and then translate them into English

1 የኔ አባት አስተማሪ ናቸው።
2 ይቺ ያንቺ መኪና ነች?
3 የሱ ትልቅ ወንድም ከአዲስ አበባ ደረሰ።
4 የርስዎ ተማሪዎች ትጉ ናቸው? አዎ፥ የኔ ተማሪዎች በጣም ትጉ ናቸው።
5 የኔ እናት ወደት ሂደች? ወደርስዎ እኅት ቤት ሂደች።
6 የነርሱ ንደኛ ብዙ ገንዘብ አለው።
7 ያንተ ስም ማን ነው? የኔ ስም ዳዊት ነው።
8 መላኩ ከርሱ ወንድም ጋር ወደ ሲኒማ ቤት ሔደ።

8 Here are some adjectives and some nouns with possessive suffixes. Combine the nouns with the adjectives to form meaningful phrases and then translate the whole phrase into English

Example _____ ልጅዋ። → ትንሹ ልጅዋ her little daughter

አዲስ addis 'new', አሮጌ aroge 'old', ሀብታም habtam 'rich', ድሀ diha 'poor', ቀይ k'äyy 'red', ጥቁር t'ik'ur 'black', ጥሩ t'iru 'good', መጥፎ mät'fo 'bad', ትልቅ tillik' 'big', ትንሽ tinniš 'little'.

1 _____ መኪናዬ።   6 _____ ንደኛችን።
2 _____ ጃኬትህ።   7 _____ ከተማው።
3 _____ ወንድማችን።   8 _____ አገሬ።
4 _____ ልብስዋ።   9 _____ ክፍላቸው።
5 _____ ቤታችሁ።   10 _____ እኅቱ።

Script

The homophonous letters

You will have noticed that in this lesson the word **tïmhïrt** was sometimes spelled ትምሕርት and sometimes ትምህርት, that is using different **h**s. In the introduction it was mentioned that there are several sounds that have more than one representation in the script; these may be called 'homophonous letters', letters that have the same sound.

The reason for these homophonous letters is historical, originally they represented different sounds that have merged together in Amharic. In Tigrinya, for example, some of them still have different sounds. Some people may use one letter in preference to another in certain words, reflecting the original 'correct' usage in Geʻez, for example. For example, the Geʻez word related to Amharic **sost** 'three' was written with **ሠ** for the first s and **ስ** for the second one, and so the 'correct' spelling should be **ሠስት**, but many people also write **ሶስት**. It would not be true to say that there are spelling rules in Amharic in the sense that there are, for example, in English. Rather, some spellings may be preferred to others by some people.

In order to distinguish these letters special names are sometimes given to them as follows:

ሰ	:	ሰ አሳት	sä ïsat	ጸ	:	ጸ ጸሎት	s'ä s'älot
ሠ	:	ሠ ንጉሥ	sä nïgus	ፀ	:	ፀ ፀሐይ	s'ä s'ähay
አ	:	አ አሌፍ	a alef	ሀ	:	ሀ ሃሌታ	ha halleta
ዐ	:	ዐ ዓይን	a ayn	ሐ	:	ሐ ሐመር	ha hamär
				ኀ	:	ኀ ብዙኀን	ha bïzuhan

The fourth **h** letter, **ኽ**, is pronounced **hä** in the first order, which is also the name by which it is called.

Exercise

9 Rewrite the following Amharic words using alternative letters where applicable. (Look up the words that you do not know)

1 ሠራተኛ ።
2 ዓለም ።
3 ጸጉረ ፄ ።
4 ውሐ ።
5 መሀንድስ ።

6 ጋይለኛ ።
7 ሲሶ ።
8 ፀሐፈ ።
9 ገለጸ ።
10 ስራ ።

11 ሥን ፀሐፍ ።
12 ስንደቅ አላማ ።
13 መስሪያ ቤት ።
14 ሀገን ።
15 ሐዝብ ።

Reading passage

የተረፈ አባት የመንግሥት ሠራተኛ ነበረ፡፡ እናቱም ባንድ
ትልቅ ቢሮ ፀሐፊ ነበረች፡፡ ሁለታቸው በከተማ ውስጥ ሥራ፡፡
አባትና እናቱ በጣም ደግ ሰዎች ነበሩ፡፡ አንድ ቀን አባትዬው
ከሥራው ገባና አንድ ትልቅ መጽሐፍ ለልጁ ሰጠው፡፡ ይህም
መጽሐፍ ገና ዛሬ አለው፡፡ በዚህም መጽሐፍ ብዙዎች ቆንጆዎች
ሥዕሎች አሉ፡፡ ስለዚህም ተረፈ መጽሐፉን በጣም ወደደ፡፡
የመጀመሪያው መጽሐፉ ነበረው፡፡

Supplementary vocabulary

ተመለሰ	tämälläsä	he returned, came back
ሰጠው	sät't'äw	he gave to him

4 ወደ ገበያ መሄድ
wädä gäbäya mähed

Going shopping

By the end of this lesson you should be able to:

- form sentences with a direct object (I saw the man)
- count up to 1,000
- use expressions of quantity
- understand and use properly the Ethiopian system of personal names

Shopping 🔲

Mr Mulugeta's wife goes shopping

ከሰዓት በኋላ ወደዘር አማረች ያቶ ሙሉጌታ ሚስት ወደ
መርካቶ ሄደች። ልዩ ልዩ ነገር ለመግዛት ፈለገች። በመጀመሪያ
ወደ ምግብ መደብር ገባች። ያቶ መሐመድ ሱቅ መርካቶ ውስጥ
ካውቶቡስ ጣቢያ አጠገብ ነው።

ወ/አማረች:	እንደምን አደርክ አቶ መሐመድ? ዛሬ እንደምን ነህ? ደኅና ነህ?
አ/መሐመድ:	ሰላም አሜቴ። ባልም አቶ ሙሉጌታ እዚህ ነበሩ።
ወ/አማረች:	እሪ፣ አሳቸውን ያያየቸው መቼ ነው?
አ/መሐመድ:	ባልዎን አቶ ሙሉጌታን ትናንትና ወይም ከትናንትና ወዲያ ነው ያያሁዋቸው። ታዲያስ እንዴት ልርዳዎ? ዛሬ ምን ይፈልጋሉ? አዲስ የመጣ ቡና አለ። ገና አሁን ከጅማ የደረሰ ነው።
ወ/አማረች:	አይደለም፣ ዛሬ ቡና አልፈልግም። ባለፈው ሳምንት እንቴ ሁለት ኪሎ ከሐረር አደረሰኝ። ሱኳርና ሩዝ አፈልጋለሁ፣ ደግሞም ምን ምን ዓይነት ሻይ አለ?
አ/መሐመድ:	ሦስት ዓይነት አለ። ይኸኛው በጣም ጥሩ ነው።
ወ/አማረች:	ዋጋው ስንት ነው? ውድ ነው?

አ/መሐመድ: አይደለም ፤ በውነት በጣም እርካሽ ነው፤ ሁለት ብር ብቻ ነው።
ወ/አማረች: እሺ ፤ ሁለት ፓኬት ሻይ ፤ አራት ኪሎ ሩዝና አንድ ኪሎ ሱኳር ስጠኝ ። ሁሉም ጥሩ ነው ፤ ተስፋ አደርጋለሁ!
አ/መሐመድ: እንዴታ! እዚህ ሁሉም ነገር ጥሩ ነው!
ወ/አማረች: እሺ ፤ ሂሳቡ ስንት ነው?
አ/መሐመድ: በጠቅላላው አሥራ ስድስት ከሃያ አምስት ነው።
ወ/አማረች: ሃያ ብር ይሐውና!
አ/መሐመድ: ከሃያ ብር አሥራ ስድስት ከሃያ አምስት ... መልሱ ሦስት ብር ከሰባ አምስት ነው። በጣም አገዙር ይስጥልኝ።
ወ/አማረች: አብር ይስጥልኝ።

käsäat bähwala wäyzäro Amaräčč yato Mulugeta mist wädä märkato hedäčč. lïyyu lïyyu nägär lämägzat fällägäčč. bämäjämmäriya wädä mïgïb mädäbbïr gäbbačč. yato Mähammäd suk˙ märkato wïst˙ kawtobus t'abiya at'ägäb näw.

W. AMARÄČČ: ïndämïn addärk, ato Mähammäd. zare ïndämïn näh? dähna näh?
A. MÄHAMMÄD: sälam, ïmmete. balwo, ato Mulugeta ïzzih näbbäru.
W. AMARÄČČ: ärä, ïssaččäwn yayyähaččäw mäče näw?
A. MÄHAMMÄD: balwon ato Mulugetan tïnantïnna . . . wäyïm kätïnantïnna wädiya näw yayyähwaččäw . . . tadiyass, ïndet lïrdawo? zare mïn yïfällïgallu? addis yämät't'a bunna allä. gäna ahun käJimma yädärräsä näw.
W. AMARÄČČ: aydälläm, zare bunna alfällïgïm. balläfäw sammïnt ïhïte hulättï kilo käHarär adärräsäččïlliñ. sukkwarïnna ruz ïfällïgallähw; dägmom mïn mïn aynät šay allä?
A. MÄHAMMÄD: sost aynät allä. yïhäññaw bät'am t'ïru näw.
W. AMARÄČČ: wagaw sïntï näw? wïddï näw?
A. MÄHAMMÄD: aydälläm, bäwnät bät'am ïrkaš näw; hulättï bïrr bïčča näw.
W. AMARÄČČ: ïšši, hulättï paket šay, arattï kilo ruzïnna andï kilo sukkwar sït'äñ. hullum t'ïru näw, täsfa adärgallähw!
A. MÄHAMMÄD: ïndeta! ïzzih hullum nägär t'ïru näw!
W. AMARÄČČ: ïšši, hisabu sïntï näw?
A. MÄHAMMÄD: bät'äk'lallaw asra sïddïst kähaya ammïstï näw.
W. AMARÄČČ: haya bïrr yïhäwïnna!
A. MÄHAMMÄD: kähaya bïrr asra sïddïst kähaya ammïst . . . mälsu sostï

A. Mähammäd: kähaya bïrr asra sïddïst kähaya ammïst . . . mälsu sostï
bïrr käsäba ammïstï näw. bät'am ïgzer yïst'ïllïñ.
W. Amaräčč: abro yïst'ïllïñ.

*In the afternoon Mrs Amarech, Mr Mulugeta's wife, went to the
market. She wanted to buy various items. First, she went to a grocery
store. Mr Mohammed's shop is inside the market close to the bus
station.*

Mrs Amarech: *Good afternoon, Mr Mohammed. How are you
today? Are you well?*
Mr Mohammed: *Salam, Madam . . . Your husband was here.*
Mrs Amarech: *Oh, when did you see him?*
Mr Mohammed: *I saw your husband, Mr Mulugeta, yesterday . . .
or the day before yesterday. Now, how may I help
you? What are you looking for today? I have
some good fresh coffee; it's only just arrived from
Jimma.*
Mrs Amarech: *No, I don't want coffee today. Last week my sister
brought me two kilos from Harar. I want some
sugar and some rice; also what brands of tea do
you have?*
Mr Mohammed: *There are three brands. This one's very good.*
Mrs Amarech: *How much is it? Is it dear?*
Mr Mohammed: *No, it's really very cheap; it's only 2 birr.*
Mrs Amarech: *OK, give me two packets of tea, four kilos of rice
and one kilo of sugar. Everything's good, I hope!*
Mr Mohammed: *Of course! Everything's good here!*
Mrs Amarech: *OK. How much is the bill?*
Mr Mohammed: *Altogether, that's birr 16.25.*
Mrs Amarech: *Here's 20 birr.*
Mr Mohammed: *16.25 from 20 . . . the change is 3.75. Thank you
very much.*
Mrs Amarech: *You're welcome!*

Vocabulary

ገበያ	gäbäya	market
መርካቶ	märkato	*the market in Addis Ababa, said to be the largest market area in Sub-Saharan Africa*
አውቶቡስ	awtobus	bus
ያውቶቡስ ጣቢያ	yawtobus t'abiya	bus station

ባቡር ጣቢያ	babur t'abiya	railway station
ሰላም	sälam	peace (*used as a greeting amongst Muslims and by young people*)
እመቴ	ïmmete	Madam (*lit.* 'my lady' *from* እመት, *variant* እመቤት ïmmäbet)
ጌታዬ	getaye	Sir (*lit.* 'my lord' *from* ጌታ)
ልዩ	lïyyu	different, special
ልዩ ልዩ	lïyyu lïyyu	various, several, miscellaneous
ነገር	nägär	thing, word
ሱቅ	suk'	shop, store
መደብር	mädäbbïr	store, bazaar
የምግብ መደብር	yämïgïb mädäbbïr	food shop, grocery store
ባል	bal	husband
ትናንትና	tïnantïnna	yesterday
ከትናንትና ወዲያ	kätïnantïnna wädiya	the day before yesterday
ቡና	bunna	coffee
ሻይ	šay	tea
ስኳር or ሱኳር	sïkkwar, sukkwar	sugar
ሩዝ	ruz	rice
ደግሞ	dägmo	also; (ደግሞም *lit.* 'and also')
ባለፈው ሳምንት	balläfäw sammïnt	last week (*lit.* 'in the week that has passed')
ዓይነት	aynät	sort, kind, brand (*of merchandise*)
ምን ምን ዓይነት	mïn mïn aynät	what kinds of . . . (*repeating the word* ምን *indicates that several kinds are expected*)
ይኸኛው	yïhäññaw	this one
ያኛው	yaññaw	that one
ዋጋ	waga	price, value
ውድ	wïdd	dear, expensive
እርካሽ	ïrkaš	cheap
በውነት	bäwnät	really, truly (*lit.* 'in truth', *from* እውነት ïwnät 'truth')
ፓኬት	paket	packet
ብቻ	bïčča	only
ብር	bïrr	birr (*Ethiopian unit of currency*), silver
ሁሉም	hullum	everything, everyone
ሁሉም ነገር	hullum nägär	everything
እንዲታ	ïndeta	of course!
ኪሎ	kilo	kilo
ሂሳብ	hisab	bill, account

ጠቅላላ	t'äk'lalla	total, overall, general
በጠቅላላው	bät'äk'lalllaw	altogether, all in all, in sum (*lit.* 'in the total')
ይኸውና	yïhäwïnna	here it is! (*compare* ይኸው *in lesson 3*)
መልስ	mäls	change (*i.e. from a bill*), answer

Numbers

አንድ	and	one
ሁለት	hulätt	two
ሦስት	sost	three
አራት	aratt	four
አምስት	ammïst	five
አሥራ ስድስት	asra sïddïst	sixteen
ሃያ	haya	twenty
ሰባ	säba	seventy

Verbs

ልርዳዎ	lïrdawo	let me help you, may I help you? (*for.*)
ረዳ	rädda	help (*2-lit'*)
ይፈልጋሉ	yïfälligallu	you want (*for.*) – *from* ፈለገ
እፈልጋለሁ	ïfälligallähw	I want
አደረሰችልኝ	adärräsäččïllïñ	she brought me (*lit.* 'she made (it) come for me'); *from* ደረሰ
ስጠኝ	sït'äñ	give me; from ሰጠ
አብሮ ይስጥልኝ	abro yïst'ïllïñ	you're welcome! (*the response to* እንዲአብሔር *or* እንዜር ይስጥልኝ); *lit.* 'may he give (you health) for my sake as well'
ተስፋ አደርጋለሁ	täsfa adärgallähw	I hope – *lit.* 'I do hope'; (አደርጋለሁ *is from* አደረገ)

Notes on the dialogue

1 The Ethiopian (Amhara and Tigrean) system of personal names is quite different from ours. A wife does not take her husband's name but keeps her own. Also, there are no surnames or family names as we know them; everyone has their own given name, of course, which is followed by their father's given name: so Mulugeta Kebede (ሙሉጌታ ከበደ) that is, Mulugeta (the son of) Kebede, or Amarech Haile Selassie (አማረች ኃይለ ሥላሴ) that is, Amarech (the daughter of) Haile Selassie. Mulugeta and Amarech's children will have Mulugeta as their second name: their son is Terefe Mulugeta (ተረፈ ሙሉጌታ) , and their daughter is Tsehay Mulugeta (ፀሐይ ሙሉጌታ). Some names contain two elements, like Haile Selassie (ኃይለ ሥላሴ), or Gebre Mikael (ገብረ ሚካኤል), or Welette Semayat (ወለተ ሰማያት). These double-barrelled names mostly have a religious origin; these last three literally mean (in Ge'ez) 'Might of the Trinity', 'Slave of Michael' and 'Daughter of Heaven', and often in ordinary usage are shortened, as for example to Hailie (ኃይሉ) or Gebrie (ገብሬ). Most Christian Amhara names mean something either in Amharic, or in Ge'ez, or are names drawn from the Bible and Christian tradition or, amongst Muslims, from Islamic tradition. Amarech, for example, means 'she is beautiful' in Amharic and Mulugeta means 'complete master'. You may find this difficult at first because there are no capital letters in the Ethiopian script and so nothing to make proper names stand out from the surrounding text.

When Ethiopians write their names in Roman letters, unfortunately they do not follow one single system, and they certainly do not use the type of transcription you find in this and other textbooks and grammars, with all the appropriate accents and diacritics. You have probably noticed that in the English translations of the dialogues so far a simpler system has been used; this will give you some idea of what you will find in practice.

Here are some names of biblical, Christian or Islamic origin. See how many you can identify:

ዮሐንስ ዳዊት ዓሊ አይሻ ኤልሳቤት ሰሎሞን መሐመድ
እዝራ ኤጥሮስ ሐና አስቴር ፋጡማ ዮዲት ዮሴፍ ዩሱፍ
ማርቆስ አዚዝ ቴዎድሮስ እሌኒ ይስሐቅ ጳውሎስ

2 ያየሃቸው መቼ ነው literally means 'when is it that you saw him'; ተናንትና ነው ያየሁዋቸው, *lit.* 'it is yesterday that I saw

him'; አዲስ የመጣ ነው, *lit.* 'it is what came recently'; ከጅማ የደረሰ ነው, *lit.* 'it is what arrived from Jimma'. Rather than use a simple sentence pattern like መቼ አየኸው 'when did you see him?', ተናንትና አየሁዋቸው 'I saw him yesterday', or አዲስ መጣ 'it came recently', Amharic likes to use this type of construction, particularly when emphasizing something within a sentence. It is especially common with question words like ማን, ምንድን, መቼ, and so on. The construction involves the verb 'to be' and the relative form of the verb, here indicated by prefixed የ-. We shall deal with this more fully in a later lesson.

Note the use of the pronoun suffix -aččäw on the verbs የአየኸው and የየሁዋቸው to denote the pronoun object 'him' (*formal*).

3 The Ethiopian unit of currency is the birr (ብር) which also used to be referred to as the Ethiopian dollar. One birr is divided into a hundred cents or santim (ሳንቲም). Normally, when you quote a price, for example birr 4.25, you just say አራት ከሃያ አምስት or አራት ብር ከሃያ አምስት aratt kähaya ammïst or arattï birr kähaya ammïst, *lit.* 'four with twenty five' or 'four birr with twenty five'. Until 1991 the birr was linked to the US Dollar at $2.05, but is now free-floating and at the time of writing there are about nine birr to the pound sterling. Denominations from 1 birr upwards are all banknotes; of the coins the 25-santim piece is popularly referred to as a ስሙኒ sïmuni.

Grammar

The direct object suffix

In the sentences ባልዎን አየሁዋቸው balwon ayyähuwaččäw 'I saw your husband' and እሳቸውን የየኸው መቼ ነው ïssaččäwn yayyähaččäw mäče näw 'when did you see him?', the suffix -ን on ባልዎን and እሳቸውን indicates that 'your husband' and 'him' are in each sentence the direct object of the verb 'to see'. The verb 'to see' is a transitive verb, which means to make a complete sentence you must 'see somebody or something', or in other words a transitive verb expects a direct object. In these sentences the direct object is the person or thing that you 'see'. In English the direct object usually comes after the verb, but this is of course not the case with Amharic since the verb is usually the last word in the sentence.

Here are some more sentences with marked direct objects:

ገንዘቡን አገኘሁ	gänzäbun agäññähw	I found the money
ዳቦውን በላህ	dabbown bällah	You ate the bread
መኪናዋን ገዙ	mäkinawan gäzzu	They bought the car
ሂሳባችንን ከፈለች	hisabaččinin käffäläčč	She paid our bill
ይህን አልፈለግሁም	yihin alfälläghum	I did not want this
ይቺን ሴት ሳመ	yiččin set samä	He kissed this woman
እሱን አላወቀም	issun alawwäk'äm	He did not know that
ከበደን አየን	Käbbädän ayyän	We saw Kebede

In Amharic the direct object is marked by adding the suffix -ን, i.e. -n after a vowel and -in after a consonant, to the end of the word. If the direct object is 'definite' it must be marked with -ን; if it is 'indefinite' the object marker is usually left off and is only added for clarity. With this in mind, contrast መጽሐፍ ገዛሁ mäs'haf gäzzahw 'I bought a book' and መጽሐፉን ገዛሁ mäs'hafun gäzzahw 'I bought the book'.

A 'definite' noun belongs to one of the following five categories:

1	noun & definite article	ገንዘቡን አገኘሁ	I found *the money*
2	noun & possessive pronoun	ሂሳባችንን ከፈለች	she paid *our bill*
3	demonstrative	ይህን አልፈለግሁም	I did not want *this*
	demonstrative + noun	ይቺን ሴት ሳመ	he kissed *this woman*
4	independent pronoun	እሱን አላወቀም	he did not know *it*
5	proper name	ከበደን አየን	we saw *Kebede*

As you can see from the example ይቺን ሴት ሳመ, the suffix -ን is not always added to the end of the noun phrase. In a complex noun phrase, the object marker (-ን) is normally placed on the first constituent only. Study the examples in the box below.

demonstrative & ን & noun	ይቺን መኪና ገዛሁ yičči*n* mäkina gäzzahw	I bought this car
definite adjective & ን & noun	ቀይዋን መኪና ገዛሁ k'äyyiwa*n* mäkina gäzzahw	I bought the red car
possessive noun & ን & noun	የከበደን መኪና ገዛሁ yäKäbbäda*n* mäkina gäzzahw	I bought Kebede's car

Similarly, in a complex noun phrase that contains more than two constituents, normally only the first will have the object marker added. If the noun phrase is extremely long, the object marker may be repeated. Consider the following examples:

የከበደን ቀይ መኪና ገዛሁ	
yäKäbbädän k'äyy mäkina gäzzahw	I bought Kebede's red car
ያቺን የከበደን ቀይ መኪና ገዛሁ	
yaččin yäKäbbädän k'äyy mäkina gäzzahw	I bought that red car of Kebede's

Exercises

1 Study the following sentences and if necessary add the object marker - ን in the correct place

Example ይህ አልፈልግም → ይህን አልፈልግም

1 ሁለት ኪሎ ቡና ገዛች።
2 አስተማሪው መጽሐፍቸ ወሰደ።
3 አባቱ ይህ ገንዘብ ሁሉ ለልጁ ሰጠ።
4 አልማዝ ቀዩ መጽሐፌ አገኘች።
5 ወይዘሮ ፀሐይ እነዚህ ደብዳቤዎች ጻፉ።
6 እቶ ተረፈ አፖስታ ቤት ውስጥ አየሁ።
7 ባለፈው ሳምንት ጥሩ ፊልም እሲኒማ ቤት አየን።

2 Construct as many sentences with direct objects as you can out of the following nouns, noun phrases and verbs. Be sure to add the object marker where necessary and try to make sure the verbs are in the correct person. (You may need to look some words up in the glossary)

ሦስት ኪሎ ሱኳር, አንድ ጥሩ መጽሐፍ, ተማሪቸ, አውቶቡስ, ቡናው, ብዙ ገንዘብ ያቾ ሙሉጌታ ጋዜጣ, እኔ, ብርጭቆው, ልጁ, ቀይዋ መኪና, ወይዘሮ ጊፉት, ይህ ሰው, ሌባው;

ፈለገ, ገዛ, ወሰደ, አየ, ሠረቀ, አገኘ, ወደደ, ጻፈ, ሰበረ.

Numbers 🔊

The numbers 1–1,000 in Amharic are as follows. Remember that only the number 1 has a special form for use with feminine nouns: እንዲት andit.

In Ethiopia both the European and indigenous numeral signs are used. There is an increasing tendency to use the European signs, but you will still need to know the Ethiopian signs as well. The Ethiopian system is different from the European system in that it has separate signs for the tens and for a hundred, so that a number is generally written as it is spoken:

ሰባ አምስት säba ammïst 75 – ፸፭, i.e. '70–5'

አራት መቶ ሳላሳ ሁለት arattï mäto sälasa hulätt 432 – ፬፻፴፪, i.e. '4–100–30–2'

አስራ ዘጠኝ መቶ ስልሳ ስድስት asra zät'äñ mäto sïlsa sïddïst 1966 – ፲፱፻፷፮, i.e. '10–9–100–60–6'.

The word for 1,000 ሺህ, ሺ ših, ši has no special numeral sign, neither does ሚሊዮን miliyon 'million': ስምንት ሺ አምስት መቶ ዘጠና ሦስት sïmmïntï ši ammïstï mäto zät'äna sost '8,593' – ፰ሺ፭፻፺፫, i.e. '8-thousand 5–100–90–3'. The signs for numbers are given more fully below.

		sign				sign
1	እንድ and	፩	11	አስራ እንድ, አስራንድ asra and, asrand		፲፩
2	ሁለት hulätt	፪	12	አስራ ሁለት asra hulätt		፲፪
3	ሦስት sost	፫	13	አስራ ሦስት asra sost		፲፫
4	አራት aratt	፬	14	አስራ አራት asra aratt, asraratt		፲፬
5	አምስት ammïst	፭	15	አስራ አምስት asra ammïst, asrammïst		፲፭
6	ስድስት sïddïst	፮	16	አስራ ስድስት asra sïddïst		፲፮
7	ሰባት säbatt	፯	17	አስራ ሰባት asra säbatt		፲፯
8	ስምንት sïmmïnt	፰	18	አስራ ስምንት asra sïmmïnt		፲፰
9	ዘጠኝ zät'äñ	፱	19	አስራ ዘጠኝ asra zät'äñ		፲፱
10	አስር assïr	፲				

			sign				sign
20	ሃያ		haya	፳	40	አርባ arba	፵
21	ሃያ እንድ		haya and	፳፩	50	አምሳ, ሃምሳ amsa, hamsa	፶
22	ሃያ ሁለት		haya hulätt	፳፪	60	ስልሳ, ስድሳ sïlsa, sïdsa	፷
23	ሃያ ሦስት		haya sost	፳፫, etc.	70	ሰባ säba	፸
30	ሳላሳ		sälasa	፴	80	ሰማንያ sämanya	፹
31	ሳላሳ እንድ		sälasa and	፴፩	90	ዘጠና zät'äna	፺
32	ሳላሳ ሁለት		sälasa hulätt	፴፪	100	መቶ mäto	፻
33	ሳላሳ ሦስት		sälasa sost	፴፫, etc.	1,000	ሺህ, ሺ ših, ši	

When using a numeral higher than 'one' with a noun you do not normally need to use the plural. So, for example: ሁለት ኪሎ ቡና **hulättï kilo bunna** 'two kilos of coffee', አምስት መቶ ሰው **ammïstï mäto säw** 'five hundred people', ኃምሳ ስድስት ብር **hamsa sïddïstï bïrr** 'fifty-six birr', አስራ ዘጠኝ ተማሪ **asra zät'äñ tämari** 'nineteen students'. The plural is used, however, when you wish to stress the separateness of each member that goes to make up a group: አስራ ዘጠኝ ተማሪዎች **asra zät'äñ tämariwočč** 'nineteen (separate) students', that is, each regarded as individuals rather than a collective group. The same principle applies to other quantifying words like ብዙ **bïzu** 'many' and ሁሉ **hullu** 'all'.

Here are a few other useful words denoting quantity and measurements:

ግማሽ	gïmmaš	half
ሢሶ	siso	a third
ሩብ	rub	a quarter
ጥቂት	t'ïk'it	few, a little (*in the plural* ጥቂቶች **t'ïk'itočč** *means* a few *as in* ጥቂቶች ሰዎች a few people)
አንዳንድ	andand	some (*i.e. an unspecified number*); *also used in the plural, for example,* አንዳንዶች ሰዎች some people *as well as* አንዳንድ ሰዎች
ልዩ ልዩ	lïyyu lïyyu	several

The word ሁሉ **hullu** 'all' is exceptional in that it can be placed either in front of or, more usually, after the noun it goes with:

ተማሪዎች ሁሉ ትጉ ናቸው **tämariwočč hullu tïgu naččäw** all students are hard-working

ገንዘቡን ሁሉ ወሰደ **gänzäbun hullu wässädä** he took all the money

Here are some special expressions that contain the word ሁሉ:

ሰው ሁሉ or ሁሉ ሰው	säw hullu / hullu säw	everyone, everybody
ነገር ሁሉ or ሁሉ ነገር	nägär hullu / hullu nägär	everything
ሁልጊዜ	hulgize	always
ሁሉ ቀን	hullu k'än	every day
ሁሉም	hullum	everything, everyone
ሁሉም ቦታ	hullum bota	everywhere

ሁለሁሉ	hullahullu	everything together, all sorts of things
ሁላችን	hullaččin	all of us
ሁላችሁ	hullaččuh	all of you
ሁላቸው	hullaččäw	all of them

Expressions of quantity

In the dialogue Mrs Amarech asks the shopkeeper, ሁለት ፓኬት ሻይ፣ አራት ኪሎ ሩዝና አንድ ኪሎ ሱኳር ስጭኝ 'give me two packets of tea, four kilos of rice and one kilo of sugar'. From this you can see that in expressions of quantity like 'two packets of tea' or 'four kilos of rice' you do not use the possessive particle የ- or the possessive construction. Instead, the quantity expression is followed directly by the name of the substance that is being measured.

Here are some more examples of useful quantity expressions:

ሁለት ብርጭቆ ሻይ አምጣልኝ	hulätti birč'ik'o šay amt'alliñ bring me two glasses of tea
አንድ ሲኒ ቡና አምጣልኝ	andï sini bunna amt'alliñ bring me a cup of coffee
ሦስት ጠርሙስ ቢራ ጠጣ	sostï t'ärmus bira t'ät't'a he drank three bottles of beer
አምስት መቶ ግራም ቅቤ ገዛች	ammïstï mäto gram k'ïbe gäzzač she bought five hundred grammes of butter
አንድ ፓኬት ሲጃራ ስጭኝ	andï paket sijara sït'äñ give me a packet of cigarettes

The ordinal numbers

The ordinal numbers, ('first','second', 'third', etc.), are formed by adding the suffix -äñña, or -ñña after a vowel. Consider the following examples:

1st	አንደኛ	andäñña	፩ኛ	
2nd	ሁለተኛ	hulättäñña	፪ኛ	፪ተኛ
3rd	ሦስተኛ	sostäñña	፫ኛ	፫ተኛ
4th	አራተኛ	arattäñña	፬ኛ	፬ተኛ
5th	አምስተኛ	ammïstäñña	፭ኛ	፭ተኛ

6th	ስድስተኛ	sïddïstäñña	፮ኛ	፮ተኛ
7th	ሰባተኛ	säbattäñña	፯ኛ	፯ተኛ
8th	ስምንተኛ	sïmmïntäñña	፰ኛ	፰ተኛ
9th	ዘጠነኛ	zät'änäñña	፱ኛ	
10th	አስረኛ	assïräñña	፲ኛ	
11th	አስራ አንደኛ	asra andäñña, *etc.*	፲፩ኛ *etc.*	

Note that 'first' may also be translated by የመጀመሪያ yämäjämmäriya and ፊተኛ fïtäñña. Also note that 'ninth' is built on the base zät'än- and not zät'äñ.

Exercises

3 Write out the following phrases in full and then say them aloud

1 23 ብር	6 40 ብር ከ50 ሳንቲም	11 ፪፻፲፯
2 5 ኪሎ	7 4 ሺህ 500 ዓመት	12 ፻፱
3 18 ሰዓት	8 33 ደቂቃ	13 ፵፭
4 160 ቀን	9 ፲፱፻፺፪	14 ፲፱፻፳፭
5 237 ኪሎሜትር	10 ፲፯፻፸፱	15 ፲፯፻፷፫

4 Do the following sums in Amharic following the examples

(a) 5 + 3 = 8   አምስት ሲደመር ሦስት ስምንት ነው ።
(b) 5 – 2 = 3   አምስት ሲቀነስ ሁለት ሦስት ነው ።

(ሲደመር siddämmär 'plus', ሲቀነስ sik'k'ännäs 'minus')

1 21 + 9 =	6 15 + 4 =
2 25 – 5 =	7 17 – 7 =
3 12 + 12 =	8 60 + 16 =
4 120 + 30 =	9 500 + 500 =
5 40 + 50 =	10 88 – 11 =

5 Imagine you are going shopping. Based on what you have learned so far, how would you ask the shopkeeper for the following items?

Example a can of oil → እባክህ አንድ ቆርቆር ዘይት ስጠኝ ።

1 3 kilos of sugar	6 ½ kilo of good flour
2 4 packets of tea	7 5 bottles of Metta beer
3 200 grammes of butter	8 2 packets of cigarettes
4 6 bottles of 'Ambo Water'	9 a can of meat
5 10 boxes of matches	10 a good brand of tea

Script

Writing the combination consonant + wa

In the introduction you were introduced to the wa letters: ኣ, ጓ, ቷ, · ኋ, etc. Some people avoid using these and instead write the 6th order of the consonant followed by the letter wa ዋ, or even the 2nd order followed by ዋ: so the word t'wat 'early morning' may be written ጧት, ትዋት or ጡዋት.

The third method can be explained because the combination of consonant + wa often arises from the addition of a suffix beginning in a to a base ending in u, such as አየሁዋቸው ayyähuwaččäw (ayyähu + aččäw) 'I saw him' in the dialogue. In rapid speech this is contracted to ayyähwaččäw and can therefore also be written as አየኋቸው, or as አየሀዋቸው. Other words, too, where the sequence of consonant + wa does not derive from a contraction may be written in the same way, such as ጧት, ጡዋት, etc., 'morning' or በኋላ, በኡዋላ, etc. 'afterwards'; or ጓደኛ, ጉዋደኛ, etc. 'friend', and so on.

The remaining w letters

Of the other letters indicating a combination, a consonant-followed w and another vowel, only those representing combinations in wä and wï are current in modern Amharic, though you may find the others in words of Ge'ez origin that are used in certain styles of Amharic.

To remind you, the wä letters are ጐ, ኰ, ኈ and ቈ, gwä, kwä, hwä and k'wä. In pronunciation these are almost identical to the 7th orders go, ko, ho and k'o, and in writing, too, may be substituted by these. So, a word like gobäz 'clever, strong' may be written both as ጎበዝ and as ጐበዝ. Here are some more words of the same kind:

ቆየ, ቈየ k'oyyä 'he waited'; ቆጠረ, ቈጠረ k'ot't'ärä 'he counted'; መኮንን, መኰንን mäkonnïn 'officer' (also a man's name)

Similarly, the wï letters, ጒ, ኲ, ኍ and ቍ are pronounced much like the 2nd orders **gu, ku, hu** and **k'u,** and may be substituted by these:

> **ቁጥር**, **ቍጥር** **k'ut'ïr** 'number'; **ኩራተኛ**, **ኵራተኛ** **kuratäñña** 'proud, vain'; **ጉድ**, **ጕድ** **gud** 'extraordinary'

Exercises

6 Here are some words and phrases containing wa, wä ***or*** wï ***letters. Read them out aloud and then rewrite them using alternative spellings. See how many you can translate into English, and don't hesitate to use the glossary for some***

1 ከዚህ በኋላ	6 ያማርኛ ቋንቋ	11 ቈረጥኩ
2 ጐረቤት	7 ቈንጆ	12 አቧራ
3 ልጆቿ	8 ጐደለ	13 የጐንደር ከተማ
4 መቈረጥ	9 ፈለጓቸው	14 የእግር ኳስ
5 ስኳር	10 ቧምቧ	15 ሄዷል

Reading passage

ዛሬ ወይዘሮ ድንቅነሽ ወደ ገበያ ሄደች። ከርሷም ጋር ከበደና ጣይቱ ሄዱ። ከበደ ትንሽ ልጅ ነው። አስር ዓመቱ ነው። ጣይቱም የወይዘሮ ድንቅነሽ ገረድ ናት። ወይዘሮ ድንቅነሽ ከሱቅ ብዙ ልዩ ልዩ ነገር ለመግዛት ፈለገች – ሩዝና ዱቄት፣ ሻይና ቅቤ፣ ከዚህም በላይ ብርቱካን፣ ፓፓያ፣ ቲማቲም፣ ሽንኩርትና ድንች። ስለዚህም ዛሬ ጣይቱ አብራ መጣች። በመጀመሪያ ወደ ምግብ መደብር ገቡ። እዚያም ዱቄት፣ ሩዝ፣ ሻይና ቅቤ ገዙ። አትክልትና ፍሬ ግን አልነበረም። ያትክልት ሱቅ ከመደብሩ አጠገብ አይደለም፤ በጣም ሩቅ ነው። ስለዚህ በእግር ለመሄድ አልቻሉም፤ በአውቶቡስ ሄዱ። ወይዘሮ ድንቅነሽ ስለገበያው በጣም ተደሰተችና ለከበደ ከረሜላ ገዛች።

Supplementary vocabulary

ገረድ	**gäräd**	maid	ሽንኩርት	**šinkurt**	onion
ብርቱካን	**birtukan**	orange	ድንች	**dinnič**	potato
ፓፓያ	**papaya**	papaya	አትክልት	**atkilt**	vegetables
ቲማቲም	**timatim**	tomato	ፍሬ	**fire**	fruit
ተደሰተ	**tädässätä**	be pleased	ከረሜላ	**kärämella**	sweets, candy

ያትክልት መሸጫ ሱቅ	yatkïlt mäšäč'a suk'	the green grocer's (*lit.* 'vegetable selling shop')
በገበየችው ገበያ	bägäbäyyäččïw gäbäya	with the shopping she has done
ገዛችለት	gäzzaččïllät	she bought for him

ድንቅነሽ Dïnk'ïnäš and ጣይቱ T'aytu *are women's names*

5 የሩቅ ጥሪ
yäruk' t'irri
A long-distance call

> **By the end of this lesson you should be able to:**
>
> - form the present-future tenses ('I go', 'am going', 'shall go', *etc.*)
> - tell the time

A long-distance telephone call 📼

Kebede receives a long-distance telephone call

ምሽት ነው። ከበደና ጊሩት እቤት ናቸው። ከበደ ጋዜጣ
ያነባል። ስልክ ይደወላል፤ ጊሩት ለስልኩ መልስ ትሰጣለች።

ጊሩት: ሀሎ! 71 56 22፤ *ያቾ ሙሉጌታ መኖሪያ ቤት። ማን*
ነህ የምትናገር?

ዮሐንስ: እኔ ነኝ፤ ዮሐንስ ነኝ። ከበደ አለ? ከሱ ጋር
ለመናገር እችላለሁ?

ጊሩት: አዎ፤ አለ። እንዴ ጠብቅ። ... ከበደ፤ ዮሐንስ ነው።
ካንተ ጋር ለመናገር ይፈልጋል። ና፤ ቶሎ በል
እንገዲህ! ይጠብቃል። የሩቅ ጥሪ ይመስለኛል።

ከበደ: እንዴ? እንዴት ይሆናል? እሱ አሜሪካ ያለው
አይደለም? ... ሀሎ ዮሐንስ፤ እንተ ነህ? ከዬት እገር
ትደውላለህ?

ዮሐንስ: ከሱንደን እደውላለሁ፤ የዛሬ ሁለት ቀን እዚህ
ደረስኩ፤ በቅርብ ጊዜ ግን ተመልሼ እሄዳለሁ። አሁን
ብዙ ለመነጋገር ጊዜ ፈጽሞ የለኝም፤ እችላለሁ።
ለመጠየቅ የምፈልገው እንተና ጊሩት ካይርፖላን
ማረፊያ እነነና እናቴን ለመቀበል ትችላላችሁ?

ከበደ: እንዴታ! ብቻ መቼ ትደርሳላችሁ?

ዮሐንስ: ማክሰኞ ከጥዋቱ በሁለት ሰዓት እንደርሳለን። በል አሁን
እዘጋለሁ። መቸኩል አለብኝ፤ ደና ሁን!

ከበደ: እሺ፤ አይርፖላን ማረፊያ እንደሳለን። ደና ሁን

ዮሐንስ፡ አስክ ማክሰኞ ድረስ! (ከበደ ስልኩን
ይዞጋል) ታዲያ ዮሐንስና እናቱ ማክሰኞ ይደርሳሉ።
ዛሬ ግን ቀጸሜ ነው። አንገዲህ ከሦስት ቀን በኋላ
መሆኑ ነው። ... አይ! የበረራ ቀኑ ጥረን
አልጠየቅሁም። ቢሆንም ከሉንደን የሚመጣ በረራ
በሁለት ሰዓት ያርፋል። አንቺስ ከኔ ጋር ወደ
አይሮፕላን ማረፊያ ትሂጃለሽ?
ሒሩት፡ በምን አንዚጻለን?
ከበደ፡ ያባተን መኪና አ዗ሳለሁ።
ሒሩት፡ አውነትህን ነው!? ... እሺ አናያለን!

mïšät näw. Kässädänna Hirut ïbet naččäw. Kässädä gazet'a yanäbbal.
sïlk yïddäwwälal; Hirut läsïlku mäls tïsät'alläčč.

HIRUT: hallo! säba and, hamsa sïddïst, haya hulätt, yato Mulugeta
mänoriya bet. man näh yämmïttïnnaggär?
YOHANNÏS: ïne näñ; Yohannïs näñ. Kässädä allä? kässu lämännagär
ïčïlallähw?
HIRUT: awo, allä. ande t'äbbïk' ... Kässädä, Yohannïs näw. kantä
gar lämännagär yïfällïgal. na, tolo bäl ïngïdih! yït'äbbïk'al.
yäruk' t'ïrri yïmäsläññal.
KÄSSÄDÄ: ïnde? ïndet yïhonal? ïssu Amerika yalläw aydälläm? ...
hallo Yohannïs, antä näh? käyet agär tïdäwwïlalläh?
YOHANNÏS: käLondon ïdäwwïlallähw. yäzare hulättï k'än ïzzih där-
räskw; bäk'ïrbï gize gïn tämällïšše ïhedallähw. ahun bïzu
lämännägagär gïze fäs's'ïmo yälläññïm, ïčäkkulallähw.
lämät'äyyäk' yämmïfällïgäw, antänna Hirut kayroplan
maräfiya ïneninna ïnnaten lämäk'k'äbäl tïčïlallaččuh?
KÄSSÄDÄ: ïndeta! bïčča mäče tïdärsallaččuh?
YOHANNÏS: maksäñño kät'watu bähulättï säat ïnnïdärsallän. bäl ahun
ïzägallähw; mäčäkkwäl alläbbïñ. dähna hun!
KÄSSÄDÄ: ïšši, ayroplan maräfiya ïnnïdärsallän. dähna hun, Yohannïs,
ïskä maksäñño dïräs! [Kässädä sïlkun yïzägal.] tadiya,
Yohannïsïnna ïnnatu maksäñño yïdärsallu. zare gïn k'ïdame
näw. ïngïdih käsostï k'än bähwala mähonu näw. ay!
yäbärära k'ut'run alt'äyyäk'hum. bihonïm käLondon
yämmimät'a bärära bähulättï säat yarfal. ančiss käne gar
wädä ayroplan maräfiya tïhejalläš?
HIRUT: bämïn ïnnïhedallän?
KÄSSÄDÄ: yabbaten mäkina ïwwasallähw.
HIRUT: ïwnätïhïn näw?! ïšši ïnnayallän!

*It is evening. Kebede and Hirut are at home. Kebede is reading the
newspaper. The telephone rings; Hirut answers the telephone*

HIRUT:		*Hello! 71 56 22. Mr Mulugeta's residence. Who's that?*
YOHANNES:		*It's me, it's Yohannes. Is Kebede there? Can I speak to him?*
HIRUT:		*Yes, he's here. Hold on a moment, please . . . Kebede, it's Yohannes. He wants to speak to you. Come on, hurry up! He's waiting. I think it's a long-distance call.*
KEBEDE:		*Oh, but how can that be? He's in America, isn't he? . . . Hello, Yohannes, is it you? Where are you calling from?*
YOHANNES:		*I am calling from London. I arrived here two days ago, but I shall be arriving in Addis Ababa soon. I don't have much time at all to talk now, I'm in a hurry. I want to ask, can you and Hirut pick me and my mother up from the airport?*
KEBEDE:		*Of course! But when are you arriving?*
YOHANNES:		*We're arriving on Tuesday, at eight o'clock in the morning. I'm hanging up now. I've got to hurry.*
KEBEDE:		*Alright, we'll come to the airport. Goodbye, Yohannes, until Tuesday! [Kebede hangs up.] Well, Yohannes and his mother are arriving on Tuesday. Today's Saturday, so that must be in three days' time. Oh, I didn't ask the number of his flight. Anyway, the flight from London lands at eight o'clock. Are you coming with me to the airport?*
HIRUT:		*How will we get there?*
KEBEDE:		*I'll borrow my father's car.*
HIRUT:		*Is that so? Well, we'll see!*

Vocabulary

ምሽት	mïsät	evening
ጥዋት	t'wat	early morning
ጋዜጣ	gazet'a	newspaper
ስልክ	sïlk	telephone
መኖሪያ ቤት	mänoriya bet	residence (*lit.* 'dwelling house')
አንዴ	ande	once, at once, for a moment
የሩቅ ጥሪ	yäruk' t'ïrri	long distance call (*lit.* 'call of far')
ፈጽሞ	fäs's'ïmo	not at all (*used with a negative verb*)
አይሮፕላን	ayroplan	aircraft; (*also* አውሮፕላን awroplan)
አይሮፕላን ማረፊያ	ayroplan maräfiya	airport
ማክሰኞ	maksäñño	Tuesday

ቅዳሜ	k'ïdame	Saturday
በረራ	bärära	flight
ቊጥር/ቁጥር	k'ut'ïr	number

Verbs

አነበበ	anäbbäbä	read [3-lit, derived stem in a-]
ያነባል	yanäbbal	he reads, he is reading
ደወለ	däwwälä	ring (a bell), call (on the telephone) [3-lit]
ይደወላል	yïddäwwälal	it is ringing (e.g. the telephone)
ይደውላል	yïdäwwïlal	he is calling (e.g. on the telephone)
ማን ነህ	man näh	who is speaking? (lit. 'who
የምትናገር	yämmïttïnnaggär	are you who are speaking?')
ለመናገር	lämmännagär	to speak
ለመናገር	lämmännagär	he wants to speak
ይፈልጋል	yïfälligal	
ቻለ	čalä	be able [2-lit³]
እችላለሁ	ičilallähw	I am able, I can
ጠበቀ	t'äbbäk'ä	wait for someone or something [3-lit]
ይጠብቃል	yït'äbbïk'al	he's waiting
ተመልሼ	tämällïšše	I shall arrive back (lit. 'I shall
እሄ ዳ ለሁ	ihedallähw	go returning')
መሰለ	mässälä	seem, resemble [3-lit]
ይመስለኛል	yïmäsläññal	it seems to me, I think (that it is)
ተነጋገረ	tänägaggärä	converse, talk (together)
ለመነጋገር	lämännägagär	I don't have time to talk
ጊዜ የለኝም	gize yäläññïm	
ቸኮለ	čäkkwälä	to be in a hurry [3-lit]
እቸኩላለሁ	ičäkkulallähw	I'm in a hurry
መቸኩል አለብኝ	mäčäkkwäl alläbbïñ	I have to hurry
ጠየቀ	t'äyyäk'ä	ask [3-lit]
ለመጠየቅ	lämät'äyyäk'	what I want to ask
የምፈልገው	yämmifälligäw	
ተቀበለ	täk'äbbälä	welcome, receive [3-lit derived stem in tä-]
መቀበል	mäk'k'äbäl	to welcome, etc.

ዘጋ	zägga	close, shut, hang up (*on the telephone*) [2-lit¹]
ተዋሰ	täwasä	borrow (*an object, not money*) [2-lit³ derived stem]
እዋሳለሁ	ïwwasallähw	I borrow

Phrases

ሀሎ/እሎ	hallo, allo	hello! (*when on the telephone*)
እንዴታ	ïndeta	of course! naturally!
በል አሁን	bäl ahun	well now
ቢሆንም	bihonïm	anyway, however, nonetheless
ማለት ነው	malät näw	it means – (*lit.* 'it is to say')
መሆኑ ነው	mähonu näw	it must be – (*lit.* 'it is its being')
ጠብቅ	t'äbbïk'	wait! (*masc. & inf. command*)
ጠብቂ	t'äbbïk'i	(fem.)
ጠብቁ	t'äbbïk'u	(pl.)
ይጠብቁ	yït'äbbïk'u	(for.)
ና	na	come! (masc. & inf. command)
ቶሎ በል	tolo bäl	be quick, hurry up!

Notes on the dialogue

1 ማን ነህ የምትናገር, *lit.* 'who are you who are speaking?'. You met a couple of constructions of this type in the fourth lesson. Another answer you can use on the telephone in this context is ማን ልበል? man lïbäl? which is literally 'whom should I say?'. Note that the word ሀሎ or እሎ is only used when answering the telephone and is not the usual expression for 'hello' in Amharic.

2 ይመስለኛል, *lit.* 'it seems to me (that it is)'. To express the idea of 'to think' in the sense of 'to have an opinion', Amharic uses the verb መሰለ 'seem' or 'seem to be' with an appropriate pronoun object; we shall look at these in lesson six.

3 እሱ አሜሪካ ያለው አይደለም?, *lit.* 'is it not that he is (in) America?'. The verb ያለው yalläw is a relative-verb form, 'that/which he is' built on the verb አለ that you already know. We shall look at relative verbs in a later lesson.

4 ከጥዋቱ በሁለት ሰዓት, *lit.* 'at two o'clock in the morning', is translated as 'at eight o'clock in the morning'. This is because Ethiopians calculate the time each day from dawn, nominally at

6.00 a.m., and not from midnight. To translate from a Western to an Ethiopian time reckoning, you have to subtract six hours. However, as in speech people use a twelve-hour clock, so this means that 5 o'clock will be 11 o'clock (አስራ አንድ በዓት) according to the Ethiopian system. Some educated Ethiopians may also use the Western system, particularly when talking to foreigners, so be sure to confirm which system is being used when you make an appointment: እንደ ኢትዮጵያ አቆጣጠር indä ityop'p'iya ak'k'ot'at'är 'according to Ethiopian calculation' or እንደ አውርፓ አቆጣጠር indä awrop'a ak'k'ot'at'är 'according to European calculation'.

Grammar

The present-future, or compound imperfect tense

So far you have met a number of verb forms like ይፈልጋሉ, አፈልጋለሁ, አደውላለሁ, ትችላላችሁ, እንደርሳለን with present- or future-tense meaning. You will notice that Amharic has no specific future tense like the English tenses in 'will . . .' or 'shall . . .'. The context alone makes it clear whether a present or a future tense is meant. So:

ዛሬ ወደ ቢሮ እሄዳለሁ	zare wädä biro ihedallähw	
	I'm going to the office today	
ነገ ወደ ቢሮ እሄዳለሁ	nägä wädä biro ihedallähw	
	I'll go to the office tomorrow	
በየቀኑ ወደ ቢሮ እሄዳለሁ	bäyyäk'änu wädä biro ihedallähw	
	I go to the office every day	

The present-future tense is usually called the compound imperfect because, though always written as one word, it is made up of two parts: the second part, the ending, you may recognize as derived from the verb አለ 'be'; the first part, እሄድ ihed in the above examples, is the simple imperfect, some uses of which you will meet in later lessons.

The persons of the compound imperfect are indicated by a combination of prefixes and suffixes. The suffixes are in most persons identical to the corresponding part of the verb አለ, but note the third person masculine.

The personal markers of the compound imperfect

Singular	Prefix	Suffix	
1st pers.	I...	ï-	-allähw
2nd pers. masc.	you ...	tï-	-alläh
2nd pers. fem.	you ...	tï-	-iyalläš/-yalläš*
3rd pers. masc.	he ...	yï-	-al
3rd pers. fem.	she ...	tï-	-alläčč

Plural	Prefix	Suffix	
1st pers.	we ..	ïnnï-	-allän
2nd pers.	you ..	tï-	-allaččuh
3rd pers.	they ..	yï-	-allu

Formal	Prefix	Suffix	
2nd pers.	you...	yï-	-allu (i.e. the 3rd pers. pl. form)
3rd pers.	he, she ...	yï-	-allu "

*The ending of the second person feminine -iyalläš is often shortened to -yalläš in speech, as in ተፈልጊያላሽ or ተፈልጊያላሽ tïfälligiyalläš or tïfälligyalläš 'you want'. (*See also below under 'palatalization'.*)

When forming the compound imperfect tense, there are several points that you have to pay attention to over and above the different personal markers. First, by comparing forms like እፈልጋለሁ ïfälligallähw 'I want', ይመጣል yïmät'al 'he'll come', እጽፋለሁ is'ïfallähw 'I'll write' with the corresponding simple past forms ፈለግሁ fälläghw 'I wanted', መጣ mät't'a 'he came' and ጻፍሁ s'afkw 'I wrote', you can also see that the stem to which the personal markers of the compound imperfect are added is different to that of the simple past. Each of the different classes of verbs, triliteral and the five biliteral types, that you have met so far has different imperfect tense stem shapes. So, for example:

prefix	stem	suffix		
ï-	fällïg	-allähw	አፈልጋለሁ	I want, shall want, *etc.*
tï-	fällïg	-alläh	ትፈልጋለህ	you want, will want, *etc.*
tï-	fällïg	-iyalläš	ትፈልጊያለሽ	you want, will want, *etc.*
yï-	fällïg	-al	ይፈልጋል	he wants, will want, *etc.*
tï-	fällïg	-alläčč	ትፈልጋለች	she wants, will want, *etc.*
ïnnï-	fällïg	-allän	እንፈልጋለን	we want, shall want, *etc.*
tï-	fällïg	-allaččuh	ትፈልጋላችሁ	you want, will want, *etc.*
yï-	fällïg	-allu	ይፈልጋሉ	they want, will want, *etc.* he, she wants,

ፈለገ is a 3-lit verb; you should note, as you go along, other examples of how other verb classes form the compound imperfect tense.

Second, the difference in the stem between two triliteral verbs like አፈልጋለሁ ïfällïgallähw 'I want' and እወስዳለሁ ïwäsdallähw 'I take' arises because there is a further refinement to the classification of verbs that was given in Lesson 3:

'Type A' and 'Type B' verbs

All triliteral verbs and biliteral verbs of groups 2-lit[1] and 2-lit[2] are further assigned either to 'Type A'- or 'Type B'-categories: therefore, 3-lit A; 3-lit B; 2-lit[1] A; 2-lit[1] B; 2-lit[2] A; 2-lit[2] B. The other classes of biliteral verbs do not have this distinction of Type A and Type B.

This distinction between Type A and Type B is not significant in the formation of the simple past tense, but is important in other tenses including the compound imperfect. Unfortunately, you cannot tell either from the meaning of a verb, or in most cases from its dictionary form (the third person masculine of the simple past), whether a verb is Type A or Type B. It is something that you have to learn whenever you meet a new verb. For example, ወሰደ 'take' is a 3-lit A verb, but ፈለገ 'want' is a 3-lit B verb.

In the imperfect, the difference in shape between Type A and Type B mostly concerns the presence or absence of a double or geminate consonant in the stem. The examples in the box below should make this clearer.

Class		Sample		Compound	Imperfect	Imperfect stem
Triliteral	A [3-lit A]	ወስደ	ይወስ ጻል	yïwäsdal	-wäsd-
	B [3-lit B]	ፈለገ	ይፈልጋል	yïfälligal	-fällig-
Biliteral Class 1	A [2-lit¹ A]	መጣ	ይመጣል	yïmät'al	-mät'a-
	B [2-lit¹ B]	ጠጣ	ይጠጣል	yït'ät't'al	-t'ät't'a-
Class 2	A [2-lit² A]	ሰጠ	ይሰጣል	yïsät'al	-sät'-
	B [2-lit² B]	ቀየ	ይቀያል	yïk'wäyyal	-k'wäyy-
Class 3	[2-lit³]	ጸፈ	ይጸፋል	yïs'ifal	-s'if-
Class 4	[2-lit⁴]	ሄደ	ይሄዳል	yïhedal	-hed-
Class 5	[2-lit⁵]	ሆነ	ይሆናል	yïhonal	-hon-

Remember that according to the rules of the 'hierarchy' of vowels, when two as come together they merge into a single a. So, from መጣ 'come' (imperfect stem -mät'a-) we have እመጣለሁ ïmät'allähw 'I come', ትመጣለህ tïmät'alläh 'you come', ይመጣል yïmät'al 'he comes', ትመጣለች tïmät'alläčč 'she comes', and so on.

Contrary to the rules given in lesson one, however, with the ending of the second person feminine -iyalläš, the initial vowel i of the ending replaces the final a of 2-lit¹ stems; so from ሰማ sämma 'hear' (Type A) we have ትሰሚያለሽ/ትሰምያለሽ tïsämiyalläš/tïsämyalläš 'you hear', or from ሰራ särra 'work' (Type A) ትሰሪያለሽ / ትሰርያለሽ tïsäriyalläš/tïsäryalläš 'you work'. Further examples are set out in the box below.

2-lit¹ A

እሰማለሁ	ïsämallähw	ï + säma + allähw	I hear, shall hear, *etc.*
ትሰማለህ	tïsämalläh	tï + säma + alläh	you hear, will hear, *etc.*
ትሰሚያለሽ	tïsämiyalläš	tï + säma + iyalläš	you hear, will hear, *etc.*
ይሰማል	yïsämal	yï + säma + al	he hears, will hear, *etc.*
ትሰማለች	tïsämalläčč	tï + säma + alläčč	she hears, will hear, *etc.*
እንሰማለን	innïsämallän	innï + säma + allän	we hear, shall hear, *etc.*
ትሰማላችሁ	tïsämallaččuh	tï + säma + allaččuh	you hear, will hear, etc.
ይሰማሉ	yïsämallu	yï + säma + allu	they hear, will hear, *etc.*

Palatalization

There is another important feature of the ending of the second person feminine -**iyalläš**. Look at the form ትመጪ ኣለሽ tïmäč'alläš 'you'll come' in the dialogue and compare it with ይመጣል yïmät'al 'he'll come'. The ending has caused a change in the final consonant of the verb stem, which is here **č'** instead of **t'**, and the ending itself is further shortened to just -**alläš**. Other consonants are affected in a similar way. This is called palatalization and is a process which occurs in a number of other places in the inflexion of the verb. Here are the consonants that are subject to palatalization and the changes that occur:

palatalization	Sample verb		Stem	2nd pers. fem.	
t → č	ከፈተ	open	3-lit A	-käft-	ትከፍቻለሽ tïkäfčalläš
d → j	ወረደ	go down	3-lit A	-wärd-	ትወርጃለሽ tïwärjalläš
t' → č'	መረጠ	choose	3-lit A	-märt'-	ትመርቻለሽ tïmärč'alläš
s → š	ጨረሰ	finish	3-lit B	-č'ärris-	ትጨርሻለሽ tïč'ärrišalläš
z → ž	ገዛ	buy	2-lit¹ A	-gäza-	ትገዛለሽ tïgäžalläš
s' → č'	ገለጸ	explain	3-lit A	-gäls'-	ትገልቻለሽ tïgälč'alläš
n → ñ	ሆነ	become	2-lit⁵	-hon-	ትሆኛለሽ tïhoñalläš
l → y	ከፈለ	pay	3-lit A	-käfl-	ትከፍያለሽ tïkäfyalläš

Verbs whose stems already end in one of the 'palatal' consonants (č, j, č', š, ž, ñ, y) just add -**alläš** in the second person feminine like palatalizing stems. So, for example, from ተኛ tänña 'go to bed, sleep' (2-lit¹ B), ትተኛለሽ tïtäññalläš 'you're going to bed', or from ቀየ / ቆየ k'wäyyä / k'oyyä 'wait' (2-lit² B), ትቆያለሽ tïk'oyyalläš 'you'll wait', and so on.

Verbs beginning in a-

The rule of the hierarchy of vowels operates on verbs whose stems begin in **a-**, like አወቀ awwäk'ä 'know', አሰበ assäbä 'think', አየ ayyä 'see', etc., so that the vowel ï of the personal prefixes is dropped. For example:

Prefix	Stem	Suffix		
–	awk'	-allähw	አውቃለሁ	I know, shall know, *etc.*
t-	awk'	-alläh	ታውቃለህ	you know, will know, *etc.*
t-	awk'	-iyalläš	ታውቂያለሽ	you know, will know, *etc.*
y-	awk'	-al	ያውቃል	he knows, will know, *etc.*
t-	awk'	-alläčč	ታውቃለች	she knows, will know, *etc.*
inn-	awk'	-allän	እናውቃለን	we know, shall know, *etc.*
t-	awk'	-allaččuh	ታውቃላችሁ	you know, will know, *etc.*
y-	awk'	-allu	ያውቃሉ	they know, will know, *etc.*
				he, she knows

Exercises

1 Convert the following simple past tense verbs into the corresponding compound-imperfect forms

1	ሔድን	6	ጨረስሽ	11	ቄየች	16	አየሁ
2	ወሰድኩ	7	አወቅን	12	ጻፍኩ	17	ሰሙ
3	መጣችሁ	8	ደወልን	13	ሼጠ	18	ጀመርክ
4	ሰማ	9	ኖሩ	14	ገዛች	19	አለፈች
5	ተኝ	10	ከፈልሽ	15	መረጣችሁ	20	አሰብሽ

2 Rewrite the following sentences so that the tense of the verb is in agreement with the time expression in brackets

> *Example:* ገበያ አሄዳለሁ (ትናንትና) → ትናንትና ገበያ ሄድኩ ።

1 ተማሪዎቹ መጽሐፋቸውን ይገዛሉ (ባለፈው ሳምንት) ።
2 ከበደ አዲሱን መኪናውን ሼጠ (ነገ) ።
3 ሥራህን መቼ ትጨርሳለህ? ጨረስኩ (ቦሎ) ።
4 አዲስ ጃኬት ተመርጫለሽ (ትናንትና)?
5 መብላት ፈለገን (አሁን) ።

3 How would you say the following in Amharic?

1 Almaz, do you want to eat lunch now?
2 When will you finish your studies, Hiywet?
3 We'll arrive in Jimma in three hours' time.
4 The teacher is starting the class now.
5 Who'll pay the bill? Will you pay, Hirut?

4 *Here are some sentences with verbs in the compound imperfect tense. Try to work out under which form you would find them in a dictionary. Then try to translate the sentences into English*

Example ተግርፔ ሥዕል ይሥላሉ → ይሥላሉ - ሣለ ('paint')
the students are painting a picture

---

1 ልጆቹ ይጫኸሉ።
2 ወዴት ትርጣላችሁ?
3 ከበደ ጊሩትን ይስማል።
4 ይህን ተረት አንተርታለን።
5 ስለምን ትፈጥኛለሽ?

Days of the week

In the dialogue you met ማክሰኞ Tuesday and ቅዳሜ Saturday. Here are the remaining names of the days of the week:

እሑድ	ïhud	Sunday	አሙስ,	amus,	Thursday
ሰኞ	säñño	Monday	ኃሙስ	hamus	
ማክሰኞ	maksäñño	Tuesday	አርብ	arb	Friday
ርብ	rob	Wednesday	ቅዳሜ	k'ïdame	Saturday

An alternative for Wednesday is ረቡዕ, ረቡ räbu. Amongst Christian Ethiopians Sunday is also sometimes called ሰንበት sänbät, *lit.* 'Sabbath', or ሰንበተ ክርስቲያን sänbätä krïstiyan 'the Sabbath of the Christians'. The phrase ቅዳሜ ሰንበት k'ïdame sänbät is the longer name for Saturday, *lit.* 'Saturday Sabbath'.

Telling the time

To ask the time in Amharic you say, ስንት ሰዓት ነው sïntï säat näw, *lit.* 'how many hours is it?' The word ሰዓት is then included in the answer, equivalent to the English 'o'clock'. Remember that the Ethiopians start reckoning the time of day from 6.00 a.m. and not from midnight. So:

አንድ ሰዓት ነው	andï säat näw	it's one o'clock	*i.e.* 7.00
አራት ሰዓት ነው	aratti säat näw	it's four o'clock	*i.e.* 10.00
ስድስት ሰዓት ነው	sïddïsti säat näw	it's six o'clock	*i.e.* 12.00

ሰባት ሰዓት ነው	säbattï säat näw	it's seven o'clock *i.e.* 1.00
ዘጠኝ ሰዓት ነው	zät'äñ säat näw	it's nine o'clock *i.e.* 3.00

In order to express the divisions of the hour the following expressions are used:

ተኩል	täkkul	half past
ከሩብ	kärub	a quarter past (*lit.* 'with a quarter')
ሩብ ጉዳይ	rub gudday	a quarter to (*lit.* 'lacking a quarter')

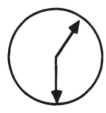  

አንድ ሰዓት ተኩል	ሁለት ሰዓት ከሩብ	ሦስት ሰዓት ሩብ ጉዳይ
andï säat täkkul	hulättï säat kärub	sostï säat rub gudday
half past one	a quarter past two	a quarter to three

Note that in the expression of 'a quarter to' you can also say **ለሦስት ሰዓት ሩብ ጉዳይ** or **ከሦስት ሰዓት ሩብ ጉዳይ**. Similarly with smaller divisions of the hour:

አራት ሰዓት ከአምስት ደቂቃ	**arattï säat kammïstï däk'ik'a**
	five past four
ስድስት ሰዓት ከሃያ	**sïddïstï säat kähaya**
	twenty past six
ከሰባት ሰዓት አስር ጉዳይ	**käsäbattï säat assïr gudday**
	ten to seven
ለዘጠኝ ሰዓት ስምንት ደቂቃ ጉዳይ	**läzät'äñ säat sïmmïntï däk'ik'a gudday**
	eight minutes to nine
ልክ አራት ሰዓት ከአምስት ደቂቃ	**likk arattï säat käammïstï däk'ik'a**
	exactly five minutes past four
ወደ ሁለት ሰዓት ከሃያ	**wädä hulättï säat kähaya**
	about twenty past two

Here are some other useful expressions for the time of day:

ጥዋት	t'wat	early morning (*from 6.00 a.m. to around 8.00 a.m.*)

ዛሬ ጥዋት	zare t'wat	this morning (lit. 'today morning')
ረፋድ	räffad	midmorning (from 8.00 a.m. to around noon)
ቀን	k'än	day, daytime
ንጋት	nïgat	dawn, daybreak
ሌሊት	lelit	night, nightime (from around midnight to dawn)
ምሽት, ምሼት	mišät, miššit	evening (from 5.00 p.m. to around 11.00 p.m.)
ማታ	mata	evening
ዛሬ ማታ	zare mata	this evening (lit. 'today evening')
ሰዓት or ቀትር	säat or k'ätïr	noon, lunchtime
እኩለ ቀን	ïkkulä k'än	midday
እኩለ ሌሊት	ïkkulä lelit	midnight (also መንፈቀ ሌሊት mänfäk'ä lelit)
ከሰዓት በኋላ	käsäat bähwala	afternoon
ደቂቃ	däk'ik'a	minute
ሰዓት	säat	hour
ሳምንት	sammïnt	week
ወር	wär	month, season
ዓመት	amät	year
ዛሬ	zare	today
ትናንትና	tïnantïnna	yesterday
ከትናንትና ወዲያ	kätïnantïnna wädiya	the day before yesterday
ነገ	nägä	tomorrow
ከነገ ወዲያ	känägä wädiya	the day after tomorrow
ዓምና	amna	last year
ዘንድሮ	zändïro	this year
ማግሥት	magïst	the next day
ሰሞኑን	sämonun	this week, recently

You will recall from lesson one that Amharic greetings often involve verbs that have a specific time reference, such as አደረ 'spend the night' and ዋለ 'spend the day'. Here are some more:

አመሸ	amäššä	spend the evening
አረፈደ	aräffädä	spend the morning
ሰነበተ	sänäbbätä	spend some days, spend a week
ከረመ	kärrämä	spend the rainy season (July, August, September), spend a long while

ደህና አመሻችሁ?	dähna amäššaččuh?	did you have a good evening?
እንደምን ሰነበትክ?	ïndämïn sänäbbätk?	how have you been keeping?

Exercises

5 Try to give the following times as far as you can. Remember to convert to the Ethiopian system

1	10.30 a.m.	
2	6.15 p.m.	
3	about 3 o'clock	
4	2.10 precisely	
5	5.45 p.m.	

6	6.25 a.m.	
7	almost five past five	
8	exactly midday	
9	4.20	
10	sorry, I haven't a watch!	

6 Imagine this is a schedule of things you plan to do tomorrow. Describe your plan for the day in Amharic, giving a time to each activity where appropriate and making use of words relating to time and sequential phrases like ከዚያም በኋላ, በጊዜ, and so on. Feel free to add anything else you think you'd like to do! (the verbs are all given in their dictionary form)

ቁርስ በላ	k'urs bälla	eat breakfast
ወደ ባንክ ሄደ	wädä bank hedä	go to the bank
ወረቀትና ቴምብር ገዛ	wäräk'ätïnna tembïr gäzza	buy paper and stamps
በቤት መጻሕፍት ሥራ	bäbetä mäs'ahïft särra	work in the library
ደብዳቤ ጻፈ	däbdabbe s'afä	write a letter
ወደ ምግብ ቤት ሄደ	wädä mïgïb bet hedä	go to a restaurant
ምሳ በላ	mïsa bälla	eat lunch
እረፍት አደረገ	ïräft adärrägä	have a rest
መናፈሻ ውስጥ ዞረ	männafäša wïst' zorä	walk round the park
ወደ ገበያ ሄደ	wädä gäbäya hedä	go to the market
ምናምን ገዛ	mïnamïn gäzza	buy some odds and ends
እቤት ገባ	ïbet gäbba	return home

ሰገብሬ ደወለ	läGäbre däwwälä	ring up Gebrie
እራት በላ	ïrat bälla	eat supper
ወደ ባር ሄደ	wädä bar hedä	go to a bar
እንድ ሁለት ቢራ ጠጣ	and hulätti bira t'ät't'a	drink one or two beers

Script

Punctuation

You will have noticed from the various dialogues and passages that you have read so far that written Amharic uses few familiar punctuation marks. The Ethiopian script has its own punctuation marks, to which in recent years have been added some signs of Western origin. Below is a list of punctuation marks in current use:

።	አራት ነጥብ	arattï nät'ïb	the end of a sentence, like a full stop
፤	ድርብ ሰረዝ	dïrrïb säräz	a marked pause, rather like a semicolon
፣	ነጠላ ሰረዝ	nät'äla säräz	a weak pause, rather like a comma
	or ሰረዝ	säräz	
፡	ነጥብ	nät'ïb	a word divider, often omitted as in this book

Some signs of Western origin that are used nowadays are:

( )	ቅንፍ	k'ïnf	brackets
-	ጭረት	č'ïrät	hyphen
/	ይዘት	yïzät	slash (also the sign of an abbreviation like ወ/አግረች for ወይዘሮ አግረች)
«»	ትእምርተ ጥቅስ	tïïmïrtä t'ïk's	quotation marks (these are often omitted when reporting quoted words so that there is no overt sign of a quotation in written Amharic)
?	ጥያቄ ምልክት	t'ïyyak'e mïlïkkït	question mark
!	ቃለ አጋኖ	k'alä aganno	exclamation mark

Reading passage

Some vocabulary which you might find useful is given below. Note that not all new words are included as you should be able to work out some for yourself

እኔና ሚስቴ ዛሬ ጥዋት አዲስ አበባ ደረስን። በኢትዮጵያ አየር መንገድ መጣን። አይሮፕላናችን ልክ አምራ ሁለት ሰዓት ተኩል ላይ ቦሌ አይሮፕላን ማረፊያ አረፈ። ከሌሎች መንገደኞች ጋር ወደ መግቢያ ክፍል ገባንና የፓስፖርታችንና የቪዛችን ሁሉንም ፈጸምን። ከዚያም በኋላ ወደ ጉምሩክ ክፍል ሄድን። አሁንም ብዙ ሰዎች መጪዎቹን ይጠብቃሉ፤ ጓደኞቻችንም እኛን ይጠብቁ ነበር። ልጃችንና ሚስቴ አበረው አሉ። «እንኳን ደኅና መጣችሁ!» አሉን። ከዚያም ዕቃችንን መኪናው ውስጥ ከጫን በኋላ አበረን ወደ ከተማ ሄድን። መኒሪያ ቤታችሁ ከመሀል ከተማ የራቀ አይደለም። ስለዚህም ከጥቂት ደቂቃዎች በኋላ ወደ ሁለት ሰዓት ከሩብ ቤት እንደርሳለን።

Supplementary vocabulary

መንገድ	mängäd	road, way
የኢትዮጵያ አየር መንገድ	Yäityop'p'ïya Ayär Mängäd	Ethiopian Airlines
መንገደኛ	mängädäñña	traveller, passenger
መግቢያ ክፍል	mägbiya kïfïl	arrivals hall (*lit.* 'entrance room')
ጉምሩክ	gumruk	customs
መጪ	mäč'	arrival, newcomer
አለ	alä say (*this is an irregular verb in Amharic; look it up in the glossary under* አለ $_2$. *Be careful not to confuse it with* አለ allä 'to be')
ዕቃ	ïk'a	thing(s), baggage, stuff, object, furniture
ጫነ	č'anä	load
ካጫን በኋላ	käč'annï bähwala	after we've loaded
መሀል	mähal	centre; መሀል ከተማ city centre

6 ሽርሽር ማቀድ
širiššir mak'k'äd

Planning a trip

By the end of this lesson you should be able to:

- form the negative of the imperfect tense ('I don't come', 'shan't come', *etc.*)
- form and use the infinitive ('to come', 'to go', *etc.*)
- construct nouns denoting occupations

Planning a trip to the country

Yohannes brings an English friend to see Hirut and Kebede, and they plan a trip

የዛሬው ቀን ቅዳሜ ነው፤ ከቀኑ ስምንት ሰዓት ነው። ካርባ ደቂቃ በፊት ዮሐንስ ለሂሩትና ለከበደ ደወለላቸው። አሁንም ይጠብቁታል።

ሂሩት:	ታዲያ ይህ የዮሐንስ ጓደኛ ማን ነው? የዛሬ ሁለት ሳምንት እሱንና እናቱን ካዮርፕላን ማረፊያ እቤት ባደረስናቸው ጊዜ ስለሱ ምንም አልነገረንም።
ከበደ:	እኔ አላውቅም። ዮሐንስ ወሬ ፈጽሞ አይነግረኝም።

[ዮሐንስና ጓደኛው ይደርሳሉ]

ዮሐንስ:	ጤና ይስጥልኝ! ሰው አለ? እኛ ነን፤ ደረስን?
ሂሩት:	ቤት ለንግዳ! ግቡ!
ዮሐንስ:	ይህ ጓደኛዬ ፒተር ነው፤ እንግሊዛዊ ነው። የተገናኘነው አዶርፕላን ውስጥ ነው። አማርኛ ትንሽ ይቻላል፤ ገማርኛ ማነጋገር አለባቸሁ።
ሂሩት:	ጤና ይስጥልኝ! እንደምን አደርክ? ኢትዮጵያ እንኳን ደና መጣህ!
ፒተር:	እግዜር ይመስገን። ደና ነኝ። እናንተስ እንደምን ናችሁ?

ከበደ፥	አማርኛ ከዩት ተማርክ? ብዙዎች ፈረንጆች ቋንቋችንን አይቾሉም። በጣም አስቸጋሪ ቋንቋ ነው ይላሉ።
ፒተር፥	እውነት ነው፤ ቀላል አይደለም። ብዙ ጊዜ አልቻልም፣ ነገር ግን እሞክራለሁ። ቋንቋችሁን በደምብ ለመናገር አፈልጋለሁ። ስለዚህ ነው ወደ ኢትዮጵያ የመጣሁት።
ከበደ፥	ጉበዝ ነህ! በጣም ጥሩ ትናገራለህ።
ጊሩት፥	አዎ፤ ከበደ እውነቱን ነው። እኛ ሁላችን እንረዳሃለን። በርግጥ እንደሚመስለኝ ባጭር ጊዜ ውስጥ እንደኛ አማርኛ ትናገራለህ።
ዮሐንስ፥	ስሙኝ፤ አሳብ አለኝ። እንደሚገላለው ቋንቋ ለማወቅ ባላገር መጉብኘትና ከተራ ሰው ጋር መናገር ያስፈልጋል። ነገ እሁድ ነው – ሸርሸር መሄድ እንቾላለን። ጊሩት፤ ካርታ አለሽ? ... መልካም፤ ስጪኝ፤ አዬት፤ ደብረ ሊባኖስ ከዚህ ሩቅ አይደለም – በገምት መቶ ኪሎ ሜትር ያህል ይሆናል። የወንድሜን መኪና አዋሳለሁ።
ፒተር፥	ደብረ ሊባኖስ ምን አለ? ስሙንም ካሁን በፊት ሰማሁት። ስፍራው ስም ጥሩ ነው?
ከበደ፥	አዎ፤ ልክ ነው። በካርታው ላይ አሳይሃለሁ ... ይኽው! ካዲስ አበባ በሰሜን በኩል ነው። እዚያ ስም ጥሩ ጥንታዊ ገዳም አለ። ቅዱስ ተክለ ሃይማኖት የሚባሉ ከኢትዮጵያ ታላላቅ ቅዱሳን አንዱ ከብዙ ክፍለ ዘመን በፊት ቆረቆሩት። ዛሬም ብዙዎች መነክሳቶች እዚህ ይኖራሉ፤ ደግሞም አዲስ ትልቅ ቤተ ክርስቲያን አለ።
ጊሩት፥	አዎ፤ ለሸርሸር ስፍራው ጥሩ ይመስላል። ፒተርም ስለ ኢትዮጵያ ታሪክና ባህል ይማራል፤ ከዚህም በላይ አማርኛ ይለማመዳል። የሆነው ሆኖ ስለ ሸርሸሩ ብዙ ነገሮች ማዘጋጀት አለብን። ታዲያ ምን ምን ያስፈልግናል? እኔ ምግብ አዘጋጃለሁ። እናንተም መኪናውን ትዋሳላችሁ። ነገ ጥዋት እንነሣለን፤ ከመሸ በኋላ ለመድረስ አንፈልግም!

Today is Saturday, and the time is about 2 o'clock in the afternoon. Forty minutes ago Yohannes rang Hirut and Kebede. Now they are waiting for him

HIRUT:	*Well, who is this friend of Yohannes's? When we brought him and his mother home from the airport two weeks ago he didn't tell us anything about him.*
KEBEDE:	*I don't know. Yohannes never tells me news.*

[Yohannes and his friend arrive]

YOHANNES: *Hello! Is there anyone at home? It's us, we've arrived.*

HIRUT: *Welcome! Come in!*

YOHANNES: *This is my friend Peter, he's English. We met on the plane. He speaks a little Amharic, so you must both speak in Amharic.*

HIRUT: *Hello, how are you? Welcome to Ethiopia!*

PETER: *I'm fine, thanks. How are you?*

KEBEDE: *Where did you learn Amharic? Not many foreigners speak our language. They say it is a very difficult language!*

PETER: *That's right, it's not easy. I can't speak much yet, but I try. I want to speak your language properly. So I've come to Ethiopia.*

KEBEDE: *You're very good, you speak very well.*

HIRUT: *Yes, Kebede is right. We'll all help you. Certainly, within a short time I think you'll be speaking Amharic like us!*

YOHANNES: *Listen everyone, I have an idea. They say, to know a language you must visit the countryside and speak with the ordinary people. Tomorrow is Sunday – we can go on a trip. Hirut, have you got a map? . . . Good, give me it. Look, Debre Libanos is not far away – the journey looks about a hundred kilometres. I'll borrow my brother's car.*

PETER: *What is there at Debre Libanos? I have heard the name before. Is it a famous place?*

KEBEDE: *Yes, that's correct. I'll show you it on the map . . . here it is! It's north of Addis Ababa. There's a famous and ancient monastery there. One of the greatest of Ethiopian saints, called St. Tekle Haymanot, founded it many centuries ago. Today many monks and nuns live there, and there's also a large new church.*

HIRUT: *Yes, it'll be a good place for a trip. Peter will learn about Ethiopian history and tradition, and he can practise Amharic as well. However, we'll have to make preparations for the trip? So, what things do we need? I'll prepare the food, and you two will borrow the car. We'll set off early tomorrow; we don't want to arrive after nightfall!*

Vocabulary

ወሬ	wäre	news, story, gossip
እንግዳ	ïngïda	guest, visitor, stranger
ፈረንጅ	färänj	foreigner, white Westerner
ደምብ	dämb	rule, principle
በደምብ	bädämb	properly, perfectly, thoroughly
ጉበዝ	gobäz	clever, smart, strong, brave; (also means a strong young man)
አጭር	ač'č'ïr	short
አሳብ	assab	thought, idea, plan
ባላገር	balagär	countryside; also means peasant
ተራ ሰው	tära säw	ordinary person
ሽርሽር	širïššïr	trip, outing, picnic
ካርታ	karta	map; also means playing card
ኪሎ ሜትር	kilo metïr	kilometre
ስፍራ	sïfra	place
ሰሜን	sämen	north
ስም ጥሩ	sïmä t'ïru	famous
ጥንታዊ	t'ïntawi	ancient
ጥንት, ጥንት ጊዜ	t'ïnt (gize)	ancient times, olden times
ገዳም	gädam	monastery, convent
ቅዱስ	k'ïddus	saint; plural ቅዱሳን k'ïddusan (the form is Ge'ez)
ታላቅ	tallak'	great, important, elder; ታላላቅ talallak' can mean the same as ታላቅ, and is also used as its plural
ክፍለ ዘመን	kïflä zämän	century
መነክሴ	mänokse	monk
መነክሲት	mänoksit	nun
መነክሳት, መነክሳቶች	mänoksat, mänoksatočč	monks, nuns
ቤተ ክርስቲያን	betä krïstiyan	church

Particles

ምንም	mïnïm(m)	nothing (with a negative verb)
በግምት	bägimmït	at a guess, approximately
ያህል	yahïl	approximately, about, as much as

Verbs

ጠበቀ	t'äbbäk'ä	wait for, expect, look after, protect [3-lit B]
ነገረ	näggärä	speak, talk, tell [3-lit A]
አነጋገረ	annägaggärä	talk together, engage in conversation [derived stem type] ማነጋገር mannägagär (infinitive)
ተናገረ	tänaggärä	speak, converse [derived stem type] ይናገራል yïnnaggäral (compound imperfect), መናገር männagär (infinitive)
ተገናኘ	tägänaññä	meet [derived stem type] ይገናኛል yïggänaññal (compound imperfect)
ቻለ	čalä	be able, be able to speak (a language)
ተማረ	tämarä	learn, study [derived stem type] ይማራል yïmmaral (compound imperfect)
ሞከረ	mokkärä	try [3-lit B]
ረዳ	rädda	help [2-lit[1] A]
ጎበኘ	gobäññä	visit: belongs to a class of verb not yet looked at; although it has three consonants note where the gemination is. ይጎበኛል yïgobäññal (compound imperfect)
አስፈለገ	asfällägä	be necessary [derived stem type] ያስፈልጋል yasfälligal (compound imperfect)
መሰለ	mässälä	seem, look like [3-lit A]
አሳየ	asayyä	show [derived stem type] ያሳያል yasayyal (compound imperfect)
ቆረቆረ	k'oräk'k'orä	found [4-lit] (see lesson seven)
ተለማመደ	tälämammädä	practise, start learning [derived stem type] – compare ለመደ 'get used to' ይለማመዳል yïllämammädal (compound imperfect)
አዘጋጀ	azzägajjä	prepare, organize [derived stem type] ያዘጋጃል yazzägajjal (compound imperfect)
ተነሣ	tänässa	get up, set off [derived stem type] ይነሣል yïnnässal (compound imperfect)

ግቡ	gïbu	come in! (pl. command *from* ገባ)
ስሙ	sïmu	listen! (pl. command *from* ሰማ)
ስጪ	sïč'i	give! (fem. command *from* ሰጠ)
እዩ	ïyu	see! (pl. command *from* አየ)

Phrases

እንደሚባለው	ïndämmibbaläw	as it is said (*from* አለ₂)
የሚባል	yämmibbal	who is called (*from* ተባለ [derived stem from አለ₂])
የሆነው ሆኖ	yähonäw hono	be that as it may, however (*lit.* 'being what is')

Notes on the dialogue

1 ደወሰላቸው däwwälällaččäw 'he rang them' is literally 'he rang to them', i.e. ደወለ + -ላቸው. There are also a number of verbs in the dialogue that involve pronoun direct objects, like ይጠብቁታል yït'äbbïk'utal 'they are waiting for him'. These will be discussed in the next lesson. For the moment, however, here are the verbs with pronoun objects that occur in the dialogue. Look at these closely and see if you can identify what element expresses the object and then compare them with what the verb would be without the object:

With object			Without object
ይጠብቁታል	yït'äbbïk'utal	they're waiting for him	ይጠብቃሉ
አደረስናቸው	adärräsnaččäw	we brought them	አደረስን
አልነገረንም	alnäggäränïm	he didn't tell us	አልነገረም
አይነግረኝም	aynägräññïm	he doesn't tell me	አይነግርም
እንረዳሃለን	ïnnïrädahallän	we'll help you	እንረዳለን
ስጪኝ	sïč'iñ	give me	ስጪ
እዩት	ïyut	look at it	እዩ
እንደሚመስለኝ	ïndämmimäslän	as it seems to me	እንደሚመስል
አሳይሃለሁ	asayyïhallähw	I'll show you	አሳያለሁ
ቆረቆሩት	k'oräk'k'orut	he founded it	ቆረቆሩ
ያስፈልገናል	yasfällïgänal	it'll be necessary for us	ያስፈልጋል

2 ቤት ለእንግዳ! bet längïda, *lit.* 'the house for the guest!' is a greeting you can say to welcome guests to your house.

3 አማርኛ ይችላል amariñña yïčilal 'he can speak Amharic': note that you do not need to use the verb 'speak' in this idiom. Amharic ቻለ means 'to be able to speak (a language)','to be able to do (something)' or 'to endure (something) as well as just 'to be able' or 'can', etc., as in, for example, መሄድ ትችላለህ mähed tïčilalläh 'you can go'.

4 ባማርኛ መነጋገር አለባችሁና bamariñña männägagär alläbbaččihunna 'so you must speak in Amharic': you have already met the suffix -ና meaning 'and'; when it is added to a verb it often has more of the sense of 'and so', 'and therefore', as it does here.

Grammar

The negative imperfect tense

You will remember that to form the negative of the simple past tense አል- is prefixed and -ም suffixed to the affirmative form: ጠጣች t'ät't'ačč 'she drank' : አልጠጣችም alt'ät't'aččim 'she didn't drink'. The formation of the negative imperfect (present-future) tense is not quite so simple. In the dialogue there are several examples of a negative imperfect: አላውቅም alawk'ïm 'I don't know'; አንፈልግም annïfälligïm 'we don't want'; አይነግረኝም aynägräññim 'he doesn't tell me'; አልችልም alčïlim 'I can't (speak)'. When you compare these with the corresponding affirmatives you can see that the transformation is not as direct. Consider the following:

Negative

አላውቅም	alawk'ïm	I don't know
አንፈልግም	annïfälligïm	we don't want
አይነግርም	aynägrïm	he doesn't tell
አልችልም	alčïlim	I can't

Affirmative

አውቃለሁ	awk'allähw	I know
እንፈልጋለን	ïnnïfälligallän	we want
ይነግራል	yïnägral	he tells
እችላለሁ	ïčïlallähw	I can

Look at these closely and you can see that the stem of the imperfect (italics) remains intact throughout, but is accompanied by different sets of prefixes and suffixes.

The negative prefix and the personal prefix merge to form a new set of prefixes, and instead of the suffix containing the verb አለ 'to be' the negative suffix -ም is added directly to the stem of the imperfect with the addition of the vowel i in the second person feminine, and u in the second and third persons plural.

Singular	Prefix	Ending	Sample		
1st pers.	al-	-[i]m	alfälligïm	አልፈልግም	I don't want
2nd pers. masc.	attï-	-[i]m	attïfälligïm	አትፈልግም	you don't want
2nd pers. fem.	attï-	-ïm	attïfälligïm	አትፈልጊም	you don't want
3rd pers. masc.	ay-	-[i]m	ayfälligïm	አይፈልግም	he doesn't want
3rd pers. fem.	attï-	-[i]m	attïfälligïm	አትፈልግም	she doesn't want
Plural					
1st pers.	annï-	-[i]m	annïfälligïm	አንፈልግም	we don't want
2nd pers.	attï-	-um	attïfälligum	አትፈልጉም	you don't want
3rd pers.	ay-	-um	ayfälligum	አይፈልጉም	they don't want; he, she doesn't want; you don't want

Some points to note:

1 When the stem ends in a consonant the vowel ï is always pronounced before the suffix -ም: አልሄድም al-hed-ïm 'I don't go', but አልሰማም al-säma-m 'I don't hear'.

2 The vowel i of the second person feminine and the vowel u of the second and third plural replace a stem final vowel: አይሰማም aysämam 'he doesn't hear', but አይሰሙም aysämum 'they don't hear'.

3 The vowel i of the second person feminine causes the palatalization of the previous consonant in exactly the same way as the ending -iyalläš of the compound imperfect: አትመጣም attïmät'am 'you [masculine] don't come', but አትመጪም/አትመጭም attïmäč'im/attïmäč'ïm 'you [feminine] don't come'. From the last example you can see that after the palatalized consonant the vowel i may either remain or be reduced to ï before the final -ም.

Here is the full set of forms of the negative imperfect of three familiar verbs, ሰማ 'hear'; መጣ 'come' and ሄደ 'go', illustrating all of the above points.

2-lit¹ A (non-palatalizing)		2-lit¹ A (palatalizing)		2-lit⁴ (palatalizing)	
አልሰማም	alsämam	አልመጣም	almät'am	አልሄድም	alhedïm
አትሰማም	attïsämam	አትመጣም	attïmät'am	አትሄድም	attïhedïm
አትሰሚም	attïsämim	አትመጪም	attïmäč'im	አትሄጂም	attïhejim
አይሰማም	aysämam	አይመጣም	aymät'am	አይሄድም	ayhedïm
አትሰማም	attïsämam	አትመጣም	attïmät'am	አትሄድም	attïhedïm
አንሰማም	annïsämam	አንመጣም	annïmät'am	አንሄድም	annïhedïm
አትሰሙም	attïsämum	አትመጡም	attïmät'um	አትሄዱም	attïhedum
አይሰሙም	aysämum	አይመጡም	aymät'um	አይሄዱም	ayhedum

As with the compound imperfect, if the stem begins in the vowel a-the ï vowel of the personal prefixes is dropped. So here is the full set of forms of the verb አወቀ 'to know':

Singular		Plural	
አላውቅም	alawk'ïm	አናውቅም	annawk'ïm
አታውቅም	attawk'ïm	አታውቁም	attawk'um
አታውቂም	attawk'im		
አያውቅም	ayawk'ïm	አያውቁም	ayawk'um
አታውቅም	attawk'ïm		

Exercises

1 Turn the following sentences into negatives and then translate them into English

1 ፒተር ነገ አሥመራ ይሄዳል።
2 እንግሊዝኛ እችላለሁ።
3 ወይዘሮ አያልነሽ ቅቤና ወተት ሰኞቷ ትገዛለች።
4 አቶ ጴጥሮስ ደብዳቤ ይጽፋል።
5 እሁን ለመብላት እንፈልጋለን።
6 ዛሬ ሠራተኞቹ ሥራቸውን ይጨርሳሉ።
7 ገንዘቡን ሁሉ ለሠራተኞቹ ለምን ትሰጣላችሁ?

*2 Rewrite the following sentences (a) in the negative past
and (b) in the negative imperfect*

Example: ከበደ ደብጻቤ ላከ → (a) ከበደ ደብጻቤ አልላከም
(b) ከበደ ደብጻቤ አይልክም

---

1 አስተማሪያችን መጽሐፍ ጻፈች ።
2 ላጊቷ በስልክ ደወልኩ ።
3 በመንገድ ላይ ብዙዎች መንገደኞች አየን ።
4 ሊኒማ በሆስት ሰዓት ተኩል ጀመረ ።
5 በየቀኑ ልክ ግሥራ አንድ ሰዓት ጸሐፊዎች ሥራ ጨረሱ ።
6 ከኛ ጋር ለምን መጣችሁ?

3 Answer the following questions in the negative

Example: ወይዘር አልማዝ ዛሬ ገበያ ትሐጻለች? → አይደለም ፣
ዛሬ ገበያ አትሐድም ።

---

1 አንተ ቡና ትጠጣለህ?
2 ነገ ከበደ ለአሜሪካ ይደውላል?
3 አሁን ምሳ መብላት ትፈልጋላችሁ?
4 አቶ መሐመድ ጥሩ ልብስ ይሺጣል?
5 ጸሐፊዋ ደብጻቤዎችን ትልካለች?
6 መንገደኞቹ ቲኬት ይገዛሉ?

Grammar

The infinitive

You have already met quite a number of infinitives, the form that
usually translates into English as 'to . . .' as in መሄድ mähed 'to go';
መብላት mäblat 'to eat' ማወቅ mawäk' 'to know', and so on. You will
see that the one thing in common is the prefix መ- mä-, or m- if the
verb stem begins with the vowel a. The prefix mä- is added to a
special infinitive stem which is often different from either the simple
past or the imperfect stems. Consider the pattern in the examples in
the box below.

Verb class	Sample	Prefix	Stem	Example		
3-lit A	ነገረ	mä-	-ngär	መንገር	mängär	to speak
3-lit B	ጠየቀ	mä-	-t'äyyäk'	መጠየቅ	mät'äyyäk'	to ask
2-lit[1] A	በላ	mä-	-blat	መብላት	mäblat	to eat
2-lit[1] B	ጠጣ	mä-	-t'ät't'at	መጠጣት	mät'ät't'at	to drink
2-lit[2] A	ሰጠ	mä-	-st'ät	መስጠት	mäst'ät	to give
2-lit[2] B	ቆየ	mä-	-k'wäyyät	መቆየት	mäk'wäyyät	to wait
2-lit[3]	ጻፈ	mä-	-s'af	መጻፍ	mäs'af	to write
2-lit[4]	ሄደ	mä-	-hed	መሄድ	mähed	to go
2-lit[5]	ሆነ	mä-	-hon	መሆን	mähon	to be, become

Some points to note

1 Types A and B are always clearly distinguished.
2 Verbs of classes 2-lit[1] and 2-lit[2] add a final -t to their infinitive stem. Make a note of this because you will see that the same classes of verbs add an 'extra' t in another tense which we shall meet later.
3 Verbs of the classes 2-lit[3], 2-lit[4] and 2-lit[5] have the same stem in the infinitive as in the simple perfect.
4 Verbs whose stems begin in a- regularly form the infinitive with the prefix m-but otherwise follow the same patterns as above:

ማወቅ	mawäk'	to know	*from* አወቀ [3-lit A]
ማለፍ	maläf	to pass	*from* አለፈ [3-lit A]
ማሰብ	massäb	to think	*from* አሰበ [3-lit B]
ማለት	malät	to say	*from* አለ (*this is an irregular verb*)
ማየት	mayät	to see	*from* አየ [2-lit[2] A]

5 A number of the verbs listed in the introduction to this section belong to different classes from those in the table. Discussion of these, as well as the infinitives of the various derived stem types, will be left until later lessons.

In some places you have met the infinitive used alone, and in other places preceded by the preposition ለ- 'to':

ቋንቋችሁን በደምብ ለመናገር እፈልጋለሁ	I want to speak your language properly
ከተራ ሰው ጋር መናገር ያስፈልጋል	it's necessary to speak with ordinary people

There are three basic uses of the infinitive in Amharic

(a) When the infinitive is used to indicate a purpose the preposition
ለ- is required, where for example in English you can use the
phrase 'in order to'.

(b) Where the infinitive is used to extend another verb, as for
instance 'want', 'begin', 'be able' or 'be necessary', as in the
example above, the use of the preposition ለ- is optional.

(c) The infinitive can be used as a noun meaning 'the act of . . .' or
'the condition of . . .', sometimes corresponding to the English
verbal noun ending in -ing. In this last instance the preposition
ለ- is not used.

The following examples illustrate each of the three uses:

(a) ጥያቄ ለመጠየቅ መጣሁ t'iyyak'e lämät'äyyäk' mät't'ahw
I've come (in order) to ask a question
ጋዜጣ ለመግዛት ሄዱ gazet'a lämägzat hedu they've gone to
buy a newspaper

(b) ጋዜጣ (ለ)መግዛት ትፈልጋለች gazet'a (lä)mägzat tïfälligalläčč
she wants to buy a newspaper
ጋዜጣ (ለ)ማንበብ ጀመርኩ gazet'a (lä)manbäb jämmärkw
I began to read the newspaper

(c) መሥራት ጥሩ ነው mäsrat t'ïru näw working is good; it's good
to work
ስለ መምጣቱ ጠየቅሁ sïlä mämt'atu t'äyyäk'hw I asked about
his coming; I asked whether he had come
መሄዳቸውን አወቀች mähedaččäwn awwäk'äčč she knew of
their going; she knew that they had gone

Exercises

**4 Into which of the above categories (a), (b) or (c) do the
infinitives in the following sentences fall?**

1 ቲኬት ለመግዛት ወደ ባቡር ጣቢያ መሄድ ያስፈልጋል ።
2 ጋዜጣ ለማንበብ አልቻልም ፣ መነጽር መግዛት አለብኝ ።
3 ብዙ መብላት ያወፍራል ፣ ብዙ መጠጣት ያስክራል ።
4 ሲኒማ ቤት ለመሄድ እንፈልጋለን ፣ እናንተስ ምን ለመሥራት
ትፈልጋላችሁ?

5 How would you say in Amharic that you want to do the following things?

1 buy a newspaper.
2 ring your husband/wife at 5 o'clock.
3 ask a question.
4 speak with Mr Aklilu.
5 choose a new jacket.
6 listen to the radio (ሬዲዮ).
7 sell your car and buy a new one.
8 write some letters to your friends.
9 visit Almaz and Terefe.

Word building

Compound nouns in   ባለ -

In the dialogue you met the word ባላገር **balagär** meaning 'country-side'. In the vocabulary list it was also glossed as 'peasant'. You may recognize the word አገር **agär** 'country' in ባላገር, which is made up of the prefixed element ባለ - **balä-** followed by አገር. The element ባለ - is connected with the noun ባል **bal** 'husband', which can also mean 'master'. There are many nouns that can be formed in this way, by prefixing ባለ - to another noun. Remember that the final vowel -ä will be dropped before another vowel higher in the 'hierarchy' system.

The usual meaning of the resultant compound is to denote a person who is in some way connected with or, in broad terms, is in possession of something. ባላገር is thus literally 'a person of the country(side)' and its second meaning 'countryside' is a little aberrant.

Here are some more useful compounds with ባለ -. Note that sometimes the two halves of the compound can be written as separate words.

ባለመሬት	balämäret	landowner	*from* መሬት land
ባላባት	balabbat	feudal landlord, nobleman	*from* አባት father
ባለቤት	baläbet	houseowner, spouse, host	*from* ቤት house
ባለ እጅ	balä ijj, baläjj	craftsman, artisan	*from* እጅ hand

ባለሱቅ	baläsuk'	shopkeeper	from ሱቅ shop
ባለሙያ	balämuya	skilled person, expert	from ሙያ skill
ባለቅኔ	baläk'ine	poet	from ቅኔ poem, poetry
ባለሥልጣን	baläsïlt'an	official	from ሥልጣን authority
ባለ ዕዳ	balä ïda	debtor	from ዕዳ debt
ባለ ብድር	balä bïddïr	creditor	from ብድር loan
ባለ ንብረት	balä nïbrät	proprieter	from ንብረት property

Here are two other useful ባለ- compounds where the relationship of meaning between the base noun and the derivative might be a little less obvious:

| ባለንጀራ | balïnjära | companion | from እንጀራ bread |
| ባለጸጋ | baläs'ägga | rich man, rich | from ጸጋ (divine) grace, beneficence |

Occupation nouns and agent nouns

There are various other ways of forming new nouns which denote occupations or human roles and activities. Think how many other such words you have met already and decide to which of the following patterns they belong.

1 Suffix -äñña (or -täñña): ጓደኛ 'friend' was the first instance of this pattern that you met. The base ጓድ gwadd means 'comrade' and was much used during the government of ጓድ ሊቀ መንበር መንግሥቱ ኃይለ ማርያም Gwadd Lik'ä Mänbär Mängïstu Haylä Maryam, Comrade Chairman Mengistu Haile Mariam. Some other examples are given below:

መንገደኛ	mängädäñña	passenger	from መንገድ road, journey
እግረኛ	ïgïräñña, ïgräñña	pedestrian	from እግር foot, leg
በሽተኛ	bäššïtäñña	patient, invalid	from በሽታ illness
ዘበኛ	zäbäñña	guard, watchman	from ዘብ sentry, guard in ዘብ ቆመ stand guard
ፈረሰኛ	färäsäñña	horseman, rider	from ፈረስ horse
መልክተኛ	mïlïktäñña	messenger	from መልክት message, errand

| ጋዜጠኛ | gazet'äñña | journalist | *from* ጋዜጣ newspaper |
| ሙዚቀኛ | muzik'äñña | musician | *from* ሙዚቃ muzik'a music |

A similar suffix with the same role is -täñña. You met this in the word ሠራተኛ 'worker' which comes from the verb ሠራ 'to work'. Another example of this pattern is the word ቀናተኛ k'ännatäñña 'jealous person, jealous' from ቀና 'to be jealous'. The same endings -äñña (sometimes -iñña) and -täñña are also used to form a number of adjectives. You have seen how -äñña is used to form the ordinal numbers, አንደኛ 'first'; ሁለተኛ 'second'; etc. Here are some ordinary adjectives constructed with these suffixes:

ፊተኛ	fitäñña	foremost, front, first	*from* ፊት face, front
ኋላኛ	hwaläñña	rear, latter, last	*from* ኋላ behind, back
ኃይለኛ	hayläñña	powerful, mighty	*from* ኃይል power, might
ጤነኛ	t'enäñña	healthy	*from* ጤና (good) health
አደገኛ	adägäñña	dangerous	*from* አደጋ danger
ቀልደኛ	k'äldäñña	funny, witty	*from* ቀልድ joke
ዕድለኛ	iddïläñña	fortunate	*from* ዕድል (good) fortune
እውነተኛ	iwnätäñña	true	*from* እውነት truth
ታችኛ	tačiñña	lower	*from* ታች below
ላይኛ	layiñña	upper	*from* ላይ on top

2 The suffix -i, usually with the vowel a in the preceding syllable: አስተማሪ and ተማሪ were amongst the first examples you met. This is a very productive pattern which can be formed from any verb, typically to denote the person who carries out the activity described by the verb. So, ተማሪ 'student' is a person who 'studies' or 'learns' – ተማሪ, and አስተማሪ 'teacher' is a person who 'teaches' – አስተማሪ. Sometimes, however, this pattern is used to provide a noun or adjective denoting a thing rather than a person. The examples of this type that you have encountered so far are አስፈላጊ 'necessary' from አስፈለገ 'to be necessary'; አስቸጋሪ 'difficult' from አስቸገረ 'to cause difficulties'; and አካባቢ 'area, surroundings' from the verb አከበበ 'walk round, surround'.

Note that the suffix -i causes the palatalization of the preceding consonant where appropriate, in exactly the same way as you have already seen in the imperfect tenses. So, other examples that have occurred already which belong here are አባይ 'liar' from አበሰ 'to break a promise'; አዲስ መጪ 'newcomer' from መጣ 'come'; and ገዢ 'governor' from ገዛ in the sense of 'rule, govern'.

This pattern is sometimes called the agent noun, because it typically denotes the agent or actor, or the person who performs the action of the verb. The patterns for the triliteral and biliteral verb classes are as illustrated in the following box.

Class	Sample		Agent noun		
3-1 it A	ነገረ	speak	ነጋሪ	nägari	speaker, talker
	ወደደ	love	ወዳጅ	wädaj	lover, friend*
3-lit B	ጨመረ	add	ጨማሪ	č'ämmari	someone who adds
	ለመነ	beg	ለማኝ	lämmañ	beggar
2-lit¹ A	መራ	lead	መሪ	märi	leader
	ነዳ	drive	ነጂ, ነጅ	näji, näj	driver
2-lit¹ B	ለካ	measure	ለኪ	läkki	someone who measures
	ጠጣ	drink	ጠጪ, ጠጪ	t'äč'č'i, t'äč'č'	drinker
2-lit² A	ቀረ	remain behind	ቀሪ	k'äri	survivor, remainder
2-lit² B	ሸኘ	escort	ሸኚ	šäñni	escort
2-lit³	ሳመ	kiss	ሳሚ	sami	kisser*
2-lit4	ሸጠ	sell	ሸያጭ	šäyač'	seller, vendor
2-lit⁵	ቆመ	stand	ቋሚ	k'wami	alive, standing*

Some points to note

1 All classes except 2-lit¹ A and B, and 2-lit² A and B have an **a** vowel in the syllable before the **-i** suffix.

2 The agent noun patterns of verbs of type 2-lit⁴ and 2-lit⁵ involve the insertion of a **y** and a **w**, respectively, before the **a** vowel. There is only a small number of verbs in the language that belong to these two classes, and few of them actively form agent nouns. Those that do show a number of variant forms, such as ሀያጅ hayaj, ሂያጅ hiyaj and even ሀጅ haj 'someone who leaves', 'someone who walks quickly', from ሄደ; or ሻጭ šač' besides ሸያጭ šäyač' 'salesperson, vendor'.

3 Sometimes the agent noun has a specialized meaning. This is the

case with the words marked with an asterisk in the box: ወ ዳ ጅ
wädaj is the ordinary word for 'friend', though in recent usage it
is often superseded by ጓደኛ, and in Addis Ababa by ዘመድ **zämäd**
which properly means 'relative, family'. ሰሚ. also means someone
who goes on a pilgrimage, that is who *lit.* 'kisses churches'. Lastly,
ቋሚ. is most often used as an adjective as in ቋሚ. ሕግ k'wami higg
'standing rule, policy'; or ቋሚ. ነገር k'wami nägär 'something
permanent'; or ቋሚ. ሰላም k'wami sälam 'lasting peace'.

Here are some more occupation names which follow the agent noun
pattern:

አስታማሚ.	astamami	nurse	*from* አስታመመ *to nurse*
ጸጉር አስተካካይ	s'ägur astäkakay	hairdresser	*from* ጸጉር *hair and* አስተካከለ *to arrange, put in order*
(ልብስ) ሰፊ	(libs) säfi	tailor	*from* ልብስ *clothes and* ሰፋ *to sew*
ዘፋኝ	zäfañ	singer, dancer	*from* ዘፈነ *to sing, dance*
ፎቶግራፍ አንሺ	fotograf anši	photographer	*from* ፎቶግራፍ አነሣ *to take a photograph*
አስተዳዳሪ	astädadari	manager, administrator	*from* አስተ ዳ ደረ *to administrate*
ሥራ አስከያጅ	sira askäyyaj	manager	*from* ሥራ *to work and* አስኬደ *to direct*
ተቀጣሪ	täk'ät'ari	employee*	*from* ተቀጠረ *to be employed*
ቀጣሪ	k'ät'ari	employer	*from* ቀጠረ *employ, hire*

*Another word for employee is ቅጥረኛ **k'it'räñña** with the -äñña
suffix.

Not all nouns describing occupations and human activities fit into
one of these patterns. Many such nouns are not derived in a regular
way, or indeed are themselves basic, non-derived forms. Here are a

few more occupations the names of which are not regularly derived nouns.

ሐኪም	hakim	doctor	ነርስ	närs	nurse
ፖሊስ	polis	policeman	ወታደር	wättaddär	soldier
መካኒክ	mäkanik	mechanic	ገበሬ	gäbäre	farmer
መሐንዲስ	mähandis	engineer	ደራሲ	därasi	author, writer
ተዋናይ	täwanay	actor	ቄስ	k'es	priest
ዳኛ	dañña	judge	ጠበቃ	t'äbäk'a	lawyer, attorney
ሾፌር	šofer	driver, chauffeur			
አለቃ	aläk'a	boss*			

*This is also the title of the principal priest of a church or the superior of a monastery.

Exercises

6 Match up the following lists of occupations and places of work and then construct a full sentence to describe where each one works. A few of the names for places of work will be new: some you'll be able to guess; some you may have to look up

> *Example:* ተማሪዎች : ትምሕርት ቤት → ተማሪዎች በትምሕርት ቤት ይማራሉ።

ሠራተኞች: ጸሐፊ   ጠበቃ   ገላሱቅ   ፖሊስ   ገበሬ
           መካኒክ   ቄስ   አስተማሪ   ተዋናይ
           የታከሲ ሾፌር   ሐኪም   አትክልት ሽያጭ   ለማኝ

የሥራ ቦታዎች: ሆስፒታል   ጋራዥ   ሱቅ ቲያትር   ቤት ክርስቲያን
            መደብር   ቢሮ   ማሳ   የከተማ መንገድ
            ትምህርት ቤት

7 Here are some statements about where people work and what they do. Using a full sentence say whether these statements are true or false

> *Example:* ሐኪም በጋራዥ ይሠራል። → እውነት አይደለም።
> ሐኪም በጋራዥ አይሠራም። በሆስፒታል ይሠራል።

1 ጋዜጠኛ በትምህርት ቤት ደሠራል።
2 ጻና በመደብር ደሠራል።
3 ተማርቶች በፖሊስ ጣቢያ ደሠራሉ።
4 ያቱክልት ሸያጭ በቢሮ ደሠራል።
5 ጸሐፊ በመንገድ ላይ ትሠራለች።
6 ፖሊስ በጸጉር ማስተካከያ ደሠራል።

Reading passage

ኢትዮጵያ በአፍሪካ አህጉር ውስጥ ሰሜን ምሥራቅ ክፍል ተገኛለች። ይህም አካባቢ የአፍሪካ ቀንድ ይባላል። የኢትዮጵያ አዋሳኝ አገሮች በሰሜን በኩል ኤርትራ፣ በመዕራብ ሱዳን፣ በደቡብ ኬንያ፣ በደቡብ ምሥራቅና በምሥራቅ ሱማልያ ናቸው። ከዚህም ሌላ በምሥራቅ በኩል ኤርትራና ሱማልያ መካከል ከምትገኘው ከጂቡቲ ጋር ትዋሰናለች።

በ፲፱፻፺፫ ዓ፣ም ኤርትራ ነጻ ወጣች። የኤርትራ ዋና ከተማ አሥመራ ናት። ከሠላሳ ዓመት በላይ የኤርትራ ሕዝብ ስለ ነጻነቱ ታግሎዋል። በፊት ግን ኤርትራ ከኢትዮጵያ ጠቅላይ ግዛቶች አንዲ ነበረች።

<u>የአቅጣጫ አመልካች</u>

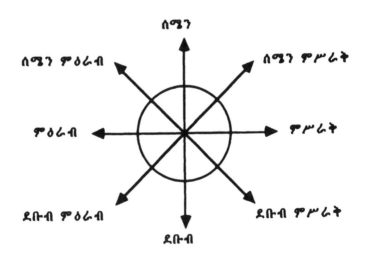

Supplementary vocabulary

አህጉር	**ahgur**	continent
ነጻ	**näs'a**	free (ነጻ ወጣ **näs'a wät't'a** gain one's freedom, *lit.* 'come out free')
ነጻነት	**näs'annät**	freedom
ተዋሰነ	**täwassänä**	adjoin, share a border
አዋሳኝ	**awwasañ**	bordering
ወሰን	**wäsän**	border
ታገለ	**taggälä**	struggle, wrestle: ታግሎዋል ፡ ታግሏል **taglowal, taglwal** it has struggled
ትግል	**tïgïl**	struggle, conflict
ጠቅላይ ግዛት	**t'äk'lay gïzat**	province
የአቅጣጫ አመልካች	**yäak't'ač'a amälkač**	points of the compass (*lit.* 'direction indicator')

7 ደብዳቤ መጻፍ
däbdabbe mäs'af
Writing a letter

By the end of this lesson you should be able to:

- use pronoun objects ('I saw *him*', 'he gave *me*', etc.)
- use prepositional pronouns ('I did it for him, I hit him with it, etc.)
- work with the Ethiopian calendar

Peter writes a letter 🔲

[የፖስታ ሣጥን ቁጥር 3267]

[አዲስ አበባ]

[ኅዳር 13 ቀን 1986]

[ለወዳጄ ለሐዲስ]

ከተለያየን ጊዜ ጀምር አስካሁን ድረስ እንደምን ሰነበትክ? እኔ ደገና ነኝ። ለመጀመሪያ ጊዜ ባማርኛ ደብዳቤ ጻፍኩልህ። ስላዚህም እንዳንድ ስህተት ይኖርበታል። ይሁን እንጂ ይህን የመጀመሪያ ደብዳቤዬን ያለምንም ድጋፍ ለመጻፍ ሞክርኩ። ዮሐንስ ግን ከመላኪ በፊት አነበበው። እሱ ምንም ስህተት የለበትም አለ። እኔ ግን አርግጠኛ አይደለሁም - መቸም ተስፋ አድርጋለሁ!

ዛሬ ኢትዮጵያ ከደረስኩ አሥር ቀኔ ነው። በጉዞዬ ላይ ዮሐንስ ከሚገባ ልጅ ጋር በደምብ ተዋወቅሁ። እሱ በጣም አዋቂ በመሆኑ ስለኢትዮጵያ ብዙ ነገር አስረዳኝ። በርግጥ አገሩን በጣም አጥብቆ ይወዳታል!

ከዚም አውርፕላናችን ካረፈ በኋላ ጌሩትና ከበደ አውርፕላን ማረፊያ በደስታ አድርገው ተቀበሉን። እነሱም የዮሐንስ የቅርብ ወዳጆች ናቸው። ሁላቸውም በጣም ደግ ናቸው። ለምሳሌ

አማርኛ ለመማር በጣም ይጠቅሙኛል - ፈረንጆችን አማርኛ
ማስተማር ቀላል አይደለም!

ትናንትና ሁላችንም ወደ ደብረ ሊባኖስ ለሽርሽር ሄድን። ቦታውን
ታውቃለህ? መነክሳቶቹ የቅዱስ ተክለ ሃይማኖትን ዋሻ አሳዩን፡
ከዚያም በኋላ ተሻገርን ወደ ገዳም ሄድን። እዚያም ቡና
አፈሉልንና የቅዱስ ተክለ ሃይማኖትን ታሪክ አወሩን። ያማርኛ
ቋንቋ ከመማር በላይ የኢትዮጵያንም ታሪክ ጭምር አማራለሁ!

[ከመልካም ምኞት ጋር]
[ፒተር]

Post box number 3267
Addis Ababa

Hidar 13th 1986 (November 22nd 1993)

Dear Haddis,

How have you been since we parted? I am fine. I am writing you a letter in Amharic for the first time. So, there may be some mistakes in it. Anyway, I have tried to write this, my first letter, without any assistance. But Yohannes has read it before I sent it. He says, there aren't any mistakes in it at all. I am not sure, though – anyway I hope so!

It's been ten days now since I arrived in Ethiopia. During my journey I met an Ethiopian boy called Yohannes. He is very knowlegeable and described to me lots of things about Ethiopia. He certainly loves his country very much indeed!

Then after our plane had landed, Hirut and Kebede welcomed us warmly at the airport. They are close friends of Yohannes. They are all very kind. For instance, they are a great help to me in learning Amharic – it isn't easy to teach foreigners Amharic!

Yesterday we all went on an outing to Debre Libanos. Do you know the place? The monks showed us St. Tekle Haymanot's cave and afterwards we went across to the monastery. There they made coffee for us and told us the history of St. Tekle Haymanot. As well as learning the Amharic language I am now also learning Ethiopian history!

[With best wishes,]
[Peter]

Vocabulary

ሣጥን	sat'ïn	box
የፖስታ ሣጥን ቁጥር	yäposta sat'ïn k'ut'ïr	post box number
ኅዳር	hïdar	*the third month of the Ethiopian year, beginning on November 10th (11th in a leap year)*
ስህተት, ስተት	sïhtät, sïtät	mistake, error
ድጋፍ	dïgaf	support, assistance
ያለምንም ድጋፍ	yalämïnïm dïgaf	without any assistance
እርግጠኛ	ïrgït'äñña	certain, sure
በረራ	bärära	flight
ጉዞ	guzo	journey
አዋቂ	awak'i	knowledgeable, expert (agent noun from አወቀ)
ደስታ	dässïta	happiness, joy; በደስታ bädässïta happily, warmly
ዋሻ	wašša	cave
ምኞት	mïññot	wish, desire; መልካም ምኞት mälkam mïññot best wishes

Verbs

ሰነበተ	sänäbbätä	spend some time [4-lit] (*see note 3*)
አነበበ	anäbbäbä	read (derived stem. Compound imperfect ያነባል yanäbbal)
አስረዳ	asrädda	describe, persuade (derived stem. Compound imperfect ያስረዳል yasräddal)
አረፈ	arräfä	rest, land (*of birds, aeroplanes*) [3-lit A]
ተቀበለ	täk'äbbälä	welcome, receive, accept (derived stem. Compound imperfect ይቀበላል yïk'k'äbbälal)
ጠቀመ	t'äk'k'ämä	be useful, benefit [3-lit A]
አስተማረ	astämarä	teach (derived stem; *compare* ተማረ 'learn, study'. Compound imperfect ያስተምር; infinitive ማስተማር)
አፈላ	afälla	boil something, make (coffee) (derived stem. Compound imperfect ያፈላል)
አወራ	awärra	tell, relate (derived stem. Compound imperfect ያወራል)

Phrases

አጥብቄ	at'bïk'k'e	very much, greatly, emphatically
አጥብቆ	at'bïk'o	" (*See note 2*)
መቸም	mäčäm	anyway, after all (*at the beginning of a sentence*)
ተሻገረን	täšagrän	across (*see note 2*)
ይሁን እንጂ	yïhun ïnji	anyway, nevertheless (*lit.* 'so be it, but . . .')
ጭምር	č'immïr	as well, in addition
ከተለያየን	kätäläyayyän	ever since we parted (*lit.* 'begin-
ጊዜ ጀምሮ	gize jämmïro	ning since the time we separated from one another')

Notes on the letter

1 Ethiopia has its own calendar which differs from the Gregorian calendar that is used in most of the rest of the world, in three fundamental respects:

(a) there are 13 months, 12 of 30 days each plus a short month of 5 or 6 days according to whether the year is a leap year or not;
(b) the year begins in what to most of the rest of the world is September, and not in January;
(c) the years are calculated from a point 7 years later than the Western Christian (AD) or Common Era used elsewhere.

The Ethiopian calendar is in regular use, in correspondence, in newspapers and magazines and in diaries.

The names of the 13 months are as follows. As well as the exact date equivalents, a rough equivalent is given for each month's name since many Ethiopians will, for example, translate መስከረም, the first month, as 'September', and so on.

Ethiopian month names		Dates (non-leap year)	Rough equivalent
መስከረም	mäskäräm	11 September–10 October	September
ጥቅምት	t'ïk'ïmt	11 October–9 November	October
ኅዳር	hïdar	10 November–9 December	November
ታህሣሥ	tahsas	10 December–8 January	December

Ethiopian month names		Dates (non-leap year)	Rough equivalent
ጥር	t'ïr	9 January–7 February	January
የካቲት	yäkkatit	8 February–9 March	February
መጋቢት	mäggabit	10 March–8 April	March
ሚያዝያ	miyazya	9 April–8 May	April
ግንቦት	gïnbot	9 May–7 June	May
ሰኔ	säne	8 June–7 July	June
ሐምሌ	hamle	8 July–6 August	July
ነሐሴ	nähase	7 August–5 September	August
ጳጉሜን	p'agumen	6 September–10 September	–

Because the Ethiopian year starts in September, this means that the Ethiopian year 1986 [፲፱፻፹፮ ዓ ፡ ም] runs from 11 September 1993 to 10 September 1994, and so if you do not know which month of the year is being talked about a date such as 1986 would be equivalent to 1993–4 in the Gregorian calendar.

The abbreviation ዓ ፡ ም which often follows the number of the year in written Amharic stands for ዓመተ ምሕረት amätä mïhrät, *lit.* 'year of mercy' in Ge'ez.

Here are some important dates from the last century and a half of Ethiopian history. The dates are given according to the Ethiopian calendar; see if you can match them up with the Gregorian dates given below:

February 1974, 10 March 1889, 13 April 1868, 1 March 1896, November 1886, 25 May 1993, 2 April 1930, 6 April 1941, 3 October 1935, May 1991

[፲፰፻፷ ሚያዝያ ፮ ቀን] suicide of Emperor Tewodros II (1855–68) at his fortress capital at Mäqdäla following the attack of the British expeditionary force led by General Napier who had come to rescue the 'Abyssinian captives'. Tewodros is still regarded as an heroic figure in Ethiopia today.

[፲፰፻፸፱ ገ ፰ c] the foundation of Addis Ababa as the new permanent capital of the kingdom of Shoa and shortly after of Ethiopia as a whole.

[፲፰፻፹፩ መጋቢት ፪ ቀን] the accession of Menilek of Shoa as Emperor Menilek II of Ethiopia (1889–1913), following the death of Emperor Yohannes IV fighting the Dervishes at Mätämma.

[፲፰፻፹፰ የአድዋ ጦር ቀን] the Battle of Adwa at which Menilek's army defeated the Italians invading from their colony of Eritrea. This defeat was widely seen as a significant check to European colonial expansion in the area and provided the pretext for the Italian invasion of Ethiopia in 1935.

[፲፱፻፳፫ መጋቢት ፪ ቀን] the accession of Ras Tafari as Emperor Haile Sellassie I (1930–74) following fourteen years as regent under Menilek's daughter, the Empress Zawditu.

[፲፱፻፳፰ መስከረም ፳፪ ቀን] the Italians invade Ethiopia crossing the Märäb river from Eritrea. Seven months later and after finally routing the Ethiopian forces at the Battle of Mayč'äw, the Italians entered Addis Ababa and seized Ethiopia. Haile Sellassie addressed the League of Nations in Geneva asking in vain for help, and then went into exile in Britain.

[፲፱፻፴፫ መጋቢት ፳፰ ቀን] the liberation of Addis Ababa during the Second World War by the British under Generals Wingate and Sandford.

[፲፱፻፷፮ የአብዮት] the start of the Ethiopian revolution, called at first a 'creeping *coup*'. By the end of the year this led to the deposition of Haile Sellassie and the establishment of what was called 'Ethiopian Socialism' under the leadership of the Committee (or ደርግ därg in Amharic, adopted into English journalese as "the Derg") headed by Colonel Mengistu Haile Mariam.

[፲፱፻፹፫ ግንቦት] the flight of Mengistu Haile Mariam and the capture of Addis Ababa by the combined forces of the EPRDF (the Ethiopian Popular Revolutionary Democratic Front) under the leadership of Meles Zenawi.

[፲፱፻፹፭ ግንቦት ፲፬] the formal recognition of Eritrean independence from Ethiopia.

2 አጥብቄ at'bïk'k'e and አጥብቆ at'bïk'o are both translated by the English adverbial phrase 'very much'. They are however in fact verbs and are in agreement with the subject of the sentence: አጥብቄ is first person singular because it goes with the verb እወደዋለሁ ïwäddäwallähw 'I like him', and አጥብቆ is third person masculine because it goes with the verb ይወዳታል yïwäddatal 'he likes it (her)'. The verb from which these two forms come is አጠበቀ at'äbbäk'a which means amongst other things 'to do something with all one's might'.

Similarly ተሻግረን täšagrän is translated as 'across', though it too is a verb form from ተሻገረ täšaggärä which means 'to go across, to cross'. አድርጎው **adrïgäw** in the phrase በደስታ አድርጎው is a similar form from the verb አደረገ **adärrägä** 'do'; also, ጀምሮ **jämmïro** in the phrase ከተለያየን ጊዜ ጀምር , from the verb ጀመረ **jämmärä** 'begin'.

All four are in a form of the verb that we have not yet discussed: the gerundive. You should note the forms of the gerundive as you work your way through the book. In the lessons that follow you'll see that the gerundive plays an important part in building up Amharic sentences and that it can sometimes be translated by an adverb and sometimes by a proper verb form in English.

In the phrase በደስታ አድርጎው the gerundive isn't translated at all! Its function is simply to "support" the adverbial በደስታ, though the whole phrase literally means 'doing [it] with happiness', i.e. 'warmly'!

3 Some Amharic verb stems consist not of two or three consonants like those you have met so far, but of four consonants like ሰነበተ **sänäbbätä** [i.e. s-n-b-t], for which the shorthand label [4-lit] will be used here. Here are a few more of this type that you may find useful to add to your vocabulary:

መረመረ	**märämmärä**	examine
ሰበሰበ	**säbässäbä**	gather, collect (something)
ደነገጠ	**dänäggät'ä**	be alarmed, scared, shocked
ከለከለ	**käläkkälä**	forbid, prevent
ጠረጠረ	**t'ärät't'ärä**	doubt, suspect
ጠቀለለ	**t'äk'ällälä**	wrap up, fold (*you may remember the phrase* በጠቅላላው, *which comes from the same root*)

The compound imperfect of this type of verbs follows the pattern ይሰነብታል **yïsänäbïtal**, and the infinitive መሰንበት **mäsänbät**. There is no separate distinction in this class between A and B types.

4 Note the idiomatic expression ከደረስኩ አሥር ቀኔ ነው **kädärräskw assïr k'äne näw**, literally 'it is my ten days since I arrived' for 'it's been ten days since I arrived'.

Grammar

Pronoun objects

In verbs like ይጠብቁታል yït'äbbïk'utal 'they're waiting for him'; አደረስናቸው asdärräsnaččäw 'we fetched them'; አይነግረኝም aynägrännïm 'he doesn't tell me'; እንረዳኻለን innïrädähallän 'we'll help you'; ይጠቁሙናል yït'äk'muññal 'they're assisting me' the direct object pronouns 'him', 'them', 'me' and 'you' are all incorporated into the verb forming a single word. This is in fact the more usual way of expressing direct objects that are pronouns, rather than using the independent pronoun with the direct object marker -ን, such as you would use if the object were a noun. So:

ከበደን ይጠብቃሉ	Käbbädän yït'äbbïk'allu	they're waiting for Kebede
ይጠብቁታል	yït'äbbïk'utal	they're waiting for him

The independent pronoun with -ን is normally only used for an emphasized object. The following pairs of sentences illustrates this:

እርሳቸውን አየን	ïrsaččäwn ayyän	we saw *them, them* we saw (but not you)
አየናቸው	ayyänaččäw	we saw them, (neutral, non-emphatic)
አንተን እረዳለሁ	antän ïrädallähw	I'll help *you, you* I'll help (but not him)
እረዳኻለሁ	ïrädahallähw	I'll help you, (neutral, non-emphatic)

From these examples and others in this and the previous lesson you can see that the object pronoun appears sometimes at the end of the verb form, and sometimes in it:

ይጠብቁታል	yït'äbbïk'u*tal*	they're waiting for *him*
አደረስናቸው	asdärräsn*aččäw*	we fetched *them*
አይነግረኝም	aynägr*äññ*m	he doesn't tell *me*
እንረዳኻለን	innïräda*h*allän	we'll help *you*
አልነገረኝም	alnäggär*äñ*m	he didn't tell *us*
ያስፈልገናል	yasfällig*äñal*	it'll be necessary for *us* (= we'll need)
ይጠቁሙናል	yït'äk'mu*ññal*	they're assisting *me*
ስጪኝ	sïč'*ïñ*	give *me*

From these you can draw the following rules about the position of the object pronoun. It occurs in the following instances:

1 on the end of the simple past tense after the personal ending: አደረስናቸው-; also on the end of the imperative: ስጪኝ;
2 before the negative -ም both in the past and the imperfect: አልነገረንም, አይነገረኝም;
3 inside the compound imperfect before the አለ ending: ያስፈልገናል. There are however some more complex changes involved here as you can see if you compare ይጠብቁታል 'they're waiting for him' with ከበደን ይጠብቃሉ 'they're waiting for Kebede'.

The affixes of the object pronoun are identical to those added to the verb አለ 'to be' to form the verb 'to have'. There the base to which the pronoun affixes are added ends in -ä, -u or -äčč. The verb bases to which the object pronoun can be added can however end in other vowels and consonants which may affect the shape of the pronoun affix.

Verb ends in:		*ä, a*	*i, e*	*u, o*	*a consonant*	*-š,-äčč*
singular						
1st pers.	me	-ñ	-ñ	-ñ	-äñ	-iñ
2nd masc.	you	-h	-h	-h	-ih	-ih
2nd fem.	you	-š	-š	-š	-iš	-iš
3rd masc.	him	-w	-w	-t	-äw	-iw
3rd fem.	her	-at	-yat	-wat	-at	-at
plural						
1st pers.	us	-n	-n	-n	-än	-in
2nd pers.	you	-ačču̇h	-yačču̇h	-wačču̇h	-ačču̇h	-ačču̇h
3rd pers.	them	-ačč̇äw	-yačč̇äw	-wačč̇äw	-ačč̇äw	-ačč̇äw
formal						
2nd pers.	you	-wo(t)	-wo(t)	-wo(t)	-wo(t)	-wo(t)
3rd pers.	him, her	-ačč̇äw	-yačč̇äw	-wačč̇äw	-ačč̇äw	-ačč̇äw

Some points to note

First person singular:
the ending is just -ñ throughout, but note the exception: when added to a verb ending in a consonant it is -äñ.

First person plural:	the ending is just **-n** throughout, but note the exception: when added to a verb ending in a consonant it is **-än**.
Third person masculine:	the ending has three shapes: **-t** after the vowels **u** and **o**; **-äw** after a consonant; **-w** elsewhere.
Third person feminine:	the ending is **-at** of which the vowel **a** is never dropped; so be careful not to confuse it with the third person masculine variant **-t**. When added to verbs ending in **i, e, o** or **u**, the ending **-at** needs a 'glide': **-y-** after **i** and **e**, **-w-** after **o** and **u**.
Second and third persons plural:	like the third person feminine suffix, **-aččuh** and **-aččäw** need a **-y-** or **-w-** 'glide' when added to verbs ending in **i** and **e**, and **o** and **u**, respectively.
Second person formal:	the ending is either **-wo** or **-wot**; only the variant **-wot** is possible when the object pronoun occurs inside a compound tense like the compound imperfect, as in እጠብቅዎታለሁ **it'äbbïk'** *wot* allähw 'I shall wait for you'.
Verbs ending in **-š** or **-ä͟čč**:	when added to the second and third persons feminine ending in **-š** and **-ä͟čč**, respectively (i.e. of the tenses you know so far, only in the simple past), the object pronoun endings for the first person singular and plural, 'me' and 'us', and the third person masculine, 'him', have the forms **-iñ, -in** and **-iw**, that is with the sixth-order and not the first-order vowel as is the case after verbs ending in other consonants. This last point should be noted carefully. As an example, contrast ጠበቅነው **t'äbbäk'n***äw* 'we waited for him' and ጠበቀችው **t'äbbäk'ä͟čč***iw* 'she waited for him'.

Here then are some examples of pronoun object suffixes added to verbs ending in different vowels or in a consonant:

	[ወደደ (he loved)]			[ወደዱ (they loved)]	
me	ወደደኝ	wäddädäñ		ወደዱኝ	wäddäduñ
you	ወደደህ	wäddädäh		ወደዱህ	wäddäduh
you	ወደደሽ	wäddädäš		ወደዱሽ	wäddäduš
him	ወደደው	wäddädäw		ወደዱት	wäddädut
her	ወደዳት	wäddädat		ወደዱዋት	wäddäduwat

[ወደደች (she loved)]

me	ወደደችኝ	wäddädäččïñ
you	ወደደችህ	wäddädäččïh
you	ወደደችሽ	wäddädäččïš
him	ወደደችው	wäddädäččïw
her	ወደደቻት	wäddädäččat

us	ወደደን	wäddädän	ወደዱን	wäddädun
you	ወደዳችሁ	wäddädaččuh	ወደዱዋችሁ	wäddäduwaččuh
them	ወደዳቸው	wäddädaččäw	ወደዱዋቸው	wäddäduwaččäw

you	ወደደዎ	wäddädäwo	ወደዱዎ	wäddäduwo
him/her	ወደዳቸው	wäddädaččäw	ወደዱዋቸው	wäddäduwaččäw

us	ወደደችን	wäddädäččïn
you	ወደደችሁ	wäddädäččaččuh
them	ወደደቻቸው	wäddädäččaččäw

you	ወደደችዎ	wäddädäččïwo
him/her	ወደደቻቸው	wäddädäččaččäw

	ሰማ (he heard)		ሰማን (we heard)		ስሚ (hear!) [2nd fem.]	
me	ሰማኝ	sämmañ	–		ስሚኝ	sïmiñ
you	ሰማህ	sämmah	ሰማንህ	sämmanïh	–	
you	ሰማሽ	sämmaš	ሰማንሽ	sämmanïš	–	
him	ሰማው	sämmaw	ሰማነው	sämmanïw	ስሚው	sïmiw
her	ሰማት	sämmat	ሰማናት	sämmanat	ስሚያት	sïmiyat
us	ሰማን	sämman	–		ስሚን	sïmin
you	ሰማችሁ	sämmaččuh	ሰማናችሁ	sämmanaččuh	–	
them	ሰማቸው	sämmaččäw	ሰማናቸው	sämmanaččäw	ስሚያቸው	sïmiyaččäw
you	ሰማዎ	sämmawo	ሰማንዎ	sämmanïwo	–	
him/her	ሰማቸው	sämmaččäw	ሰማናቸው	sämmanaččäw	ስሚያቸው	sïmiyaččäw

You may have noticed that a few of the verb forms in the above tables are ambiguous: **ሰማህ sämmah,** for instance, can mean both 'he heard you' (**ሰማ** + object pronoun **-ህ**) and 'you heard' (**ሰማህ** with no object pronoun suffix). These ambiguities are not really very frequent, and, in any case, it will always be clear from the context which is meant.

Object pronouns on verbs of 'saying' and 'giving'

When added to verbs like **አለ alä** 'he said', **ነገረ nägärä** 'tell, speak', and **ሰጠ sät't'ä** 'give', the object pronoun suffixes usually express not the direct object, the thing said or given, but the indirect object, the person to whom something is said or given. So, for example, **አልኩት alkut** 'I said to him, I told him', **ነገሩን näggärun** 'they spoke to us, told us', **ሰጣት sät't'at** 'he gave [it] to her, he gave her (as recipient)', and so on.

Remember, though, that if the indirect object is a noun then you have to use the preposition **ለ- lä-: ለከበደ ሰጠሁት lä-Käbbädä sät't'ähut** 'I gave it to Kebede', **ወሬውን ለኛ ነገሩን wärewn läñña näggärun** 'they told *us* the news'.

You will notice from these examples that you can still keep the suffix on the verb, 'in agreement' with the indirect object noun. It's quite usual in Amharic to do this with direct object nouns, too: **ሌቦቹ ገንዘቡን ሁሉ ሠረቁት lebočču gänzäbun hullu särräk'ut** 'the thieves stole all the money', *lit.* '. . . stole it, all the money'.

Exercises

1 Substitute a verb plus an object pronoun suffix ('I saw him') for the independent pronoun object or noun object plus verb ('I saw the man') in the following sentences

Example: ይህን ታሪክ መቼ ሰማሽ? → መቼ ሰማሽው?

1 ከበደንና ጊሩትን በሲኒማ ቤት አገኘሁ።
2 ጊሩት አስተማሪውን ስለ ትምሕርቷ ጠየቀች።
3 እኔን ወደድሽ?
4 አቶ ሙሉጌታ ጸሐፊያቸውን ፈለጉ።
5 ተማሪዎቹ ሁሉ መጽሐፋቸውን አሁን ገዙ?

6 ይህን ነገር አላወቅንም።
7 ገንዘቡን ከዬት አገኘህ?
8 ወንድምሽን በትምሕርቱ አልረዳሽም እንዴ?
9 እኛን አልሰሙም?

2 Rewrite the following sentences using noun or independent pronoun objects. Select your answers from amongst the nouns and phrases listed below

ሬዲዮን, መኪናዬን, መልሱን, ተማሪውን, ለኔ, ወይዘር አልማዝን, እኔን, ተማሪዎቹን

1 ባለፈው ዓመት አንድ ሌባ ሠረቀው።
2 አቶ ሙሉጌታ አምስት ብር ሰጡኝ።
3 በክፍላቸው ውስጥ አገኘናቸው።
4 ትናንትና ማታ አልሰማሁትም።
5 ባለፈው ሳምንት ሲኒማ ቤት አየሁዎት።
6 ስለምን መረጥከኝ?
7 በትምሕርቱ ረዳሁት።
8 ስለምን ጠየቅከኝ? አላወቅሁትም።

3 Here are some things you might want to do and some dates when you might want to do them. Construct Amharic sentences to express your intentions, translating the dates into the Ethiopian calendar. You may need to do a little arithmetic!

Activities:

sell your car	buy a new house	fly to America
go into hospital	write a book	visit your friends
learn Amharic	lose some weight[1]	paint your house[2]

[1] Use **ክብደት ቀነሰ** [3-lit B] **kïbdät k'ännäsä,** *lit.* 'lessen weight'
[2] Use **ቀባ** [2-lit[1] B] **k'äbba,** 'smear, spread (butter); paint (a house)

Dates:

in the month of July	at the beginning of April	before the end of May
August 10th	Monday, January 1st	December 15th
before May 20th	in the month of March	by (*lit.* 'until') November

Grammar

Object pronouns and the compound imperfect tense

When an object pronoun suffix is added to a compound imperfect tense verb it has to come in front of the ኣለ element, that is, the ending of the verb that closely resembles, and indeed is derived from the verb ኣለ 'to be'. This means that the compound tense is split into two halves and the object pronoun is inserted between them. Study the pattern as set out in the box below.

Comp. imperfect:	yïwäddal	ይወዳል	he loves
→	yïwädd -al		
	verb base + ኣለ		
Add pronoun object:	yïwäddatal	ይወዳታል	he loves her
→	yïwädd -at -al		
	verb base + object pronoun + ኣለ		

This is quite straightforward, but note in the third person plural where the ኣለ element (-allu) is reduced to -al when an object pronoun is inserted and the 'verb base' has a vowel -u added in

	Without object	*With object*	
1st pers. sing.	አወዳለሁ	አወዳታለሁ	I love her
	ïwadd-allähw	ïwädd-at-allähw	
2nd pers. masc.	ተወዳለህ	ተወዳታለህ	you love her
	tïwädd-alläh	tïwädd-at-alläh	
2nd pers. fem.	ተወጃለሽ	ተወጃታለሽ	you love her
	tïwäjj-alläš	tïwäjj-at-alläš	
3rd pers. masc.	ይወዳል	ይወዳታል	he loves her
	yïwädd-al	yïwädd-at-al	
3rd pers. fem.	ተወዳለች	ተወዳታለች	she loves her
	tïwädd-alläčč	tïwädd-at-alläčč	
1st pers. pl.	እንወዳለን	እንወዳታለን	we love her
	innïwädd-allän	innïwädd-at-allän	
2nd pers. pl.	ተወዳላችሁ	ተወዱዋታላችሁ	you love her
	tïwädd-allaččuh	tïwädd*u*-wat-*allaččuh*	
3rd pers. pl.	ይወዳሉ	ይወዱዋታል	they love her
	yïwädd-allu	yïwädd*u*-wat-*al*	

compensation. This same -u also appears in the second person plural. Examine the following box and compare the second and third plural forms with and without an object pronoun.

Exercises

4 Convert the sentences with pronoun objects in exercise one into the compound imperfect tense

---

Examples መቼ ሰማሸው? → መቼ ትሰሚዋለሽ?

በሲኒማ ቤት አገኘሁዋቸው→ በሲኒማ ቤት
አገኛቸዋለሁ

---

5 The following sentences all contain verbs with object pronoun suffixes. Rewrite them substituting a suitable noun, independent pronoun or name for the object pronoun suffix, and then translate your answer into English.

Example: መቼ አያችሁት? → ወንድሜን መቼ አያችሁ?
When did you see my brother?

---

1 የታከሲ ሾፌር ፖስታ ቤት አጠገብ ደጠብቃታል።
2 ነገ የፈተናውን መልስ አሳያችሁዋለሁ።
3 ከበደና ጊሩት ያማርኛ ቋንቋ ያስተምሩታል።
4 እማማ፡ ወደ ገበያ መቼ ትወስጂናለሽ?
5 እናቴ በጣም ብዙ ትወደዋለች።
6 ከሳምንቱ መጨረሻ በፊት ለናንተ አልከዋለሁ።

Grammar

Prepositional pronoun suffixes

In his letter, Peter used the following verbs አጽፍልሃለሁ is'ïfïllïhallähw 'I am writing to you'; አፈሱልን afällullïn 'they made [coffee] for us'; ይሆንበታል yïhonïbbätal 'there will be in it'; and አይገኘበትም ayïggäññïbbätïm 'there is not found in it'. These verbs all have in common a pronoun suffix very similar to the object pronoun suffix, but following an additional element with 'l' or 'b'. Compare the pairs of words set out below.

አጽፋለሁ	ïs'ïfallähw	I am writing
አጽፍልሃለሁ	ïs'ïfi*llï*hallähw	I am writing *to you*
አፈሉ	afällu	they boiled/made [coffee]
አፈሉልን	afällu*llïn*	they boiled/made . . . *for us*
ይሆናል	yïhonal	there will be
ይሆንበታል	yïhonï*bbä*tal	there will be *in it*
ደወለ	däwwälä	he rang
ደወለላቸው	däwwälä*llaččä*w	he rang *to them* (= he rang them)
አምጣ	amt'a	bring!
አምጣልኝ	amt'a*llïñ*	bring *to me!* or bring *for me!*
አደረጉ	adärrägu	they did
አደረጉላት	adärrägu*llat*	they did [it] *for her*
ይቀመጣሉ	yïk'k'ämmät'allu	they are sitting
ይቀመጡበታል	yïk'k'ämmät'u*bbä*tal	they are sitting *in it*

You can see that these suffixes occupy the same place as the object pronoun suffixes:

- on the end of simple past and imperative forms;
- before the -ም of the negative;
- inside the compound imperfect in front of the አለ element; note the same changes in the second and third persons plural.

Notice that the prepositional element is always either a geminate **ll** or a geminate **bb**, and that if the verb base to which this is added ends in a consonant (i.e. sixth order) then a sixth-order vowel ï has to be pronounced between the base and the suffix: አጽፍልሃለሁ ïs'ïfillïhallähw.

The two sets of prepositional pronoun suffixes are built on the elements -ll- and -bb-, which basically correspond in their meanings to the prepositions ለ- lä- and በ- bä- that you have already met. So, the -ll- set can be translated into English with 'to' or 'for'; the -bb- set with 'at', 'in', or 'with' in the sense of an instrument 'he hit him with it': መታበት mättabbät. In practice, you will find many other ways in which these suffixes are rendered in English, but for the present you should think of them as having the same meanings as the corresponding prepositions.

You should be careful to note, however, that the use of the Amharic prepositional pronoun suffixes and English pronoun phrases like 'for him', 'to me' and so on do not always correspond one to one. For example, the verb ጠበቀ t'äbbäk'ä is itself translatable by English 'wait for', so 'him' in 'I waited for him' is expressed as a direct object: ጠበቁሁት t'äbbäk'hut.

A verb cannot have both an object pronoun and a prepositional pronoun suffix added to it, only the one or the other. This is why a verb like መታበት mättabbät in the preceding paragraph can be translated as 'he hit him with it' though it literally means 'he hit with it'; the object pronoun is 'understood'. Similarly, አምጣልኝ amt'alliñ may render English 'bring it to me' or 'fetch it for me'; or አደረጉላት adärrägullat 'they did it for her', and so on.

A special and quite common use of the prepositional pronoun suffixes is to denote whether an event is to someone's favour or otherwise. Contrast, for example, ነገረልኝ näggärä*lliñ* 'he spoke *for me*' and ነገረብኝ näggärä*bbiñ* 'he spoke *against me*'. A special use of the **-bb-** suffixes is with the verb ጠፋ t'äffa [2lit[1] A] 'disappear, get lost' to form the idiom ጠፋብኝ t'äffabbiñ 'I've lost it', *lit.* 'it has disappeared against me', and so on.

The endings that mark the various persons are practically identical to the object pronoun suffixes, but take note of the third person masculine form which ends in -**ät** (-**llät**, -**bbät**).

	[*-ll-* + *pronoun*]		[*-bb-* + *pronoun*]	
me	ነገረልኝ	näggärälliñ	ነገረብኝ	näggäräbbiñ
you	ነገረልህ	näggärällih	ነገረብህ	näggäräbbih
you	ነገረልሽ	näggärälliš	ነገረብሽ	näggäräbbiš
him	ነገረለት	näggärällät	ነገረበት	näggäräbbät
her	ነገረላት	näggärällat	ነገረባት	näggäräbbat
us	ነገረልን	näggärällin	ነገረብን	näggäräbbin
you	ነገረላችሁ	näggärällaččuh	ነገረባችሁ	näggäräbbaččuh
them	ነገረላቸው	näggärällaččäw	ነገረባቸው	näggäräbbaččäw
you	ነገረልዎ	näggärälliwo	ነገረብዎ	näggäräbbiwo
him/her	ነገረላቸው	näggärällaččäw	ነገረባቸው	näggäräbbaččäw

Exercises

6(a) In the Amharic versions of the following English sentences say whether you would use a -bb- or an -ll- prepositional pronoun suffix

1 I lost all my money.
2 He hit the boy with it.
3 My father mended it for me.
4 What bad luck we've had!
5 The judge condemned the prisoner.
6 Peter's sitting on it.
7 I'll tell you about them tomorrow.
8 Where did you lose it?

6(b) Using the following new vocabulary, now translate the sentences in exercise six into Amharic

አሳደሰ	asaddäsä	repair, mend [derived stem]
ክፉ ዕድል	kïfu ïdïl	bad luck
ደረሰ	därräsä	*in the sense of* happen
ፈረደ	färrädä	judge (*used for both* condemn *and* acquit *according to which prepositional pronoun suffix is used*) [3-lit A]
አስረኛ	ïsränña	prisoner

7 Replace the underlined phrases in the following sentences with the appropriate prepositional pronoun suffix

1 በዚህ ደብዳቤ ብዙ ስተት ይገኛል ፡፡
2 ደብዳቤውን ላንተ እመረምራለሁ ፡፡
3 ለኔ አልግዝ ሁለት ኪሎ ብርቱካን ገዛች ፡፡
4 በቤቱ ውስጥ ምን ያደርጋሉ? በቤቱ ውስጥ ዝም ብለው ይቀመጣሉ ፡፡
5 የኔ ብዕር ዬት ነው? ሐዲስ በብዕርህ ይጽፋል ፡፡
6 ነገ ከሰዓት በኋላ ላባትና እናታችን እንደውላለን ፡፡

Reading passage

ይህ የኛ መንደር ነው ፡፡ አጠገባችን እንድ ሰፊ ሽለቆ ይገኛል ፡፡ እመንደራችን አሥር ቤቶች አሉ ፡፡ እመንደሩም መሀል ሜዳ አለ ፡፡ ወንዶች ልጆች እሜዳው ላይ የእግር ኳስ

ለመጫወት ይወጻሉ። ልጃገረዶች ግን በየጓቱ ውሀ ከምንጭ
ለናቶቻቸው ያመጡላቸዋል። ምንጩ ከመንደሩ ሩቅ አይደለም ፡
ስለዚህም አያስቸግራቸውም። ከጥዋቱ ሁለት ሰዓት ተኩል
ጀምሮ በየቀኑ የመንደሩ ልጆች ሁሉ ወደ ትምሕርት ቤት
ይሔዱና ይማራሉ። ትምሕርት ቤቱ በቅርብ ነው። ልጆቹም
አስተማሪያቸውን በጣም ይወጻሉ፣ ደግ ሰው ናቸው ይላሉ።
እመንደራችን ትልቅ ሱቅ አለ። ከሱቁ ቡና ፡ ጨው ፡ ስኳር
እንገዛለን። ከዚህም በላይ ፖሊስ ጣቢያና ትንሽ የጤና ጣቢያ
አለን። የኤሌክትሪክ መብራት ግን ለጊዜው የለንም። ከጥቂት
ዓምነት በኋላ ግን መብራት ያስገቡልናል ብለን ተስፋ
እናደርጋለን።

Supplementary vocabulary

መንደር	mändär	village
ምንጭ	minč'	spring, fountain, source
የእግር ኳስ	yäigïr kwas, yägïr kwas	football
አስቸገረ	asčäggärä	cause (*someone*) trouble [derived stem]
አስገባ	asgäbba	bring in, introduce [derived stem]

Note that ይሔዱና ይማራሉ is said instead of ይሔዳሉና ይማራሉ።

8 ቱሪዝም በኢትዮጵያ
turizm
bäityop'p'ïya
Tourism in Ethiopia

By the end of this lesson you should be able to:

- form simple relative clauses ('the man *who came*', 'the book *that I read*')
- use expressions of obligation ('must', 'have to', 'got to', *etc.*)
- display a basic knowledge of the geography of Ethiopia

Tourism in Ethiopia 📼

Peter, who's just returned from a trip to Harar, is discussing tourism in Ethiopia with Hirut and her father, Mr Mulugeta

ፒተር ፦ አቶ ሙሉጌታ እርስዎ እንደነገርኩዎት ትናንትና ሐረር ለጉብኝት ሔጄ ተመለስኩ፡፡ ያስገረመኝ ነገር እንዳንድ ፈረንጆች አገኘሁ - እነዚ ከስንግሊዝ አገር፤ ከጀርማን አገርና ከአሜሪካ የመጡ ቱብኞች የሚሆኑ ናቸው፡፡ ፈረንጆች በብዛት ወደ ኢትዮጵያ ይመጣሉ ማለት ነው?

አ/ሙሉጌታ ፦ አዎ፤ በያመቱ ከውጭ አገር የሚመጡ እንግዶች በብዙ ሺ የሚቆጠሩ ናቸው፡፡ ለሥራ፤ ለጉብኝት ወይም ለስብሰባ ነው የሚመጡ፡፡ በተለይም ባሁኑ ጊዜ ኢትዮጵያን የሚጎበኙ የውጭ አገር ዘጌዎች ብዛት አያደገ ሔጻል፡፡

ሒሩት ፦ ኢትዮጵያ ለቱሪዝም በጣም የምታመች አገር ናት፡፡ ከተፈጥሮ ሀብቷዋ ሌላ በታሪክዋና በሕዝቦችዋ ባህል በጣም ተደናቂ አገር ናት፡፡

ፒተር ፦ እውነቱን ነው፡፡ ያገኘሁዋቸው ፈረንጆች አብዛኞቻቸው እንዳንቺው አሉኝ፡፡

አ/ሙሉጌታ ፦ አዎ፤ ልክ ነው፡፡ መጀመሪያ ነገር እንደ አክሱም፤ እንደ ላሊበላና እንደ ጉንደር የሆኑ በታሪክ

<table>
<tr><td></td><td>ምክንያት የታወቁ ሥፍራዎች አሉ። ከዚያም ሌላ
በስተደቡብ በኩል ትልልቅ ሐይቆችና በስምጥ ሸለቆ
አካባቢም ለአደን፥ ለዓሣ ማጥመድና ለሸርሸር
የሚያመቹ ብዙ ሥፍራዎች አሉ።</td></tr>
<tr><td>ሂሩት :</td><td>አገግ፣ ስለ አደን መናገር አይጠቅምም! በዛሪ ጊዜ
ሰው የዱር አራዊትን ፈቶግራፍ ያነሣል እንጂ
አያድንም።</td></tr>
<tr><td>አ/ሙሉጌታ:</td><td>የሆነው ሆኖ፣ ለአደንም ይሁን ፈቶግራፍ ለማንሣት
ኢትዮጵያ በአገር ቤተዋ ውብነትና በአየርዋ ንብረት
ምክንያት የበዙ ቱሪስቶች መማረክ ትችላለች።</td></tr>
<tr><td>ፒተር :</td><td>እውነት ነው። ብቻ እንደሚመስለኝ ለመዘዋወር
አስቸጋሪ ይመስላል። ለምሳሌ ሐረር በሄድን ጊዜ
መንገድ ላይ አውቶቡሳችን ተበላሸ፣ እስኪጠገንት
ድረስ ሁለት ሰዓት ነው መጠበቅ የነበረብን!</td></tr>
<tr><td>አ/ሙሉጌታ:</td><td>አይ እሱማ ኢትዮጵያ እንዳውርፓ አይደለችም ፣
ይህን መቀበል አለብህ።</td></tr>
<tr><td>ፒተር :</td><td>እሱስ ልክ ነው ፣ ይገባኛል!</td></tr>
</table>

Note

From here on, the translations of the dialogues adopt a less literal, more colloquial English style. Compare the translation with the Amharic and see if you can identify where the idiomatic expressions differ. You may need to study the notes first.

PETER: *As you know, Mr Mulugeta, yesterday I returned from a visit to Harar. What surprised me, was I came across several foreigners – they were visitors like me coming from England, or Germany and America. Does this mean very many foreigners come to Ethiopia?*

MR MULUGETA: *Yes, each year visitors coming from abroad can be numbered in the thousands. They come for work, and visits or conferences, too. Nowadays, the number of foreign nationals who visit Ethiopia has especially gone on increasing.*

HIRUT: *Ethiopia is a very suitable country for tourism. As well as its natural resources, it's an impressive country because of its history and folk customs.*

PETER: *You're right. Most of the foreigners I came across told me just that.*

MR MULUGETA: *Yes, that's correct. In the first place, there are places like Axum, Lalibala and Gondar which are famous because of their history. In addition,*

HIRUT:|towards the south of the country in the area of the big lakes and the Rift Valley there are many places suitable for hunting, fishing and picnics.

HIRUT: *Daddy, it's no use talking about hunting! People take photos of animals these days, they don't hunt them.*

MR MULUGETA: *All the same, whether it's hunting or photography, because of the beauty of its countryside and the quality of its climate Ethiopia attracts lots of tourists.*

PETER: *That's true. But it seems to be difficult to get around, I think. For instance, when we were going to Harar on the way our bus broke down. We had to wait two hours before it was repaired.*

MR MULUGETA: *No but then, Ethiopia is not like Europe; you've got to accept that.*

PETER: *That's correct; I understand!*

Vocabulary

ጉብኝት	gubïññït	visit, trip (*cf. the verb* ጉብኝ gwäbäññä visit *in the verb section of this vocabulary*)
ጉብኝ	gwäbïñ	visitor
ቱሪስት	turist	tourist
ቱሪዝም	turizm	tourism
ብዛት	bïzat	large number, quantity (*cf.* ብዙ many)
በብዛት	bäbïzat	in large numbers
እንግዳ	ingïda	visitor, guest, stranger
ዜጌ	zäge	citizen, subject
ስብሰባ	sïbsäba	meeting, gathering, conference
ተፈጥሮ	täfät'ro	nature
ሀብት	habt	wealth, riches
የተፈጥሮ ሀብት	yätäfät'ro habt	natural resources
ሕዝብ	hïzb	people, nation
ባህል	bahïl	custom
አብዛኛ	abzañña	majority
አብዛኞቻቸው	abzaññoččaččäw	most of them
ምክንያት	mïkïnyat	reason, cause
በ- . . . ምክንያት	bä- . . . mïkïnyat	by reason of, because of

ሐይቅ	hayk'	lake
ሸለቆ	šäläk'o	valley
ስምጥ ሸለቆ	sïmt' šäläk'o	the Rift Valley
አባባ	abbabba	daddy, papa
አደን	adän	hunting
ዓሣ	asa	fish
አራዊት	arawit	(wild) animals, beasts
አገር ቤት	agär bet	countryside
ዱር	dur	forest
ፎቶግራፍ	fotograf	photograph
ፎቶግራፍ አነሣ	fotograf anässa	take a photo
ውብነት	wïbbïnnät	beauty (cf. ውብ wibb beautiful)
አየር	ayyär	climate (also means air as in የኢትዮጵያ አየር መንገድ Ethiopian Airlines)
ንብረት	nïbrät	belongings, possessions
የአየር ንብረት	yäayyär nïbrät	climatic features, climate

Adverbs, particles

በያመቱ	bäyyamätu	every year (cf. ዓመት year; see note 5)
በተለይ	bätäläyy	especially, in particular
ባሁኑ ጊዜ	bahunu gize	at the present time, nowadays (cf. አሁን now and ጊዜ time)
ከ- ... ሌላ	kä- ... lela	other than, aside from
እንዲሁም	ïndihum	likewise, similarly
ማለትም	malätïmm	that is, that's to say (lit. 'and to say')
የሆነው ይሁን	yähonäw yïhun	nonetheless, all the same (lit. 'be it what it is')
ብቻ	bïčča	only, but (at the beginning of a sentence)

Verbs

ተመለሰ	tämälläsä	return, come back, go back [derived stem] (cf. መለሰ [3-lit B] return, give back)
አስገረመ	asgärrämä	surprise, amaze [derived stem] (cf. ገረመ [3-lit A] be wonderful, surprising)
አገኘ	agäññä	find, come across [derived stem]

ተቆጠረ	täk'wät't'ärä	be counted [derived stem] (compound imperfect ይቆጠራል yïk'k'wät't'äral; *cf.* ቆጠረ [3-lit A] count)
ጐበኘ	gwäbäññä	visit (*see note 2*)
አደገ	addägä	grow, increase [3-lit A]
እያደገ ይሄዳል	ïyyaddägä yïhedal	it is increasing, it goes on increasing (*lit.* 'it goes while it increases')
አመቸ	amäčča	be suitable, comfortable [derived stem] (*another derived stem of this verb has the same meaning:* ተመቸ tämäčča be suitable, convenient)
ተደነቀ	tädännäk'ä	be admired, impressive; (*also means* be impressed, astonished [derived stem]; compound imperfect ይደነቃል yïddännäk'al. Agent noun ተደናቂ tädänak'i impressive)
ታወቀ	tawwäk'ä	be known, be famous [derived stem] (*cf.* አወቀ know)
አጠመደ	at'ämmädä	trap, catch (fish) [derived stem]
ሆነ	honä	be, become [2-lit⁵] (*see note 4*)
ማረከ	marräkä	capture, captivate, attract [3-lit C] (*see note 3*)
ተቻለ	täčalä	be possible [derived stem] (compound imperfect ይቻላል yïččalal; *and so* ይቻላታል yïččalatal *is literally* 'it is possible for her'; *cf.* ቻለ be able)
ተበላሸ	täbälaššä	be spoiled, go wrong, break down [derived stem]
ጠገነ	t'äggänä	mend, repair, fix [3-lit B]
ገባኝ	gäbbañ	I have understood (*lit.* 'it has entered me')

Phrases

ሄጄ ተመለስኩ	hejje tämälläskw	I went and came back (*see note 1*)
እንዳንቺው	ïndančiw	the same as you (*lit.* 'like yours')
እንደነገርኩዎት	ïndänäggärkuwot	as I told you (*lit.* 'like what I told you')
እያደገ ሄዷል	ïyyaddägä hedwal	it has gone on increasing (*lit.* 'it has gone while growing')

እንደሚመስለኝ   ïndämmimäsläñ   in my opinion, as I think (*lit.* 'like what it seems to me')

እሱማ   ïssumma   for all that, but then (*lit.* 'but that'; -ማ -mma is a more emphatic form of -ም -mm.)

Notes on the dialogue

1 To express 'I went and came back' it is better Amharic to say ሔጄ ተመለስኩ hejje tämälläskw rather than the literal ሔድኩና ተመለስኩ hedkunna tämälläskw. The form ሔጄ is another gerundive like those we met in the last lesson. We shall look at gerundives in greater detail in a later lesson.

2 The verb ጐበኘ gwäbäññä 'to visit' belongs to a type you have not yet met; you can tell this from the fact that though it has three root consonants, gw–b–ñ, the gemination does not fall on the middle one as in 'genuine' triliteral verbs, such as you met in lesson three, but on the third and final consonant. Can you find another verb of this type in the dialogue? (ተበላሸ täbälaššä 'to break down' is of the same class though it is a derived stem – its three root consonants are b–l–š.) This class of verb may be called 3-lit Y. There are not very many verbs of this type, but here are a few that you may find useful:

ሰለቸ   säläččä   be boring   ገበየ   gäbäyyä   go to market, go shopping

ዘገየ   zägäyyä   be late, delayed

and like ተበላሸ:

ተበሳጨ   täbäsač'č'ä   be annoyed, in a bad mood

ተዘጋጀ   täzägajjä   be prepared, ready (*cf.* አዘጋጀ azzägajjä prepare, make ready)

Their compound imperfect is formed following the patterns (i) ይሰለቻል yïsäläččal and (ii) ይበላሻል yïbbälaššal, and the infinitives follow the patterns (i) መሰልቸት mäsälčät and (ii) መበላሸት mäbbälašät, adding an extra -t just like the 2-lit[1] and 2-lit[2] classes. Similarly, ያዘጋጃል yazzägajjal 'he prepares' and ማዘጋጀት mazzägajät 'to prepare'.

A related class of verbs, which we can call 3-lit X, end in -a rather than -ä,

ዘነጋ	zänägga	forget	*ፈነዳ*	fänädda burst, split
ዘረጋ	zärägga	spread something out, unroll	*በረታ*	bärätta be strong, try hard

The compound imperfect and infinitive of this class follow the patterns *ይዘናጋል* yïzänäggal and *መዘንጋት* mäzängat.

3 Yet another verb type is represented by the word *ማረከ* marräkä 'attract' in the dialogue. This also has three consonants, m-r-k, but this time has gemination on the middle one just like 'genuine' triliterals. It differs from these, however, in that the first consonant is followed by the vowel **a**, i.e. it is in the fourth order.

Here are a few verbs of this class to add to your vocabulary:

ጣፈጠ	t'affät'ä	taste sweet, taste good
ጋበዘ	gabbäzä	invite someone to a meal, treat, entertain someone
ማለደ	mallädä	be (too) early
ባረከ	barräkä	bless

In the simple stem the compound imperfect and the infinitive follow the patterns *ይጣፍጣል* yït'affit'al and *መጣፈጥ* mät'afät', respectively. This class of verb is called the C type, parallel to the A and B types you have already learned; so, *ማረከ* is a 3-lit C-type verb.

4 The verb *ሆነ* honä has a wider range of meanings than the simple translation 'become' suggests. Firstly, it 'supplies' many parts of the verb 'to be', such as the infinitive *መሆን* mähon 'to be' and the imperative or command form *ሁን* hun 'be!'. It is also used in a large number of idiomatic phrases such as, *የሆነው ይሁን* yähonäw yïhun and *ይሁን እንጂ* yïhun ïnji, that you have already met. The compound imperfect tense *ይሆናል* yïhonal also has the meaning 'it may be, it will be'. Second, *ሆነ* also sometimes has the implied sense of 'be right or proper' particularly in the negative imperfect *አይሆንም* ayhonïm 'it won't do, it isn't right'.

5 The expression *በያመቱ* bäyyamätu 'every year' is formed in the same way as *በየቀኑ* bäyyäk'änu 'every day' which occurred in lesson five. Both words are made up of the following parts:

preposition *በ-* bä- + prefix *አየ-* ïyyä- + noun (*ዓመት* 'year', *ቀን* 'day') + article -u

The prefix *አየ-* ïyyä- is added to nouns and corresponds to

English 'each' or 'every' and usually requires the article -**u** or an appropriate possessive pronoun suffix added at the end. Here are some other useful expressions which include አየ- ïyyä-:

አያንዳንዱ	ïyyandandu	each one
በየጊዜው	bäyyägizew	on each occasion, regularly
በየጥዋቱ	bäyyät'watu	each morning
በየሳምንቱ	bäyyäsammïntu	each week, weekly
በየወሩ	bäyyäwäru	each month, monthly
በያይነቱ	bäyyaynätu	of all sorts, of every kind

Look at the following examples to see how አየ- ïyyä- may be used in a sentence. It often has no direct equivalent in English.

እየሥራችን እንሔዳ ለን	ïyyäsïraččïn ïnnïhedallän
	we're (each) going to our work
ሁሉም እየገንዘቡን ወሰደ	hullum ïyyägänzäbun wässädä
	everyone (each) took their money
ወደየቤታቸው ተመለሱ	wädäyyäbetaččäw tämälläsu
	they (each) went back home
እየወምበራችሁ ተቀመጡ	ïyyäwämbäraččuh täk'ämät'u
	(each) sit down on your chairs!

Grammar

Relative verbs

There are a large number of verb forms in this dialogue which begin in የ- or የም- or የሚ- such as: የሁ ኑ, የሚመጡ and የምታመች. See if you can find the rest – there's one which begins in ያ- where የ- is added to a verb with initial a-. Have a look back across other dialogues you've read so far and you should find others, too. For example, from lesson four መቼ ነው ያየኸው 'when did you see him?', ተናንትና ነው ያየሁዋቸው 'I saw him yesterday', አዲስ የመጣ ነው 'it came recently', ከጂማ የደረሰ ነው 'it arrived from Jimma', and from lesson five ማን ነህ የምትናገር 'who is speaking?'

These are all relative verb forms, though in the translation they do not always correspond to English relative clauses which often begin with 'who', 'what', 'which', 'that', and so on. Amharic makes great use of relative verbs and in order to adopt a truly colloquial style you will need to know how to form and use them.

There are only two tenses of relative verbs: the relative past and the relative imperfect. As their names suggest, they are built on the simple past and the imperfect tenses that you have already learned. The relative past is simply formed by prefixing f- yä- to the simple past tense. So, in the example above, የመጣ yämät't'a 'that came' is formed from መጣ mät't'a 'it came'; and ያየሃቸው yayyähaččäw 'that you saw him' is from አየሃቸው ayyähaččäw 'you saw him', and so on. Remember that if the verb begins in a- like አየሃቸው the ä vowel of the prefix is dropped before the a. The same applies to the negative past, which of course always begins in a because of the negative prefix አል- al-. What you must watch here, however, is that the suffix -ም -m of the negative tenses is always dropped in the relative verb, and in other subordinate verb forms as well. So, from አልመጣም almät't'am 'it didn't come' the corresponding relative is ያልመጣ yalmät't'a 'which didn't come' without the final -ም -m. Here then are the relative forms of the verb መጣ 'come':

Relative past

person	*affirmative*		*negative*	
	'I who came, which I came'		'I who did not come . . .', etc.	
1st sing.	የመጣሁ	yämät't'ahw	ያልመጣሁ	yalmät't'ahw
2nd masc.	የመጣህ	yämät't'ah	ያልመጣህ	yalmät't'ah
2nd fem.	የመጣሽ	yämät't'aš	ያልመጣሽ	yalmät't'aš
3rd masc.	የመጣ	yämät't'a	ያልመጣ	yalmät't'a
3rd fem.	የመጣች	yämät't'ačč	ያልመጣች	yalmät't'ačč
1st pl.	የመጣን	yämät't'an	ያልመጣን	yalmät't'an
2nd pl.	የመጣችሁ	yämät't'aččuh	ያልመጣችሁ	yalmät't'aččuh
3rd pl.	የመጡ	yämät't'u	ያልመጡ	yalmät't'u

The relative imperfect is a little more complicated. In the first place, it is not built on the compound imperfect tense but on the simple imperfect. The simple imperfect is the tense that forms the basis of the compound imperfect – the 'verb base' in the grammar in lesson seven – and on which the negative imperfect is built.

Second, the relative prefix added to make the relative imperfect is የም- yämmi- which combines with the person markers in the following way:

የም- yämmi- + አ- i-	→	የም- yämmi-	[1st pers. sing.]
ት- ti-	→	የምት-yämmitti-	[2nd pers. sing./pl.; 3rd pers. fem.]
ይ- yi-	→	የሚ. yämmi-	[3rd pers. masc./pl.]
እን- inni-	→	የምን-yämminni-	[1st pers. pl.]

Points to note

1 In the second persons singular and plural, and in the third person feminine, the **t** of the person marker is usually geminated, but it may also be pronounced as a single consonant: የምትሰማ yämmïttïsäma or yämmïtsäma 'you who hear ..., which you hear ...', *etc.*

2 In the third person masculine the relative prefix የም- yämmï- and the person marker ይ- yï- combine to form የሚ- yämmï-.

The relative prefix የም- yämmï- combines with the negative imperfect in the way that you would expect, but remember that as with the relative past the final -ም -m is dropped: አይመጣም aymät'am 'he doesn't come, isn't coming'; የማይመጣ yämmaymät'a 'he who doesn't come, which doesn't come ...' *etc.*

Relative imperfect

	affirmative		*negative*
	'I who come, am coming ...' etc.		'I who do not come, am not coming ...' etc.
የምመጣ	yämmïmät'a	የማልመጣ	yämmalmät'a
የምትመጣ	yämmïttïmät'a	የማትመጣ	yämmattïmät'a
የምትመጪ	yämmïttïmäč'i	የማትመጪ	yämmattïmäč'i
የሚመጣ	yämmïmät'a	የማይመጣ	yämmaymät'a
የምትመጣ	yämmïttïmät'a	የማትመጣ	yämmattïmät'a
የምንመጣ	yämmïnnïmät'a	የማንመጣ	yämmannïmät'a
የምትመጡ	yämmïttïmät'u	የማትመጡ	yämmattïmät'u
የሚመጡ	yämmïmät'u	የማይመጡ	yämmaymät'u

Note
In most persons the affirmative and the negative are distinguished only by the presence of the vowel **a** in the latter following the **mm** of the relative prefix: የምንሰማ yämmïnnïsäma 'which we hear' and የማንሰማ yämmannïsäma 'which we don't hear'. The exceptions are the first person singular, and the third persons masculine and plural.

Uses of the relative verb: simple relative clauses

The most obvious use of the Amharic relative tenses is in relative clauses, corresponding to English relative clauses which often begin with 'who, what, which' and other 'wh- words', or with 'that', all describing or qualifying a noun: 'the man who came'; 'the book that I bought'; 'the house where I live' and so on.

There are, however, some fundamental differences between Amharic and English relative clauses. The principal differences are set as below:

1 Amharic relative clauses precede the noun that they describe:

የመጣው ሰውዬ	yämät't'aw säwïyye	the man who came
የመታቸው ልጅ	yämättaččïw lïjj	the boy whom she hit
የገዛሁት መጽሐፍ	yägäzzahut mäs'haf	the book that I bought
የሰጠሁዋት ሴትዮ	yäsät't'ähuwat setïyyo	the woman to whom I gave it
ያደረጉላት ሰውዬ	yadärrägullät säwïyye	the person for whom they did it
የምኖርበት ቤት	yämminorïbbät bet	the house where I live
የመረጡበት ምክንያት	yämärrät'ubbät mïkinyat	the reason why they chose him

2 In English the relative pronoun tells you what the grammatical relationship is between itself and the noun that is being described by the relative clause. That is, whether it is the subject – 'the man who came'; the direct object – 'the boy whom she hit'; the indirect object or beneficiary – 'the woman to whom I gave it'; or in any other adverbial relationship – 'the house in which/where I live'.

In Amharic, on the other hand, the relative prefixes የ- and የም- remain 'fixed' and cannot show this kind of relationship. Instead, an appropriate pronoun 'link' is added to the relative verb in the shape of an object pronoun suffix or a prepositional pronoun suffix:

የመታቸው ልጅ	yämättaččïwlïjj	*lit.* 'the boy which she hit *him*'
የገዛሁት መጽሐፍ	yägäzzahut mäs'haf	*lit.* 'the book which I bought *it*'
የሰጣሁዋት ሴትዮ	yäsät't'ahu wat setïyyo	*lit.* 'the woman which I gave (it) *her*'
ያደረጉላት ሰውዬ	yadärrägullät säwïyye	*lit.* 'the man which they did (it) *for him*'
የምኖርበት ቤት	yämmïnorïbbät bet	*lit.* 'the house which I live *in it*'
የመረጡበት ምክንያት	yämärrät'ubbät mïkïnyat	*lit.* the reason which they chose (him) *by it*'

If the relationship between the relative clause and the described noun is a possessive one, such as is expressed in English by 'whose' – 'the boy *whose* book they stole' – then the pronoun 'link' in Amharic takes the form of the appropriate possessive pronoun suffix added to the possessed noun inside the relative clause. In other words, the Amharic construction says literally 'the boy which they stole it *his* book': መጽሐፉን የሠረቁት ልጅ mäs'hafun yäsär-räk'ut lïjj – in this example the -ት -t 'it' is added to the relative verb because 'his book' is the direct object of 'which they stole'.

When the connection between the noun described and the relative clause is simply that of subject, and the noun is definite, as in the example 'the man who came', then as long as no other pronoun suffix is added to the relative verb a definite article suffix is added. The shape of this definite article suffix, however, is rather different from that added to nouns.

The form of the definite article added to relative verbs resembles the third person masculine object pronoun suffix which you met in lesson seven. As with the object suffix, the shape of the article depends on what the verb ends in: -t after the vowel u; -äw after a consonant, but -ïw after the endings -š and -čč; -w elsewhere (i.e. the vowels ä, a and ï). You will notice that there is no special feminine form of the article added to relative verbs. Consider the following examples:

የመጣው ሰው	yämät't'aw säw	the man who came
የመጣችው ሴት	yämät't'aččïw set	the woman who came
የመጡት ሰዎች	yämät't'ut säwoč	the persons who came

Remember that if there is already a pronoun suffix added to the verb you do not add the article, as well. So:

ገንዘቡን የሰጠኝ ሰው   gänzäbun yäsät't'äñ säw
                        the man who gave me the money
ቤቴን የምትጠርግልኝ ገረድ   beten yämmïttït'ärgïllïñ gäräd
                        the maid who sweeps my house for me

A relative verb can also be used on its own without a following noun in the sense of English 'the person who . . ., he who . . ., I who . . .', and so on. In this case it is usual to add the definite article suffix to the verb:

እንደዚህ የሚነግረው ወዳጄ አይደለም   indäzzih   yämminägräw
                            wädaje aydälläm
                            he who speaks like this is not my friend
መኪና የሚሠርቁት ይታሰራሉ   mäkina   yämmisärk'ut
                            yïttassärallu
                            people who steal cars will be arrested

Relative clauses in Amharic are treated rather like adjectives. This is why the definite article in a phrase like የመጣው ሰውዬ yämät't'aw säwïyye 'the man who came' appears on the relative verb and not on the noun, just as in the phrase ትልቁ ሰውዬ tïllik'u säwïyye 'the big (*i.e.* important) man'.

For the same reason, if the noun that is being described by a relative clause is a direct object in the overall sentence, then the object marker -ን -n is added not to the noun, but to the relative verb. Compare the following pairs of sentences:

ከበደ ቀይዋን መኪና ሸጠ ፡፡   Käbbädä k'äyyiwan mäkina šet'ä
                        Kebbede sold the red car
ከበደ ትናንትና የገዛትን መኪና ሸጠ ፡፡
                        Käbbädä tïnantïnna yägäzzatïn mäkina šet'ä
                        Kebbede sold the car that he bought yesterday
አሮጌውን ቤት ገዛሁ   arogewn bet gäzzahw
                        I bought the old house
የተወለድኩበትን ቤት ገዛሁ   yätäwällädkubbätïn bet gäzzahw
                        I bought the house in which I was born

The relative verb and ነው

The majority of the occurrences of relative verbs that you have encountered in the dialogues so far are not, however, in simple relative clauses. If you look back at them you will see that they are mostly combined with the verb ነው· 'is'. Here are some examples from earlier lessons together with their translations:

ማን ነው· የሚናገር	who is speaking?
መቼ ነው· ያየኸዉ·	when did you see him?
ትናንትና ነው· ያየሁዋቸዉ·	I saw him yesterday
የተገናኘን ባይሮፕላን ነዉ·	we met on the plane
ስለዚህ ነዉ· ወደ ኢትዮጵያ የመጣሁት	this is why I came to Ethiopia

All the examples contain a short phrase ending in ነው· which is either preceded or followed by a relative clause which contains the main verbal idea of the sentence. In addition, the word or phrase preceding ነው· is in some sense highlighted or emphasized; it is what the speaker wishes to stress. Consider the following:

ማን ነው· የሚናገር	*lit.* 'who is it that is speaking?'
መቼ ነው· ያየኸዉ·	*lit.* 'when is it that you saw him?'
ትናንትና ነው· ያየሁዋቸዉ·	*lit.* 'it is yesterday that I saw him'
የተገናኘን ባይሮፕላን ነዉ·	*lit.* 'it is on the plane that we met'
ስለዚህ ነዉ· ወደ ኢትዮጵያ የመጣሁት	*lit.* 'it is because of this that I came to Ethiopia'

This is why this sentence pattern is especially prevalent with question words, like ማን 'who?'; መቼ 'when?'; የት 'where?', and so on, because question words are naturally stressed or highlighted. To ask 'who is speaking?' it's not incorrect Amharic to say literally ማን ይናገራል?, but it is more natural to say ማን ነው· የሚናገር?

Here are some more examples with other kinds of question words:

የትኛዉን ዓይነት ነው· የምትፈልገዉ·?
        yätiññawn aynät näw **yämmittïfälligäw**?
        lit. 'what kind is it that you want?'
ምንድን ነው· የሚያስፈልገን?
        mindin näw **yämmiyasfälligän**?
        lit. 'what is it that is necessary to us = that we need?'
ከዬት ነው· የደረስኸዉ·?
        käyet näw **yädärräshäw**?
        lit. 'from where is it that you arrived?'
እንዴት ነው· የሚያደርገዉ·?
        indet näw **yämmiyadärgäw**?
        lit. 'how is it that he does it?'

To see how the relative + ነው sentence pattern is used to emphasize one part of a statement compare the following pairs of statements:

ከበደ ጥያቄ ይጠይቃል	Käbbädä t'ïyyak'e yït'äyyïk'al
	Kebbede's asking a question
ጥያቄ የሚጠይቀው ከበደ ነው	t'ïyyak'e yämmit'äyyïk'äw *Käbbädä näw*
	it's Kebbede who's asking a question; Kebede's asking a question (i.e. and not someone else)
ብርጭቆ ሰበርኩ	bïrč'ïk'k'o säbbärkw
	I broke a glass
ብርጭቆ ነው የሰበርኩ	*bïrč'ïk'k'o näw* yäsäbbärkw
	it was a glass that I broke, I broke a glass (i.e. and not something else)

You will notice that you have a choice as to the sequence of the parts of the sentence:

stressed phrase + ነው	+	relative clause
ማን ነው		የሚናገር

relative clause	+	stressed phrase + ነው
የተገኘኘን		ባይርጥላን ነው

When the highlighted word is a feminine or a plural noun then ናት/ነች and ናቸው are used instead of ነው. Similarly, if the highlighted word is a first or second person pronoun then the appropriate person of the copula ነው is used:

ጥያቄ የምትጠይቀው ዘነበች ናት	t'ïyyak'e yämmïttit'äyyïk'äw *Zännäbäčč nat*
	it's Zennebech who's asking questions
ገንዘቡን ያገኘሁት እኔ ነኝ	gänzäbun yagäññähut *ine näñ*
	it was me who found the money
ቦርሳዬን የሠረቅኸው አንተ ነህ	borsayen yäsärräk'häw *antä näh*
	it was you who stole my briefcase

Exercises

1 Convert the relative past verbs in the following phrases into the relative imperfect, and then translate the whole phrase into English

1 የሰማነው ወሬ
2 የጠየቅሽን ጥያቄ
3 የጻፈችን ደብዳቤ
4 የደወልኩለት ጓደኛዬ
5 ጓዝ የወደደው ሰውዬ

6 መንገድ ላይ የቆመው መኪና
7 የገዙትን ዳቦ
8 የጀመራችሁት ሥራ
9 ያደረጉብኝን ጥሬ
10 የጠጡ ቡና

2 Rewrite the following sentences using the correct relative verb form of the verb in brackets

1 አልማዝ (ለበሰ) ልብስ ቀይ ነው ቡናማ?
2 ሠራተኞቹ ትናንትና (ጀመረ) ሥራ መቼ ይጨርሳሉ?
3 ሚስትህ (ገዛ) ቀሚስ ቀለሙ ምን ዓይነት ነው?
4 ከአሥመራ (ደረሰ) አድርፕላን መቼ ያርፋል?
5 እናንተ (ቀጠረ) ሰውዬ አሁን መጣ?
6 ከበደ ዕቃውን (ወሰደ) መኪና የማን ነው?
7 አሁን አንተ ከመንገዱ ወደ ግራ (አየ) ቤት ፖሊስ ጣቢያ ነው ።

3 Combine the following pairs of short sentences using a relative verb construction

> *Example:* ልጅ መጣ – ከበደ ነው → የመጣው ልጅ ከበደ ነው ።

1 ጋለፈው ዓመት የዩኒቨርሲቲ ገባች – አማረች ናት ።
2 ሲኒማ ቤት በየቀኑ እሔዳለሁ – እኔ ነኝ ።
3 አስተማሪ ለመሆን ይፈልጋል – አየለ ነው ።
4 ፎቶግራፍ አንሺ ለመሆን ይፈልጋሉ – ማምና ከበደ ናቸው ።
5 ሰውዬው ሞተ – የሙሉጌታ አባት ነው ።
6 ሻይ በወተት ጠጣን – እኛ ነን ።
7 ሙሉ ቀን እገበያ ዋለች – ወይዘሮ አበበች ናት ።

4 Rewrite the following simple sentences so as to highlight the underlined word or phrase

> *Example:* ጊፉት   ሪዲዮን   መስማት   ትፈልጋለች   →   ጊፉት
> የምትፈልገው ሪዲዮን መስማት ነው ፡፡

1 ያማርኛ ቋንቋ እንግሪሳለን ፡፡
2 ሁሉም መጽሐፍ ማንበብ ይወዳል ፡፡
3 ከበደ ለመኪናው ስንት ከፈለ?
4 ፒተር ለማን ይጽፋል?
5 ትናንትና ማን መጣ?
6 ስለዚህ ያቺ ሙሉጊታን አሳብ አልወድም ፡፡
7 በፉን መቼ ዘጋህ?
8 ይህን ወረ ስለምን አወራሽኝ?
9 ለኛ ተማርቼ ሥራቸውን ይጀምራሉ ፡፡
10 አልማዝ ቡና አፈላች ፡፡

Grammar

'Must', 'have to'

Mr Mulugeta tells Peter, ይህን   መረዳት   አለብህ yihïn märrädat alläbbïh 'you must realize this'. Also, do you remember the expression መሄድ አለብኝ mähed alläbbïñ 'I've got to go' from lesson one? Both expressions of obligation are made in the same way, using the infinitive followed by the verb አለ allä 'be' with the appropriate person of the prepositional pronoun suffix in -bb-. So, መሄድ አለብኝ mähed alläbbïñ is literally 'it is upon me to go'.

The negative is formed of course, by substituting የለም yälläm for አለ allä – but remember that the suffix -ም -m comes right at the end of the verb after any other suffix:

	'I must . . .; have to . . .'		'I mustn't . . .; don't have to . . .'	
1st pers. sing.	አለብኝ	alläbbïñ	የለብኝም	yälläbbïññïm
2nd pers. masc.	አለብህ	alläbbïh	የለብህም	yälläbbïhïm
2nd pers. fem.	አለብሽ	alläbbïš	የለብሽም	yälläbbïšïm
3rd pers. masc.	አለበት	alläbbät	የለበትም	yälläbbätïm
3rd pers. fem.	አለባት	alläbbat	የለባትም	yälläbbatïm

1st pers. pl.	አለብን	alläbbïn	የለብንም	yälläbbïnïm
2nd pers. pl.	አለባችሁ	alläbbaččuh	የለባችሁም	yälläbbaččïhum
3rd pers. pl.	አለባቸው	alläbbaččäw	የለባቸውም	yälläbbaččäwm
2nd pers. for.	አለብዎ	alläbbïwo	የለብዎም	yälläbbïwom
3rd pers. for.	አለባቸው	alläbbaččäw	የለባቸውም	yälläbbaččäwm

Expression of obligation in the past is formed by substituting ነበረ näbbärä for አለ allä, and አልነበረ-ም alnäbbärä-m for የለ-ም yällä-m:

ዮሐንስ መኪናውን መሸጥ ነበረበት
    Yohannïs mäkinawn mäšet' näbbäräbbät
    Yohannes had to sell his car
እኛም ለቲኬት መክፈል አልነበረብንም
    ïññam lätiket mäkfäl alnäbbäräbbïnïm
    we didn't have to pay for the tickets either

Another way of saying 'have to' or 'must' is to use the verb አስፈለገ asfällägä 'be necessary' with the infinitive. The person who 'has to do something' is indicated by the object suffix pronoun. A general obligation is expressed either by using the verb without an object pronoun, or by using the agent noun from አስፈለገ with the verb ነው: አስፈላጊ ነው asfällagi näw 'it is necessary, one must . . .'. Consider the following examples:

መሄድ ያስፈልገኛል	mähed yasfälligäññal
	I've got to go, I need to go
አዲስ መኪና መግዛት ያስፈልገዋል	addis mäkina mägzat
	yasfälligäwal
	he will have to buy a new car
አልማዝ ሥራ ማግኘት ያስፈልጋታል	Almaz sïra magñät yasfälligatal
	Almaz has to get a job
እንደዚህ ማድረግ ያስፈልጋል	ïndäzzih madräg yasfälligal, or
እንደዚህ ማድረግ አስፈላጊ ነው	ïndäzzih madräg asfällagi näw
	one has to do it like this

Impersonal verbs

You have already met a number of expressions like ያስፈልገኛል yasfälligäññal in the sense of 'I need', where the subject 'I' in English is indicated in Amharic by an object suffix pronoun added to a verb in the third person masculine. You can think of

ያስፈልገኛል as being literally 'it is necessary to me'. This kind of verb is called an impersonal verb. Here are some more, some of which you've already met, together with others that you will find useful to add to your vocabulary.

ራበኝ	rabäñ	I am hungry	[ራበ 2-lit³]
ጠማኝ	t'ämmañ	I am thirsty	[ጠማ 2-lit¹ A]
ደከመኝ	däkkämäñ	I am tired	[ደከመ 3-lit A]
አመመኝ	ammämäñ	I am ill	[አመመ 3-lit A]
መሰለኝ	mässäläñ	I thought	[መሰለ 3-lit A]
ገባኝ	gäbbañ	I understand	[ገባ 2-lit¹ A]
ገረመኝ	gärrämäñ	I am surprised	[ገረመ 3-lit A]
በቃኝ	bäk'k'añ	I have enough	[በቃ 2-lit¹ A]
ሰለቸኝ	säläčäñ	I am bored	[ሰለቸ – see note 2 to the dialogue in this lesson]
ተቻለኝ	täčaläñ	I am able	[ተቻለ derived stem: ይቻለኛል yïččaläññal]
ተሰማኝ	täsämmañ	I feel, sense	[ተሰማ derived stem: ይሰማኛል yïssämmaññal]
ተረዳኝ	täräddañ	I realize	[ተረዳ derived stem: ይረዳኛል yïrräddaññal]
ተገባኝ	tägäbbañ	I ought	[ተገባ derived stem: ይገባኛል yïggäbbaññal]
ደስ አለኝ	däss aläñ	I am happy	[ደስ አለ – አለ here is the verb say alä, not be allä; the word ደስ which precedes it remains unchanged: ደስ ይለኛል däss yïläññal]
ትዝ አለኝ	tïzz aläñ	I recall, remember	[ትዝ አለ is like ደስ አለ]

Notice that most of these expressions are translated as English present tenses though in Amharic they are expressed in the simple past tense. If you use the compound imperfect tense instead it gives a future meaning: ይበቃኛል yïbäk'aññal 'I'll have enough'; ይቻላታል yïččalatal 'she'll be able'; ይርበናል yïrïbänal 'we'll be hungry'; ደስ ይለዋል däss yïläwal 'he'll be pleased'; and so on.

Exercises

5 Match up the following part sentences so as to make a coherent and sensible whole

1 ሙሉ ቀን ምንም ያልበላው ሰው...   1 ደስ ይለዋል ፡፡
2 ብዙ ሥራ የሠራው ሰው...   2 ጥሩ ሥራ ይቾለዋለ ፡፡
3 መቶ ብር በድንገት የሚያገኘው ሰው... 3 እሁን ጠማው ፡፡
4 ማንበብ ያወቀ ሰው...   4 ራሱን አመመው ፡፡
5 ትናንትና ከሆስፒታል የገባው ልጅ...   5 አጥብቆ ደከመው ፡፡
6 ከጥዋት ጀምሮ ልጁ ስላልጠጣ...   6 በጣም ራበው ፡፡

6 Complete the following sentences using a relative clause of the form 'the person who' or 'the place where'

> *Example:* _____ ደራሲ ይባላል ፡፡ → መጽሐፍ የሚጸፈው ሰው ደራሲ ይባላል ፡፡
> The person who writes books is called an author

1 _____ አስተማሪ ይባላል ፡፡   7 _____ ቲኬት ቆራጭ ይባላል ፡፡

2 _____ መካኒክ ይባላል ፡፡   8 _____ አጋላፊ ይባላል ፡፡
3 _____ ሐኪም ይባላል ፡፡   9 _____ የታክሲ ሾፌር ይባላል ፡፡

4 _____ ሌባ ይባላል ፡፡   10 _____ ትምሕርት ቤት ይባላል ፡፡

5 _____ አዋቂ ይባላል ፡፡   11 _____ እስር ቤት ይባላል ፡፡
6 _____ ፍቶ አንሺ ይባላል ፡፡   12 _____ አይርፕላን ማረፊያ ይባላል ፡፡

7 Complete the following sentences in Amharic using (a) አለ + ብ-, and (b) አስፈለገ

1 ነገ ገበያ I have to go.
2 ከበደ ፡ ለቢርቱ you have to phone.
3 ተጨማሪ ቲኬት we had to buy.
4 ሕይወት ሃስት ሥዕል ለትርኪት had to choose.
5 ቲኬቱን ለቲኬት ቆራጭ they have to show.
6 አልማዝ አምስት መቶ ብር had to pay.
7 እናንተ ልጆች ካባቸሁን ላስተማሪው didn't you have to give?

After the fall of the Marxist government of Mengistu Haile Mariam and the coming to power of the EPRDF in May 1991, the internal political map of Ethiopia was completely redrawn. Eritrea gained her independence and the old provinces of Ethiopia, the precise boundaries of which were finally drawn around the end of the last century, but the names of many of which had existed for many more centuries, were swept away. The map of Ethiopia was recast along ethnic lines and the country was divided into fourteen regions or zones. Below are the fourteen zones and the names by which they are also known:

ዞን 1 ትግራይ	Tigray	ዞን 8 ሲዳማ	Sidama
ዞን 2 ዐፋር	Afar	ዞን 9 ወላይታ	Wälayïtta
ዞን 3 አማራ	Amara	ዞን 10 ኦሞ	Omo
ዞን 4 ኦሮሞ	Oromo	ዞን 11 ከፋ	Käffa
ዞን 5 ሶማሌ	Somale	ዞን 12 ጋምቤላ	Gambela
ዞን 6 በኒሻንጉል	Bänišangul	ዞን 13 ሐረር	Harär
ዞን 7 ጉራጌ/ሃዲያ	Gurage/Hadiyya	ዞን 14 አዲስ አበባ	Addis Abäba

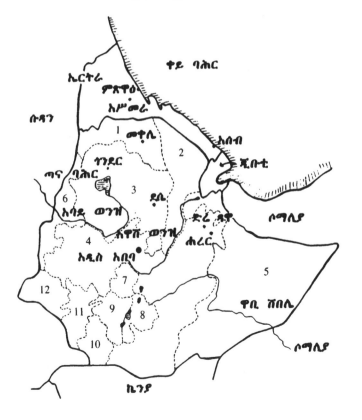

*8 Imagine that you are describing to an Ethiopian friend
what you enjoy – or don't enjoy – about the countryside in
the area where you live. Write down some of the views that
you might develop using the vocabulary below to help you*

አገር ቤት	agär bet	countryside, rural area
መንደር	mändär	village
ወንዝ	wänz	river, stream
ሸለቆ	šäläk'o	valley, gorge
ገደል	gädäl	cliff, precipice, canyon
ሃይቅ	hayk'	lake
ባሕር	bahïr	sea, (large) lake
እርሻ	ïrša	farm, field, cultivated land
በረሃ	bäräha	desert, wilderness
መሬት	märet	earth, ground, soil
ጭቃ	č'ïk'a	mud
አሸዋ	ašäwa	sand
የባሕር ዳር	yäbahïr dar	sea or lake shore
ደሴት	däset	island
ተራራ	tärara	mountain
ኮረብታ	koräbta	hill
ሜዳ	meda	plain
ጫካ	č'akka	forest, wood, bush
ደንጊያ	dängiya	rock, stone
ዛፍ	zaf	tree
አበባ	abäba	flower
ለምለም	lämläm	fertile, green (*of landscape*)

Reading passage

ኢትዮጵያ በአፍሪካ አህጉር በሰሜን ምሥራቅ በኩል ትገኛለች ፡፡
ኢትዮጵያን አዋሳኝ አገሮች በሰሜን ኤርትራ፤ በምዕራብ
ሱዳን፤ በደቡብ ኬንያ፤ በደቡብ ምሥራቅና በምሥራቅ
ሱማሊያና ጂቡቲ ናቸው ፡፡

ኢትዮጵያ በጣም ውብ የሆነች አገር ናት ፡፡ በነገሪቱ ውስጥ
የተፈጠሩ ሀብቶች በያይነቱ ድንቅባታል ፡፡ ለምሳሌ ኢትዮጵያ
በአብዛኛው ተራራማ አገር ናት ፡፡ የኢትዮጵያ ከፍተኛ ተራራ
ራስዳሽን ይባላል ፡፡ እሱም የሚገኘው በሰሜን በኩል ነው ፡፡
እዚያም ማለትም በስተሰሜንና በአገሪቱ መካከል ጥልቀት
ያላቸው ሸለቆዎችና ገደሎች አሉ ፡፡ በደቡብ በምሥራቅም በኩል
ያለው አካባቢ ግን በረሃ የሆነ አሸዋማ ሜዳ ነው ፡፡

አገሪቱ በታላቁ ስምጥ ሸለቆ የተገመሰች ሲሆን ብዙ ሃይቆች
አሉባት። ከኢትዮጵያ ሃይቆች መካከል ሰፊ የሆነውና
የታወቀው ጣና ነው። እሱም በሰሜን በኩል ነው
የሚገኘው። ከኢትዮጵያ ወንዞች መሀከል አባይ፣ አዋሽ፣ ዋቢ
ሸበሌና ኦሞ የታወቁ ናቸው።

Supplementary vocabulary

ሀብት	habt	wealth, resource
የተፈጥሮ ሀብቶች	yätäfät'ro habtoč	natural resources
አዋሳኝ	awwasañ	neighbouring, bordering
ጥልቀት	t'ilk'ät	depth
የተገመሰች ሲሆን	yätägämmäsäčč sihon	whilst it (she) is divided

9 ብሔራዊ ምግብ ቤት
bïherawi mïgïb bet

An Ethiopian restaurant

By the end of this lesson you should be able to:

- form and use the gerundive ('having eaten'; 'after eating' . . . etc.),
- form and use the compound gerundive tense ('I have eaten' . . . etc.)
- use some constructions equivalent to English 'when' . . ., 'because' . . ., 'as' . . . etc.

A visit to an Ethiopian restaurant

ከበደና ጌሩት ፒተርን በብሔራዊ ምግብ ቤት ይጋብዙታል።

ከበደ: ዛሬ ማታ እኔና ጌሩት አንድ ጥሩ ብሔራዊ ምግብ ቤት ልናሳድህ እንፈልጋለን። የምንወስድህ ምግብ ቤት ስም «ካራ ማራ ምግብ ቤት» ይባላል። ነገር ግን የሣር ቤት ስለ መሰለ ሁሉም የሚለው «ጎጆ» ነው።

ፒተር: ካሁን ቀደም አንድም ብሔራዊ ምግብ ቤት ሄጄ አላውቅም።

ታክሲ ጠርተው ተሳፈረው ከፕቶት ጊዜ በኋላ ምግብ ቤቱ ይደርሳሉ። አደርፕላን ማረፊያ በሚወስደው መንገድ ላይ ነው የሚገኘው።

ከበደ: ቆዩ አንድ ጊዜ። ቦታ እንዳለ መጠየቅ አለብኝ . . .
አሳላፊ: ቦታ አለ። ለስንት ሰው ነው?
ከበደ: ለሦስት ነው። ዛሬ ማታ ምን ምን አላችሁ? እንጋ አምጥተናል ያገር ባህል ምግብ ምን እንደሆነ ልናሳየው እንፈልጋለን።
አሳላፊ: ሁሉም አለን: የደር ወጥ: የበግ ወጥ: የበግ አልጫ:

ጥብስ፡ ክትር በአይብ፡ ምንድን ነው የምትመርጡት?

ከበደ፡ የዶሮ ወጡ እንዴት ነው?

አሳላፊ፡ ዛሬ በጣም ለስላሳ ነው።

ከበደ፡ እሺ፡ ለንግግዳችን ዶር ወጥ፡ አልጫና ትንሽ ክትር በአይብ፡ ለኛ ደግሞ ዶር ወጥና ቃሪያ አምጣልን።

አሳላፊ፡ በጻሎ ይሁን ወይስ በንጀራ?

ፒተር፡ እኔ የምፈልገው እንጀራ ነው።

ከበደ፡ ምን ለመጠጣት ትፈልጋለህ? ... ምን የሚጠጣ ነገር አላችሁ? ጠጅ አለ ዛሬ?

አሳላፊ፡ አልቋል። ጠላና ሜታ ቢራ እንዲሁም ለስላሳ መጠጥ አለ።

ከበደ፡ ኧረ! ያሳዝናል፡ ጥሩ ዓይነት የማር ጠጅ የኢትዮጵያ ብሔራዊ መጠጥ ነው። በአውርኔ የሚገኝ አይመስለኝም።

ፒተር፡ ከማር የተሠራ ጠጅ አለን፡ ግን አብዛኛውን ጊዜ ከወይን ነው ጠጃችንን የምንሠራው። የሆነ ሆኖ እኔ አምሎ ውሃ ልጠጣ።

ከበደ፡ እንዴ? ሌላ መጠጥ ለምን አትጠጣም?

ፒተር፡ መጠጥ አልጠጣም።

ከበደ፡ እንገዲያውስ እስቲ ለእንግዳችን አንድ ጠርሙስ አምሎ ውሃ አምጣለት። እኔና ጌሩት ሜታ ቢራ ነው የምንጠጣ ...

ጌሩት፡ በል! ወጡ እንዴት ነው? ይፋጃል?

ከበደ፡ አይ፡ በውነት በጣም ጥሩ ነው። ምንም አይፈጅም። ብቻ ምንላባት ለፒተር በርበሬው ትንሽ የበዛበት ይመስላል?

ፒተር፡ አዎ፡ ትንሽ ይፈጅብኛል፡ ግን ይጣፍጣል ... ለመሆኑ ጋገራችሁ ከምግቡ በኋላ ቡና ይጠጣል?

ጌሩት፡ እንዴታ! እኔና ከበደ ምሳ ከበላን በኋላ ነው ቡና የምንጠጣው። ቡና በወተት ይሻላሃል ወይስ ያለ ወተት? አብዛኛውን ጊዜ ጋገራችን ቡና ያለ ወተት በሱኳር ነው የሚጠጣው።

ቡና ጠጥተው ሲጨርሱ ከበደ ሂሳብ ይጠይቃል።

ከበደ፡ ጋሼ፡ እስቲ የምገቡ ሂሳብ ስንት ነው?

አሳላፊ፡ ሃያ ዘጠኝ ብር ከሃምሳ ስንቲም ነው።

ከበደ፡ ዋጋው በጣም ጥሩ ነው።

አሳላፊ፡ መልሱ ይኸውና።

ከበደ፡ እሺ፡ እንካ፡ ሁለት ብር ጉርሻ ልጨምርህ።

አሳላፊ፡ እግዜር ይስጥልኝ። አመሰግናለሁ።

KEBEDE: *This evening Hirut and I want to show you a good national restaurant. The restaurant we're taking you to is called the 'Kara Mara Restaurant'. But because it looks like a grass house, everyone calls it the 'hut'.*

PETER: *I've never been to a national restaurant before.*

They call a taxi, get in and after a while they arrive at the restaurant. It's on the road leading to the airport.

KEBEDE: *Just a minute, I'll ask if they're full . . .*

WAITER: *There is room. How many is it for?*

KEBEDE: *For three . . . What do you have this evening? We've brought a guest and want to show him what national food is like.*

WAITER: *We have everything. Chicken* wot, *mutton* wot, *mutton* allitcha, *fried meat,* kitfo *with cheese. What would you like?*

KEBEDE: *What is the chicken* wot *like?*

WAITER: *It's very mild today.*

KEBEDE: *OK, bring some chicket* wot, *some* allitcha *and a little* kitfo *with cheese for our guest, and then for us bring some chicken* wot *and some chillies.*

WAITER: *With bread or with* injera?

PETER: *I would like* injera.

KEBEDE: *What would you like to drink? . . . What drinks do you have? Is there any* tejj *today?*

WAITER: *It's finished. There's* tella *and Metta beer and likewise soft drinks.*

KEBEDE: *Oh, that's a pity! The best quality honey tejj is the national drink of Ethiopia. I don't think it's something that exists in Europe.*

PETER: *We have wine made from honey, but most of the time we make our wine from grapes. Anyway, let me drink Ambo Water.*

KEBEDE: *Why won't you drink something stronger?*

PETER: *I don't like strong drinks.*

KEBEDE: *In that case, please bring a bottle of Ambo Water for our guest. Hirut and I will drink Metta beer . . .*

Hirut: *Well, how is the* wot? *Is it too hot?*

KEBEDE: *No, it's really very good. It's not too hot at all. But perhaps there's too much pepper in it for Peter?*

PETER: *Yes, it is a little too hot for me, but it tastes very good . . .*

> *By the way, in your country do people drink coffee after food?*
>
> Hirut: *Of course, both Kebbede and I drink coffee after eating dinner. Do you prefer coffee with or without milk? Usually in our country people drink coffee without milk and with lots of sugar.*

When they have finished drinking coffee Kebbede asks for the bill.

KEBEDE: *Waiter, how much is the bill for the meal, please?*
WAITER: *29 birr and 50 Santim.*
KEBEDE: *The price is very good.*
WAITER: *Here's your change.*
KEBEDE: *OK, here you are, and let me add 2 birr as a tip for you.*
WAITER: *Thank you. Goodbye.*

Vocabulary

ብሔራዊ	biherawi	national (cf. ብሔር biher nation)
ጎጆ	gojo	hut
ሣር	sar	grass
ባህል	bahïl	custom
ያገር ባህል ምግብ	yagär bahïl mïgïb	indigenous, national cuisine
ዶሮ	doro	chicken
በግ	bäg	sheep
ወጥ	wät'	spiced stew, meat sauce containing **bärbärre** (red chilli) pepper
(የ)ዶሮ ወጥ	(yä)doro wät'	chicken stew, chicken **wot**
(የ)በግ ወጥ	(yä)bäg wät'	mutton stew, mutton **wot**
በርበሬ	bärbärre	dried red chillies, 'pepper'
አልጫ	allïč'č'a	spiced stew without **bärbärre** (red chilli) pepper
ጥብስ	t'ïbs	*anything roasted or fried, usually fried pieces of meat*
ክትፎ	kïtfo	chopped or minced raw beef
አይብ	ayb	*kind of fresh cheese, like cottage or curd cheese*
ለስላሳ	läslassa	soft, smooth, mild (*of foods*), non-alcoholic (*of drinks*)
ቃሪያ	k'ariya	fresh green chilli pepper
ዳቦ	dabbo	raised bread similar to European bread

እንጀራ	injära	flat pancake-like bread (*see note 1*)
መጅ	t'äjj	mead, honey wine
ጠላ	t'älla	Ethiopian beer
ቢራ	bira	European (lager) beer
ማር	mar	honey
ወይን	wäyn	grape
ወይን መጅ	wäyn t'äjj	(grape) wine
መጠጥ	mät'ät't'	drink (*the word on its own usually refers to alcoholic drinks*)
ለስላሳ (መጠጥ)	läslassa (mät'ät't')	soft drinks
ሂሳብ	hisab	bill, check, account
ጉርሻ	gurša	tip (*see also note 1*)
መልስ	mäls	(*here*) change

Adverbs, particles

ከ- ቀደም	kä- k'ädäm	before (*in time*)
ምን ምን	mïn mïn	what? (*expecting that the answer will include several items*)
ደግሞ	dägmo	then, also
ይሁን	yïhun	(*here*) or (*lit.* 'let it be'; 'be it')
አብዛኛውን ጊዜ	abzaññawn gize	most of the time
እንጊዲያውስ	ïngïdiyawiss	in that case
ለመሆኑ	lämähonu	by the way
እስቲ	ïsti	please (*see note 4*)
በል	bäl	well, come on, go on . . . (*lit.* 'say!'; *see note 5*)
ምንም	mïnïmm	(*with a negative verb*) nothing, not at all
እንካ	ïnka	here you are! (*see note 5*)

Verbs

ጋበዘ	gabbäzä	invite to a meal, treat [3-lit C]
ተሳፈረ	täsaffärä	get into, on to (*a vehicle*) [derived stem]
አመጣ	amät't'a	bring [derived stem]
አምጣ	amt'a	bring! (command form or imperative, masc. sing.)
ተሠራ	täsärra	be made (derived stem from ሠራ särra make)

ተፋጀ	täfajjä	be too spicy, hot (*lit.* 'destroy'; 'exterminate!' [derived stem], compound imperfect ይፋጃል yiffajjal)
ተሻለ	täšalä	be better, preferable; (*as an impersonal verb* ተሻለኝ täšaläñ I preferred; compound imperfect ይሻለኛል yiššaläññal; I prefer)
አመሰገነ	amäsäggänä	thank, praise [derived stem], compound imperfect ያመሰግናል yamäsäginal

Phrases

ልናሳይህ	linnasayyih	so that we show you
ሂጀ አላውቅም	hejje alawk'im	I have never gone (*see note 2*)
የሚገኘው	yämmiggäññaw	which is located (*lit.* 'found'); *from* ተገኘ tägäññä be found [derived stem] (*see note 3*)
እንደሆነ	indähonä	(*here*) how it is
እንዳለ	indallä	(*here*) whether there is
አልቋል	alk'wal	it's finished (*from* አለቀ alläk'ä be finished)
ያሳዝናል	yasazzinal	it's a pity; (አሳዘነ asazzänä make sad derived stem from አዘነ azzänä be sad)
ልጠጣ	lit'ät't'a	let me drink
ይጠጣል	yit't'ät't'al	it is drunk, (*i.e.* people drink, one drinks)
ልጨምርህ	lič'ämmirih	let me add for you

Notes on the dialogue

1 Ethiopian cooking is one of the most distinctive and interesting cuisines in Sub-Saharan Africa. Food is almost always served with እንጀራ injära, a large round pancake-like bread preferably made of ጤፍ t'ef flour. The various stews or sauces – such as ወጥ wät' – are served in small bowls which are tipped out on to a pile of two or three injära. Sometimes rolled up strips of injära are also served. The food is eaten by tearing off pieces of injära with the right hand, which are then used to scoop up mouthfuls of meat and sauce. As a special sign of honour your host may do

this for you and feed you directly with often oversized portions! This is called **ጉርሻ** gurša – the same word is now used for 'tip'! Everyday Ethiopian (Amhara-Tigrean) food consists chiefly of meat dishes, except on fast days – which are called **ጾም** s'om – of which there around 180 a year obligatory for observant lay Christians, including every Wednesday and Friday, and as many as 250 for monks and the clergy. On these days no animal products are consumed. At other times Ethiopia can be a difficult place for vegetarians, especially away from the big towns!

Ambo Water (**አምቦ ውሃ**) is the principal Ethiopian mineral water which comes from the springs at Ambo to the west of Addis Ababa. Metta Beer (**ሜታ ቢራ**) is one of the brands of Ethiopian lager-type beer. The indigenous Ethiopian alcoholic drinks are **ጠጅ** t'äjj, a sort of mead or honey wine, which is usually not very sweet; **ጠላ** t'älla, a light beer made from barley or sorghum, and **አራቄ** arak'e, a very potent spirit, which also appears in a home-made version as **ካቲካላ** katikala !

2 The phrase **ሄጄ አላውቅም** hejje alawk'ïm 'I never went; I have never gone' illustrates an idiomatic use of the verb **አወቀ** 'know'. The construction consists of the gerundive (see the grammar section in this lesson) followed by the negative imperfective tense of **አወቀ** . The corresponding positive phrase – gerundive followed by the compound imperfective of **አወቀ** – expresses 'ever':

ወሬውን ሰምቶ አያውቅም	wärewn sämto ayawk'ïm
	he never heard the news
ወሬውን ሰምቶ ያውቃል?	wärewn sämto yawk'al?
	did he ever hear the news?

3 The verb **ተገኘ** tägäññä 'be found' is often used in the sense of 'be situated, located' or just 'be (in a place)', as in the sentence in the dialogue **እስከ አይሮፕላን ማረፊያ በሚያስከደው መንገድ ነው የሚገኘው** iskä ayroplan maräfiya bämmiyaskedäw mängäd näw yämmiggäññäw, which is literally 'it's on the road which leads up to the airport that it is found'. **ተገኘ** tägäññä is a derived stem type:

ይገኛል	yïggäññal	compound imperfective
መገኘት	mäggäññät	infinitive
ተገኝቶ	tägäñto	gerundive (*see below*)

4 You have already learned in lesson three that one way to say 'please' in Amharic is to use the base **እባክ**- followed by the appropriate second person ending: **እባክህ** ïbakkïh, **እባክሽ** ïbakkïš,

አባካችሁ ïbakkaččuh, አባከም ïbakkïwo. This is the usual and more polite way of saying 'please'. አስት ïsti is less formal, more casual and is commonly used to soften the force of a direct command and give it a less abrupt feeling: እንጀራ አምጣልኝ ïnjära amt'allïñ 'bring me some injera!'; አስት እንጀራ አምጣልኝ ïsti ïnjära amt'allïñ 'bring me some injera, please'.

5 The little word በል bäl is often used as an informal introduction to a request or a suggestion, or as a way of getting someone to volunteer information. It is literally the command form or imperative of the verb አለ alä 'say', and therefore has three forms according to who is being addressed:

በል	bäl	masculine singular
በይ, በዪ	bäy, bäyi	feminine singular
በሉ	bälu	plural

Another similar little word which can introduce a sentence is እንክ ïnka. It is said when offering something to someone and is equivalent to the English 'here!' or 'here you are!'. Like በል bäl it was originally a command form or imperative and so 'agrees' with the person who is being addressed:

እንክ	ïnka	masculine singular
እንኪ, እንቺ	ïnki, ïnči	feminine singular
እንኩ	ïnku	plural

Yet another useful command or imperative form which can be used to introduce a sentence is ተው täw 'wait'; 'just a minute'; 'hang on':

ተው	täw	masculine singular
ተይ, ተዪ	täy, täyi	feminine singular
ተዉ	täwu	plural

Grammar

The gerundive

The gerundive is a form or 'tense' of the Amharic verb that has no direct correspondent in English. There are several gerundives in the dialogue in this lesson: ጠርተው t'ärtäw; ገብተው gäbtäw; አምጥተን amt'ïtän. You have already encountered a few others in earlier lessons: አጥብቆ at'bïk'o; አጥብቄ at'bïk'k'e; ሄጄ hejje; ተመልሼ

tämällišše; ሁኖ hono; አሻገረን aššagrän; ጀምሮ jämmïro; and so on. If you look back and see how these were translated into English you will see that there are quite a number of possibilities:

ሂጄ ተመለስኩ	*hejje* tämälläskw	I have (*gone and*) returned
አብረን	*abrän* ïnnïmät'allän	we'll come *together*
እንመጣለን		
ታክሲ ተሳፍረው	taksi *täsafräw*	they *get into* a taxi *and ...*
...ይደርሳሉ	... *yïdärsallu*	arrive
አጥብቆ ያሳዘነን	*at'bïk'o* yasazzänä	it was a *very great* pity
ተመለሺ ደርስኩ	*tämällïšše* därräskw	I arrived *back*

The gerundive is formed by adding a special set of endings (which are similar but not everywhere identical to others that you know) to a special gerundive stem. The gerundive stems of each of the verb classes (excluding derived stems) you have met so far are as follows: each verb class is given with a sample gerundive, in the third person masculine form; the accompanying English translation is only a guideline. You have already seen how it is difficult to give the gerundive a genuine one-to-one English translation.

verb class	gerundive stem		sample		
3-lit A	[ነገረ]	nägr-	ነገሮ	nägro	*lit.* 'he speaking'
	[አወቀ]	awk'-	አወቆ	awk'o	*lit.* 'he knowing'
3-lit B	[ፈለገ]	fällïg-	ፈለጎ	fällïgo	*lit.* 'he wanting'
3-lit C	[ማረከ]	mark-	ማርኮ	marko	*lit.* 'he capturing'
2-lit[1] A	[ሰማ]	sämt-	ሰምቶ	sämto	*lit.* 'he hearing'
2-lit[1] B	[ጠጣ]	t'ät't'*ït*-	ጠጥቶ	t'ät't'ïto	*lit.* 'he drinking'
2-lit[2] A	[ሰጠ]	sät'*t*-	ሰጥቶ	sät'to	*lit.* 'he giving'
2-lit[2] B	[ቆየ]	k'oyy*ït*-	ቆይቶ	k'oyyïto	*lit.* 'he waiting'
2-lit[3]	[ጻፈ]	s'ïf-	ጽፎ	s'ïfo	*lit.* 'he writing'
2-lit[4]	[ሄደ]	hed-	ሄዶ	hedo	*lit.* 'he going'
2-lit[5]	[ሆነ]	hon-	ሁኖ	hono	*lit.* 'he being'
4-lit	[መረመረ]	märmïr-	መርምሮ	märmïro	*lit.* 'he examining'
3-lit Y	[ጐበኘ]	gwäbñï*t*-	ጐብኝቶ	gwäbñïto	*lit.* 'he visiting'
3-lit X	[ዘነጋ]	zängï*t*-	ዘንግቶ	zängïto	*lit.* 'he forgetting'
irregular	አለ 'say'	bïl-	ብሎ	bïlo	*lit.* 'he saying'

Points to note

1 Verbs which add -t in their infinitives also add -t in the formation of the gerundive stem: 2-lit¹, 2-lit², 3-lit Y and 3-lit X.
2 The gerundive stem is modified in the first person singular: e.g. **ነግሮ** nägro 'he speaking' but **ነግሬ** nägïrre 'I speaking'; **ሰምቶ** sämto 'he hearing' but **ሰምቼ** sämïčče 'I hearing'; **ደርሶ** därso 'he arriving' but **ደርሼ** därïšše 'I arriving'. To derive the first singular stem from the basic stem two steps are involved:
  (a) geminate the last consonant: **ነግር** nägr-o → **ነግሬ** nägïrr-e
  (b) if that consonant is one that palatalizes (**t, d, t', s, z, n, l**) then palatalize it: **ሰምት** sämt-o → **ሰምቼ** sämïčč-e, **ደርስ** därs-o → **ደርሼ** därïšš-e; **መርጥ** märt'-o → **መርጪ** märïč'č'-e, **ከፍሎ** käfl-o → **ከፍዬ** käfïyy-e; and so on. (See lesson five to remind yourself of the palatalization process.)
Remember Amharic doesn't like three consonants in a row, so you have to pronounce the preceding sixth order vowel: **ነግሬ** nägïrre; **ሰምቼ** sämïčče; and so on.
3 In the case of those verb types that add a t in the formation of their gerundive stems, when the verb base itself ends in **t, d,** or **t'** some people pronounce a short sixth order vowel ï to separate the two; others don't: **መጥቶ** mät'ïto or mät'to.

The personal endings of the gerundive are as follows:

	ending	sample stem		
		gäbt- [2-lit¹ A]		
1st pers. sing.	-e	ገብቼ	gäbïčče	*lit.* 'I entering'
2nd pers. masc.	-äh	ገብተህ	gäbtäh	*lit.* 'you entering'
2nd pers. fem.	-äš	ገብተሽ	gäbtäš	*lit.* 'you entering'
3rd pers. masc.	-o	ገብቶ	gäbto	*lit.* 'he entering'
3rd pers. fem.	-a	ገብታ	gäbta	*lit.* 'she entering'
1st pers. pl.	-än	ገብተን	gäbtän	*lit.* 'we entering'
2nd pers. pl.	-aččuh	ገብታችሁ	gäbtaččuh	*lit.* 'you entering'
3rd pers. pl.	-äw	ገብተው	gäbtäw	*lit.* 'they entering, etc.'

Points to note

1 Remember that the ending of the first person singular modifies the gerundive stem: **አይቶ** ayto 'he seeing' but **አይቼ** ayïčče 'I seeing'.

2 As in the simple past tense, the ending of the second person plural is pronounced -ačču only when no further suffix is added; otherwise it is pronounced as written -aččïhu-: አይታችሁ aytaččuh 'you seeing' but አይታችሁኝ aytaččïhuñ 'you seeing me'.

3 Be careful in your pronunciation to distinguish the third person masculine from the third person plural: ገብቶ gäbto: ገብተው gäbtäw.

Use of the gerundive

In English you can say things like 'he came in and sat down', 'I went to the shop and bought some coffee', where two consecutive actions are joined by 'and'. In Amharic, however, the first action in each of the examples would normally be expressed by a gerundive, because it precedes and is somehow subordinate to the second or 'main' action. In other words, he has to come in *before* he sits down, and I have to go to the shop *before* I buy the coffee. In these examples only the main verb in Amharic will be expressed by the simple past tense:

ገብቶ ተቀመጠ	gäbto täk'ämmät'ä
	he came in and sat down
ሱቁ ሂጄ ቡና ገዛሁ	suk'u hejje bunna gäzzahw
	I went to the shop and bought coffee
ተረፈ ገብቶ ተማሪዎቹ ወጡ	Tärräfä gäbto tämariwočču wät't'u
	Terrefe came in and the students left

The gerundive corresponds to other English sentence types besides simple phrases linked by 'and'. For example, ገብቶ ተቀመጠ gäbto täk'ämmät'ä would also be equivalent to the English 'coming in, he sat down', or 'after coming in he sat down', or 'when he came in he sat down', and so on.

It is not wrong to say literally ገብና ተቀመጠ gäbba*nna* täk'ämmät'ä 'he came in *and* sat down' or ሱቁ ሂድኩና ቡና ገዛሁ suk'u hedku*nna* bunna gäzzahw 'I went to the shop *and* bought coffee' But if you do this though, the implication given here by the -ና -nna is usually more like 'and so . . ., and as a result . . ., and therefore . . .', or even 'because . . .'. For cases where you can join verbs with -ና -nna see also the section below on simultaneous actions.

The main verb can however be in any tense, but the action expressed in the gerundive still remains antecedent and subordinate to the main action:

በሩን ከፍታ ተገባለች	bärrun käfta tïgäballäčč
	she opens the door and goes in
ሥራዬን ጨርሼ እተኛለሁ	sïrayen č'ärrïšše ïtäññallähw
	I'll finish my work and go to bed
ቀሚስ መርጠሽ ግዢላት	k'ämis märt'äš gïžillat
	choose a dress and buy it for her!
ነገ ደውዬ ልንገርህ	nägä däwwïyye lïngärïh
	let me call and tell you tomorrow

Sometimes the action expressed in the gerundive is so closely linked with that of the main verb that you cannot really say that it occurs 'before' it. Consider the following sentences:

ልጁ ሮጦ ገባ	lïjju rot'o gäbba
	the boy came in running
ቤት ተመልሰን ደረስን	bet tämällïsän därräsïn
	we arrived back home
ሲኒማ ቤት አብረን እንሂድ	sinima bet abrän ïnnïhid
	let's go to the cinema together
እንደዚህ አድርገው ገደሉት	ïndäzzih adrïgäw gäddälut
	they killed him like this

These are literally:

the boy entered *(he) running* [ሮጦ rot'o from ሮጠ rot'ä]
we arrived *(we) returning* home [ተመልሰን tämällïsän from ተመለሰ tämälläsä]
let's go to the cinema *(we) being together* [አብረን abrän from አበረ abbärä]
they killed him *(he) doing* like this [አድርገው adrïgäw from አደረገ adärrägä]

Sometimes an Amharic gerundive corresponds to a simple adverb in English, like 'together' for አብረን abrän or 'back' for ተመልሰን tämällïsän in the sentences above. Below are some further examples of this kind.

ፈጽሞ አጠፋው	fäs's'imo at'äffaw	he completely destroyed it
አጥብቆ ከለከለኝ	at'bïk'o käläkkälañ	he strictly forbade me
ደስ ብሎት አደረገው	däss bïlot adärrägäw	he did it willingly
ዝም ብሎ ተቀመጠ	zïmm bïlo täk'ämmät'ä	he sat quietly
ከቶ አልፈለገውም	kätto alfällägäwm	he didn't want it at all, he never wanted it

ፈጸመ **fäs's'ämä** [3-lit B] 'complete'; አጠበቀ **at'äbbäk'ä** [derived stem] 'tighten'; ደስ አለው **däss aläw** [impersonal irregular] 'be happy'; ዝም አለ **zïmm alä** [irregular] 'be silent'; ከተተ [3-lit A] **kättätä** 'gather'.

The gerundive of the verb ያዘ **yazä** 'hold, take' is sometimes used in a similar adverbial sense often corresponding to English 'with':

ወረቀቱን ይዞ መጣ	**wäräk'ätun yïzo mät't'a**
	he brought the papers
	lit. 'he came taking the paper'
እንግዶች ይዤ መጣሁ	**ïngïdočč yïžže mät't'ahw**
	I brought some guests
	lit. 'I came taking guests'
ቦርሳየን ይዘው አመለጡ	**borsayen yïzäw amällät'u**
	they ran away with my bag
	lit. 'they ran away taking my bag'
እቃህን ይዤልህ እሄዳለሁ	**ïk'ahïn yïžžellïh ïhedallähw**
	I'll take your things away for you
	lit. 'I'll go taking your things for you'

Simultaneous actions and events

You can join two verbs by -ና **-nna** when the actions are simultaneous or co-temporaneous (i.e. occurring at the same time). Consider the following:

በሉና ጠጡ	**bällunna t'ät't'u**	they ate and drank

Note: they hadn't finished eating before they began drinking, but the two events are carried on together.

Note also that you cannot join two compound imperfect verbs directly with -ና **-nna**. Instead, the first verb is put into the simple imperfect, the 'verb base' form described in the previous lesson:

ይበሉና ይጠጣሉ	**yïbälunna yït'ät't'allu**	they're eating and drinking

You can, however, join two compound imperfect verbs directly with -ም **-m(m)**, the other Amharic suffix meaning 'and'. Remember that -ም is added to the second word and not the first.

ይበላሉ ይጠጣሉም	**yïbälallu yït'ät't'allum**	they're eating and drinking

Exercises

1 Say whether the following English sentences would be more likely to use (a) a gerundive + a main verb tense, or (b) two main verb tenses joined by -ና when translated into Amharic

1 Peter sat down and wrote a letter.
2 The children were singing and dancing.
3 Why aren't the students reading and writing today?
4 I'll ring and book a taxi this afternoon.
5 Go and sit in the corner quietly!
6 Aisha bought the cloth and made this dress herself.

2 Substitute the correct form of the gerundive for the verb in brackets in the following sentences

1 ገረዲቱ ከሦስት ሰዓት በፊት ሥራዋን (ጨረሰ) ሂደች።
2 ከበደ ከዩኒቨርሲቲ (ገባ) ሒሳብ ለመማር ወሰነ።
3 ነገ ገንዘቡን (ያዘ) ወደ ቤትህ እመጣለሁ።
4 እንደነ (አደረገ) መጽፍ ይገባሃል።
5 ትምሕርቴን (ጨረሰ) አገንክ ደሆናል የምሥራ።
6 ቲያትር (አየ) አታውቁም እንዴ?
7 ታክሲ (ጠራ) ሲኒማ ቤት እንሂድ!
8 ምሳዬን (ጨረሰ በላ) ሥራ እመለጋለሁ።

3 Fill in the blanks in the following sentences using one of the gerundive phrases listed below so as to make a sensible sentence in Amharic

1 አይሻ ገበያ _____ የሚያስፈልጋትን ትገዛለች።
2 አቶ ሙሉጌታ _____ ተቀመጡ።
3 ከነገ ወዲያ ገንዘቡን _____ እመጣለሁ።
4 አስተማሪው _____ ከለከላቸው።
5 እናንተ ልጆች፤ ሮጣችሁን _____ ወዴት ነው የምትሄዱ?
6 ትናንትና ጸሐፊዋ ዘጠኝ ደብዳቤ _____ ላከች።
7 ትንሽ ቅይ፤ አፕስታ ቤት _____ ቴምበር አገዛለሁ።
8 ምሳ _____ ከበደን ለመጠየቅ እንሂድ!

[ይዤ, ዝም ብለው, በልተን, ጽፋ, አጥብቆ, ሄጃ, ይዛችሁ, ገብቼ.]

4 Imagine you are describing to an Ethiopian friend a picnic that you have recently been on. Tell him or her what you did, what you ate and drank, using gerundives where appropriate rather than sequences of verbs joined by -ና. Below are some new words and phrases that you might find useful

ባለፈው እሁድ	balläfäw ïhud	last Sunday
ሽርሽር ሔደ	širïššïr hedä	go on a picnic
ምግብ ሠራ	mïgïb särra	prepare food
የመድኃኒት ዕቃ	yämädhanit ïk'a	first aid things
ዝናብ ዘነበ	zïnab zännäbä	it rained (*lit.* 'it rained rain'; ዘነበ [3-lit A])
ሳህን	sahïn	plate
ቢላዋ	billawa	knife
ኩባያ	kubbayya	cup
ፔርሙዝ	permuz	Thermos flask
ማንኪያ	mankiya	spoon
ሹካ	šukka	fork
ሰንድዊች	sändwič	sandwich

The compound gerundive tense

Another important use of the gerundive is to provide the base for the compound gerundive tense. An example of this tense is አልቋል **alk'wal** 'it's finished', which you met in the dialogue in this lesson. Quite often the compound gerundive tense has the same meaning as the simple past tense: አለቀ **alläk'ä** 'it's finished'.

	stem	*ending*	*sample*	
1st pers. sing.	gäbïčč-	-eyallähw, -[y]allähw	ገብቻለሁ, ገብቻለሁ	gäbïččallähw
2nd pers. masc.	gäbt-	-ähal	ገብተሃል	gäbtähal
2nd pers. fem.	"	-äšal	ገብተሻል	gäbtäšal
3rd pers. masc.	"	-owal, -wal	ገብቶዋል, ገብቷል	gäbtwal
3rd pers. fem.	"	-alläčč	ገብታለች	gäbtalläčč
1st pers. pl.	"	-änal	ገብተናል	gäbtänal
2nd pers. pl.	"	-aččïhwal	ገብታችኋል	gäbtaččïhwal
3rd pers. pl.	"	-äwal	ገብተዋል	gäbtäwal

Points to note

1 To make the compound gerundive the suffix **-al** is added to the gerundive in all persons except the first person singular, which has **-allähw**, and the third person feminine, which has **-alläčč**. Be careful that these '**ኣለ**' endings are **not** quite the same as those of the compound imperfect.

2 The first person singular is formed by adding **-allähw** to the gerundive which ends in the vowel **-e**. This means that according to the rules of 'vowel hierarchy' something has to happen when the **e** meets the **a**: either a 'glide' consonant **y** is placed between the two vowels, as in **ገብቻ*ያ*ለሁ** gäbiččeyallähw, or more usually in spoken Amharic a contraction takes place and the ending **-eyallähw** becomes **-yallähw**, or in certain circumstances simply **-allähw**. The contraction to **-allähw** occurs only when the consonant before the ending is a palatal one: š, ž, č, č', j, ñ, or y. Otherwise, the contraction is simply to **-yallähw**.

-eyallähw ➙ (a) **-yallähw** (following a non-palatal consonant)
(b) **-allähw** (following a palatal consonant: š, ž, č, č', j, ñ, y)

In practice you will find that there are various ways of writing the first person singular form which reflect the 'history' of these different contractions: **ገብቻኣለሁ**, **ገብቻ*ያ*ለሁ** [both pronounced **gäbiččeyallähw**]; **ገቢቻ*ያ*ለሁ**, **ገብ*ቻ*ለሁ**, **ገብቻለሁ** [all pronounced as **gäbiččallähw** in normal spoken Amharic]. You will not go far wrong, however, if you keep to the basic principal that Amharic is mostly written as it sounds. Below are some examples of contracted forms:

ነገርያለሁ	nägïrryallähw	I have spoken	from	**ነገረ** näggärä
አለፍያለሁ	alïffyallähw	I have passed	"	**አለፈ** alläfä
ጀምርያለሁ	jämmïrryallähw	I have begun	"	**ጀመረ** jämmärä
አሰብ*ያ*ለሁ	assïbbyallähw	I have thought	"	**አሰበ** assäbä
አዝዣለሁ	azïžžallähw	I have ordered	"	**አዘዘ** azzäzä
ወስ*ኟ*ለሁ	wäsïjjallähw	I have taken	"	**ወሰደ** wässädä
ከፍያለሁ	käfiyyallähw	I have paid	"	**ከፈለ** käffälä
ደርሻለሁ	därïššallähw	I have arrived	"	**ደረሰ** därräsä
ገለፅ'ጫለሁ	gälïč'č'allähw	I have explained	"	**ገለፀ** gälläs'ä
ለምኛለሁ	lämmïññallähw	I have begged	"	**ለመነ** lämmänä
ደውይያለሁ	däwwïyyallähw	I have rung	"	**ደወለ** däwwälä
ተርቻለሁ	tärrïččallähw	I have told a story	"	**ተረተ** tärrätä

ሰምቻለሁ	sämïččallähw	I have heard	"	ሰማ	sämma
ጠጥቻለሁ	t'ät't'ïččallähw	I have drunk	"	ጠጣ	t'ät't'a
ብያለሁ	bïyyallähw	I have said	"	አለ	alä

3 The third person masculine also has an uncontracted and a contracted form. As the gerundive base here ends in -o, this time a 'glide' w has to be inserted before the ending -al of the compound gerundive. The resultant compound ending -owal may be contracted to -wal, which can either be written as -ዋል, or using one of the "wa" letters.

As with the first person singular, then, there are various ways of writing the third person masculine form, though the usual spoken form is the one in -wal. Here are some examples:

ነግሮአል, ነግሯል, ነግሮል, ነግሯል	nägrowal, nägrwal
	he has spoken
ወስዶአል, ወስዷል, ወስድዋል, ወስዷል	wäsdowal, wäsdwal
	he has taken
ደርሶአል, ደርሷል, ደርስዋል, ደርሷል	därsowal, därswal
	he has arrived
አዞአል, አዟል, አዝዋል, አዟል	azzowal, azzwal
	he has ordered
ፈልቶአል, ፈልቷል, ፈልትዋል, ፈልቷል	fältowal, fältwal
	it has boiled
ብሎአል, ብሏል, ብልዋል, ብሏል	bïlowal, bïlwal
	he has said

4 As with the simple gerundive, be careful to distinguish the third person masculine from the third person plural: ነግሯል, ነግሯል nägrowal or nägrwal 'he has spoken' and ነግረዋል nägräwal 'they have spoken'.

5 As with the compound imperfective, object pronoun and prepositional pronoun suffixes are placed between the base and the 'አለ' element. Unlike and simpler than the compound imperfective, the 'አለ' element (-allähw, -alläčč or -al) in the compound gerundive is not changed in any way when a pronoun suffix is inserted. Remember to pay attention to the ending of the gerundive base in selecting the correct form of the object pronoun suffix.

gerundive + object pronoun + -allähw / -alläčč / -al

Here are some examples:

ነገርኛል	nägronñal	he has told *me*
ነገርታል	nägro*t*al	he has told *him*
ነገርዋታል	nägro*wat*al	he has told *her*
ነገርዋቸዋል	nägro*waččä*wal	he has told *them*

| አይቼዋለሁ | ayïčče*w*allähw | I have seen *him* |
| አይቼያችኋለሁ | ayïčče*yaččïh*wallähw | I have seen *you* |

ሰጥተኸኛል	sät'ïtäh*äññal*	you have given *me* (it)
ሰጥተኸዋል	sät'ïtäh*äwal*	you have given *him* (it)
ሰጥታናለች	sät'ïta*n*alläčč	she has given *us* (it)
ሰጥታቸዋለች	sät'ïta*ččä*walläčč	she has given *them* (it)

The meaning of the compound gerundive tense

As the English translations of the examples of this tense suggest, the compound gerundive tense is generally used to indicate the continuing result of a past event, or in other words to suggest the present relevance of a past action in contrast to the simple past tense which simply describes an action in the past. In some ways, this is rather like the difference in English between a simple past 'he went' and a present perfect 'he has gone': ሄደ **hedä** as against ሄዷል **hedwal**. The comparison is not, however, exact – Amharic does not always use a compound gerundive (ሄዷል **hedwal**) where English uses a present perfect (he has gone), and vice versa. In many instances you can use either tense in Amharic without altering the meaning. For example, imagine you have been waiting for someone and when you see them arriving you can say either:

| ደረሰ | därräsä | he's arrived |

or

| ደርሷል | därswal | " |

The second phrase, however, implies '. . . and here he is at last'. Or again, imagine you are talking in Amharic with an Ethiopian friend and find your Amharic is not as good as it should be! You can make an excuse and say either:

| ብዙ ረሳሁ | bïzu rässahw | I've forgotten a lot |

or

| ብዙ ረስቻለሁ | bïzu räsïččallähw | " |

Here the second phrase stresses the fact that your bad memory has the present result of your not being able to speak so well.

However, if the event you are talking about happened some time ago, and especially if that time is mentioned, you can only use the simple past:

ከሦስት ሳምንት በፊት ደረሰ käsost sammïnt bäfit därräsä
he arrived three weeks ago

It is, of course, easier to learn the compound gerundive tense by observing how it is used in the dialogues, rather than by giving complicated rules here.

One point that it is important to note about the compound gerundive tense is that it has no corresponding negative form of its own. Instead, the negative simple past is used as the negative counterpart of both the simple past and the compound gerundive tenses. So, if in the previous scenario you have not in fact forgotten much Amharic, you need only say:

ብዙ አልረሳሁም bïzu alrässahum   I haven't forgotten a lot

Exercises

5 Rewrite the following sentences using the compound gerundive tense

1 ሙሉ ቀን እዚህ ቆየን፡፡
2 ወደ አሥመራ ሔዱ፡፡
3 ተማሪዎቹ በዚዛ ደረሱ?
4 እናቷን ለመጠየቅ ሂደች፡፡
5 ባቡሩ ተነሣ፡፡
6 ወረዉን ሰማችሁ?
7 እሬ፡ ወተት አለቀ!
8 አማረች ረጅም ደብዳቤ ጻፈች፡፡

6 Rewrite the following sentences to include the time expression given in brackets. Be careful to change the compound gerundive into the correct tense

> *Example:* እስከ አይርፖላን ማረፊያ ደርሰናል (ትናንትና)
> → ትናንትና እስከ አይርፖላን ማረፊያ ደረስን፡፡

1 እናታችን ጥሩ ምሳ ሠርታልናለች ። (ከትናንትና ወዲያ)
2 ጸሐፊዋ አምስት ደብዳቤዎች ጽፋለች ። (ዛሬ ከሰዓት በፊት)
3 ጥላሽን አገኘተውልሻል? (ገለፈው ሳምንት)
4 ከበደ መኪናውን ሼጧል? (ነገ)
5 ልጆቹ ተኝተዋል ። (ካንድ ሰዓት በፊት)
6 ስልሳ ብር ሰጥቼያታለሁ (ተነገ ወዲያ)
7 ሐኪሙ ወረውን ነገረውኛል ። (ዛሬ ማታ)
8 በሸተኞቹ አዲስ ሆስፒታል ሂደዋል ። (ከጥቂት ቀን በኋላ)

Grammar

Relative clauses with prepositions

In the last lesson you learned how to construct and use relative clauses in Amharic such as የምኖርበት ቤት yämminoribbät bet 'the house in which/where I live'. How, though, do you now go on to form phrases such as 'in the house where I live'? You have had an example of this type of phrase in the dialogue in this lesson:

እስከ አይሮፕላን ማረፊያ በሚያስከደው መንገድ
iskä ayroplan maräfiya bämmiyaskedäw mängäd
on the road which leads (leading) to the airport

It was suggested in the last lesson that in Amharic relative clauses work rather like adjectives. You saw, for instance, how a relative verb can occupy the same place as an adjective, and it may have a definite article and an object marker added to it. So, compare the following two phrases:

በረጅሙ መንገድ	bäräjjïmu mängäd	on the long road
በሚያስከደው መንገድ	bämmiyaskedäw mängäd	on the road which takes (you)

Both phrases can be described schematically as:

Preposition +	Adjective Relative Clause	+ Article	+ Noun
በ-	ረጅም	-u	መንገድ
በ-	(የ)ሚያስከድ	-äw	መንገድ

This is why in the phrase በሚያስከደው መንገድ, the preposition በ- bä- 'in, on, by' is added to the front of the relative verb and the article -ው- -w is added to the end, and not simply to the noun itself as in the simple phrase በመንገዱ **bämängädu** 'on the road'.

One important point that you may have noticed, however, is that when the preposition is added to the relative verb, the የ- yä- element of the relative prefix is lost:

በ- + የሚያስከደው መንገድ → በሚያስከደው መንገድ

bä- + yämmiyaskedäw mängäd → bämmiyaskedäw mängäd

This is similar to the rule that says the possessive prefix የ- yä- 'of' is dropped when a preposition is added to a possessive phrase (see lesson three).

In the case of relative verbs, this means that if the verb is a relative past the relative prefix የ- yä- is lost entirely, and if the verb is a relative imperfective only the -ም- -mmi- element remains of the relative prefix የም- yämmi-. Here are some more examples:

Relative past

በተወለድኩበት ቤት	bä*täwällädkubbät* bet
	in the house *where I was born*
ለሰጠኸው ሰውዬ	lä*sät't'ähäw* säwïyye
	to the man *to whom you gave it*
በገዛችው መኪና	bä*gäzzaččïw* mäkina
	in the car *which she bought*
ካየነው ሰው ጋር	ka*yyänäw* säw gar
	together with the man *whom we saw*

Relative imperfective

በምኖርበት ቤት	bä*mmïnoríbbä* bet
	in the house *where I'm living*
በምንጠብቀው ማዘን	bä*mminnit'äbbik'äw* mazän
	on the corner *where we're waiting*
ለምታየው ሰውዬ	lä*mmittayäw* säwïyye
	to the man *whom you'll see*
ከሚያውቁት ተማሪዎች	kä*mmiyawk'ut* tämariwočč
	from the students *who know it*

Further uses of relative verbs

This construction of preposition + relative verb is also used in Amharic to provide the equivalent of a number of subordinate conjunctions in English, such as 'when . . .'. 'after . . .', 'because . . .', 'until . . .', and so on. Here are some useful examples:

(a) Conjunctions with relative past or relative imperfective

Consider the following examples:

ስለ-	sïlä-	because
እንደ-	ïndä-	as (of similarity), according to
		as, as soon as, when (of time, in the past only)

The relative past is used when talking about events that are completed before the 'main' event. Consider the following examples.

ስለመጣህ በጣም ደስ አለኝ	silämät't'ah bät'am däss aläñ
	I am very happy *because you came*
እንዳልኩሽ አደረግሽ?	indalkuš adärrägš?
	did you do *as I told you?*
እንደሰማሁት እንደገና አይመጡም	indäsämmahut indägäna aymät'um
	as I heard, they're not coming again
መስኮቱን እንደከፈትኩ ድመቷ ወጣች	mäskotun indäkäffätkw dïmmätwa wät't'ačč
	the cat went out *as I opened the window*
ክፍሉ እንደገባሁ ሁሉም ተነሣ	kïflu indägäbbahw hullum tänässa
	everyone stood up *when I entered the room*
እንግዶች እንደገቡ ምሳ ይቀርባል	ingïdočč indägäbbu misa yïk'ärbal
	lunch will be served *as soon as the guests have arrived*

The relative imperfective is used when talking about events that are not completed before the 'main' event. Consider the following examples.

ውጭ አገር ስለሚኖሩ እጽፍላቸዋለሁ	wič'č' agär silämminoru is'ifillaččäwallähw
	I'm writing to them *because they're living abroad*

እንደሚመስለኝ ይህ ጥሩ አሳብ ነው·   *indämmimäsläñ* yïh t'ïru assab näw
as it seems to me, this is a good idea

እንደምላችሁ ታደርጋላችሁ·   *indämmilaččuh* tadärgallaččuh you will do *as I tell you*

(b) Conjunctions only with relative past

Consider the following useful examples.

ከ-	kä-	if, since (*of time*), as, since (*of cause*)
ከ- + negative	kä- + negative	unless (*with the same meaning you can also use* ከ- በቀር kä- bäk'är)
ከ- በኋላ	kä- bähwala	after
ከ- በፊት	kä- bäfit	before
በ- ጊዜ	bä- gize	when
በ- ቁጥር	bä- k'ut'ïr	as often as, every time that, whenever
ከ- ወዲህ	kä- wädih	ever since
ከ- ጀምሮ	kä- jämmïro	since, ever since

Examples:

ወደዚህ ከመጣሁ ብዙ ዓመት ነው·   *wädäzzih kämät't'ahw* bïzu amät näw
it's many years *since I came here*

ገንዘቡ ከጠፋበት እቤት ቆይቷል   *gänzäbu kät'äffabbät* ibet k'oyyïtwal
he's been staying at home *since he's lost his money*

ይህን ካልበላህ (በቀር) አትድንም   *yïhïn kalbällah* (bäk'är) attïdïnïm
you won't get well *unless you eat this*

አስተማሪው ከመጡ ጊዜ በሩን ከፈትኩላቸው·   *astämariw kämät't'u gize* bärrun käffätkullaččäw
when the teacher came I opened the door for him

ሐረር በደረስኩ ጊዜ ከሱ ጋር እገናኛለሁ·   *Harär bädärräskw gize* kässu gar iggänaññallähw
I'll meet him *when I arrive/have arrived in Harar*

እንግዶች ከደረሱ በኋላ ቡና ጠጣን	*ingïdočč kädärräsu bähwala bunna t'ät't'an*
	we drank coffee *after the guests arrived*
አልማዝ ከተወለደች በፊት አባትዋ የሞቱባት ናቸው	Almaz *kätäwällädäčč bäfit abbatwa yämotubbat naččäw*
	Almaz's father died *before she was born*
ከተማ በመጣሁ ቁጥር ሲኒማ ቤት እሄዳለሁ	*kätäma bämät'ahw k'ut'ïr* sinima bet ïhedallähw
	I go to the cinema *whenever I come to town*
አደጋ ላይ ከወደቀች ወዲህ ጤና የላትም	*adäga lay käwäddäk'äčč wädih t'ena yällatïm*
	she's not had good health *ever since she had an accident*
እንግሊዝ አገር ከደረስን ጀምሮ ዝናብ ይዘንባል	*Ïngïliz agär kädärräsïn jämmïro zïnab yïzänbal*
	it's been raining *ever since we arrived in England*

Another useful 'conjunction-like' prefix which combines only with the relative past is እየ- *ïyyä-* which means 'while, all the time that'. Do not confuse this እየ- with the እየ- that is added to nouns meaning 'each, every'!

ሁልጊዜ እየሠራ ሲጃራ ያጨሳል	hulgize *ïyyäsärra* sijara yač'äsal
	he always smokes a cigarette *while he's working*

There are other constructions in Amharic corresponding to English conjunctions of this type. You will meet some of these in the next lesson.

Exercises

7 Rewrite the following sentences so that the relative verb in brackets appears in the correct form

1 ነገ ለ(የሚመጡት) እንግዶች ዊስኪ አለ?
2 ባለፈው ሳምንት ከ(የደረሰው) ሰውዬ ጋር ለመናገር እፈልጋለሁ ::

3 በ(የሚመጣው) አሕድ አባትና እናቴን ለመጠየቅ አሔዳለሁ።
4 ለወንድምሽ በ(የምትልኪው) ደብዳቤ ውስጥ ምንድን ነው የተጻፈ?
5 አስቲ ስለ(የምንገማረው) መጽሐፍ ልንገርዎ!
6 አሁን ስለ(ደረስንበት) ቦታ ምንም አላውቅም።

8 Fill in the blanks in the following sentences using the appropriate form of the verb in brackets

1 ትናንትና ዝናብ ስለ_____ ከቤት ውጭ አልወጣሁም። (ዘነበ)
2 ምሳህን እየ_____ መንገር አይገባም! (በላ)
3 ትምህርትህን ደህና አድርገህ ከ_____ በቀር ዩኒቨርሲቲ አትገባም። (ተማረ)
4 ጥዋት ከ_____ በፊት ሬዲዮ እከፍታለሁ። (ነሃ)
5 ጊሩት ገበያ ከ_____ ቁጥር ቡና ትገዛለች። (ሄደ)
6 ነገ ከበደ አብርዋችሁ ስለ_____ እኔ አልሄድም። (መጣ)
7 አሁን እንደ_____ ይህ ያንተ አሳብ ጥሩ አይደለም። (መሰለ)
8 ደብዳቤ በ_____ ጊዜ ሰላምታዬን አልክለታለሁ። (ጻፈ)

Reading passage

የአቶ ንጉሡ ቤተሰብ ማታ ማታ ቴሌቪዥን ከበው እስከ ፕሮግራሙ መጨረሻ ድረስ ማየት በጣም ይወዳሉ። አቶ ንጉሡ ግን ቴሌቪዥን ለማየት ወይም ራዲዮ ለመስማት ፍላጎት የላቸውም። ስለዚህም ዛሬ ማታ እንደልማዳቸው ልጆቻቸው ቴሌቪዥን በከፈቱበት ጊዜ አሳቸው ቶሎ ብለው ወደ ማንበቢያ ክፍላቸው ገብተው መጽሐፍ ወይም መጽሔት ማንበብ ጀመሩ።

አቶ ንጉሡ ሀብታም ነጋዴ ናቸው። አንድ ትልቅ ሆቴል አላቸው። አባታቸውም ነጋዴ፣ እሳቸውም ነጋዴ ሆነው በመቀረታቸው አዝነው ነበር። ነገር ግን ልጃቸው የሕግ ትምህርት ተምር የክፍተኛ ፍርድ ቤትዳኛ ለመሆን ስለሚያስብ በጣም ደስ ብላቸዋል። እሳቸው ራሳቸውም እንደሚሉት፥ «ያለኝ ሀብት ሁሉ ቀርቶብኝ ተራ ሰው ሆኜ ብኖር እወዳለሁ! እውነት ነው፥ ከገላም ሀብት ከገንዘብም ትምህርት ይሻላል።»

Supplementary vocabulary

ቴሊቪዥን, ፕሮግራም and ሆቴል you can easily work out for yourself!

ማታ ማታ	mata mata	every evening
ቤተሰብ	betäsäb	household, family
ፍላጎት	fïllagot	need, want, desire
ልማድ	lïmad	habit, custom
ማንበቢያ ክፍል	manbäbiya kïfïl	reading room, study
መጽሔት	mäs'het	magazine, journal
ቀረ	k'ärrä	remain, be left behind [2-lit² A]
አዘነ	azzänä	be sad [3-lit A]; አዝነው ነበር aznäw näbbär he was sad
ተራ ሰው	tära säw	ordinary, common person
እሳቸው ራሳቸው	ïssaččäw rasaččäw	he himself (*the noun* ራስ ras *literally means* 'head', *but with the possessive pronoun suffixes corresponds to the English emphatic use of* 'self': እኔ ራሴ ine rase I myself; አንተ ራስህ antä rasïh you yourself; እሱ ራሱ ïssu rasu he himself; *and so on.*)
ብኖር	bïnor	*here means* if I was

10 ወደ ሆስፒታል መሔድ
wädä hospital mähed
Going to the hospital

By the end of this lesson you should be able to:

- form the simple imperfect tense and use it in complex sentences equivalent to English 'when', 'if', 'so that', *etc*
- form and use the instrument noun denoting 'the thing with which', or 'the place where you do something'

A visit to the doctor's 📼

Hirut is ill. Kebede is going to take her to hospital. Peter also needs to go to the hospital to get an injection. So he decides to go with them

ጊሩት ታማለች:: ከበደ ወደ ሆስፒታል ሊያደርሳት ነው:: ፒተር ደግሞ መርፌ ለመወጋት ወደ ሆስፒታል መሔድ ያስፈልገዋል:: ስለዚህም አብሮዋቸው ሊሄድ ይወስናል::

ጊሩት: ራቤን አምኛል:: ባለፈው ሳምንት ጉንፋን ይዞኝ ነበር: ራስ ምታቱ ግን እስካሁን አለቀቀኝም:: በጤንነት አይሰማኝም:: እባክህ ሆስፒታል ውሰደኝ::

ከበደ: አሁን ሆስፒታል ልወስድሽ አልቻልም:: ኮሊጅ ልሄድ ነኝ::

ፒተር: እኔም ሆስፒታል ሒጄ መርፌ ለመወጋት አፈልግ ነበር:: ጊሩትንም እኔ ልወስዳት እችላለሁ::

ከበደ: አይ! ግድ የለም: እወስዳታለሁ::

ፒተር: አብሪያቸሁ ልመጣ እችላለሁ?

ከበደ: እንዴታ! ብቻ እስቲ ንገረኝ: ለምንድን ነው መርፌ መወጋት የምትፈልግ? ሰው «መርፌ» ብሎ ሲለኝ ዝም ብዬ መሸሽ ነው!

እሆስፒታል ሲደርሱ ጊሩትን ይዘዋት ወደ መመዘገቢያ ክፍል ሄዱ::

ከበደ፡ ጤና ይስጥልኝ። እህቴ ታማብኛለችና ዶክተር
እንዲያዩዋት እፈልጋለሁ።
አስታማሚ፡ እሺ። ስማቸውን ማን ልበል?
ከበደ፡ ኂሩት ሙሉጌታ።
አስታማሚ፡ እድሜያቸውስ?
ከበደ፡ ሠላሳ ሦስት ዓመት። እባክዎ፡ በጤናዋ አይደለችም።
እባክዎ መጠበቁ ምን ያህል ጊዜ ይፈጃል?
አስታማሚ፡ ዶክተር እስኪጠሩዎ እማረፊያው ክፍል ውስጥ ትንሽ
ይጠብቁ። ብዙ ጊዜ አይፈጅም፡ ምናልባት ቢበዛ
ከአሥር ደቂቃ በላይ አይሆንም።

ከአንድ ሰዓት በኋላ አስተማሚዋ መጥታ ለኂሩት ዶክተር አሁን
ያዩዎታል ትላታለች።

ፒተር፡ አስተማሚዋ ያለችን ካሥር ደቂቃ በላይ አይፈጅም ነው።
ቢያንስ አንድ ሰዓት ነው እዚህ የምንቆይ!
ከበደ፡ በኛ አገር ብቻ ሳይሆን በሌላው አገር እንደዚህ ነው
አይደለም?
ዶክተር፡ ጤና ይስጥልኝ። ምን ይሰማዎታል? ትኩሳት አለብዎ?
ዬት ላይ ነው የሚሰማዎት?
ኂሩት፡ ራሴን በኃይል ያመኛል። ደግሞም ሣል አለብኝ።
በምሥል ጊዜ ጉሮሮዬን ያመኛል።
ዶክተር፡ ትኩሳትዎን እለካልዎታለሁ። ... እባክዎ አሁን ምርመራ
እንዳደርግልዎ እዚህ ላይ ጋደም ይበሉ። ልብስ ማውልቅ
አያስፈልግም። ...እሺ ሕመምዎ ከባድ አይደለም -
መድኃኒት እሰጥዎታለሁ፡ አንድ ኪኒን ጥዋት ሲነሡ
አንድ ደግሞ ሌሊት ሲተኙ ይዋጡ።
ኂሩት፡ እንደገና ለመመለስ ያስፈልገኛል?
ዶክተር፡ የለም፡ ካልጻኑ በቀር ለመመለስ አያስፈልግም።

Hirut: *My head hurts. Last week I caught a cold, but the headache hasn't disappeared so far! I don't feel well. Please take me to hospital.*
Kebbede: *I can't take you to hospital now. I'm on my way to college.*
Peter: *I have to go to hospital, too. I'd like to get an injection. I can take Hirut if she wants.*
Kebbede: *No, don't worry, I'll take her.*
Peter: *In that case, can I come too?*
Kebbede: *Of course! But tell me, why do you want an injection? When someone says 'injection' to me I've just got to run away!*

When they arrive at the hospital, they take Hirut to the registration

KEBBEDE: *Hello, can you help us please? My sister has fallen ill on me and I'd like the doctor to see her.*

NURSE: *Alright. What's her name?*

KEBBEDE: *Hirut Mulugeta.*

NURSE: *And her age?*

KEBBEDE: *Thirty-three years. Please, she isn't well. About how long will we have to wait?*

NURSE: *Wait a little in the waiting room until the doctor calls you. It won't take long, perhaps at most it'll be ten minutes.*

After an hour the nurse comes and tells Hirut that the doctor will see her now

PETER: *The nurse told us that it wouldn't take more than ten minutes. We've been waiting at least an hour!*

KEBBEDE: *It's like this in other countries, isn't it, not only in our country?*

DOCTOR: *Hello. How are you feeling? Do you have a temperature? And are you in pain?*

HIRUT: *My head hurts a great deal. I've got a cough as well, so that when I cough my throat hurts me.*

DOCTOR: *I'll take your temperature for you . . . Now please lie down for me so that I can give you an examination. There's no need to undress . . . Alright, your sickness is not serious – I'll give you some medicine. Take one pill in the morning when you get up, one pill at night when you go to bed.*

HIRUT: *Do I need to come back another time?*

DOCTOR: *No, there's no need to come back unless you're no better.*

Vocabulary

መርፌ	märfe	needle, injection
መርፌ ወጋ	märfe wägga	give an injection (ወጋ wägga *lit.* 'stab, prick' [2-lit¹ A])
መርፌ ተወጋ	märfe täwägga	be given, receive an injection (ተወጋ [derived stem from ወጋ]: infinitive መወጋት mäwwägat)
ጉንፋን	gunfan	cold, flu
ጉንፋን ያዘኝ	gunfan yazäñ	I caught a cold (*lit.* 'a cold caught me')
ራስ ምታት	ras mïtat	headache
እድሜ	ïdme	age

መመዝገቢያ ክፍል	mämäzgäbiya kifil	registration (room)
ማረፊያ ክፍል	maräfiya kifil	waiting room
ትኩሳት, ትኵሳት	tïkkusat	fever
ሙቀት	muk'ät	heat, temperature
ሙቀት ለካ	muk'ät läkka	measure, take (someone's) temperature; *you can also say:* ትኩሳት ለካ tïkkusat läkka
ሙቀት/ትኩሳት	muk'ät / tïkkusat	thermometer
መለኪያ	mäläkkiya	
ምርመራ	mïrmära	check up, examination (*cf. the verb* መረመረ märämmärä examine [4-lit])
(የሕክምና)	[yähïkmïnna]	mïrmära adärrägä – give someone a
ምርመራ አደረገ		(medical) check up
ሕክምና	hïkmïnna	medicine (*the science*), medical treatment
መድኃኒት, መዳኒት	mädhanit, mädanit	medicine, drug, remedy
ጉሮሮ	gurorro	throat
ከባድ	käbbad	difficult, serious, heavy
ኪኒን	kinin	pill
ሕመም	hïmäm	illness

Particles

ደግሞ, ደም	dägmo, dämmo	also, besides, moreover, too
ያህል	yahïl	about, approximately (*see note 3*)
በኃይል	bähayl	extremely, strongly, vehemently (*lit.* 'with strength')

Verbs

አመመ	ammämä	hurt, ache, be sore [3-lit A]; *remember the use of* አመመ *as an impersonal verb* አመመኝ ammämäñ I am ill and ራሴን አመመኝ rasen ammämäñ my head hurts (*lit.* 'I am ill in the head' (*see note 1*))
ታመመ	tammämä	fall ill, become ill [derived stem from አመመ] gerundive ታሞ tammo
ወሰነ	wässänä	decide, delimit [3-lit A]
ለቀቀ	läk'k'äk'ä	leave, abandon [3-lit A]
ተሰማ	täsämma	feel [impersonal verb, derived stem] compound imperfect ይሰማኛል yïssämmaññal I feel

በጤንነት አይሰማኝም	bät'enïnnät ayïssämmaññïm	I don't feel well – 'I do not feel in (good) health'
ሸሸ	šäššä	run away, flee [2-lit² B] – NB infinitive መሸሸ mäšäš
ፈጀ	fäjjä	use up, take (time) [2-lit² A]
ለካ	läkka	measure [2-lit¹ B]
ሳለ	salä	cough [2-lit³] – compare the noun ሳል sal 'a cough' (see note 4)
አወለቀ	awälläk'ä	undress, take something off – ልብስ አወለቀ lïbs awälläk'ä 'take one's clothes off'. አወለቀ is a derived stem – infinitive ማውለቅ mawläk'
ዋጠ	wat'ä	swallow, take medicine [2-lit³]
ተነሳ	tänässa	get up, set out [derived stem] – compound imperfect ይነሳል yïnnässal; ሲነሱ sinnässu 'when you (formal) get up (see grammar section)
ዳነ	danä	get well, be saved [2-lit³]

Phrases

ግድ የለም	gïdd yälläm	never mind, don't worry (lit. 'there's no compulsion')
ስማቸውን ማን ልበል	sïmaččäwn man lïbäl	what's her name (lit. 'whom should I say her name is?'). ልበል lïbäl is from the irregular verb አለ alä say.
ቢበዛ	bibäza	at most (lit. 'if it is a lot' – see grammar section – from በዛ bäzza [2-lit¹ A])
ቢያንስ	biyans	at least – lit. 'if it is a little' from አነሰ annäsä [3-lit A]
ብቻ ሳይሆን	bičča sayhon	not only (lit. 'without it being only' – see grammar section)
ጋደም ይበሉ	gadämm yïbälu	lie down (formal request form) from ጋደም አለ gadämm alä [composite verb with አለ 'say']

Notes on the dialogue

1 The expression ራሴን አሞኛል **rasen ammoññal** 'my head hurts, I have a pain in my head' means literally 'it has hurt me in my head'. The direct object suffix -ን **-n** is used here in an adverbial or specifying sense. Below are some other idioms that use -ን **-n** in a similar way.

እጇዋን ታጠበች	**ïjwan tat't'äbäčč**	she washed her hands (*lit.* 'she washed herself on her hand')
ልቤን ታመምኩ	**lïbben tammämkw**	I fell ill in my heart
እግሩን ተጉዳ	**ïgrun tägwädda**	he injured his leg (*lit.* 'he injured himself in his leg')
ልጇዋን ልብሱን አለበሰች	**lïjwan lïbsun aläbbäsäčč**	she dressed her child in his clothes
ብርጭቆውን ሻይ ሞላች	**bïrč'ïk'k'own šay mollačč**	she filled his glass with tea
ብቻዬን ተመለስኩ	**bïččayen tämälläskw**	I returned on my own

2 Remember that doubled or geminate consonants are not written separately in the Ethiopian script, even when they arise where a prefix or suffix is added. So, for example, the word አለቀቀኝም in the dialogue represents **alläk'k'äk'äññïm**, the negative of ለቀቀኝ **läk'k'äk'äñ**, in which the **l** of the negative prefix አል- **al-** comes into direct contact with the **l** of the verb base.

3 Note that the word ያህል **yahïl**, which means 'about, approximately', always follows the word or words which indicate the quantity approximated:

ሦስት ያህል ቀን ትቆያለች	**sost yahïl k'än tïk'wäyyalläčč** she'll be staying for about three days
መቶ ያህል ብር አወጡ	**mäto yahïl bïrr awät't'u** they spent about a hundred birr
ሠላሳ ሺ ያህል ሰው አልቋል	**sälasa ši yahïl säw alk'wal** about thirty thousand people have perished

ያህል is also used in the expression ይህን ያህል **yïhïn yahïl** 'this much, so much':

ይህን ያህል ገንዘብ አወጣች yïhïn yahïl gänzäb awät't'ačč
she spent this much money
(*lit.* 'she spent about this money')

And in the phrase ምን ያህል mïn yahïl, as in the question Kebbede asks:

ምን ያህል ጊዜ ይፈጃል?   mïn yahïl gize yïfäjal?
how long will it take?
(*lit.* 'about what time will it take?')

4 There are two verbs salä – (i) ሣለ salä 'cough', and (ii) ሳለ salä 'paint'. In order to make it quite clear in speech which one you mean, it is usual to add the corresponding noun associated with each verb as a direct object: ሣል ሣለ sal salä – *lit.* 'he coughed a cough'; but ስዕል (ስል) ሳለ sïil (sïl) salä – *lit.* 'he painted a picture'.

Grammar

The simple imperfect tense

So far you have encountered various uses of the simple imperfect tense:

(a) as the base of the compound imperfect (ይበላል yïbä*la*l he eats)
(b) as the base of the negative imperfect (አይበላም ay*bä*lam he doesn't eat)
(c) as the base of the relative imperfect (የሚበላ yämmi*bä*la who eats)
(d) joined by -ና to a compound imperfect (ይበላና ይጠጣል yïbä*la*nna yït'ät't'al he eats and drinks)

Another important use of the simple imperfect is to combine with prefixes that are equivalent to English conjunctions such as 'when', 'if', 'so that', and the like. You will see that this is quite different from English, where 'if', 'when', and so on, are separate words. Below are some examples of this use of the simple imperfect that you have met so far:

ልናሳይህ እንፈልጋለን	*lïnnasayyïh innïfälligallän*	we want to show you
የተገመሰች ሲሆን	*yätägämmäsäčč sihon*	whilst it is divided

ለያደርሳት ነው	liyadärsat näw	he is going to take her
እንዲሄድ ይቀርጣል	indihed yïk'wärt'al	he decides to go
ልወስድሽ አይቻልም	lïwäsdiš ayïččalïm	it isn't possible for me to take you
ሰው «መርፌ» ሲለኝ	säw 'märfe' silän	when someone says 'injection' to me
እንዲያዩዋት ይቻላል	indiyayuwat yïččalal	is it possible for him to see her

See if you can find some more similar to these in the dialogue in this lesson.

This use of the simple imperfect and the first three uses in the list above are the commonest ones, which means that more often than not you will not come across a simple imperfect tense in its 'bare' form without some additional prefixed or suffixed element. However, to remind you, here is the simple imperfect of ደረሰ där-räsä 'to arrive' [3-lit A]:

			person marker	stem
1st pers. sing.	እደርስ	ïdärs	ï-	-därs-
2nd pers. masc.	ትደርስ	tïdärs	tï-	"
2nd pers. fem.	ትደርሺ	tïdärši	tï- . . . -i	"
3rd pers. masc.	ይደርስ	yïdärs	yï-	"
3rd pers. fem.	ትደርስ	tïdärs	tï-	"
1st pers. pl.	እንደርስ	ïnnïdärs	ïnnï-	"
2nd pers. pl.	ትደርሱ	tïdärsu	tï- . . . -u	"
3rd pers. pl.	ይደርሱ	yïdärsu	yï- . . . -u	"

Points to note

1 The second person masculine and third person feminine forms are always identical: ትደርስ tïdärs 'you (አንተ) arrive' or 'she arrives'.

2 If the stem ends in one of the palatalizable consonants (t, d, t', s', s, z, n, l) then this consonant is palatalized in the second person feminine form: ትደርሺ tïdärši 'you (አንቺ) arrive'; ትወስሺ tïwäsji 'you take'; ትከፍዪ tïkäfyi 'you pay'; ትመርጪ tïmärč'i 'you choose'; and so on.

3 Remember to add the -u suffix in the second and third persons plural.

There are five of these prefixes in Amharic that combine directly
with the simple imperfect tense and which are equivalent to English
conjunctions:

ብ-	bï-	if	ብንመጣ	bïnnïmät'a	if we come, came ...
ስ-	sï-	when, while	ስንመጣ	sïnnïmät'a	when we come, came ...
ል-	lï-	so that	ልንመጣ	lïnnïmät'a	so that we come
እንድ-	indï-	so that	እንድንመጣ	indïnnïmät'a	so that we come
እስከ-	iskï-	until	እስከንመጣ	iskïnnïmät'a	until we come

ል- lï- and እንድ- ïndï- basically have the same meaning and are
sometimes interchangeable. Generally speaking, however, ል- lï- is
used when its subject and that of the main verb are the same, whilst
እንድ- ïndï- is preferred when the two subjects are different. To see
what this means compare the following pair of sentences:

ገበያ ልሄድ እፈልጋለሁ   gäbäya lïhed ïfälligallähw
                                         I want to go to market (*lit.* '*I* want
                                         that *I* go ...')

ገበያ እንድትሄድ እፈልጋለሁ   gäbäya ïndïttïhed ïfälligallähw
                                         I want her to go to market (*lit.* '*I*
                                         want that *she* goes ...')

These prefixes combine with the simple imperfect in exactly the
same way as the relative prefix የም- yämmï-, which you met in
lesson eight. So, if you substitute b- for yämm- in the table in lesson
eight you arrive at the following set of forms from the verb መጣ
mät't'a 'come'.

ብመጣ	bïmät'a	if I come ...
ብትመጣ	bïttïmät'a, bïtmät'a	if you come ...
ብትመጪ	bïttïmäč'i, bïtmäč'i	if you come ...
ቢመጣ	bïmät'a	if he comes ...
ብትመጣ	bïttïmät'a, bïtmät'a	if she comes ...
ብንመጣ	bïnnïmät'a	if we come ...
ብትመጡ	bïttïmät'u, bïtmät'u	if you come ...
ቢመጡ	bïmät'u	if they come ...

ባልመጣ	balmät'a	if I don't come ...
ባትመጣ	battïmät'a	if you don't come ...

ባትመጪ	battïmäč'i	if you don't come . . .
ባይመጣ	baymät'a	if he doesn't come . . .
ባትመጣ	battïmät'a	if she doesn't come . . .
ባንመጣ	bannïmät'a	if we don't come . . .
ባትመጡ	battïmät'u	if you don't come . . .
ባይመጡ	baymät'u	if they don't come . . .

Please note that negative tenses after prefix conjunctions do not have the final -ም -m: አይመጣም aymät'am 'he isn't coming' but ባይመጣ baymät'a 'if he isn't coming', etc.

Remember that with verbs beginning in a- the rules of vowel hierarchy will apply, just as they do in combination with the relative prefix የም-. Here, too, you need to pay special attention to the third person masculine and third person plural forms! To remind you what this involves have a look at the affirmative simple imperfect of አወቀ 'know' with ብ-:

ባውቅ	bawk'	if I know	ብናውቅ	bïnnawk'	if we know
ብታውቅ	bïttawk'	if you know	ብታውቁ	bïttawk'u	if you know
ብታውቂ	bïttawk'i	if you know			
ቢያውቅ	biyawk'	if he knows	ቢያውቁ	biyawk'u	if they know
ብታወቅ	bïttawk'	if she knows			

Similarly:

with ስ-	→ ስመጣ	sïmät'a	when I come, when I came
with ል-	→ ልመጣ	lïmät'a	so that I come, in order for me to come, (for me) to come
with እንድ-	→ እንድመጣ	indïmät'a	so that I come, in order for me to come, (for me) to come
with እስክ-	→ እስክመጣ	iskïmät'a	until I come

These prefixes are always attached to the simple imperfect tense. Whether you are talking about present, future or past events, in Amharic the verb remains in the simple imperfect tense. Look at the following examples, notice how the equivalent of the Amharic verb with ብ-, ስ-, ል-, etc., can appear in the English in various tenses.

ሐዲስ ቢመጣ ወዲያው ንገረኝ   Haddis *bimät'a* wädiyaw nïgärañ
                              if Haddis comes tell me at once

ሥራዋን በደንብ ብትሠራ ነገ እከፍላታለሁ	sïrawan bädänb *bïttïsära* nägä ïkäflatallähw *if she's done* her work properly I'll pay her tomorrow
ገንዘቡን ባገኝ እሰጣት ነበC	gänzäbun *bagäñ* ïsät'at näbbär *if I had found* the money I would give it to her
እቃውን ሲያመጣ እከፍለዋለሁ	ïk'awn *siyamät'a* ïkäfläwallähw I'll pay him *when he brings* the things
ስሥል (ጊዜ) ጉርC ያመኛል	*sïsïl* (gize) gurorro yammäññal *when I cough* my throat hurts (me)
ጋዜጣ ሳነብ እልማዝ መጣች	gazet'a *sanäbb* Almaz mät't'ačč Almaz came *when I was reading* the paper
ከበደ ከተማ ሲሄድ ከረሜላ ይዞ መጣ	Käbbädä kätäma *sihed* kärämella yïzo mät't'a *when Kebbede went* to town he brought some sweets back
እስኪደክመው ሙሉ ቀን ሠራ	*ïskidäkmäw* mulu k'än särra he worked the whole day *until he was* tired
እስኪመጡ እዚህ እቆያለሁ	*ïskimät'u* ïzzih ïk'wäyyallähw I'll wait here *until they come*
ልበላ እሠራለሁ	*lïbäla* ïsärallähw I work *in order to eat*
ወረቀት ልንገዛ ከተማ ሄድን	wäräk'ät *lïnnïgäza* kätäma hedïn we went to town *to buy* some paper
ጉንፋን እንዳይዘው ኪኒን ዋጠ	gunfan *ïndayyïzäw* kinin wat'ä he took pills *so as not to catch* a cold

It is worth recalling here that we now have three different ways of expressing '(in order) to':

ለ- + simple imperfect

እባቱን ሊረዳ ይፈልጋል	abbatun lïräda yïfälligal he wants to help his father

እንድ- + simple imperfect

እናትዋን እንድረዳ ትፈልጋለች   innatwan indïräda tïfällïgalläčč
                she wants me to help her mother

ለ- + infinitive

ልጆቻችንን ለመርዳት እንፈልጋለን   lïjjoččaččïnïn lämärdat
                ïnnïfällïgallän
                we want to help our children

Translating 'before', 'without'

You will need to pay particular attention to the meaning of the combination of ስ- sï- and the negative simple imperfect, as for example ሳይበላ saybäla. This does not mean 'when he doesn't/didn't eat', but 'before he eats/ate' or 'without (him) eating'. Consider the following:

እራቱን ሳይበላ ተኛ   ïratun saybäla tänña
                      he went to bed without eating his
                      supper
መስጊድ ሳንገባ (በፊት)   mäsgid sannïgäba (bäfit) č'amma
ጫማ እናወልቃለን   ïnnawälk'allän
                      we take our shoes off before going
                      into a mosque

Some further uses of the simple imperfect

One place where the simple imperfect is used without any additions is in combination with a small number of what are called 'auxiliary' verbs. You have already met one example in the dialogue where Peter says መርፌ ለመወጋት እፈልግ ነበር märfe lämäwwägat ïfällïg näbbär 'I would like to get an injection'. The combination of the simple imperfect tense (here እፈልግ) and ነበር usually implies a continuous or habitual event in the past, such as is expressed in English by phrases like 'he was going' or 'he used to go' – in Amharic, ይሄድ ነበር yïhed näbbär. Below are some examples of this usage:

በየሳምንቱ አስተማሪያችን ፈትና ይሰጠን ነበር   bäyyäsammïntu
                astämariyaččïn fätäna yïsät'än näbbär
                our teacher used to give us a test every week
ገበሬው እርሻውን ይቆፍር ነበር   gäbärew ïršawn yïk'offïr näbbär
                  the farmer was digging his field

The particular example in the dialogue, አፈለግ ነበር, illustrates another use of this combination, corresponding to English 'would'. In other words, አፈለግ ነበር is also a more polite way of saying አፈልጋለሁ, rather like English 'I would like' as against 'I want'.

አፈለግ ነበር	ïfällīg näbbär	I was wanting, I would like
ተፈለግ ነበር	tïfällïg näbbär	you were wanting, you would like
ተፈለጊ ነበር	tïfällïgi näbbär	you were wanting, you would like
ይፈለግ ነበር	yïfällïg näbbär	he was wanting, he would like
ተፈለግ ነበር	tïfällïg näbbär	she was wanting, she would like
እንፈለግ ነበር	ïnnïfällïg näbbär	we were wanting, we would like
ተፈለት ነበር	tïfällïgu näbbär	you were wanting, you would like
ይፈለት ነበር	yïfällïgu näbbär	they were wanting, they would like

You can see that the word ነበር näbbär remains unchanged throughout and only the simple imperfect changes according to which person is the subject.

The simple imperfect in the expression of 'began to . . .'

Another similar use of the simple imperfect is in combination with ጀመር jämmär, which also remains unchanged, in the meaning 'began to'.

አልማዝ ቡና ታፈላ ጀመር   Almaz bunna tafäla jämmär
Almaz started to make coffee

ልጆች ይሮጡ ጀመር   lïjjočču yïrot'u jämmär
the children began to run

In order to say 'begin to', however, you are not restricted to this construction; you can also use the infinitive + ጀመረ, or ል- + simple imperfect + ጀመረ. Be careful, though, to remember that in these patterns the verb ጀመረ is fully inflected:

አልማዝ ቡና ማፍላት ጀመረች   Almaz bunna maflat jämmäräčč
Almaz started to make coffee

ገዲቱ ቤቱን መጥረግ ትጀምራለች   gärädïtu betun mät'räg tïjämmïralläčč
the maid is starting to sweep the house

The expression of 'may, might . . .'

A third combination of the simple imperfect and a fixed auxiliary verb is with ይሆናል **yïhonal** or ይሆን **yïhon**, expressing doubt about whether something will happen or not – 'probably will' or 'may possibly'. Consider these examples:

ነገ አመለስ ይሆናል	nägä ïmmälläs yïhonal
	I'll probably come back tomorrow
ዛሬ ማታ አማረች አትወጣም ይሆናል	zare mata Amaräčč attïwät'am yïhonal
	Amarech may not go out this evening
እዚያ ጥሩ ሙዚቃ እንሰማ ይሆናል	ïzziya t'ïru muzik'a ïnnïsäma yïhonal
	we'll maybe hear some good music there
ነገ ይዘንብ ይሆን?	nägä yïzänb yïhon?
	Is it likely to rain tomorrow?

The expression 'be about to'

Kebbede tells Hirut ኮሌጅ ልሄድ ነኝ **kolej lïhed näñ** 'I'm about to go to college', illustrating yet another construction involving the simple imperfect. This time the pattern is:

ል- + simple imperfect + ነው, etc.
ልሄድ ነኝ

The verb ነው can either remain as a fixed form, or can be in the same person as the ል- + simple imperfect, as in the example. When talking about the past, ነበር **näbbär** is substituted for ነው:

በቅርቡ አሜሪካን	bäk'ïrbu amerikan	we're shortly to be going
አገር ልንሄድ ነው	agär lïnnïhed näw	to America
ልጠራችሁ ነበር	lït'äraččuh näbbär	I was about to call you

The same idea of an event that is about to happen, or one that has to be done, can be expressed by using the infinitive and ነው. In this case you can add the appropriate possessive pronoun suffix to the infinitive to indicate the subject. Look at the following examples:

አዲስ መኪና መግዛት ነው   addis mäkina mägzat näw
you (I, we . . .) must buy a new car

ምሳ መብላታችን ነው   mïsa mäblataččïn näw
we're about to have lunch

ይኸው መሄዴ ነው   yïhäw mähede näw
look, I'm just about to go

Exercises

1 Substitute the verb in brackets for a 'when' clause with ስ-
to complete the sentences

> *Example:* አልማዝ ከተማ (ሔደ) አዲስ ጫማ ትገዛለች።
> → አልማዝ ከተማ ስትሔድ አዲስ ጫማ ትገዛለች።

1 አንተ ደብዳቤ (ጻፈ) ብዙ ጊዜ ይፈጃል።
2 ተረፈ ወደ ጂማ (ሔደ) በርበሬ ይዞ መጣ።
3 ገረዲቱ ቤቱን (ጠረገ) ከመምበር በታች ሃያ ብር አገኘች።
4 እኛ ግሜሪካን አገር (ሔደ) ጊዜ ገራንድ ካንዮን ለማየት ፈለግን።
5 እነዚህ ተማሪዎች ጥያቄ (ጠየቀ) ሌሎች ይስቃሉ።
6 ድንቅነሽ ሙዚቃ (ሰማ) ልትዘፍን ትፈልጋለች።
7 አውቶቡስ (መጣ) ሁሉም ገንዶ ላይ ለመውጣት ሞከረ።

2 Use one of the constructions meaning 'in order to' to
complete the following sentences. Be sure to vary the
construction you use

1 እርስዎ አዲስ መኪና _____ ይፈልጋሉ?
2 ቲያትር _____ ነው የመጣነው።
3 ሙዚቃ _____ ትወጃለሽ?
4 ወደ ትምሕርት ቤት _____ አልፈለግንም።
5 ልጁን _____ የማታስቡ ስለምን ነው?
6 ሊጋው እንጀራ _____ ገንዘቡን ሠረቀ።

3 Turn the underlined verbs in the following sentences into
the negative form and then translate them into English. (You
might need to look some vocabulary up in the glossary)

1 ዛሬ ቢዘንብ ካባትና እናቴ ጋር ወደ መናፈሻ ቦታ አብረን እንሄዳለን ፡፡

2 ይህን ለማድረግ <u>ብትፈልግ</u> ፈቃድ ያስፈልጋል ፡፡

3 ይህን የመሰለ ነገር <u>እንዲደርስብህ</u> ተስፋ አደርጋለሁ ፡፡

4 ጋዜጣ <u>ሲያነብ</u> እንቅልፍ ወሰደው ፡፡

5 ወደ ውጭ አገር <u>እንድንንዝ</u> ተፈቅዶልናል ፡፡

4 Rewrite the following statements and questions following the pattern of the examples, and then translate them into English

> *Example:* ነገ ይደውልልሻል → ነገ ይደውልልሽ ይሆናል
> he might ring you tomorrow

1 ነገ ከሰዓት በኋላ አቶ ለማ ፋብሪካ ይጎበኟሉ ፡፡

2 የተማሪዎች ቁጥር አየተጨመረ ይሄዳል ፡፡

3 አዚህ ሆቴል ውስጥ በጣም ጥሩ መዚቃ እንሰማለን?

4 ቱንፋን ስለያዘኝ ቤቱ ውስጥ አቤያለሁ ፡፡

> *Example:* ምሳዋን በልታለች → ምሳዋን ትበላ ጀመር
> she began to eat her lunch

1 ገረዲቱ እጅዋን ታጠበች ፡፡

2 አጎላፈው ላሕኑን በጨርቅ ጠረገ ፡፡

3 ትናንትና ቤቱን ቀባሁት ፡፡

4 ልጆቹ የገዛ አልጋቸውን ዘረጉ ፡፡

> *Example:* አዲስ ቀሚስ አፈልጋለሁ → አዲስ ቀሚስ አፈልግ ነበር
> I would like a new dress

1 ለዮሐንስ ደብዳቤ አጽፋለሁ ፡፡

2 አቶ አብዱልመጂድ የቤቱን ኪራይ ይከፍላሉ ፡፡

3 አልማዝ መኪና ቶሎ ቶሎ ትነዳለች ፡፡

4 ተረፈ ቢገባ አኛ ሬዲዮን እንሰማለን? ፡፡

5 Here are a few Amharic proverbs, each of which contains a simple imperfect verb with ብ-, ስ- or እ-. Identify the verb(s) in each case, give the dictionary form, and then try and translate the proverb into English. (Note: the language of Amharic proverbs is often highly condensed. Also, the normal patterns of word order are frequently disrupted)

1 በሬ ሆይ ሣሩን እየህ ገደሉን ሳታይ ::
2 ሃብታም ሲወድቅ ከስገነት ፣ ድሃ ሲወድቅ ከመሬት ::
3 ለሰው ብትል ትጠፋለህ ፣ ለገዛር ብትል ትለማለህ ::
4 ሳይጣሩ ማንበብ ፣ ሳይበሉ መጥገብ ::
5 ዝምብ ሲሰበሰብ መግላሊት አይከፍት ::
6 ወንድ ለበላ ቤት ሊግ ::
7 ዓሣ ብለምነው ዘንዶ ፣ ዝናም ብለምነው በረዶ ::

Here is some vocabulary to help you

ሆይ	hoy	*a vocative particle*: በሬ ሆይ bäre hoy oh ox!
ሰገነት	sägännät	balcony
መሬት	märet	ground, earth
ለማ	lämma	prosper, flourish [2-lit[1] A]
ጠገበ	t'äggäbä	be satisfied, full (*of food and drink*) [3-lit A]
ዝምብ	zïmb	fly (*insect*)
መግላሊት	mäglalit	lid
ዘንዶ	zändo	python
በረዶ	bärädo	hail

Grammar

The instrument noun

In the dialogue you met the word መመዝገቢያ in the phrase መመዝገቢያ ክፍል mämäzgäbiya kïfïl 'registration room'. This is a regular derivation from the verb መዘገበ mäzäggäbä [4-lit] 'register' and is called the instrument noun, because it designates the means or instrument with which, or sometimes, as here, the place where you do something.

So, for example, መጀመሪያ mäjämmäriya is literally 'the means by which you begin something', in other words 'the beginning'. You have already met a few other examples of instrument nouns: ማረፊያ

maräfiya in አድርፕላን ማረፊያ 'airport', or ማረፊያ ክፍል 'waiting room' from አረፈ arräfä 'rest'; መለኪያ mäläkkiya in ትኩሳት መለኪያ 'thermometer' from ለካ läkka 'measure'; ማዘጋጃ mazzägajja in ማዘጋጃቤት 'town hall' from አዘጋጀ azzägajjä 'arrange'; መናፈሻ män-nafäša in መናፈሻ ቦታ 'park' from ተናፈሰ tänaffäsä 'go for a stroll, take the air' (ነፋስ näfas is 'wind').

Here are some more examples that you will find useful:

መግቢያ	mägbiya	entrance	from ገባ gäbba come in
መውጫ	mäwč'a	exit	from ወጣ wät't'a go out
መጨረሻ	mäč'ärräša	end	from ጨረሰ č'ärräsä finish
መጀመሪያ	mäjämmäriya	beginning	from ጀመረ jämmärä begin
መክፈቻ	mäkfäča	(can/bottle) opener	from ከፈተ käffätä open
መክደኛ	mäkdäña	lid, cover	from ከደነ käddänä cover
መጥረጊያ	mät'rägiya	broom	from ጠረገ t'ärrägä sweep
መስቀያ	mäsk'äya	(coat) hanger	from ሰቀለ säk'k'älä hang
መላጫ	mälač'a	razor	from ላጨ lač'ä shave
ማቆሚያ	mak'omiya	stop, stopping place	from አቆመ ak'omä stop
መሳቂያ	mäsak'iya	laughing stock	from ሳቀ sak'ä laugh
መቀመጫ	mäk'k'ämäč'a	seat, stool	from ተቀመጠ täk'ämmät'ä sit
ማስታወቂያ	mastawäk'iya	information, notice	from አስታወቀ astawwäk'ä inform
መሥሪያ (ቤት)	mäsriya (bet)	office	from ሠራ särra work
መሣሪያ	mässariya	tool, equipment	also from ሠራ särra work, but slightly irregular in formation

Sometimes the instrumental noun is joined to another noun with the possessive preposition የ-, or is used as an adjective with another noun to form a compound:

የማጠቢያ መኪና	yämat'äbiya mäkina	washing machine
ያውቶቡስ መቆሚያ	yawtobus mäk'omiya	bus stop
የመገንቢያ መሣሪያ	yämägänbiya mässariya	building materials
መኖሪያ ቤት	mänoriya bet	dwelling, residence

The instrumental noun is formed on the same stem as the infinitive by means of the prefix **mä-** together with the suffix **-iya / -ya**. If the verb stem ends in one of the palatalizable consonants (**t, t', d, s, s', z, n, l**) then it is palatalized and the suffix **-ya** is shortened to **-a**. Also, if the verb stem already ends in a palatal consonant (**č, č', j, š, ž, ñ, y**) the suffix **-ya** is shortened to **-a**.

On stems which do not palatalize, it is optional whether you use **-iya** or simply **-ya**: መፕረጊያ mät'rägiya, or መፕረጋያ mät'rägya. For convenience, only **-iya** forms are given in the table.

	Example		Prefix stem	Suffix	Infinitive
3-lit A	መፕረጊያ	mät'rägiya	mä-	-t'räg-	-(i)ya	መፕረግ
3-lit B	መጀመሪያ	mäjämmäriya	mä-	-jämmär-	-(i)ya	መጀመር
2-lit¹ A	መሥሪያ	mäsriya	mä-	-sr-	-iya	መሥራት
2-lit¹ B	መለኪያ	mäläkkiya	mä-	-läkk-	-iya	መለካት
2-lit² A	መስጫ	mäsč'a	mä-	-st'-	-ya	መስጣት
2-lit² B	መለያ	mäläyya	mä-	-läyy-	-(y)a	መለየት
2-lit³	መሳቂያ	mäsak'iya	mä-	-sak'-	-(i)ya	መሳቅ
2-lit⁴	መሄጃ	mäheja	mä-	-hed-	-ya	መሄድ
2-lit⁵	መኖሪያ	mänoriya	mä-	-nor-	-(i)ya	መኖር
4-lit	መመዝገቢያ	mämäzgäbiya	mä-	mäzgäb-	-(i)iya	መመዝገብ
3-lit X	መገንቢያ	mägänbiya	mä-	gänb-	-iya	መገንባት
3-lit Y	መጉብኛ	mägwäbña	mä-	gwäbñ-	-(y)a	መጉብኘት

Exercises

6 Match up the list of instrument nouns with the common nouns that follow and then form sentences following the pattern of the example to describe what each is used for (you will need to look some words up in the glossary at the end of the book)

> *Example:* መግቢያ : ሰው በመግቢያ ይገባል፡ ለምሳሌ በር መግቢያ ነው ።

---

1 መቀመጫ	5 መተኛ	9 የሰዓት መቁጠሪያ
2 ሜሒ ዣ	6 መጻፊያ	10 መክፈቻ
3 መጠጫ	7 መስፊያ	11 መኖሪያ
4 ማንበቢያ	8 የዕቃ መግዣ	12 መለኪያ

ሰዓት፡ አልጋ፡ ወንበር፡ ቁልፍ፡ ቤት፡ ብርጭቆ፡ መርፌ፡ ሜትር፡ እርሳስ፡ ገንዘብ፡ መንገድ፡ መጽሐፍ ።

7 Translate the short passage below into English and then answer the following questions about it in Amharic

አብዛኛውን ጊዜ አንድ ሰው ጉንፋን ሲይዘው ብዙ ያነጥስና ጉርርሩን ያሞታል ። ከዚህም በላይ ምናልባት ትኩሳት ይሰማዋል ። እንጻንደቾም ጉንፋን እንደያዛቸው ከሥራ ቀርተው አልጋ ላይ ወጥተው ይተኛሉ ። ጉንፋን የያዘው ሰው ደግሞ ሲስልና ሲያጥስ አፋንና አፍንጫውን በመሐረብ መሸፈን አለበት ። ያለዚያም በሽታው ወደ ሌላ ሰው ይተላለፍ ይሆናል ።

Here is some vocabulary to help you

አነጠሰ	anät't'äsä	sneeze [derived stem]
አፍ	af	mouth
አፍንጫ	afinč'a	nose
መሐረብ	mäharräb	handkerchief
ሸፈን	šäffänä	cover [3-lit B]
በሽታ	bäššita	sickness, disease
ተላለፈ	tälalläfä	be passed on [derived stem]

1 ሰው ጉንፋን ሲይዘው ምን ያደርጋል?
2 የጉንፋን በሽታ ተላላፊ ነው?
3 በሽተኛው አፋንና አፍንጫውን የሚሸፍን ስለምን ነው?
4 ጉንፋን ለያዘ ሰው ምን ማድረግ አስፈላጊ ነው?

Reading passage

ይህም
እሌ!

የሰው አካል የማዕድናት ጉድኝድ ነው?

በሰው ልጅ አካል 60% ውጋ፤ 39% አካላዊ ተፈጥር፤ 1% ማዕድናዊ ጨው ሲሆን 70 ኪሉ ግራም በሚመዝን ሰው አካል ውስጥ ደግሞ የሚከተሉት ማዕድናት እንደሚገኙ ተረጋግጧል

45.5 ኪ.ግ ኦክሲጅን

12.6 ኪ.ግ ካርቦን

7 ኪ.ግ ሐይድሮጅን

2.1 ኪ.ግ እዮተ

1 ኪ.ግ ካልሲየም

0.7 ኪ.ግ ፎስፈረስ

0.214 ኪ.ግ ፖታሲየም

3 ግራም ብረት

3 ግራም ማገነዚየም

2 ግራም ዚንክና ሌሎች ማዕድናት እናገኛለን። እንድ ጀርመናዊ ሊቅ እንዳስቀመጡት ከሆነ በሰው አካል ውስጥ ከሚገኙ ማዕድናት ልዩ ልዩ ነገሮችን መሠራት እንደሚቻል ታውቋል።

ለምሳሌ 5 ኪሉ ግራም ሻማ

        65 ደርዘን ደረቅ እርሳስ

         7 ሚስማር

       820 ሺ ከብሪት እንጨት

        20 የሻይ ማንኪያ ጨው

        50 ቁርጥራጭ ስኳር

        42 ሊተር ውጋ!!!

Supplementary vocabulary

ማዕድን	maïdïn	mineral (ማዕድናት maïdïnat minerals)
ጉድጓድ	gudgwad	pit, well, mine
የሰው ልጅ	yäsäw lïjj	human being
አካል	akal	body
አካላዊ	akalawi	physical (አካላዊ ተፈጥር akalawi täfät'ro physical matter)
መዘነ	mäzzänä	weigh [3-lit B]
ተከተለ	täkättälä	follow [derived stem] (imperfect ይከተል yïkkättäl)
ተረጋገጠ	tärägaggät'ä	be verified, ascertained (cf. እርግጥ ïrgït' certain)
አዞት	azot	azote (an old word for nitrogen)
ብረት	bïrät	iron
ሊቅ	lik'	expert, scholar, scientist
አስቀመጠ	ask'ämmät'ä	set down, establish [derived stem] (cf. ተቀመጠ täk'ämmät'ä sit)
ነገር	nägär	thing
ታወቀ	tawwäk'ä	be known [derived stem] (ታውቋል tawk'wal it is known, recognized)
ሻማ	šama	candle
(ደረቅ) እርሳስ	(däräk') ïrsas	pencil (እርሳስ alone can mean both pencil and lead; ደረቅ እርሳስ lit. 'dry pencil')
ደርዘን	därzän	dozen
ሚስማር	mismar	nail
ቁርጥራጭ	k'urït'rač'	piece, bit, lump
% = በመቶ	bämäto	percent
ኪ.ግ = ኪሎግራም		
አሥራ ሁለት	asra hulätt	= 12.6
ነጥብ ስድስት	nät'ïb siddïst	
ነጥብ	nät'ïb	point, dot
ዜሮ	zero	zero (= 0)

11 ብሔራዊ በዓል
bïherawi bäal
A national holiday

By the end of this lesson you should be able to:

- form and use command forms ('go', 'let's go', *etc.*)
- use the verb አለ 'say' in various ways
- greet your Ethiopian friends on national holidays

A national holiday

Peter and his girlfriend, Tsehay, meet Kebbede by chance as they are walking along Adwa Avenue in the direction of Piasa

ፒተርና ፀሐይ የተባሉትው ወዳጃ አድዋ ጉዳና ላይ በፒያሳ
በኩል ቢሔዱ ግጋጣሚ ከበደን ያገኛሉ።

ከበደ ፡ እናንተ እንደምን አላችሁ? ወዴትስ ነው የምትሔዱ?

ፒተር ፡ እኔ ደገና ነኝ ። አገዛC ይመስገን። እንተስ እንዴት
ነህ? ጌሩትስ እንዴት ናት? ተሻላት? ሃሉ ለቀቃት?

ከበደ ፡ አዎ ። እኔ ደገና ነኝ ። ጌሩትም እግዜC ይመስገን
ድናለች ።

ፒተር ፡ መሃል ከተማ ውስጥ በየቦታው ተሰቅሉ ስለሚታየው
ሰንደቅ ዓላማ አስቲ ንገረኝ ። ምክንያቱ ምንድን ነው?
ዛሬ በዓል ነው እንዴ!

ከበደ ፡ እንዴት አታውቅም? ነገ የመስቀል በዓል እኮ ነው!
በዓሉ የሚከበረው በመላ ኢትዮጵያ ነው ። በያመቱ
ከሚከበሩት ትልልቅ በዓሎች መካከል አንዱ ስለሆነ
ሕዝቡ አንድ ሙሉ ቀን እረፍት ነው ። አስቲ! አዚህ
ቡና ቤት እንግባ! ዛሬ የመስቀል ዋዜማ ስለሆነ እኔ
ልጋብዛችሁ ።

ከበደ ፡ በሉ እንግዲህ ምን መጠጣት ትፈልጋላችሁ?

ፒተር ፡ በጣም አመሰግናለሁ ። እኔ ቀዝቃዛ ቢራ ልጠጣ ።

ከበደ ፡ እንቺስ ፀሐይ ምን ትጠጫለሽ?

ፀሐይ: እኔ ቡና በወተት ብጠጣ ይሻለኛል።

ፒተር: እስቲ እባክህ ነገ በዓሉ እንደት እንደሚከበር ንገረኝ።

ከበደ: ቀኑ ከመድረሱ በፊት ብዙ ነገሮች ቀደም ብለው መዘጋጀት አለባቸው። ለምሳሌ ያህል በየቤቱ ሴቶች እንጀራ ይጋግራሉ፣ ወጥ ይሠራሉ፤ ጠጅ ይጥላሉ እንዲሁም ጠላ ይጠምቃሉ። ከዚያም በኅላ ማንኛውም ሰው ዘመዶቹንና ወዳጆቹን ለገብዝ ጠርቶ በዓሉን አብሮ ለማክበር ከዋዜማው ጀምሮ ድንኳን በመትከል በደስታ ይጠብቃል።

ፀሐይ: እሪ እባገሁ! እኔ የሚገርመኝ እኛ ሴቶች ሁልጊዜ ሁሉን ነገር መሥራት ለምን እንዳለብን ነው። እናንተ ወንዶች ገን ምንም ሳትሠሩ ዝም ብላችሁ መቀመጥ ብቻ!

ከበደ: ለምን እንደዚህ ትያለሽ ፀሐይ?

ፒተር: እስቲ እባካችሁ አትጨቃጨቁ እናንተ! እኔ የምፈልገው በዓሉ እንዴት እንደሚከበር ማወቅ ነው። ሌላ ጥቅጥቅ አልፈልግም።

ከበደ: ጎህ ሲቀድ ሰው ሁሉ ይሰበሰብና ወደ ደመራው ቦታ ይሄዳል።

ፒተር: ደመራ ምንድን ነው?

ፀሐይ: በመጀመሪያ ሰዎች እንድ ረጅም እንጨት ይተክላሉ። ከዚያም በኅላ በዙሪያው ብዙ እንጨቶች አብረው ይደረድራሉ። ያም ደመራ ይባጋል።

ፒተር: ረጅም እንጨት ለምን ከመካከል ላይ ይተከላሉ?

ከበደ: መካከል ላይ ያለው ረጅም እንጨት የመስቀል ምልክት አለበት። ይህም ንግሥት እሌኒ ያገኘችው መስቀል ምሳሌ ነው።

ፒተር: ሰው ሁሉ ወደ ደመራ ቦታ ለምን ይሄዳል?

ፀሐይ: ደመራ ለማቃጠል ነዋ!

ከበደ: አዎ፣ እውነትዋን ነው። በናንተ አገር የደመራ በዓል የለም እንዴ?

ፒተር: አይ! አለ እንጂ። ነገር ግን በዚህ አይነት አይከበርም።

ፀሐይ: ታዲያ እንዴት አድርጋችሁ ነው የምታከብሩት?

ፒተር: እኛ የምንከብረው ከሃይማኖት ጋር በማያያዝ አይደለም።

ከበደ: ለማንኛውም በዓሉን እንዴት እንደምናከብረው ነገ ከጥዋቱ ጀምረህ ታያለህ። ስለሄሀ ካሜራህን ይዘህ ና!

ፒተር: እንዴ በደስታ ነው እንጂ! ለማየት ቸኩያለሁ!

KEBBEDE: *How are you? And where are you going?*

PETER: *I'm fine, thanks. How are you? And how is Hirut? Is she better? Has her cough gone?*

KEBBEDE: *Yes, I'm fine. Hirut, too, is better, thanks.*

PETER: *Tell me please about the flags that can be seen hanging everywhere in the city centre. Is today a holiday, then! What's the reason for it?*

KEBBEDE: *How come you don't know? Tomorrow is of course the Feast of Meskel! The holiday's celebrated throughout the whole of Ethiopia. Since it's one of the biggest festivals celebrated every year the people have a day's holiday. Look! Let's go into this café! As it's a holiday let me treat you.*

KEBBEDE: *Well now, what do you want to drink?*

PETER: *Thank you very much. Let me have a cold beer.*

KEBBEDE: *And what will you have, Tsehay?*

TSEHAY: *I'd prefer a milky coffee.*

PETER: *So then, please tell me how the festival will be celebrated tomorrow.*

KEBBEDE: *Before the day arrives a lot of preparations have to be made in advance. By way of example, in every house the women bake* injera, *make* wot, *brew* tejj *and brew* tella. *After that, everyone invites their friends and relatives to a party; and then eagerly waits for them, setting up a marquee on the eve so as to celebrate the holiday with them.*

TSEHAY: *Oh please! What amazes me is why we women always have to do everything. You men, though, merely sit around without doing anything!*

KEBBEDE: *Why do you talk like this, Tsehay?*

PETER: *Please don't argue! What I want to know is how the day of the holiday is celebrated. I don't want any more argument!*

KEBBEDE: *Well, at daybreak everyone gathers and goes to the Meskel bonfire site.*

PETER: *What's a Meskel bonfire?*

TSEHAY: *First people plant a long piece of wood. Then they stack lots of pieces of wood together around it. That is called the Meskel bonfire.*

PETER: *Why do they plant a long piece of wood in the middle?*

KEBBEDE: *The long piece of wood in the middle has the symbol of the cross on it. This is a representation of the cross which Queen Helena found.*

PETER: *Why does everyone go to the bonfire site?*

TSEHAY: *To light the bonfire of course!*

KEBBEDE: *Yes, she's right. Isn't there a bonfire festival in your country, then?*

PETER: *Yes, there is indeed! But it's not celebrated in this manner.*
TSEHAY: *Well then, how do you celebrate it?*
PETER: *The celebration that we have has no connection with religion.*
KEBBEDE: *In any case, you'll see how we celebrate the festival from tomorrow. So bring your camera with you.*
PETER: *Well yes, but gladly! I'm eager to see it!*

Vocabulary

ወዳጅ	wädaj	(girl/boy) friend, lover
ጉዳና	gwädana	road, avenue
አድዋ ጉዳና	Adwa Gwädana	one of the main shopping streets in Addis Ababa leading to the area called ፒያሳ Piyassa, *from the Italian* **piazza**
ሰንደቅ ዓላማ	sändäk' alama	flag
መስቀል	mäsk'äl	cross (የመስቀል በዓል yämäsk'äl bäal The Feast of Meskel or The Feast of the Invention of the Cross (*see note 1*))
በዓል	bäal	festival
እረፍት	iräft	rest, holiday
ዋዜማ	wazema	eve (*of a holiday*)
ሙሉ	mulu	whole, full, entire
ዘመድ	zämäd	relative, relation
ግብዣ	gibža	party, reception, invitation (*cf. the verb* ጋበዘ gabbäzä invite)
ድንኳን	dinkwan	tent, marquee
ወንድ	wänd	male, man
ጭቅጭቅ	č'ik'ič'č'ik'	argument, quarrel (*cf. the verb* ተጫቃጨ täč'äk'ač'č'äk'ä *below*)
ጎህ	goh	daybreak, dawn (*in the idiom* ጎህ ሲቀድ (*see* ቀደደ *in the verbs below*). *You can also say* ንጋት ሲከ'ädd nigat sik'ädd)
ደመራ	dämära	(Meskel) bonfire
እንጨት	inč'ät	(*piece of*) wood
ዙሪያ	zuriya	surrounding area, environs
በዙሪያው	bäzuriyaw	around him/it (*lit.* 'in his/its surroundings')
ምልክት	milikkit	symbol, sign
ንግሥት	nigist	queen (ንግሥት እሌኒ Nigist Ileni Queen Helena – *see note 1*)

ነጉሥ	nïgus	king (*cf.* ነጉሠ ነገሥት nïgusä nägäst emperor *lit.* 'king of kings' – in Ge'ez)
ሃይማኖት	haymanot	faith, religion
ካሜራ	kamera	camera

Verbs

ተሻለ	täšalä	be better [derived stem]; (*as an impersonal verb with an object suffix pronoun, e.g.* ተሻለው täšaläw, *it can mean* feel better, get well; *but remember* ይሻለኛል yïššaläññal *means* I prefer *lit.* it will be better for me)
ተሰቀለ	täsäk'k'älä	hang, be hung [derived stem]; gerundive ተሰቅሎ täsäk'lo
ታየ	tayyä	be seen [derived stem]; (*cf.* አየ 'see', simple imperfect ይታይ yïttayy)
ተከበረ	täkäbbärä	be celebrated (*festivals*) [derived stem]; (simple imperfect ይከበር yïkkäbbär)
አከበረ	akäbbärä	celebrate (*a festival*) [derived stem]; (simple imperfect ያከብር yakäbïr)
ቀደም አለ	k'ädämm alä	be early, precede [አለ verb] (*see grammar section*)
ቀደም ብሎ	k'ädämm bïlo	earlier, ahead of time, in advance
ጋገረ	gaggärä	make **injera** [3-lit C]
ጣለ	t'alä	besides meaning 'throw down', here means make **tejj** [2-lit³]
ጠመቀ	t'ämmäk'ä	brew **tella** [3-lit A]
ተከለ	täkkälä	plant, pitch (*a tent*) [3-lit A]
ዝም አለ	zïmm alä	be quiet, keep still [አለ verb] (*see grammar section*)
ዝም ብሎ	zïmm bïlo	quietly, merely, just (*without purpose*)
ተጨቃጨቀ	täč'äk'ač'č'äk'ä	argue, quarrel [derived stem]; (simple imperfect ይጨቃጨቅ yïč'č'äk'ač'č'äk')
ቀደደ	k'äddädä	cut, make a hole (*but note the idiom* ጎህ ሲቀድ goh sik'ädd when day breaks; at day break – *lit.* 'when dawn cuts (*the sky*)'

ተሰበሰበ	täsäbässäbä	gather, assemble [derived stem]; (simple imperfect ይሰበሰብ yïssäbässäb – *cf.* ሰበሰበ säbässäbä gather (*something or somebody*) together [4-lit])
ደረደረ	däräddärä	put in a row, stack [4-lit]
አቃጠለ	ak'k'at't'älä	burn, set fire to [derived stem]; (infinitive ማቃጠል mak'k'at'äl)

Particles

ባጋጣሚ	baggat'ami	by chance
እኮ	ïkko	in fact, actually (*see note 2*)
መካከል	mäkakkäl	amongst (*postposition*); middle (*noun*)
ማንኛውም	manniññawm	each, every, all
[-a] e.g. ነዋ	näwa	it is indeed, it certainly is (*see note 2*)
ከ- — ጋር በማያያዝ	kä- — gar bämayyayaz	in connection with
ለማንኛውም	lämanniññawm	in any case

Notes on the dialogue

1 The Feast of the Cross (የመስቀል በዓል yämäsk'äl bäal) is one of several Ethiopian national holidays. Some of these are Christian festivals, some are Muslim, and others celebrate important days in the history of Ethiopia. You may find the following details of Ethiopian national holidays of interest.

(a) የዘመን መለወጫ በዓል yäzämän mäläwwäč'a bäal (also called አውደ ዓመት awdä amät, or simply አዲስ ዓመት addis amät) New Year (መስከረም 1)

(b) የመስቀል በዓል yämäsk'äl bäal the Feast of the Invention of the Cross, celebrating the finding of the True Cross by Queen Helena, mother of the Roman Emperor Constantine (መስከረም 17)

(c) የገና በዓል yägänna bäal the Feast of Christmas (ታሕሣሥ 29); Ethiopian Christmas falls on 7 January

(d) የጥምቀት በዓል yät'imk'ät bäal the Feast of Epiphany, celebrating the baptism of Christ in the River Jordan (ጥር 11)

(e) የአድዋ ድል በዓል yäAdwa dïl bäal Adwa Victory Day, celebrating Menilek II's victory over the Italians in 1896 (የካቲት 23)

(f) የኢትዮጵያ ነጻነት በዓል yältyop'p'ïya näs'annät bäal Ethiopian Independence Day, also called የድል በዓል yädïl bäal Victory Day, celebrating the defeat of the Italian occupying forces in 1941 (መጋቢት 24)

(g) የፋሲካ በዓል yäfasika bäal Easter (a moveable feast occurring between የካቲት 25 and ሚያዝያ 30). The name ፋሲካ applies to the whole week

There are three Muslim festivals which are celebrated as national holidays in Ethiopia. The dates of these are calculated according to the Muslim calendar and so do not always occur on the same day of the year in the Ethiopian calendar.

(a) መውሊድ mäwlid, or የመሐመድ ልደት yäMähammäd lïdät, the birthday of the Prophet Mohammed

(b) ያረፋ በዓል yaräfa bäal, also called by its Arabic name ኢድ አል አድሐ id al adha, the Feast of Immolation

(c) ኢድ አል ፍጥር id al fit'ïr, the Feast of the Breaking of the Ramadan Fast

There are quite a number of set expressions in Amharic for greeting people on national holidays. These usually follow the pattern:

እንኳን ለበዓሉ በደኅና አደረሰዎ*	inkwan läbäalu bädähna adärräsäwo*

lit. 'congratulations that He (*God*) has brought you safely to the feast!'

Here are some other examples and variants:

እንኳን ከዘመን ወደ ዘመን አሻጋገረዎ	inkwan käzämän wädä zämän aššägaggäräwo

'Happy New Year!' (*lit.* 'congratulations He has brought you across from year to year!')

እንኳን ለአዲሱ ዓመት በሰላምና በደስታ አደረሰዎ	inkwan läaddisu amät bäsälaminna bädässïta adärräsäwo

'Happy New Year!' (*lit.* 'congratulations He has brought you to the new year in peace and happiness!')

እንኳን ለልደቱ በዓል በደኅና አደረሰዎ	inkwan lälïdätu bäal bädähna adärräsäwo

'Happy Christmas!' (*lit.* 'congratulations He has brought you safely to the Feast of His Birth!')

እንኳን ለብርሃነ ትንሣዔው ያደረሰዎ   ïnkwan läbïrhanä tïnsaew yadärräsäwo

'Happy Easter!' (*lit.* 'congratulations He has brought you to the Light of His Resurrection!')

እንኳን ለልደት በዓል በደኅና ያደረሰዎ   ïnkwan lälïdät bäal bädähna yadärräsäwo

'Happy birthday!' (*lit.* 'congratulations He has brought you safely to the feast of (your) birth!')

* Of course, you can change this to አደረሰህ, አደረሰሽ or አደረሳችሁ according to the person you are greeting. More simply, you can also say መልካም በዓል mälkam bäal 'happy holiday!'. Below are some further, more formal expressions of good wishes, that you will find useful.

መልካም ጤንነትን፡ ዕድገትንና ብልጽግናን እመኝልዎታለሁ
mälkam t'enïnnätïn, ïdgätïnïnna bïls'ïgïnnan ïmmäññïllïwotallähw
I wish you good health, prosperity and wealth!

አዲሱ ዓመት የዕድገት፡ የብልጽግናና የሰላም እንዲሆንልዎ እመኛለሁ
addis amät yäïdgät, yäbïls'ïgïnnanna yäsälam ïndihonïllïwo ïmmäññallähw
I wish that the New Year will be one of prosperity, wealth and peace for you!

2 In the dialogue, several discourse particles occur: እኮ ïkko, እንጂ ïnji and -a on ነዋ näwa. It is important to know how to use these correctly if you want to develop a good use of spoken Amharic, as it is these which will give your Amharic a lively and expressive character. You have already met እንጂ ïnji in the phrase ይሁን እንጂ yïhun ïnji 'nevertheless', *lit.* 'so be it, but . . .'. You can see from how it is used in the dialogue in this lesson that እንጂ is used to mark a contrast or protestation of some kind:

(a) when Peter confirms that there is a bonfire festival in his country in response to Kebbede's doubtful question: አለ እንጂ allä ïnji 'but (*of course*) there is!'

(b) when Peter affirms that he will of course bring his camera, dispelling any doubt that he might forget it: በደስታ ነው እንጂ bädässïta näw ïnji 'but gladly (*I shall bring it*)!'

You can also use አንጂ after an imperative or jussive (command forms of a verb) to stress or emphasize the command, or as a protestation:

ብላ አንጂ   bïla ïnji   eat, why don't you!; do eat!
ሂድ አንጂ   hid ïnji   do get a move on!; go, for goodness' sake!
እንሂድ አንጂ   ïnnïhid ïnji   let's go then! (*i.e.* why are we waiting?)

When used inside a sentence, አንጂ usually contrasts two ideas and corresponds to English 'but'; 'on the other hand'; 'on the contrary':

ይራበኝ አንጂ ይህን አልበላም   yïrabäñ ïnji yïhïn albälam
I may starve, but I shan't eat this (*lit.* 'let me go hungry, but . . .')
ጠጉሩ ነጭ ነው አንጂ ገና ወጣት   t'äguru näč'č' näw ïnji gäna
ነው   wät'at näw
his hair is white, but he's still young
ነገ አንጂ ዛሬ አንጨርስም   nägä ïnji zare annïč'ärrisïm
we shan't finish today, but rather tomorrow

The little particle እኮ ïkko is rather like አንጂ in that it also indicates a kind of protestation, but rather that something is indeed true, and not so much in contrast to another idea that is expressed or understood. It corresponds to English expressions like 'exactly'; 'quite, indeed'; 'in fact'; 'actually' and so on. Unlike አንጂ it can also be used on its own as a response.

እንዲህ ላድርገው? እኮ!   ïndih ladrïgäw? ïkko!
    should I do it like this? – Of course!
በል እኮ ስጠኝ!   bäl ïkko sït'äñ!
    come on then, give it to me! (*to assure someone who's reluctant*)
ይገርማል እኮ!   yïgärmal ïkko!
    it's truly amazing!
አንተ አዋቂ ነህ እኮ!   antä awak'i näh ïkko!
    you are really intelligent!

The little suffix particle -a, which is always written joined on to the preceding word has a similar function to እኮ. It is very commonly found added to ነው as in the dialogue: ነዋ näwa, meaning 'of course it is!'

Grammar

The command forms (imperative and jussive)

In the dialogues so far you have met quite a few jussive and imperative forms of the verb. Here are some examples:

እንሂድ	innïhid	let's go	ልጠይቀው	lit'äyyïk'äw	let me ask him
ጠብቅ	t'äbbïk'	wait	ልጋብዛችሁ	lïgabzaččuh	let me invite you
ግቡ	gïbu	come in	ልጠጣ	lït'ät't'a	let me drink
አምጣ	amt'a	bring	ይሁን	yïhun	so be it

ይሁኑ yïhunu may you be *in the phrase* ደኅና ይሁኑ dähna yïhunu goodbye

The imperative expresses a direct command to the person you are talking to. It therefore can only be in the second person, masculine, feminine or plural, corresponding to the three pronouns አንተ, አንቺ, and እናንተ. For a less abrupt request, and to be more polite, the jussive is used in the third person plural, corresponding to the pronoun እርሶ, as in the phrase ደኅና ይሁኑ above.

The jussive expresses a request or a wish and is used only in the first and third persons. This can be equivalent to the English use of 'let me . . .'; 'let us . . .'; 'let him . . .'; and so on, or sometimes is equivalent to 'may. . .' or 'should . . .'. For example:

ልሂድ	lïhid	let me go!	ልደውል	lïdäwwïl	should I ring?
እንብላ	innïbla	let's eat!	ልግባ	lïgba	may I come in?

In the negative, the situation is a little different. The negative of the imperative, i.e. a direct prohibition such as 'don't go!', is expressed by what is formally the second person forms of the negative jussive. For example:

ብላ	bïla	eat!	*but*	አትብላ	attïbla	don't eat!
ሂጂ	hiji	go!	*but*	አትሂጂ	attïhiji	don't go!
ስሙ	sïmu	listen!	*but*	አትስሙ	attïsmu	don't listen!

The jussive and the imperative are both formed on the same stem, which in many but not all classes of verb is different from the imperfect stem. The three persons of the imperative are marked by suffixes, whilst the jussive has a set of combined prefixes and suffixes *almost* identical to those of the simple imperfect tense.

Here are the full sets of forms of the imperative and the jussive, affirmative and negative, from the verb ሂደ **hedä** 'go', built on the stem **-hid-** :

Imperative (affirmative only)

	affix	example	
2nd pers. masc.	—	ሂድ	hid
2nd pers. fem.	-i	ሂጂ, ሂጅ	hiji, hij
2nd pers. plur.	-u	ሂዱ	hidu

Jussive (affirmative)   *(Negative)*

	affix	example		affix	example	
1st pers. sing.	li-	ልሂድ	lïhid	al-	አልሂድ	alhid
2nd pers. masc.				attï-	አትሂድ	attïhid
2nd pers. fem.				attï- – -i	አትሂጅ	attïhij
3rd pers. masc.	yï-	ይሂድ	yïhid	ay-	አይሂድ	ayhid
3rd pers. fem.	tï-	ትሂድ	tïhid	attï-	አትሂድ	attïhid
1st pers. plur.	ïnnï-	እንሂድ	ïnnïhid	annï-	አንሂድ	annïhid
2nd pers. plur.				attï- – -u	አትሂዱ	attïhidu
3rd pers. plur.	yï- – -u	ይሂዱ	yïhidu	ay – -u	አይሂዱ	ayhidu

Points to note

1 The ending of the second person feminine in the imperative and the negative jussive, **-i,** causes palatalization in exactly the same way as in the simple imperfect tense. So:

ጨርሽ č'ärriš finish from ጨረሰ   ምራጭ mïräč' choose from መረጠ
ግዢ gïži buy from ገዛ   ግላጭ gïläč' explain from ገለጸ
ክፋች kïfäč open from ከፈተ   ክፈይ kïfäy pay from ከፈለ
ውስጅ wïsäj take from ወሰደ   እማኝ ïmäñ believe from አመነ

2 The first person singular affix in the affirmative jussive is **li-,** otherwise the personal affixes in the jussive are the same as in the simple imperfect tense. So:

እሂድ ነበር   ïhed näbbär   I was going
but
ልሂድ   lïhid   let me go

3 Unlike in the negative imperfect tense, in the negative jussive there is no -ም **-m** suffix. So:

አትሂድም	attïhedim	you don't go
but		
አትሂድ	attïhid	don't go!
አንበላም	annïbälam	we don't eat
but		
አንብላ	annïbla	let's not eat
አይጀምርም	ayjämmïrïm	he won't start
but		
አይጀምር	ayjämmïr	don't let him start

The jussive and imperative stem

Verb class		Imperative sample stem			
3-lit A	[ወሰደ]	-wsäd-	ውሰድ	wïsäd	take!
			ይውሰድ	yïwsäd	let him take
	[አወቀ]	-iwäk'-	አወቅ	iwäk'	know!
			ይወቅ	yïwäk'	let him know
3-lit B	[ጠረሰ]	-č'ärris-	ጨርስ	č'ärris	finish!
			ይጨርስ	yïč'ärris	let him finish
3-lit C	[ጋበዘ]	-gab(ï)z-	ጋብዝ	gabïz	invite!
			ይጋብዝ	yïgabïz	let him invite
2-lit¹ A	[ሰማ]	-sma-	ስማ	sïma	listen!
			ይስማ	yïsma	let him listen
2-lit¹ B	[ጠጣ]	-t'ät't'a-	ጠጣ	t'ät't'a	drink!
			ይጠጣ	yït'ät't'a	let him drink
2-lit² A	[ሰጠ]	-s(ï)t'-	ስጥ	sït'	give!
			ይስጥ	yïst'	let him give
2-lit² B	[ቀየ]	-k'wäyy-	ቁይ	k'wäyy	wait!
			ይቁይ	yïk'wäyy	let him wait
2-lit³	[ጻፈ]	-s'af-	ጻፍ	s'af	write!
			ይጻፍ	yïs'af	let him write
2-lit⁴	[ሄደ]	-hid-	ሂድ	hid	go!
			ይሂድ	yïhid	let him go
2-lit⁵	[ኖረ]	-nur-	ኑር	nur	stay!
			ይኑር	yïnur	let him stay
4-lit	[መረመረ]	-märmïr-	መርምር	märmïr	examine!
			ይመርምር	yïmärmïr	let him examine
3-lit Y	[ጐብኘ]	-gwäb(ï)ñ-	ጐብኝ	gwäbïñ	visit!
			ይጐብኝ	yïgwäbïñ	let him visit

Verb class	Imperative sample stem			
3-lit X [ሀነጋ]	-zänga-	ሀነጋ	zänga	forget!
		ይሀነጋ	yïzänga	let him forget
irregular አለ say	-bäl-	በል	bäl	say!
		ይበል	yïbäl	let him say

Points to note

1 In all B-type verbs the imperfect stem and imperative–jussive stem are identical.

2 In all A-type verbs the imperative–jussive stem begins with a sixth-order letter, such as ው·በድ, ስማ, ስጥ. Whether that sixth-order letter is pronounced with the vowel ï, or not, basically depends on the shape of the word.

   (a) when there is no prefix it is always pronounced, i.e. in the imperative:

ስማ	sïma	listen!
ስጪኝ	sïč'iñ	give me it! (እንቺ)
ንገረው	nïgäräw	tell him!
ው·በዱት	wïsädut	take it!

   (b) where there is a prefix it is usually not pronounced, i.e. in the jussive:

ይስማ	yïsma	let him hear
አትስጪኝ	attïsč'iñ	don't give me it! (እንቺ)
ልንገረው	lïngäräw	let me tell him
አይውሰዱት	aywsädut	don't let them take it

Remember, however, that Amharic does not normally like more than two consonants in a row, so an example like the last one above (አይው·በዱት) can also be pronounced as ayïwsädut in careful speech. Similarly አልንገረው 'don't let me tell him' is pronounced alïngäräw, and not as alngäräw, which would be very difficult to say anyway!

3 In verbs beginning in a- the initial vowel of the stem is absorbed after a prefix, following the normal rules of vowel hierarchy. This will mean of course that as in the imperfect tense so in the jussive there will be no separate letter:

from አወቀ awwäk'ä know [3-lit A]:

| አወቀው | ïwäk'äw | know it! |

but

| የወቀው | yïwäk'äw | may he know it |

from አከመ akkämä treat medically [3-lit B]:

| አከመው | akkïmäw | treat him! |

but

| ያከመው | yakkïmäw | let him treat him |

4 The verb መጣ mät't'a 'come' has an irregular imperative. The jussive of መጣ, however, is formed perfectly regularly.

Imperative
masc.	ና	na	come!
fem.	ነይ	näy	
pl.	ኑ	nu	

Jussive
| e.g. 3rd pers. masc. | ይምጣ | yïmt'a | let him come |
| 2nd pers. masc. neg. | አትምጣ | attïmt'a | don't come! |

Exercises

1 Complete the following sentences using an imperative or jussive form as appropriate. (You may find the verbs listed beneath the exercise useful)

1 አንቺ በሩን _____ ።
2 እናንተ ልጆች መጽሐፎቻችሁን ይዛችሁ _____ ።
3 አኔ ዛሬ ማታ ስልክ _____ ።
4 አሁን ለጤናችን _____ ።
5 ነገ ገረዲቱ አንጇራ በወጥ _____ ።
6 አቶ ዓለማየሁ አገሩን ከፍል ውስጥ _____ ።
7 ገንዘቡን _____ ብዬ አዘዝኩት ።
8 አንዴ _____ ብሎ ተናገራት ።

ጠበቀ, ከፈተ, ነጋ, ደወለ, መጣ, ጠጣ, ሠራ, ሰጠ, ዘጋ, ከፈለ, አዘጋጀ

2 Convert the following commands into the negative

1 ነገ ስልክ ደውዱልኝ ።

2 መስኮቱን ዝጋ።
3 እስቲ ስልኩን ንገረኝ።
4 አባባ ኪራዩን ይከፍሉልኝ።
5 በቀኝ በኩል ውጣ።
6 የቤት ሥራችሁን ጨርሱ።
7 የሱን ስልክ ቁጥር ስጪኝ።
8 እንጨቱን እዚህ ይትከሉ።

3 (a) How would you ask a little boy to do the following things in Amharic

1 wash the car.	5 go to the shop and buy a bottle of Ambo Water.
2 answer the phone.	6 wait a bit.
3 finish eating his supper.	7 wipe the table.
4 close the door.	8 be quiet.

3 (b) Now how would you ask a little girl to do the same things?

Reading passage (1)

ስለ ሙዚቃ መሣሪያዎች

በሙዚቃ መሣሪያዎች መጫወት ትወዳላችሁ? በኢትዮጵያ
ውስጥ ብዙውን ጊዜ የምትሰሟቸው ያገር መሣሪያዎች ሶስት
ዓይነት ናቸው: ማስንቆ፣ ከራርና ከበር ናቸው። ከራር
የተባለው ከሶስቱ መሣሪያዎች ትልቅ የሆነው ስድስት የጅማት
ገመድ ያለው ነው። ማስንቆ የተባለውም አንድ የፈረስ ጭራ
ገመድ ያለው ሆኖ በማስንቆ መምቻ የሚጫወቱት ነው። ብዙ
ሰዎች እነዚህን በገመድ የተሠሩ መሣሪያዎች እየተጫወቱባቸው
ይዘፍናሉ። አንድ ሌላ ዋሽንት የተባለ መሣሪያ አለ። ዋሽንት
ደግሞ በትንፋሽ የሚጫወቱት ሲሆን ለመጫወት ቀላል
አይደለም። ለጫወቱበት ከሞከሩ በፊት ብዙ ማጥናት አስፈላጊ
ነው: ያለዚያ ጥሩ ድምፅ አይሰጥም። ከበር የተባለው ገን
ያው እንደሌሎቹ ከበሮዎች ዓይነት ነው።

Here is some vocabulary to help you

ተጫወት	täč'awwätä	play (*a game or a musical instrument*), as well as chat [derived stem]; infinitive መጫወት

		mäč'č'awät; simple imperfect, **ይጫወት** yïč'č'awwät
ገመድ	gämäd	string
ጅማት	jïmmat	sinew
ፈረስ	färäs	horse
ጭራ	č'ïra	hair *(from an animal's tail)*; *also means* fly whisk: **የፈረስ ጭራ** horsehair
ማሲንቆ መምቻ	masïnk'o mämča	masinqo bow (*cf.* **መታ** hit, strike)
ትንፋሽ	tïnfaš	breath
አጠና	at'änna	study [derived stem]. Infinitive **ማጥናት** mat'nat
ያለዚያ	yaläzziya	otherwise (*lit.* 'without that')
ያው	yaw	the same
ከበሮ	käbäro	(*large*) drum

ክራር kïrar, **ማሲንቆ** masïnk'o, **ከበሮ** käbäro *and* **ዋሽንት** wašint *are the names of the four musical instruments described in this passage.*

4 Now answer the following questions in Amharic about the passage you have just read

1 ማስንቆ ስንት ገመድ አለው?
2 ዋሽንት መጫወት ቀላል ነው ወይስ አስቸጋሪ?
3 በኢትዮጵያ የሚጫወቱት ከበሮ እንደ ሌላ አገሮች ከበሮ ነው?
4 ኢትዮጵያ በዬትኛው መሣሪያ ሲጫወቱ ይዘፍናሉ?
5 ክራር የተባለውን መሣሪያ በጣት ነው የሚጫወቱት ወይስ በመምቻ?

Grammar

The verb አለ *alä*

Aside from the verb 'be', **አለ** is the major irregular verb in Amharic. Whilst the prefixes and suffixes that it takes in the various tenses are the same as those used with regular verbs, it is irregular inasmuch as the stems for each of those tenses are not formed following one of the regular patterns. You have now met all of the tenses of **አለ**, but here they are again in table format to remind you. You can see from the table that this irregularity mainly consists in the presence of a **b** in some tenses, which is missing in others.

Be careful not to confuse አለ alä 'he said' with አለ allä 'he is', which forms part of the truly irregular verb 'be', which we shall be reviewing in the next lesson.

Tense			Stem	Gloss
simple past	አለ	alä	al-	he said
simple imperfect	ይል	yïl	-ïl-	(he says, will say)
compound imperfect	ይላል	yïlal	"	he says, will say
jussive	ይበል	yïbäl	-bäl-	let him say
imperative	በል	bäl	"	say
gerundive	ብሎ	bïlo	bïl-	he saying ...
compound gerundive	ብሏል	bïlwal	"	he has said
infinitive	ማለት	malät	-alät	to say
agent noun	ባይ	bay		someone who says

You have also met in recent lessons some parts of the passive derivative ተባለ täbalä 'be said, be called', such as the compound imperfect ይባላል yïbbalal 'it is called'. Although we have not yet described this derived stem (it will be covered in lesson thirteen), you can see that the same **b** appears as occurs in some parts of the simple stem. The verb አለ 'say' is especially important in Amharic as it is used in a variety of ways that go far beyond its English equivalent.

First, of course, it is used like English 'say', as for instance in the dialogue when Kebbede asks Tsehay, ለምን እንደዚህ ትያለሽ lämin ïndäzzih tïyalläš 'why do you say this? (*lit.* 'like this'). Similarly, ምን አልክ? : ምንም አላልኩም min alk – minïmm alalkum 'what did you say? – I didn't say anything'. አለ does not necessarily imply 'saying' something, it can also mean 'thinking' or 'intending'. Have a look at the following examples:

አዲስ ቀሚስ እገዛለሁ ብላ ገበያ ሄዳች addis k'ämis ïgäzallähw bïla gäbäya hedäčč
'she went to market intending to buy a new dress' (*lit.* '... saying, "I'll buy a new dress"')

ዛሬ ትምህርት የለም ብዬ ቀርቻለሁ zare tïmhïrt yälläm bïyye k'äriččallähw
I stayed away thinking that there was no class today

In Amharic, it is normal practice to quote directly words that are spoken or thought, rather than put them into what is called 'indirect speech' as we often do in English. If the verb of 'saying' is itself አለ then you can simply quote the words directly:

ነገ ቢሮ አልሄድም አለ   nägä biro alhedïm alä
he said, 'I am not going to the office
tomorrow'
he said he wasn't going to the office
tomorrow

Otherwise, it is usual to 'finish off' the quoted words with an appropriate part of አለ, most frequently the gerundive. In this case the
verb of 'saying' is something like ነገረ 'speak'; ጠየቀ 'ask'; መለሰ
'reply'; አሰበ 'think'; ጻፈ 'write'; ጮኸ 'shout'; and so on. Look at the
examples below.

ነገ ቢሮ ትሄጻለህ ብላ ጠየቀችኝ   nägä biro tïhedalläh bïla
t'äyyäk'äččïñ
she asked me, 'Are you going to
the office tomorrow?'
she asked me whether I was going
to the office tomorrow
ደሞዙን እጨምርለታለሁ   dämozun   ič'ämmïrïllätallähw
ብዬ አሰብኩ   bïyye assäbkw
I thought, 'I will increase his
salary for him'
I thought that I would increase
his salary for him

Second, the infinitive ማለት malät and the imperative በል bäl we
have also met with special uses: ማለት in the phrase ምን ማለት ነው
mïn malät näw 'what does it mean?' (lit. 'it is to say what?'); and በል
as the introductory particle equivalent to English 'well'; 'come on';
and so on. Here are some more examples:

(ማለት)

ይህ ምን ማለት ነው?   yïh mïn malät näw?
what does this mean?
ባማርኛ ችግር ማለት በንግሊዝኛ   bamarïñña čïggïr malät
ምን ማለት ነው?   bängïlizïñña mïn malät näw?
what is the English for the
Amharic ችግር? (lit. 'to say ችግር
in Amharic is to say what in
English?')

(በለ)

በዪ ከበደን ሰላም አትዪም እንዴ? bäyi, Kābbädän sälam attïyim ïnde?
well, won't you say hello to Kebbede, uh?

በል እንዒሂድ! bäl ïnnïhid!
come on, let's go!

Third, as in the examples ዝም ብላችሁ zïmm bïlaččuh '(you) being quiet' and ቀደም ብሎ k'ädämm bïlo '(it) being earlier', which occur in the dialogue, and as in ደስ አለኝ däss alän 'I am happy' and ትዝ አለኝ tïzz alän 'I recall' which you have met before, the verb አለ forms compounds in which it no longer appears to have any meaning of 'saying'. The word immediately in front of the verb አለ remains unchanged, while person, tense, and so on, are indicated in the verb አለ. We can call these compound or composite verbs 'አለ verbs'. There are very many of these 'አለ verbs' and they are particularly common in spoken Amharic. Below are some more examples which you will find useful to add to your vocabulary.

እምቢ አለ	ïmbi alä	refuse, say no
አሺ አለ	ïšši alä	agree, say yes
ይቅር አለ	yïk'ïr alä	forgive
አደራ አለ	adära alä	implore, entreat, entrust
ከፍ አለ	käff alä	be high, important
ዝቅ አለ	zïk'k' alä	be low
ቁጭ አለ	k'uč'č' alä	sit down
ቀስ አለ	k'äss alä	be careful
ቶሎ አለ	tolo alä	be quick
ጸጥ አለ	s'ät't' alä	be quiet, still, peaceful

There are others like ቀደም አለ which are derived from existing verb stems. There are set patterns which these derived 'አለ verbs' follow, but rather than list these here it will be simpler if you make a note of these new items when you meet them.

Exercises

5 How would you say the following in Amharic? You will find it easier if you try to recover first the original words that were spoken or thought

> *Example:* he told me he was hungry ➡ he told me, saying 'I'm
> hungry'
>
> ራብኝ ብሎ ነገረኝ።

1 Almaz told me she would come with the gifts tomorrow.
2 I replied to her that I didn't know at all.
3 He asked me what the time was.
4 Let me ask him what time we'll arrive at Langano.
5 We thought we'd go to Awasa next week.
6 He told me he'd ring this evening at 7 o'clock.

6 Answer the following questions in Amharic

1 ጋማርኛ ስልክ ማለት በንግሊዝኛ ምን ማለት ነው?
2 ደመራ የተባለው ምንድን ነው? በንግሊዝኛ አንዴት ይባላል?
3 በንግሊዝኛ wood ማለት ጋማርኛ ምን ማለት ነው?
4 ስምፖ ማን ይባላል?
5 ሰው ራብኝ ቢል ለመብላት አፈልጋለሁ ማለቱ ነው ወይስ ለመጠጣት አፈልጋለሁ?
6 የኢትዮጵያ ዋና ከተማ ስምዋ ምን ይባላል?

Reading passage (2)

ዮሴፍና ማርቆስ

ሁለት ጓደኞች ነበሩ። ማርቆስና ዮሴፍ ይባላሉ። በጣም ይዋደዱ ነበር። ትንሽም ሆነ ትልቅ አውሬ ለማደን ወደ ጫካ አብረው ይሄዱ ነበር። አንድ ቀን አደን ሄደው ምንም ነገር ሳያገኙ ቆዩ። ተስፋ በመቁረጥ ወደቤታቸው ለመለሱ ቢሉ ከአንድ ዛፍ ሥር ማርቆስ አንድ ማሰር አየ። ዮሴፍ ደግሞ ማሰርውን ከፍቶ ሲያይ በወርቅ የተሞላ ሆነ አገኘው። ሁለቱም እኩል በመካፈል ፈንታ አብር ጓደኝነታቸውን ረስተው የነ ነው። የነ ነው በሚል ትንቅንቅ ጀመሩ። ማርቆስ ማሰርውን መጀመሪያ ያየሁት እኔ ስለሆንኩ ወርቁ የነ ነው አለና በቦክስ ለማታ ተጋጀ። ዮሴፍም ከማርቆስ አልተሻለም። ማሰርውን መጀመሪያ የነካሁትና ከፍቼ ያየሁት እኔ ነኝና ለነ ይገባል አለ። ብዙ ተጨቃጨቁ። ማርቆስ አንድ ዘዴ ባይፈጥር ኖር በድንገተኛው ጠብ እርስ በርሳቸው በቦክስ ላናረቱ ነበር።

(ይቀጥላል)

Here is some vocabulary to help you

ጓደኛሞች	gwadäññamoč	good friends (*cf.* ጓደኛ gwadäñña friend)
ጓደኝነት	gwadäññïnnät	friendship
ተዋደደ	täwaddädä	love one another [derived stem]; (*cf.* ወደደ wäddädä love); simple imperfect ይዋደዱ yïwwaddädu
ማሰሮ	masäro	small pot
ወርቅ	wärk'	gold
ተሞላ	tämolla	be full [derived stem]
እኩል	ïkkul	equal
ተካፈለ	täkaffälä	share [derived stem] (*cf.* ከፈለ käffälä 'divide, pay'; infinitive መካፈል mäkkafäl.)
ትንቅንቅ	tïnïk'nïk'	struggle, contest
ቦክስ	boks	boxing; (በቦክስ ተማታ bäboks tämatta box one another; ተማታ 'fight, hit one another' [derived stem]; *cf.*, ማታ mätta 'hit'. Simple imperfect ይማታ yïmmatta)
ተሻለ	täšalä	be better (than)
ነካ	näkka	touch [2-lit[1] A]
ተገባ	tägäbba	deserve [impersonal, derived stem]; simple imperfect ይገባ yïggäbba – ለኔ ይገባል läne yïggäbbal 'I deserve. . .'
ተጨቃጨቀ	täč'äk'ač'č'äk'ä	argue, quarrel [derived stem]
ዛዴ	zäde	plan, scheme
ኖሮ	noro	in ባይፈጥር ኖሮ bayfät'ïr noro 'if he had not invented . . .' – cf. ፈጠረ fät't'ärä 'create, invent' [3-lit A]
ድንገተኛ	dïngätäñña	sudden, unexpected – cf. ድንገት dïngät 'sudden(ly)'
ጠብ	t'äb	quarrel, fight
ተናረተ	tänarrätä	thrash one another [derived stem] – cf. ነረተ närrätä 'thrash' [3-lit B]. simple imperfect ይናረት yïnnarrät

12 ጉብኝት በአዲስ አበባ

gubïññït bäAddis Abäba

A tour of Addis Ababa

By the end of this lesson you should be able to:

- conjugate and use derived stem verbs in a- and as-
- form comparative constructions (e.g. 'bigger than this')

A tour of Addis Ababa 📼

Tsehay takes Peter to show him some of the sights of Addis Ababa

ፀሐይ ፒተርን አዲስ አበባ ውስጥ ያሉ አንዳንድ ቦታዎችን ልታሳይ ትወስደዋለች ፡፡

ፀሐይ ፦ ፒተር ዛሬ ትርፍ ጊዜ ስላለኝ አንዳንድ ቦታዎችን ወስጄ ላሳይህ መጥቻለሁ ፡፡

ፒተር ፦ አስበሽ በመምጣትሽ በጣም አመሰግናለሁ ፡፡ አንዳንድ ቦታዎችን እኔው ራሴ አይቻለሁ ፡፡

ፀሐይ ፦ ዬት ሄድክ? ምንስ አየህ?

ፒተር ፦ መርካቶ ሄጄ ገበያውን አየሁ ፡፡ ከዚያም ስመለስ ያዲስ አበባን ማዘጋጃቤት ዙሬ አየሁት ፡፡ በጣም ደስ ይላል ፡፡

ፀሐይ ፦ በጣም ጥሩ ነው ፡፡ ዛሬ ደግሞ የቅድስት ሥላሴ ካቴድራልን፣ ብሔራዊ መዚዬምን፣ ስድስት ኪሎ አካባቢ ያለትን ሌሎች ቦታዎች ለምሳሌም ስድስት ኪሎ ዩኒቨርሲቲን አሳይሀለሁ ፡፡

ፒተር ፦ አንዴ ጠብቂኝና እንወጣለን ፡፡

ፀሐይ ፦ ይኸ በጣም የታወቀው ካቴድራላችን ነው ፡፡ አዲስ አበባ ውስጥ ካሉት ቤተ ክርስቲያኖች መካከል ትልቁ ይህ

ነው። በኖንተ አገርስ እንደዚህ አይነት አለ እንዴ?
መቼም እንደሚኖር አርገጧኝ ነኝ።

ፒተር: ሁሉም ቤት ክርስቲያኖች እንደዚህ አይነት ናቸው አንዴ?

ፀሐይ: አይ! ይኸኛው የተለየ ነው። ነገር ግን ሌሎች ቤት
ክርስቲያኖች አሠራራቸው ተመሳሳይ ነው። ስለዚህ በሊላ
ቀን ደግሞ እነሱን ላሳይህ እሞክራለሁ። ምናልባትም
የተመቸኝ እንደሆን በሜቀጥለው እሑድ እንጦጦ ኪዳነ
ምሕረት ቤተ ክርስቲያን እወስድሃለሁ። ምክንያቱም
የሚቀጥለው ሰንበት ያመቱ ኪዳነ ምሕረት በዓል ነው።
በከፍተኛ ደረጃ በደማቅ ሁኔታ እናከብራለን።

ፒተር: በኞም አገር ያሉት ቤተ ክርስቲያኖች ይህንን ይመስላሉ።
ብዙ ካቴድራሎች በዚህ መልክ የተሠሩ ናቸው። የንጦጦ
ኪዳነ ምሕረት ቤተ ክርስቲያን ያልሸዉስ አሠራሩ
እንደዚህ አይነት አይደለም እንዴ?

ፀሐይ: ያኞው አሠራሩ የተለየ ነው። በመጀመሪያ ደረጃ ቤተ
ክርስቲያንዋ የምትገኘው እንጦጦ ተራራ ላይ ሲሆን
አካባቢዉም በደን የተሸፈነ ከመሆንም በላይ ከከተማ
መሃል የራቀ በመሆኑ ፀጥታ የሰፈነበት ነው። አሠራሩ
ደግሞ ክብ ሆኖ ጣራው ቆርቆሮ የለበሰ በመሆኑ ሲያዩት
በጣም ያምራል።

ፒተር: ይህ ደግሞ ምንድን ነው? መዚዬሙ መሆኑ ነው?
በጣም ደስ ይላል አይደለም እንዴ?

ፀሐይ: አዎ ልክ ነህ። ይህ ደግሞ ብሔራዊ መዚዬም ሲሆን
በዉስጡ እጅግ ብዙ ታሪካዊ ቅርሶችን የያዘ በመሆኑ
ከፍተኛ እንክብካቤ ያደርጉለታል። በዉስጡ የተለያዩ
የታሪክ መረጃዎች ለምሳሌ ያህል ቅርጻቅርጾች፡ ጥንታዊ
የብራና ጽሑፎች፡ ረጅም ዕድሜ ያላቸው የሰዉ
አፅንቶች እንዲሁም ደግሞ ሌሎች ተመሳሳይ የሆኑ
ለታሪክ፡ ለማኅበረሰብ፡ ለቋንቋና ለዘህል ጥናት የሚረዱ
ወደም የሚያገዙ ነገሮች ይገኙበታል።

ፒተር: ወይ ጉድ! በጣም የሚገርም ነው። አሁን ግን እነን
በጣም ስለደከመኝ ሁሉን ለማየት ስለሚከብደኝ ነገ
እነዉ ራሴ ተመልሼ ጊዜ ወስጄ እመለከተዋለሁ።

ፀሐይ: እነም ያሰብከዉ እንደሱ ሲሆን ዛሬ ያመጣሁህ ቦታዉን
እንድታይ ብቻ ነው። ስለዚህ አሁን ና እንኂድና
የድርጅቱን ጓላፈ ላስተዋዉቅህ ምክንያቱም ነገ ስትመጣ
በሚገባ ገለጻ እንዲያደርግልህ።

ፒተር: እዚህ አካባቢ መጽሐፍ የያዙ ብዙ ወጣቶች አሉ።
መናፈሻ መሆኑ ነው እንዴ?

ፀሐይ: አይ! አይደለም። ስድስት ኪሎ ዩኒቨርሲቲ ነው። በፊት
ቤተ መንግሥት የነበረ ሲሆን በኋላ ግን ዩኒቨርሲቲ

ሆነ፡፡ በውስጡ ብዙ መናፈሻዎች ከመናራቸውም በላይ የመማሪያ ክፍሎችና የተማሪዎች መናሪያ ቤትም አዚሁ ጊቢ ውስጥ ይገኛል፡፡ እንዲሁም ደግሞ ተማሪዎች የሚበሉበት ምገብ ቤት፡ የሚዝናኑባቸው መጠጥ መሸጫ ቤቶችና ልዩ ልዩ የስፖርት እንቅስቃሴ የሚያደርጉባቸው መጫወቻ ቦታዎች አሉ፡፡ በተጨማሪም ድንገተኛ ሕመምና አደጋ በደረስ ጊዜ የሕክምና እርዳታ የሚሰጥ ክሊኒክ ይገኛል፡፡

ፒተር፡ ምገብ ቤት ስትኩ ራብኝ፡፡ ስለዚህ እንጂድና እንብላ፡፡ በዚያውም ካንዳንድ ተማሪዎች ጋር ለመገናኘት ያመቻል፡፡

TSEHAY: *Peter, since I've some free time today I've come to take you and show you some of the sights.*

PETER: *Thanks very much for coming and thinking of me. I have already seen several places by myself.*

TSEHAY: *Where did you go, and what did you see?*

PETER: *I went to the Merkato and saw the market. Then on my way back I looked round the City Hall. It was very nice.*

TSEHAY: *That's very good. Today, though, I'll show you Holy Trinity Cathedral, the National Museum and other sights in the Siddist Kilo area, the Siddist Kilo campus for example.*

PETER: *Wait for me a moment and then we'll go out.*

TSEHAY: *This is our well-known cathedral. This is the biggest of the churches in Addis Ababa. Are there any of this kind in your country, then? I'm sure there must be.*

PETER: *Are all the churches of this kind, then?*

TSEHAY: *No, this one's different. The other churches are all alike in construction. So I'll try to show you those another day. Maybe if I can manage it, I'll take you to Entotto Kidane Mihret church next Sunday, because next Sunday is the annual feast of Kidane Mihret. We celebrate it fully and in a most lively way.*

PETER: *The churches in our country do look like this. Many churches are built in this style. And the style of the church of Entotto Kidane Mihret which you mentioned to me is of this kind, too, isn't it?*

TSEHAY: *The style of that one is different. In the first place, whereas the church is situated on Entotto mountain, it's a place where peace prevails because it's far from the city centre, and also because the location is covered in forest, as well. It's also very beautiful to look at because the style of building is circular and the roof's covered in corrugated iron.*

PETER: *What's this, then? It must be the museum? It's very nice, isn't it?*

TSEHAY: *Yes, you're right. As this is the National Museum, they take very great care of it since inside it holds very many historical remains. There are various historical items inside, for example, sculptures, ancient vellum manuscripts, very old human bones, and likewise other similar objects that aid historical, social, linguistic and folkloric studies.*

PETER: *Wow! That's amazing. But because I'm very tired now, and because it's too much for me to see everything at once, I'll come back tomorrow by myself and take time and have a look.*

TSEHAY: *I thought that too and only brought you today to see the place. So, come now, let's go so I can introduce you to the curator of the organization, and then when you come tomorrow he can give you a proper tour.*

PETER: *There are lots of young people around here carrying books. It must be a park, then?*

TSEHAY: *No, it's not. It's Siddist Kilo campus. It was previously a royal palace, but has since become the university. Inside, as well as having many gardens, there are classrooms and student residences within the compound. Likewise, there are canteens where the students eat; snack bars where they relax; and several games locations where they can practice sports activities. In addition, there's a clinic which provides medical aid when sudden illness or accidents happen.*

PETER: *When you mention a canteen, I feel hungry. So let's go and eat. In that way it'll be an opportunity to meet some students.*

Vocabulary

ጉርፍ	tïrf	spare, free (*time*)
ቅድስት ሥላሴ	k'ïddïst sïllase	Holy Trinity
ካቴድራል	katedral	cathedral
ሙዚየም	muziyem	museum
ስድስት ኪሎ	Sïddïst Kilo	*the name of the square and surrounding area where the Social Science Faculty of Addis Ababa University is to be found. (See note 2)*

አሠራር	assärar	manner of construction
ተመሳሳይ	tämäsasay	similar, alike (cf. the verb መሰለ mässälä be like)
እንጦጦ	Ïnt'ot't'o	the name of the mountain to the north of Addis Ababa.
ኪዳነ ምሕረት	Kidänä Mïhrät	a common title given to the Virgin Mary, lit. Covenant of Mercy. Here it is the name of one of the churches on Entotto. (See note 3)
ሰንበት	sänbät	another name for እሑድ Sunday. (See lesson five)
ከፍተኛ	käffïtäñña	high, important, topmost, extreme (cf. the verb ከፍ አለ käff alä be high)
ደረጃ	däräja	step, stairs, level, grade
በከፍተኛ ደረጃ	bäkäffïtäñña däräja	at the topmost level
በመጀመሪያ ደረጃ	bämäjämmäriya däräja	in the first place
ደማቅ	dämmak'	bright, animated, lively
ሁኔታ	huneta	situation, attitude, manner, way
መልክ	mälk	appearance, style, look
ደን	dän	forest, woodland
ጸጥታ	s'ät't'ïta	quiet, calm, peace (cf. the verb ጸጥ አለ s'ät't' alä be quiet, still)
ክብ	kïbb	round, circular
ጣራ	t'ara	roof
ቆርቆሮ	k'ork'orro	corrugated iron, zinc roofing (also means tin can)
ልክ	lïkk	correct, right
ታሪካዊ	tarikawi	historical (cf. ታሪክ tarik history)
ቅርስ	k'ïrs	remains, legacy, heritage
እንክብካቤ	ïnkïbïkkabe	care, special treatment
መርጃ	märräja	proof, evidence, fact, (piece of) information (cf. the verb ተረዳ tärädda realize, understand, be persuaded)
ቅርጽ	k'ïrs'	image, model, sculpture, carving
ቅርጽቅርጽ	k'ïrs'ak'ïrs'	sculptures
ጥንታዊ	t'ïntawi	ancient (cf. ጥንት t'ïnt ancient times)
ብራና	bïranna, branna	parchment
የብራና መጽሐፍ	yäbranna mäs'haf	vellum book, vellum manuscript
ዕድሜ	ïdme	age
አጥንት	at'ïnt	bone
ማኅበረሰብ	mahbäräsäb	society
ጥናት	t'ïnat	study

የማኅበረሰብ ጥናት yämahbäräsäb t'inat		social studies, sociology
ድርጅት	dirijjit	organization, firm, institution
ጓላፊ	halafi	curator, keeper, someone in charge
ገላፅ	gäläs'a	description, briefing (*cf. the verb* ገላፅ gälläs'ä reveal, describe, explain)
ገላፅ አደረገ	gäläs'a adärrägä	give a briefing, show someone round
ቤተ መንግሥት	betä mängïst	royal palace
መማሪያ ክፍል	mämmariya kïfil	classroom, study room (*cf. the verb* ተማረ tämarä learn, study)
ግቢ	gïbbi	compound (*i.e. a collection of buildings surrounded by a wall or fence.*) (*See note 2*)
እንቅስቃሴ	ïnk'ïsïk'k'ase	movement, activity
የስፖርት እንቅስቃሴ	yäsport ïnk'ïsïk'k'ase	sports activities, sports
አደጋ	adäga	accident, danger
ክሊኒክ	klinik	clinic (*the same as* የሕክምና ጣቢያ yähïkmïnna t'abiya, *lit.* 'medical station')

Verbs

አሳየ	asayyä	show [derived stem in as-]. (*See grammar section*)
አመሰገነ	amäsäggänä	thank [derived stem in a-]. (*See grammar section*)
ዞረ	zorä	go round [2-lit[5]]
ተለየ	täläyyä	be different, distinguished from [derived stem]
ተለያየ	täläyayyä	be different from one another, be various [derived stem]
ተመቸ	tämäččä	be convenient [derived stem]
ተሠራ	täsärra	be built, made [derived stem]
ተገኘ	tägäññä	be found, located [derived stem]. Simple imperfect, ይገኝ yïggäññ
ተሸፈነ	täšäffänä	be covered [derived stem]
ራቀ	rak'ä	be far away [2-lit[3]] (*cf. the adjective* ሩቅ ruk' far)
ሰፈነ	säffänä	be dominant, prevail, reign [3-lit B]
አማረ	amarä	be beautiful [derived stem in a-]
አደረገ	adärrägä	do, make [derived stem in a-]

አገዘ	aggäzä	help, aid, assist [3-lit B]
ከበደ	käbbädä	be heavy, serious, severe, respected [3-lit A]. (*As an impersonal verb* ከበደኝ **käbbädäñ** I am overawed; it's too much for me)
ተመለከተ	tämäläkkätä	look at [derived stem]. Simple imperfect, ይመለከት **yïmmäläkkät**
አመጣ	amät't'a	bring [derived stem in a-]
አስተዋወቀ	astäwawwäk'ä	introduce someone to somebody [derived stem in **astä-**]
ተዝናና	täznanna	relax [derived stem]. Simple imperfect, ይዝናና **yïznanna**
አመቸ	amäččä	be suitable, comfortable, opportune [derived stem in **a-**] (*cf.* ተመቸ **tämäččä** *in this vocabulary*)

Particles, phrases, etc.

እንደሁን	ïndähon	if (*following a relative verb*)
የተመቸኝ እንደሁን	yätämäččäñ ïndähon	if it is convenient for me
እጅግ	ïjjïg	*means the same as* በጣም **bät'am** very
ወይ ጉድ	wäy gud	how amazing! how strange! wow! (an exclamation of astonishment, surprise or dismay)
በሚገባ	bämmïggäbba	properly, duly, appropriately (*cf. the verb* ተገባ **tägäbba** be right, fitting)
በተጨማሪ	bätäč'ämmari	in addition, what's more, moreover (*cf. the verb* ጨመረ **č'ämmärä** add)

Notes on the dialogue

1 The dialogues in this and the next lesson are framed in an ordinary Amharic conversational style. You will see that this can be quite complicated and can have many turns of phrase that are rather different from what we might say in English.

  Although these dialogues may at first seem difficult to you, if you follow the Amharic using the vocabulary and the grammar rather than at first trying an English translation, you will get a better feel for the language. They should also provide you with a model for your own Amharic conversation!

2 Only the largest thoroughfares (ጉዳና gwädana) and the squares (አደባባይ addäbabay) in Addis Ababa have names, and even then people often don't use these official names at all. Instead there are popular terms for areas and districts, some of which date back to the early days of the city (Addis Ababa was founded by Menilek II as a new, fixed capital in 1889). For instance, ስድስት ኪሎ Sïddïst Kilo and አራት ኪሎ Aratt Kilo are the popular names for the two large squares which are officially called የካቲት 12 አደባባይ and መጋቢት 28 አደባባይ, respectively. No one knows for sure why they are commonly called 'Six Kilos' and 'Four Kilos'! The university campus is split between these two areas which are connected by a wide thoroughfare – the Social Science Faculty and the Institute of Ethiopian Studies are located at Siddist Kilo, whilst the Science Faculty is at Aratt Kilo. The area of the Graduate School, which lies between the two, is jokingly called አምስት ኪሎ Ammïst Kilo – 'Five Kilos'! The Siddist Kilo campus is within the old palace grounds, which Haile Sellassie gave to the university after 1960 when he built a newer palace downtown. This was called ኢዮቤልዩ ቤተ መንግሥት Iyobelyu Betä Mängïst 'The Jubilee Palace', and is still used for official receptions and state occasions. The oldest palace in Addis Ababa is the one built by Menilek II, which is popularly known by the simple name ግቢ Gïbbi 'The Ghebbi', from the Amharic word for a compound. The Ghebbi covers a wide area and from the outside, like the Siddist Kilo campus, looks like a park surrounded by high railings with various buildings dotted amongst the trees.

3 Ethiopian churches are commonly called simply after the saint in whose name they are consecrated, usually without the accompanying title of ቅዱስ k'ïddus '(male) saint' or ቅድስት k'ïddïst '(female) saint'. The name of the district or village where the church stands may also be prefixed. So, እንጦጦ ኪዳን ምሕረት Ïnt'ot't'o Kidanä Mïhrät is how you speak of the Church of Kidane Mihret (The Virgin Mary) on top of Entotto Mountain. Similarly, አራዳ ጊዮርጊስ Arada Giyorgis is the Cathedral of St. George in the district of Arada, one of the largest and oldest churches in Addis Ababa.

Whilst St. George's Cathedral is built in a traditional Ethiopian style, Trinity Cathedral (ቅድስት ሥላሴ) is constructed in an ornate Baroque style imitating a Southern European cathedral.

Grammar

Derived stems

Amongst the vocabulary of the more recent lessons you have
encountered quite a number of verbs that have been described simply as 'derived stems'. This means that in forming the various tenses they do not follow the basic patterns that you have learned so far
(3-lit, 2-lit[1], 2-lit[2], 4-lit, and so on). Instead, they are 'derived' from
one or another of these patterns by some additional element that is
added to the basic root. This additional element may be a prefix,
like **a-, as-,** or **tä-**, if you look back over the vocabularies you will see
that most of the derived stems there begin with one of these. The
additional element may also involve some internal change, as in
አስተዋወቀ astäwawwäk'ä 'introduce' from simple **አወቀ awwäk'ä**
'know' in the new vocabulary in this lesson; or **ተገናኘ tägänaññä**
'meet' from **አገኘ agäññä** 'find'; or the set **ተናገረ tänaggärä** 'talk';
ተነጋገረ tänägaggärä 'converse, talk together'; and **አነጋገረ annä-
gaggärä** 'engage in conversation', all from the simple stem **ነገረ näg-
gärä** 'speak', all of which you have encountered in previous lessons.
   It has to be said there is a very large number of these derived
stems in Amharic. They give the verbal system of the language a
high degree of complexity, but at the same time allow for a great
deal of subtlety and richness of expression. In the remaining lessons
of this book we shall look at only the simplest derived stems,
essentially those formed by prefixes. As you go on to expand your
knowledge of Amharic, the more you get to speak it and read it, you
will soon discover how to form and use the remaining derived stems
by practice.

Derived stems in a- and as-

In this lesson we shall look at derived stems formed by the prefixes
a- and **as-**. Here is a list of some such derived stems that you have
met already. See how many others you can find by going over the
vocabularies of past lessons. Remember, though, that not all verbs
that begin with the vowel **a** are necessarily derived stems!

አገኘ	agäññä	find	**አሳየ**	asayyä	show
አነበበ	anäbbäbä	read	**አስገረመ**	asgärrämä	surprise
አደረሰ	adärräsä	take	**አስፈለገ**	asfällägä	be necessary

| አወራ | awärra | tell news | አመጣ | amät't'a | bring |
| አመቸ | amäččä | suit | አደረገ | adärrägä | do |

1 a- *stems*

Most **a-** stems are derived from simple stems, like አደረስ 'take' from ደረሰ 'arrive' in the list above. The meaning of the derived stem in these cases is usually 'to make happen', 'to cause to happen', and therefore the **a-** stem is sometimes called the 'causative'. Typically, the simple stem is an 'intransitive' verb, that is one that cannot logically have a direct object, and the derived **a-** stem produces a 'transitive' verb, that is one that can and normally does have a direct object. You have to be careful here, however, because in English we sometimes use the same word in both instances where Amharic makes a clear distinction. The pairs of sentences below should make this clearer:

ቡና ፈላ	bunna fälla	the coffee boiled	[intrans.]
ቡናውን አፈላች	bunnawn afällačč	she boiled the coffee	[trans.]
ቁስሉ ዳነ	k'uslu danä	his wound healed	[intrans.]
ቁስሉን አዳነ	k'uslun adanä	he healed his wound	[trans.]
ወተት ፈሰሰ	wätät fässäsä	the milk spilled	[intrans.]
ወተቱን አፈሰሰ	wätätun afässäsä	he spilled the milk	[trans.]
እሳት ጨስ	ïsat č'äsä	the fire smoked	[intrans.]
ሲጃራ አጨስ	sijara ač'äsä	he smoked a cigarette	[trans.]

In a few instances English uses a related word to express the transitive or 'causative' notion just as Amharic uses an **a-** stem derivative of a simple stem. You can see this clearly from the examples below:

ማሰሪያው ጠበቀ	masäriyaw t'äbbäk'ä	the fastening is tight [intrans.]
ማሰሪያውን አጠበቀ	masäriyawn at'äbbäk'ä	he tightened the fastening [caus.]
ጌቶች ወፍረዋል	getočč wäffiräwal	the boss has grown fat [intrans.]
ስኳር ያወፍራል	sïkkwar yawäffiral	sugar is fattening [caus.]
ደክሞኛል	däkmoññal	I am tired [intrans.]
ሥራ አድክሞኛል	sïra adkïmoññal	work has tired me out [caus.]

As you can see from these examples this is especially common with what we may call 'adjective verbs', that is verbs like ጠበቀ [3-lit A] 'be tight'* and ወፈረ [3-lit B] 'be fat' which in their English translations are often rendered by 'be' and an adjective.

* This is a different verb from ጠበቀ [3-lit B] 'wait (for)' which you know already.

At other times, English uses a quite different word to express the transitive or 'causative' idea that is expressed in Amharic by the a- stem derivative. Again, consider the pairs of sentences below:

ልጁ በላ	lïjju bälla	the child ate	[intrans.]
ልጇን አበላቸ	lïjjwan abällačč	she fed her child	[trans.]
አልማዝ መጣች	Almaz mät't'ačč	Almaz came	[intrans.]
ምግቡን አመጣች	mïgïbun amät't'ačč	she brought the food	[trans.]
ደሴ ደረስኩ	Dässe därräskw	I arrived in Dessie	[intrans.]
ደሴ አደረሱኝ	Dässe adärräsuñ	they took me to Dessie	[trans.]
ምሳ ቀረበ	mïsa k'ärräbä	lunch arrived/was served	[intrans.]
ምሳ አቀረበች	mïsa ak'ärräbäčč	she served lunch	[trans.]
ሌቦቹ በረሩ	leboččnu bärräru	the thieves fled	[intrans.]
ሌቦቹን አበረሩ	leboččun abärräru	they chased the thieves off	[trans.]

Yet again, we sometimes have to use in English a whole phrase where Amharic expresses a 'causative' idea by the a- stem derivative. So:

መቼ መሸ	mäče mässä	when did it become evening?	[intrans.]
ሲጠጣ አመሸ	sit'ät't'a amässä	he spent the evening drinking	[caus.]
እዚህ ቆመ	ïzzih k'omä	it stood here	[intrans.]
እዚህ አቆመው	ïzzih ak'omäw	he set it up here	[caus.]

Lastly, the basic or simple meaning of a verbal idea may be expressed in Amharic by an a- stem derivative, and the corresponding simple stem either has no apparent connection in meaning with the derivative, or in a few instances is not used at all. There are some very important and basic pieces of vocabulary amongst the latter category, some of which you have already learned. Consider the examples below.

ገባ	gäbba	'enter'	*but*	አገባ	agäbba	'marry' as well as 'put in'
መለጠ	mällät'ä	'peel'	*but*	አመለጠ	amällät'ä	'escape'
ረዳ	rädda	'help'	*but*	አረዳ	arädda	'announce a death'
አደረገ	adärrägä	'do'	*but no*	*ረደገ		
አገኘ	agäññä	'find'	*but no*	*ገኘ		
አበደረ	abäddärä	'lend'	*but no*	*በደረ		
አለቀሰ	aläk'k'äsä	'weep, cry'	*but no*	*ለቀሰ		

As with all derived stems, you cannot form **a-** stems at random. In other words, even though you know a simple stem, like መለሰ **mälläsä** 'answer, give back' or ቀረ **k'ärrä** 'remain behind', you cannot predict for certain whether it will have an **a-** stem derivative, even when the meaning would suggest one. In fact, both of the verbs just mentioned form their 'causatives' by means of the **as-** stem and not the **a-** stem: አስመለሰ **asmälläsä** 'make someone give back, recover something'; and አስቀረ **ask'ärrä** 'exclude, abolish, keep out'. You will need to use a dictionary to see not only what derived stems mean, but also whether a particular one is in fact used.

The inflexion of a- stem derivatives

Each of the derived stems has its own patterns of inflexion. This means that you will need to learn new stem shapes for each class of verb in each tense. This is not such an enormous task as it may sound, as often the patterns are similar to those you learned for the simple stems.

The personal markers for each of the various tenses and the prefixes and suffixes that form the non-finite parts of the verb (i.e. infinitive, instrument and agent nouns) are the same as you have already learned. In the tables that follow, therefore, only the third person masculine singular form of each tense will be given. You can easily form the other persons from this.

As an example, the various tenses, etc., of the **a-** stem of trilteral verbs, illustrated by አደከመ **adäkkämä** 'tire' [A-type] and አበደረ **abäddärä** 'lend' [B-type] are set out below.

	3-lit A		3-lit B	
s. past	አደከመ	adäkkämä	አበደረ	abäddärä
s. impf.	ያደክም	yadäk(ï)m	ያበድር	yabäddïr
c. impf.	ያደክማል	yadäkmal	ያበድራል	yabäddïral
juss.	ያድክም	yadkïm	ያበድር	yabäddïr
imp.	አድክም	adkïm	አበድር	abäddïr
ger.	አድክሞ	adkïmo	አበድሮ	abäddïro
c. ger.	አድክማል	adkïmwal	አበድሯል	abäddïrwal
inf.	ማድከም	madkäm	ማበደር	mabäddär
inst.	ማድከሚያ	madkämiya	ማበደሪያ	mabäddäriya
ag.	አድካሚ	adkami	አበዳሪ	abäddari

Points to note

1 The vowel **a** of the 'causative' prefix is present in all tenses.
2 In B-type verbs the shape of the stem following the **a-** prefix is the same as in simple stems, which you have learned already.
3 However, in A-type verbs the shape of the stem following the **a-** prefix differs in several places from that of the corresponding simple stem: in the jussive and imperative; in the gerundive; in the infinitive and instrument noun; in the agent noun.
4 All the usual rules (a) of vowel hierarchy between stems and suffixes, and (b) of palatalization apply.

Similarly with other stem types (biliterals, quadriliterals, etc.):

	2-lit^l A		2-lit^l B	
s. past	አበላ	abälla	አጠጣ	at'ät't'a
s. impf.	ያበላ	yabäla	ያጠጣ	yat'ät't'a
c. impf.	ያበላል	yabälal	ያጠጣል	yat'ät't'al
juss.	ያብላ	yabla	ያጠጣ	yat'ät't'a
imp.	አብላ	abla	አጠጣ	at'ät't'a
ger.	አብልቶ	ablïto	አጠጥቶ	at'ät't'ïto
c. ger.	አብልቷል	ablïtwal	አጠጥቷል	at'ät't'ïtwal
inf.	ማብላት	mablat	ማጠጣት	mat'ät't'at
inst.	ማብያ	mabya	ማጠጫ	mat'äč'č'a
ag.	አብዪ	abyi	አጠጪ	at'äč'č'i

	2-lit² A		2-lit² B	
s. past	አገኘ	agäññä	አቴየ	ak'wäyyä
s. impf.	ያገኝ	yagäñ	ያቴይ	yak'wäyy
c. impf.	ያገኛል	yagäñal	ያቴያል	yak'wäyyal
juss.	ያገኝ	yagiñ	ያቴይ	yak'wäyy
imp.	አገኝ	agiñ	አቴይ	ak'wäyy
ger.	አገኝቶ	agiñto	አቴይቶ	ak'wäyyïto
c. ger.	አገኝቷል	agiñtwal	አቴይቷል	ak'wäyyïtwal
inf.	ማገኘት	magñät	ማቴየት	mak'wäyyät
inst.	ማገኛ	magña	ማቴያ	mak'wäyya
ag.	አገኚ	agñi	አቴዪ	ak'wäyyi

	2-lit³		2-lit⁴	
s. past	አዳነ	adanä	አጨሰ	ač'esä
s. impf.	ያድን	yadïn	ያጨስ	yač'es
c. impf.	ያድናል	yadïnal	ያጨሳል	yač'esal
juss.	ያድን	yadïn	ያጪስ	yač'is
imp.	አድን	adïn	አጪስ	ač'is
ger.	አድኖ	adïno	አጪሶ	ač'iso
c. ger.	አድኗል	adïnwal	አጪኳል	ač'iswal
inf.	ማዳን	madan	ማጨስ	mač'es
inst.	ማዳኛ	madaña	ማጨሻ	mač'eša
ag.	አዳኝ	adañ	አጭያሽ	ačyaš

	2-lit⁵	
s. past	አቆመ	ak'omä
s. impf.	ያቆም	yak'om
c. impf.	ያቆማል	yak'omal
juss.	ያቁም	yak'um
imp.	አቁም	ak'um
ger.	አቁሞ	ak'umo
c. ger.	አቁማል	ak'umwal
inf.	ማቆም	mak'om
inst.	ማቆሚያ	mak'omiya
ag.	አቋሚ	ak'wami

አበላ 'feed', አጠጣ 'give to drink'; አገኝ 'find'; አቴየ 'keep, detain'; አዳነ 'cure'; አጨሰ/አጪስ 'smoke'; አቆመ 'stop, erect'.

	4-lit	
s. past	አሠለጠነ	asälät't'änä
s. impf.	ያሠለጥን	yasälät't'in
c. impf.	ያሠለጥናል	yasälät't'inal
juss.	ያሠልጥን	yasält'in
imp.	አሠልጥን	asält'in
ger.	አሠልጥኖ	asält'ino
c. ger.	አሠልጥኗል	asält'inwal
inf.	ማሠልጠን	masält'än
inst.	ማሠልጠኛ	masält'äña
ag.	አሠልጣኝ	asält'añ

	3-lit X		3-lit Y	
s. past	አመነታ	amänätta	አዘጋየ	azägäyyä
s. impf.	ያመነታ	yamänätta	ያዘጋይ	yazägäyy
c. impf.	ያመነታል	yamänättal	ያዘጋያል	yazägäyyal
juss.	ያመንታ	yamänta	ያዘጋይ	yazäg(i)y
imp.	አመንታ	amänta	አዘጋይ	azäg(i)y
ger.	አመንትቶ	amäntito	አዘጋይቶ	azägyïto
c. ger.	አመንትቷል	amäntïtwal	አዘጋይቷል	azägyïtwal
inf.	ማመንታት	mamäntat	ማዘጋየት	mazägyät
inst.	ማመንጫ	mamänča	ማዘጋያ	mazägya
ag.	አመንቺ	amänči	አዘጋዪ	azägyi

አሠለጠነ 'train'; አመነታ 'hesitate'; አዘጋየ 'detain, postpone'.

2 as- *stems*

The derived stem in as- has a similar meaning to that in a-. It is also a kind of 'causative', but frequently implies that you cause, make or get someone else to do the action of the base verb.

ሥራውን አስጨረስኩት	sïrawn asč'ärräskut	I got him to finish his work
ጩኸቱ አላስተኛም	č'uhätu alastäññam	the noise didn't let one sleep
ቆሎ አስበላቸው	k'olo asbällaččïw	she made him eat the *qolo*

If the person whom you get to do the action is mentioned, then he/she is expressed as a direct object, and as the object of the action itself may also be expressed, this means that as- stem verbs can have two direct objects. The examples below should make this clear.

ቤቱን ጠረገችፕ	betun t'ärrägäčč
	she cleaned the house
ቤቱን አስጠረገችፕ	betun ast'ärrägäčč
	she had the house cleaned
ገረድዋን ቤቱን አስጠረገችፕ	gärädwan betun ast'ärrägäčč
	she had her maid clean the house

Intransitive verbs that form a transitive derivation by means of the prefix a- can, in turn, build a 'causative' of this by means of the as- prefix. In these instances, therefore, a simple stem can have both an a- and an as- derived stem. So:

ከበደ መጣ	Käbbädä mät't'a
	Kebbede came
ከበደ ገንዘቡን አመጣ	Käbbädä gänzäbun amät't'a
	Kebbede brought the money
ከበደ ገንዘቡን አስመጣ	Käbbädä gänzäbun asmät't'a
	Kebbede had the money brought

You will note that you cannot normally have more than one derivational prefix on the same verb base: as- replaces a- in the pair አስመጣ and አመጣ. The same thing happens when you want to make a 'causative' of a verb whose basic meaning is expressed by a derived stem, like አገኘ agäññä 'find, obtain, get' and አደረገ adärrägä 'do'. The 'causatives' of these are, respectively:

አስገኘ asgäññä produce, provide (*i.e. cause someone to obtain*)
አስደረገ asdärrägä have something done

Verbs whose simple stems begin in a cannot of course form 'causatives' by means of the a- prefix as this would break the rule about having two vowels together. Instead, verbs of this shape use the as- derivative.

አደሰ addäsä	be new	አሳደሰ asaddäsä	renew, repair
አረፈ arräfä	rest, land	አሳረፈ asarräfä	bring to rest, land [trans.]
አወቀ awwäk'ä	know	አሳወቀ asawwäk'ä	inform, acquaint
አሰበ assäbä	think	አሳሰበ asassäbä	remind, recommend
አጠበ at't'äbä	wash	አሳጠበ asat't'äbä	have something washed
አየ ayyä	see	አሳየ asayyä	show

አጣ **at't'a** be without   አሳጣ **asat't'a** deprive, cause to be without

አደረ **addärä** spend the night   አሳደረ **asaddärä** put someone up for the night

In verbs whose simple stems begin in s, z, š or s' the s of the **as-** prefix merges with this initial consonant to form a double or geminate **ss, zz, šš** or **s's'**. This means that from the written dictionary form (the third person masculine simple past) you cannot tell whether such a verb is an **a-** or an **as-** stem derivative:

ጻፈ	**s'afä**	write	አጻፈ	**as's'afä**	have something written
ሠራ	**särra**	build, make	አሠራ	**assärra**	have something built, made
ሳመ	**samä**	kiss	አሳመ	**assamä**	offer (*e.g. one's hand*) to be kissed
ሸጠ	**šät'ä**	sell	አሸጠ	**aššät'ä**	offer for sale
ዘረፈ	**zärräfä**	rob	አዘረፈ	**azzärräfä**	have someone robbed

Sometimes both **a-** and **as-** stem derivatives occur. Of course, in context there is not likely to be any real confusion:

ሠለጠነ	**sälät't'änä**	be skilled, efficient, trained
አሠለጠነ	**asälät't'änä**	train
አሠለጠነ	**assälät't'änä**	have someone trained

The inflexion of as- stems

There is no distinction between A- and B-type verbs in the **as-** stem.

	3-lit		*3-lit in 'a'*	
s. past	አስፈለገ	asfällägä	አሳደሰ	asaddäsä
s. impf.	ያስፈልግ	yasfällig	ያሳድስ	yasaddïs
c. impf.	ያስፈልጋል	yasfälligal	ያሳድሳል	yasaddïsal
juss.	ያስፈልግ	yasfällig	ያሳድስ	yasaddïs
imp.	አስፈልግ	asfällig	አሳድስ	asaddïs
ger.	አስፈልጎ	asfälligo	አሳድሶ	asaddïso
c. ger.	አስፈልጓል	asfälligwal	አሳድጓል	asaddïswal
inf.	ማስፈለግ	masfälläg	ማሳደስ	masaddäs
inst.	ማስፈለጊያ	masfällägiya	ማሳደሻ	masaddäša
ag.	አስፈላጊ	asfällagi	አሳዳሺ	asaddaši

አስፈለገ 'be neccesary'; አሳደሰ 'renew, repair'

Points to note

1 The syllable -as- is present throughout.
2 The pattern of stem shapes following the as- prefix is identical to the B-type pattern of simple stems.

	2-lit¹		2-lit²	
s. past	አስበላ	asbälla	አስቀረ	ask'ärrä
s. impf.	ያስበላ	yasbälla	ያስቀር	yask'ärr
c. impf.	ያስበላል	yasbällal	ያስቀራል	yask'ärral
juss.	ያስበላ	yasbälla	ያስቀር	yask'ärr
imp.	አስበላ	asbälla	አስቀር	ask'ärr
ger.	አስበልቶ	asbällïto	አስቀርቶ	ask'ärrïto
c. ger.	አስበልቷል	asbällïtwal	አስቀርቷል	ask'ärrïtwal
inf.	ማስበላት	masbällat	ማስቀረት	mask'ärrät
inst.	ማስበያ	masbäyya	ማስቀሪያ	mask'ärriya
ag.	አስበዪ	asbäyyi	አስቀሪ	ask'ärri

	2-lit³	
s. past	አስዳነ	asdanä
s. impf.	ያስድን	yasdïn
c. impf.	ያስድናል	yasdïnal
juss.	ያስድን	yasdïn
imp.	አስድን	asdïn
ger.	አስድኖ	asdïno
c. ger.	አስድኗል	asdïnwal
inf.	ማስዳን	masdan
inst.	ማስዳኛ	masdañña
ag.	አስዳኝ	asdañ

	2-lit⁴		2-lit⁵	
s. past	አስኪደ	askedä	አስቆመ	ask'omä
s. impf.	ያስኪድ	yasked	ያስቆም	yask'om
c. impf.	ያስኪዳል	yaskedal	ያስቆማል	yask'omal
juss.	ያስኪድ	yaskid	ያስቁም	yask'um
imp.	አስኪድ	askid	አስቁም	ask'um
ger.	አስኪዶ	askido	አስቁሞ	ask'umo
c. ger.	አስኪ ዳል	askidwal	አስቁማል	ask'umwal
inf.	ማስኪድ	masked	ማስቆም	mask'om
inst.	ማስኪ ጃ	maskejja	ማስቆሚያ	mask'omiya
ag.	አስኪያጅ	askiyaj	አስቋሚ	ask'wami

	4-lit	
s. past	አስመረመረ	asmärämmärä
s. impf.	ያስመረምር	yasmärämmïr
c. impf.	ያስመረምራል	yasmärämmïral
juss.	ያስመርምር	yasmärmïr
imp.	አስመርምር	asmärmïr
ger.	አስመርምሮ	asmärmïro
c. ger.	አስመርምሯል	asmärmïrwal
inf.	ማስመርመር	masmärmär
inst.	ማስመርመሪያ	masmärmäriya
ag.	አስመርማሪ	asmärmari

	3-lit X		3-lit Y	
s. past	አዘረጋ	azzärägga	አስጐበኛ	asgwäbäññä
s. impf.	ያዘረጋ	yazzärägga	ያስጐብኝ	yasgwäbäññ
c. impf.	ያዘረጋል	yazzäräggal	ያስጐብኛል	yasgwäbäññal
juss.	ያዘርጋ	yazzärga	ያስጐብኝ	yasgwäbïñ
imp.	አዘርጋ	azzärga	አስጐብኝ	asgwäbïñ
ger.	አዘርጌቶ	azzärgïto	አስጐብኝቶ	asgwäbïñto
c. ger.	አዘርጌቷል	azzärgïtwal	አስጐብኝቷል	asgwäbïñtwal
inf.	ማዘርጋት	mazzärgat	ማስጐብኘት	masgwäbñät
inst.	ማዘርጊያ	mazzärgiya	ማስጐብኛ	masgwäbña
ag.	አዘርጊ	azzärgi	አስጐብኚ	asgwäbñi

አስበላ 'have something eaten, get someone to eat'; አስቀረ 'leave out'; አስዳነ 'have someone cured'; አስኬደ 'let go, lead'; አስቆመ 'stop something'; አስመረመረ 'have someone or something examined'; አዘረጋ 'have something laid out'; አስጐበኝ 'let someone visit'.

The 'causative' of 'አለ verbs'

'አለ verbs', that is, those composed of a fixed element and አለ alä 'to say' (which we met in the previous lesson) form their 'causatives' by replacing አለ with አደረገ adärrägä 'do' (or sometimes አሰኘ assäññä [2-lit[2] as- stem]) in the case of a direct transitivization, and with አስደረገ asdärrägä 'have someone do' if a third party is involved. The following example should make this clear:

ምርት ከፍ ብLዋል	mïrt käff bïlwal	production is high
ምርት ከፍ አድርጓል	mïrt käff adrïgwal	he has raised production

ምርት ከፍ አስደርጓል mïrt käff asdärrïgwal he has had production raised

'አለ verbs' that denote a sensation or emotion usually form their 'causatives' with the verb አሰኝ assäññä, which is chiefly only used in this context. On its own አሰኝ means 'call, name', or as an impersonal verb 'feel like doing'.

ደስ አለኝ	däss aläñ	I am happy, pleased
ደስ ያሰኛል	däss yassäññal	it will be pleasing, nice
አማርኛሽ በጣም ደስ የሚያሰኝ ነው	amarïññaš bät'am däss yämmiyassäññ näw	
		your Amharic is very nice

Exercises

1 Here are some short statements. Using the word in brackets as a subject, turn them into transitive statements, first in the simple past, and then in the compound imperfect

---

Example: ቡና ፈላ። (አልማዝ) → አልማዝ ቡናውን አፈላች
አልማዝ ቡናውን ታፈላለች

---

1 ሻይ ቀረበ (አሳላፊው)
2 ዕቃው ወረደ (ኩሊ)
3 ሠራተኞቹ ሠለጠኑ (የድርጅቱ ጎላፊ)
4 መኪና በቀይ መብራት ቆመ። (እኔ)
5 ፈረስ ጠጣ። (አሽከርቹ)
6 ክፍሉ ጨለመ። (አንተ)
7 ቁስሉ ዳነለት። (ሐኪም)
8 የሊጋው ቤት ፈረሰ። (ባላገርቹ)

2 In the same way as in exercise one rewrite the following sentences so that the person denoted by the word in brackets becomes the initiator of the action. This time use the same tense in your answer as in the original sentence

---

Example: ገረዲቱ ቤቱን ጠረገች (ወይዘሮ ድንቀነሽ) →
ወይዘሮ ድንቀነሽ ገረዲቱን ቤቱን አስጠረገቻዋት

1 ተማሪዎቹ ፈተናውን አለፉ። (አስተማሪው)
2 ከበደ በሩን ይከፍታል። (እኔ)
3 አልማዝ የቤት ኪራይ ከፍላለች። (አቶ ሙሉጌታ)
4 ዘበኛው ድንኳኑን ይተክላል። (እኛ)
5 ተረፈ ጠርሙዙን ከፍቷል። (አልማዝ)
6 ሶስት ሰዓት ላይ ሥራ ጨረስኩ። (ጌቶች)
7 አስታማሚዋ ልጅዋን መርምራለች። (እናቱ)
8 ብሔራዊ ሙዚዬምን አየህ? (ፀሐይ)

3 How would you say the following in Amharic? Each one will require either an a- or an as- stem derivative.

1 Ali showed me the photos he took last week.
2 They gave us a lot to eat and drink at the party.
3 The director of the factory raised production last year.
4 It's very nice to listen to music in the evening.
5 Can you put these guests up for the night?

4 Imagine you're showing an Ethiopian visitor round your town. How would you answer the following questions that your visitor asks about the town?

— የከተማውን ሙዚዬም መጉብኘት ይቻላል?
— በሙዚዬምስ ውስጥ ምን ምን አይነት ቅርስ አለ?
— ከተማው በዬትኛው ክፍለ ዘመን ነው የተቆረቆረ?
— ግንት ከተማ ውስጥ የስፖርት ሜዳ አለ?
— የከተማስ ነዋሪ ቁጥር ስንት ነው?
— ጥሩ ቡና ቤት ታውቃለህ/ታውቂያለሽ?
   በል እንግዲህ ቡና እንጠጣ!

Grammar

Expressions of comparison

In the dialogue Tsehay told Peter, አዲስ አበባ ውስጥ ካሉት ቤተ ክርስቲያኖች መካከል ትልቁ ይህ ነው Addis Abäba wïst' kallut betä krïstiyanoč mäkakkäl tïllïk'u yïh näw 'this is the biggest of the churches in Addis Ababa'. Literally translated this is, 'from amongst the churches which are in Addis Ababa this is the big one'. Below are some more sentences which illustrate how Amharic expresses comparative statements.

አዲስ አበባ ከጉንደር ትልቅ   Addis Abäba käGwändär tïllïk' näw
ነው   Addis Ababa is bigger than Gondar
አልጋዬ ከገድጓዳው   algaye kägïdgïddaw räjjïm näw
ረጂም ነው   my bed is longer than the wall
ድሬ ዳዋ ከመቀሌ የሞቀ ነው Dire Dawa käMäk'älle yämok'ä näw
                     Dire-Dawa is warmer than Mekelle

From these you can say two things about comparative statements in
Amharic: (a) the preposition ከ- kä- is used in the sense of English
'than'; (b) that in Amharic adjectives do not alter in the comparative, or for that matter, in the superlative either. Where English
would say, for instance, 'big, bigger, biggest' the Amharic ትልቅ
tïllïk' by itself conveys all of these. In this respect, Amharic is for
once simpler than English! By the way, you will also notice that
adjective verbs like ሞቀ 'be warm' can be used as well as simple
adjectives.

To stress the degree of comparison you can place one of the
words ይልቅ yïlïk' 'more', ይበልጥ yïbält', or የበለጠ yäbällät'ä after
the noun against which the comparison is made:

ካባቱ ይልቅ እናቱን   kabbatu yïlïk' ïnnatun yïwäddal
ይወዳል   he loves his mother more than his
                      father
ከዚያ መጽሐፍ ይልቅ   käzziya mäs'haf yïlïk' yïh mäs'het
ይህ መጽሔት ጥሩ ነው   t'ïru näw
                      this magazine is better than that book
ከኛ የበለጠ አንተ   känña yäbällät'ä anta bägïls'
በግልጽ ትናገራለህ   tïnnaggäralläh
                      you speak more plainly than us
ከጓደኞችዋ ይበልጥ   kägwaddäññoččwa yïbält'
አሰዋ ትማራለች   ïsswa tïmmarallächč
                      she studies more than her friends

Amharic also has a few adjective verbs which have an inherently
comparative meaning:

በለጠ	bällät'ä	be bigger, greater	[3-lit A]
እነሰ	annäsä	be less, smaller	[3-lit A]
ተሻለ	täšalä	be better	[2-lit³ derived stem in tä-]; *you have already met this as an impersonal verb meaning* to prefer

So the first example above could also be expressed as:

አዲስ አበባ ከጎንደር ይበልጣል   Addis Abäba käGwändär yïbält'al
                               Addis Ababa is bigger than Gondar

አልማዝ ከፀሐይ በቁመት   Almaz käS'ähay bäk'umät tansal-
ታንሳለች   läčč
                                Almaz is shorter in stature than
                                Tsehay

ይኸኛው ይሻላል   yïhäññaw yïššalal
                                this one is better

Superlative statements can also employ the preposition ከ- and the unaltered adjective. This time, however, the definite article is added to the adjective, as in the sentence from the dialogue. You can also use the word ሁሉ hullu 'all' to express the range of the comparison. The examples below illustrate various 'superlative' statement types.

ከልጆቻችን ወፍራሙ እሱ ነው   kälïjjoččaččïn wäframu ïssu näw
                                he is the fattest of our children

ከተማሪዎቹ ሁሉ ታላቅዋ እስዋ ናት   kätämariwoččhu hullu tallak'wa
                                ïsswa nat
                                she is the eldest of all the students

Having said all this, however, you should remember that Amharic does not have comparative and superlative adjectives as such. There are quite a few constructions which can be used as equivalents of English comparatives, only some of which we have mentioned here. Frequently the context alone will indicate whether a comparison is being made.

በፍጥነት የነዳሁት እኔ ነኝ   bäfit'nät yänäddahut ïne näñ
                                I drove fast/*I* drove the fastest (*lit.* 'I
                                am the one who drove with speed')

ዮትኛው አጭሩ ነው?   yetïññaw ač'č'ïru näw?
                                which one is the shorter/the shortest?
                                (*lit.* 'which is the short one')

Exercises

5 The following passage contains a number of comparative expressions. Translate it into English and then answer in Amharic the questions set out below

ባለፈው ሳምንት ታላቅ ወንድሜ እኖን ለመጠየቅ መጣ። በትልቅ ፋብሪካ ነው የሚሠራው። ፋብሪካው የጫማ ፋብሪካ ሲሆን ከተማው ውስጥ ከሚገኙት ድርጅቶች መካከል ትልቁ ነው። ወንድሜ ሶስት ትንንሽ ልጆች አሉት። ጥሩነሽ የምታባለው ታናሿቱ ከወንድሞቻዋ በዕድሜ ብታንስም በቁመት ደግሞ ትበልጣቸዋለች። ክልጆቹም ሁሉ እስዋ ብልህዋ ናት። ለምሳሌ ማታ ማታ ከትምሕርት ቤት ስትመለስ መጽሐፍ ታነባለች ወይም ድርሰት ትጽፋለች። ወንድሞቻዋ ግን የቤት ሥራቸውን ሳይሠሩ ቴሌቪዥን ብቻ ያያሉ።

1 ጥሩነሽ ቴሌቪዥን ለማየት ትወዳለች?
2 ከወንድሜ ልጆች መካከል ታናሹ ማን ነው?
3 ወንድሜ የሚሠራበት ፋብሪካ ትንሽ ነው?
4 ወንደቾ ማታ ማታ የቤት ሥራቸውን ይሠራሉ?
5 ወንደቹስ ከጥሩነሽ ብልህ ናቸው?

6 Here's an advertisement from a magazine. Using the vocabulary supplied read the advert and then answer the questions below about the 'Tsedey Auto and Real Estate Company'

ፀደይ የመኪናና የቤት አሻሻጭ ድርጅት

ሁሉንም ይመለከታል!

ፀደይን ይወቁት

☆ፀደይ ዘመናዊ የመኪናና የቤት አሻሻጭ ድርጅት በአይነቱም ሆነ በይዘቱ ልዩና የመጀመሪያ ነው።

☆ጊዜዎን በአግባቡ ተጠቅመው ውጣ ውረድ ሳይገጥምዎ ያገለገሉና ጥሩ ይዞታ ያላቸው
- የቤት፡ የጭነትና የሕዝብ ማመላለሻ መኪኖች

- ለመኖሪያ፡ ለድርጅትና ለቢሮ አገልግሎት የሚውሉ ቤቶችን ለመግዛት፡ ለመሸጥ፡ ለማከራየት ቢፈልጉ

θደይን ይጠይቁ

☆☆☆☆☆

አድራሻ:-

ደብረዘይት መንገድ ከገብርና
ሚኒስቴር ወረድ ብሎ ወደ
ቲርቆስ በሚወስደው መንገድ
ላይ ነው θደይን የሚያገኙት ::
ስልክ   75 63 23
ፋክስ   251 - 1 - 626556
ፖ.ሣ.ቁ.   22608

Supplementary vocabulary

አሻሻጭ	aššašač'	selling, dealing (agent noun from አሻሻጠ aššašat'ä help to sell, sell off, deal in [derived stem from ሻጠ, ሸጠ 'sell']; *also means* sales clerk, broker)
አሻሻጭ ድርጅት		dealer, broker (*company*)
ተመለከተ	tämäläkkätä	watch, look at, notice, pay attention to [derived stem in tä- 4-lit]; compound imperfect ይመለከታል yïmmäläkkätal
ዘመናዊ	zämänawi	modern, contemporary (ዘመን zämän time, era, period)
ይዘት	yïzät	content, activity
በአይነትም ሆነ በይዘቱ		either in kind or in content
አገባብ	agbab	procedure, proper conduct
በአገባቡ	bäagbabu	properly, duly, suitably
ተጠቀመ	tät'äk'k'ämä	use
ውጣ ውረድ	wït'a wiräd	fuss, bother, 'ups and downs'

አወጣ አወረደ	awät't'a awärrädä	ponder, weigh something up in one's mind (*lit.* 'take it up and down' [derived stems in a-])
አገለገለ	agäläggälä	serve [derived stem in a-]
አገልግሎት	agälgïlot	service
ይዞታ	yïzota	condition, attitude. control
ጭነት	č'ïnät	load, cargo, freight
አከራየ	akkärayyä	rent out, lease [derived stem in a-] (*cf. the noun* ኪራይ kiray rent)
አድራሻ	adrašša	address
ደብረዘይት	Däbrä-Zäyt	a town south of Addis Ababa, also called ቢሾፍቱ Bišoftu
የግብርና	yägïbrïnna	Ministry of Agriculture
ሚኒስቴር	minister	
ቂርቆስ	K'irk'os	= የቅዱስ ቂርቆስ ቤተ ክርስቲያን
ወረድ አለ	wärädd alä	go down a little
ወረድ ብሎ	wärädd bïlo	a little way down

ጥያቄዎች

1 ፀደይ የሚገባለው ድርጅት ምን አይነት ነገር ይሸጣል?
2 አንድ መኪና ከዚህ ድርጅት መግዛት ቀላል ነው እንዴ?
3 ደግሞስ መኪና ለመከራየት ይቻላል?
4 ቢሮው ስ ከፒያሳ አጠገብ ነው?
5 ድርጅቱ አዲስ ነው ወይስ ከብዙ ዘመን ነው የተቋቋመው?

Reading passage (2)

የቤፍ ማርቆስ
(... ካሥራ አንደኛ ትምሕረት የሚቀጥል ነው)

ማርቆስ ያቀረበው ሀሳብ እንዲህ የሚል ነው። «ጓደኛዬ መተሳሰብ አለብን። ወረቁን ለመውሰድ ስንል መጣላቱ ጥቅም የለውም። ወደ ቤታችን ወስደን እንካፈለው። መውሰጃ ደግሞ ደህና ክረጢት ያስፈልገናል። ከተማ ሂደና ክረጢት ገዝ፣ ምግብም አምጣ። ይህን ከገድ ነገር ለመሽከም መብላት ያስፈልገናል» አለ። የቤፍ አመነታ። ማርቆስን ከወርቁ ጋር ጥሎት ሲሄድ ይዞበት ይጠፋ ይሆናል፣ ግን ካጠጣ ካወረደ በኋላ በሀሳቡ ተስማማ። የቤፍ ወደ ከተማ ሂደ። ማርቆስ ሌላ ሀሳብም ነበረው። የቤፍ ክረጢቱንና ምግቡን ይዞ ሲመለስ አድፍጦ ለገድለው ፈልጓል! ወርቁም የሱ ብቻ

ይሆናል፤ ስለዚህ ⦿ቤውን አዘጋኛ። የሌፍም በበኩሉ
ማርቆስን በምን መልክ እንደሚገድለው ያስብ ነበር! «አዎ!
ከረጢቴንና ምግቡን ይዤ እመለሳለሁ። ምግቡን ግን መርዝ
እ⦿ምርበትና ማርቆስ ምግቡን በልቶ ይሞታል። እኔ ወርቁን
ለብቻዬ እወስዳለሁ» አለ ለራሱ።

ማርቆስ የሌፍን ⦿ክ ውስጥ ተደብቆ ጠበቀው። የሌፍ
ስለዘገየበት የቀረ መስሎት ተቤጥቶ ነበር። የሌፍ ባንድ እጁ
ከረጢት፤ በሌላው እጁ ምግብ ይዞ መጣ። የሌፍ ማርቆስን
አየፈለገ ነበር። ማርቆስ ግን ከተደበቀበት ቦታ ዘሎ ክኋላው
ተከመረበትና ገደለው። ማርቆስ ወርቁን ከነማሰሮው በከረጢቱ
ከተተ። ስለራበው ግን የሌፍ ያመጣውን ምግብ ሊበላና
ወደቤቱ ሊሄድ ተዘጋኛ። ምግቡን ቀምሶ በጣም ይጣፍጣል
አለ። በልቶ ሲጨርስ ሆዱን ውጋት ያዘው። በጥቂት ደቂቃ
ውስጥ ከየሌፍ ሬሳ ጎን ዝርግት አለና ሞተ። የማሰሮው
ወርቅ በከረጢቱ ውስጥ ቀረ። አንዳቸውም ወረቁን
አላገኙትም።

Here is some additional vocabulary to help you

ተሳሰበ	täsässäbä	consider one another [derived stem from አሰበ]; infinitive መተሳሰብ mättäsasäb
ተጣላ	tät'alla	quarrel [derived stem from ጠላ 'hate']; infinitive መጣላት mät't'alat
ጥቅም	t'ïk'ïm	use, benefit
ከረጢት	kärät'it	bag
ተስማማ	täsmamma	agree [derived stem from ሰማ]
አደፈጠ	adäffät'ä	lie in wait for, ambush [a- stem 3-lit A]
⦿ቤ	č'ube	small dagger
መርዝ	märz	poison
ተደበቀ	tädäbbäk'ä	be concealed, be hidden, hide (oneself) [derived stem]
ተቤጣ	täk'wät't'a	get angry [derived stem]
ዘለለ	zällälä	jump, leap [3-lit A]
ተከመረ	täkämmärä	pounce, jump on top of [derived stem]
ከን-	kännä-	together with, along with
ከተተ	kättätä	put something inside a receptacle [3-lit A]
ውጋት	wïgat	sharp pain (*cf.* ወጋ wägga prick, stab [2-lit[1] A])
ሬሳ	resa	(dead) body, corpse
ዝርግት አለ	zïrïggïtt alä	stretch (oneself) out ['አለ' verb from ዘረጋ]
አንዳቸውም	andaččäwm	(here with a negative verb) nobody

13 መጽሔትና ጋዜጣ
mäs'hetïnna gazet'a

Magazines and newspapers

By the end of this lesson you should be able to:

- conjugate and use derived stems in tä-
- form adverbs ('happily', 'eagerly', 'quickly', etc.)
- use all parts of the verb 'to be' correctly

Amharic magazines and newspapers

Abbebe is one of the people Peter has made friends with. In the passage, he comes to Peter's house to pay him a visit

ፒተር ከተዋወቃቸው ሰዎች መካከል አንዱ አበበ ነው።
ስለሆነም ሊጠይቀው ወደፒተር መኖሪያ ይመጣል።

ፒተር: አበበ እንደምን አለህ? ትናንትና ጓደኛህን ፒያሳ
        አግኝቼው ዛሬ እንደምትመጣ ነግሮኝ ስለነበር እኔም
        ከስዓት በኋላ ጀምሮ በጉጉት ስጠብቅህ ቁየሁ።

አበበ: እሪ! ማን ነው የነገረህ? ከበደ ነው እንዴ? እሱን
        ባለፈው ሳምንት አግኝቼው ዛሬ ወዳንተ እንደምመጣ
        ተነጋግረን ነበር።

ፒተር: አዎ እሱ ነው የነገረኝ። ለመሆኑ ይህ የያዝከው
        የመጽሔት ከምር ምንድን ነው? አስቲ ስጠኝ
        ልመልከተው።

አበበ: እንካ! ይኸ በጣም ተወዳጅ መጽሔት ነው። «ሙዳይ»
        ይባላል። ብዙ ማህበራዊ ጉዳዮችን በስፋት ያነሣል።
        ነገር ግን የተጻፈው ባማርኛ በመሆኑ ምንልባት
        ለከብድህ ይችላል። ለማንኛውም ውሰድና ተመልከተው።

ፒተር: በእንግሊዝኛ ቋንቋ እየተጻፈ የሚወጣ መጽሔት የለም
        እንዴ? ባለፈው ጊዜ አንድ «አብሲኒያ» በሚል ስም
        የወጣ አንብቢያለሁ።

አበበ: አይ! ሌሎች የተለያዩ መጽሔቶች አማርኛና እንግሊዝኛን

ያቀፉ የሚወጡ አሉ። እንሱንም ደጄልህ መጥቻለሁ።
ስለዚህ አንብበህ ስትጨርስ ትመልስልኛለህ።

ፒተር፡ በጣም አመሰግናለሁ። እንደስማሁት ከሆነ ባሁኑ ጊዜ
በመገናኛ ብዙኃን ስለ አገር ጉዳይ በሰፊው ይጻፋል።
ቀደም ሲል ይህ አይነቱ የጽሑፍ ነፃነት እድል
እንዳልነበረ ውጭ አገር ሁኜ ሰምቻለሁ።

አበበ፡ አዎ፡ አውነትህን ነው። በጣም ብዙ ችግር ነበር። እኛ
ደግሞ እዚህ ሆነን በናንተ አገር የመጻፍም ሆነ የመናገር
ነፃነት ያለ ገደብ የሚሰጥ መሆኑን እንሰማለን።

ፒተር፡ ሁሉም መጽሔቶች በግለሰብ ብቻ የሚወጡ ናቸው ወይስ
የመንግሥት መጽሔቶችም አሉበት?

አበበ፡ በግልም ሆነ በመንግሥት እያታተው የሚወጡ ናቸው።
ነገር ግን አብዛኛዎቹ ከማህበራዊ የዕለት ተዕለት ጉዳይ
ላይ ከማተኩር ይልቅ ስለ ፖለቲካ ነው የሚያወሩት።
ቢሆንም ሕዝቡ የማንበብ እድል በሰፊው ስላገኘ ቢያንስ
ቢያንስ የንባብ ችሎታውን እንዲያዳብር ከፍተኛ
አስተዋጽኦ ያበረከታል።

ፒተር፡ አንዳንዶቹ መጽሔቶች የሚጠቀሙበት የቋንቋ ደረጃ
ከበድ ያለ በመሆኑ በቀላሉ ለመረዳት አይቻልም።
ከመጽሔቶች ይልቅ ለኔ የሚቀለኝ ጋዜጦችን ማንበብ
እንደሆነ ተረድቻለሁ።

አበበ፡ አይ! አሁን የማንበብም ሆነ የመረዳት ችሎታህ ስላደገ
የምትቸገረው ለጥቂት ጊዜ ብቻ ነው። በቅርቡ ሁሉንም
አይነት ጽሑፍ በቀላሉ ለማንበብና ለመረዳት ትችላለህ።

ፒተር፡ እኔም ተስፋ አደርጋለሁ። ግን ያንተና የጓደኞችህን
እርዳታ ከምን ጊዜውም በበለጠ አፈልጋለሁ። እንዲያውም
ሰሞኑን ካነበብኩት መጣጥፍ ውስጥ አንዱን ወስጄ ምን
ያህል ተረድቸው እንደሆነ ለማወቅ ብዬ ወደ እንግሊዘኛ
ቋንቋ ለመተርጎም ሞክሬያለሁ።

አበበ፡ እንዲ! በጣም ግሩም ነው! በጣም ጉበዝ ነህ! በዚህ
አይነትማ የኛንም እርዳታ የምትፈልግ አይመስለኝም። ያለ
ምንም ስሕተት በቀጥታ ነው የተረጉምከው።

ፒተር፡ እንደውነቱ ከሆነ ከናንተ ከጓደኞቹ ሌላ በአብዛኛው
የረዳኝ በየቀኑ የማጻምጠው የሬድዮ ፕርግራም ነው።
ቴሌቪዥንም በተከፈተ ቁጥር በጥሞና ተከታትያለሁ።
ነገር ግን የቴሌቪዥን ፕርግራም ከዜናውና ከስፖርቱ
ዝንጀት በስተቀር ሌላው ፕርግራም ለኔ ብዙ ጠቃሚ
ሆኖ አላገኘሁትም።

አበበ፡ ከኛ ቤት እንኳን ቴሌቪዥን ቢኖርም አይከፈትም።
ምክንያቱም አገቴ በቴሌቪዥን የሚተላለፍ ፕርግራም ማየት
ፈጽሞ አይፈልጉም። እኔም ስፖርትም ሆነ ዜና ከቴሌቪዠን
የማየው ወደ ጉረቤቶቼ ቤት ሄጄ ብቻ ነው።

PETER: *Abbebe, how are you? Since I met a friend of yours yesterday in Piyassa and he told me you were coming today, I've been waiting for you eagerly ever since midday.*

ABBEBE: *Oh, who was it that told you? Was it Kebbede, eh? I met him last week and we discussed whether I should come to your place today.*

PETER: *Yes, it was him who told me. By the way, what's this pile of magazines you're carrying? Please, give me them and let me have a look.*

ABBEBE: *Here you are! This one's a very popular magazine. It's called* Muday. *It broadly deals with many social matters. But as it's written in Amharic it may perhaps be too difficult for you. Anyway, take it and have a look.*

PETER: *Aren't there any magazines written and published in English, then? Last time I read one published under the name of* Abyssinia.

ABBEBE: *Oh well, there are various other magazines covering both Amharic and English. I'll bring you them. You can give them back to me when you've finished reading.*

PETER: *Thanks very much. If it's true what I heard, at the present time a lot's being written in the mass media about national affairs. Previously, I heard when I was abroad that there wasn't this kind of freedom of writing.*

ABBEBE: *Yes, you're right. There were very many difficulties. Over here, though, we hear that in your country freedom of both writing and speech is granted without restriction.*

PETER: *Are all magazines published only by individuals or are there government magazines too amongst them?*

ABBEBE: *They're printed and published both privately and by the government. But most of those report on politics rather than focusing on day-to-day social matters. However, as the people have largely got the opportunity to read, it at least makes a great contribution towards them developing their reading skills.*

PETER: *As the level of language that some of the magazines use is a little difficult, it isn't possible to understand them easily. I've come to realize that reading newspapers is easier for me than magazines.*

ABBEBE: *Oh well, now as your ability both to read and to understand has grown, it'll only be for a little while that you have any trouble. You'll soon be able to read and understand all kinds of writing.*

PETER: *I hope so, too. But I need your and your friends' help more than ever. In any case, I've taken one of the articles I read this week and have tried to translate it into English so as to find out how much I have understood it.*

. . .

ABBEBE: *What! That's really wonderful! You're very clever! In this case I don't think you'll need our help. You've translated it straight off without any mistakes.*

PETER: *As a matter of fact, what's helped me most aside from you, my friends, is the radio programmes that I listen to every day. And whenever the television's turned on I follow it carefully. But aside from the news and sports programmes I haven't found the other TV programmes very useful.*

ABBEBE: *Though there is a television at our house it's not turned on. This is because my father doesn't want to see the programmes that are transmitted on the TV at all. It's only by going to the neighbours' house that I see both the sport and the news on TV.*

Vocabulary

ጉጉት	guggut	desire, longing
በጉጉት	bäguggut	eagerly
ክምር	kïmmïr	pile, heap
ጉዳይ	gudday	affair, business, matter
ስፋት	sïfat	width, breadth, extent
ሰፊ	säffi	wide, broad
በስፋት,	bäsïfat,	widely, extensively
በሰፊው	bäsäffiw	
መገናኛ	mäggänaña	junction, connection, means of communication [instrument noun from ተገናኘ tägänaññä meet]
መገናኛ ብዙሃን	mäggänaña bïzuhan	mass media (*lit.* 'communication of the many')
ጽሑፍ	s'ïhuf	(*piece of*) writing, anything written (*cf.* ጻፈ s'afä write; ጸሐፊ s'ähafi secretary)
ዕድል	ïddïl	luck, fortune, chance
ችግር	čïggïr	trouble, difficulty, hardship (ችግረ čäggärä be in difficulties (*impersonal*); ተቸገረ täčäggärä be hard pressed, bother, trouble oneself, አስቸገረ asčäggärä cause difficulty)

ገደብ	gädäb	barrier, obstacle, drawback; *also means* dam
ግለሰብ	gïlläsäb	individual (*person*)
ግል	gïll	private, solitary
ዕለት	ïlät	day
የዕለት ተዕለት	yäïlät täïlät	daily
ፖለቲካ	polätika	politics
ንባብ	nïbab	reading, literacy (*cf.* አነበበ anäbbäbä read)
አስተዋጽኦ	astäwas'ïo	contribution
ቀላል	k'ällal	easy, light (*cf.* ቀለለ k'ällälä be easy *amongst the verbs listed in this vocabulary*)
በቀላሉ	bäk'ällalu	easily
እርዳታ	ïrdata	help, assistance (*cf.* ረ rädda help)
መጣጥፍ	mät'at'ïf	article (*in a newspaper or magazine*)
ቀጥታ	k'ät't'ïta	straightness, straightforwardness (*cf.* ቀጥ አለ k'ät't' alä be straight, upright, steep ['አለ verb'])
በቀጥታ	bäk'ät't'ïta	directly, straightaway
ጥሞና	t'immona	calm, care, quiet
በጥሞና	bät'immona	quietly, carefully, attentively
ዜና	zena	news, report
ዝግጅት	zïgïjjït	preparation, arrangement (*also means* programme (radio, TV); *cf.* አዘጋጀ azzägajjä prepare)
ጎረቤት	goräbet	neighbour

Verbs

ተዋወቀ	täwawwäk'ä	be acquainted, friendly with (*several people*) [derived stem from አወቀ]
ተነጋገረ	tänäggagärä	talk together (*implies more than one person*) [derived stem from ነገረ]
ተመለከተ	tämäläkkätä	look at, notice [4-lit derived stem in tä-] (*see grammar section for details of* tä- stems)
ተወደደ	täwäddädä	be liked, loved [3-lit A derived stem in tä-]
ተወዳጅ	täwädaj	liked, loved, popular
አነሣ	anässa	raise, take up [2-lit[1] A derived stem in a-]
ተጻፈ	täs'afä	be written [2-lit[3] derived stem in tä-]
ተሰጠ	täsät't'ä	be given [2-lit[2] A derived stem in tä-]
ወጣ	wät't'a	be published (*in addition to* come out, go out, go up) [2-lit[1] A] (*cf.* አወጣ awät't'a [2-lit[1] A derived stem in a-] publish)

አቀፈ	ak'k'äfä	embrace, envelop, include [3-lit A]
ታተመ	tattämä	be printed [3-lit B derived stem in tä-]; (*cf.* አተመ attämä print, stamp)
አተኩረ	atäkkwärä	focus on, stare at [3-lit A derived stem in a-]; (*cf.* ተኩረ täkkwärä *which also means* stare at)
አወራ	awärra	tell, relate, give news [2-lit[1] A derived stem in a-]
አጸበረ	adabbärä	develop, enrich [3-lit C derived stem in a-]
አበረከተ	abäräkkätä	provide, present [4-lit derived stem in a-]
ተጠቀመ	tät'äk'k'ämä	use, make use of, take advantage of [all with the preposition በ- bä-] [3-lit A derived stem in tä-]
ከበድ አለ	käbädd alä	be a little hard, rather difficult ['አለ verb' derivative of ከበደ käbbädä be heavy, hard]
ተረዳ	tärädda	understand, realize, be persuaded [2-lit[1] A derived stem in tä-]
ተቻለ	täčalä	be possible [2-lit[3] derived stem in tä-]; (*cf.* ቻለ čalä be able)
ቀለለ	k'ällälä	be easy, light [3-lit A]
አደገ	addägä	grow, increase [3-lit A]
ተቸገረ	täčäggärä	be hard pressed, have trouble; *also means* bother, trouble oneself [3-lit B derived stem in tä-]
ተረጐመ	täräggwämä	translate [4-lit]
አጸመጠ	addammät'ä	listen to something [derived stem]; simple imperfect ያጸምጥ yaddammit'
ተከፈተ	täkäffätä	be opened, turned on (*a radio, TV, etc.*) [3-lit A derived stem in tä-]
ተከታተለ	täkätattälä	follow after, keep up with [derived stem from ተከተለ täkättälä 'follow' which is itself a derived stem: 3-lit A tä- stem]; gerundive ተከታትሎ täkätatlo
ተላለፈ	tälalläfä	be transmitted, broadcast [derived stem from አላፈ alläfä 'pass']; simple imperfect ይተላለፍ yittälalläf

Particles, phrases, etc.

አንደ-	ïndä-	that . . . (*see note 1*)
አንደሆነ	ïndähonä	(here) that it is
በሚል ስም	bämmil sïm	under the name of (*lit.* 'in a name which says . . .')
ባሁት ጊዜ	bahunu gize	at the present time (*lit.* 'at the now time')
ከ- - ይልቅ	kä- - yïlïk'	rather than, more than
ቢሆንም	bihonïm	however (*lit.* 'even though it is (so)')
ምን ጊዜውም	mïn gizewm	at any time, ever
አንደውነቱ ከሆነ	ïndäwnätu kähonä	as a matter of fact. (*lit.* 'if it is like the truth')
አንኳን	ïnkwan	even (*follows the word or phrase it goes with*)
ብ- - -ም	bï- - -m(m)	although (*with the simple imperfect tense*)
ቢኖርም	binorïm	although there is

Notes on the dialogue

1 The conversation between Peter and Abbebe contains a number of uses of the prefix 'conjunction' አንደ- ïndä- which correspond to English 'that . . .'. You already know this word in the sense of 'like' added either to nouns or to relative verbs: for example, አንደሚሉት ïndämmilut 'as they say', *lit.* 'like what they say it'.

It is also used to correspond to English 'that' in such situations as 'I heard that', 'I see that', 'I know that', and so on. Go through the dialogue and collect the instances of አንደ- used in this way. Note that sometimes it is combined with ሆነ honä to make አንደሆነ ïndähonä.

2 In the last couple of years a very large number of new magazines have appeared in Ethiopia, mostly in Amharic, though there are some in English like *Abyssinia* which Peter mentions in the dialogue, as well as some with articles in both English and Amharic. At present there are as many as fifty such publications. This is very different from the situation under the previous regime which controlled the press very tightly.

Many of the new magazines cover social and topical questions, such as the monthly ሙዳይ *Muday* (*lit.* 'a small basket used for storing personal items'), which Abbebe mentions. Others have a more political flavour, such as the independent የአፍሪካ ቀንድ 'YäAfrika K'änd' *The Horn of Africa*; or the government magazine ንጋት 'Nïgat' (*Dawn*). Others are business orientated, or focus on literary and cultural topics, like አሌፍ *Alef*.

The Amharic daily newspaper, which has been published for over fifty years, is called አዲስ ዘመን 'Addis Zämän', *New Times*. There's also a weekly paper of long standing called የዛሬዪቱ ኢትዮጵያ 'Yäzareyitu Ityop'p'ïya' *Today's Ethiopia*.

Ethiopian television broadcasts for only six hours a day and is not received everywhere in the country. The radio is a much more significant force in the broadcast media in Ethiopia.

Grammar

Derived stems in tä-

Like the derived stems in **a-**, those formed by means of the prefix **tä-** are very common and very important in Amharic. You have already encountered a large number of **tä-** stems, even from as early on as the first lesson. There, you learned the expression እግዚር ይመin igzer yïmmäsgän, which literally means 'may God be praised'. The verb ይመበ *ïmmäsgän* 'may he be praised' is the third person masculine form of the jussive of ተመሰገነ tämäsäggänä 'be praised'; the **tä-** stem derivative corresponding to አመሰገነ amäsäggänä 'praise, thank', itself an **a-** stem 4-lit verb. All of this illustrates a number of important points about **tä-** stem derived verbs, which are listed below.

1 The meaning of the **tä-** stem is often to express a 'passive' notion, that is that something 'is done' rather than someone 'does' something. For instance, compare the following pairs of verbs which occur in the dialogue:

ከፈተ	käffätä	open:	ተከፈተ	täkäffätä	be opened
ወደደ	wäddädä	love:	ተወደደ	täwäddädä	be loved
ጻፈ	s'afä	write:	ተጻፈ	täs'afä	be written
ሰጠ	sät't'ä	give:	ተሰጠ	täsät't'ä	be given

2 Unlike the prefixes **a-** and **as-**, which we looked at in the previous lesson, the prefix **tä-** is not 'visible' as such in all tenses. Instead, there is a different pattern which always involves doubling or

'gemination' of the first consonant of the stem. Compare the following pairs of forms, also from the dialogue:

ተከፈተ	täkäffätä	it was opened, switched on
አይከፈትም	ayïkkäffätïm	it isn't opened, switched on
ተጻፈ	täs'afä	it was written
ይጻፋል	yïs's'afal	it is being written

3 To form the 'passive' of a verb whose basic, transitive meaning is expressed by an a- stem derivative, the prefix tä- replaces the prefix a- and is *not* added to it. So, for example:

አመሰገነ	amäsäggänä	thank:	ተመሰገነ	tämäsäggänä	be thanked
አገኘ	agäññä	find:	ተገኘ	tägäññä	be found
አደረገ	adärrägä	do:	ተደረገ	tädärrägä	be done

Of course, if the verb root begins in the vowel a- (in other words if the verb is a basic stem type and not a derived stem) then tä- is added to this producing ta-, as in the following examples:

አወቀ	awwäk'ä	know →	ታወቀ	tawwäk'ä	be known
አየ	ayyä	see →	ታየ	tayyä	be seen
አሰበ	assäbä	think →	ታሰበ	tassäbä	be thought, remembered

As you can see from the examples you have looked at so far, the usual meaning of the tä- stem is to express a passive event, that is, to turn a transitive verb into an intransitive: to say that something 'is done' rather than someone 'does' something. For this reason the tä- stem is often called the 'passive', but as with a- and as- stems there are exceptions to this. Not all tä- stem derivatives are passives. Sometimes the tä- stem expresses the basic idea and the simple, underived stem is not used. Below are some examples of this kind, many of which have occurred in the lessons so far.

ተቀመጠ	täk'ämmät'ä	sit	[3-lit B derived stem in tä-]
ተሸከመ	täšäkkämä	carry	[3-lit B " tä-]
ተቀበለ	täk'äbbälä	receive	[3-lit B " tä-]
ተከተለ	täkättälä	follow	[3-lit B " tä-]
ታገለ	taggälä	struggle	[3-lit A " tä-]
ተቈጣ	täk'wät't'a	get angry	[2-lit[1] A " tä-]
ተመኘ	tämäññä	wish	[2-lit[2] A " tä-]
ተመቸ	tämäčča	be convenient	[2-lit[2] B " tä-]
ተሻለ	täšalä	be better	[2-lit[3] " tä-]
ተማረ	tämarä	learn	[2-lit[3] " tä-]

| ተጓዘ | tägwazä | travel | [2-lit³ | " | tä-] |
| ተገናዘበ | tägänäzzäbä | realize | [4-lit | " | tä-] |

In other instances, the **tä-** stem does not have an obvious 'passive' connection with the simple stem, but has quite a different meaning. For example:

ገባ **gäbba** enter → ተገባ **tägäbba** be right, proper
ረዳ **rädda** help → ተረዳ **tärädda** understand, be persuaded
ሰማ **sämma** hear → ተሰማ **täsämma** feel (as an impersonal verb), *as well as* be heard

Below are some examples of **tä-** stems, some pairing with simple stems, others with **a-** stems, where the meaning is not strictly speaking 'passive':

አመለከተ	amäläkkätä	notify, point out	→ ተመለከተ	tämäläkkätä	look at
አበደረ	abäddärä	lend (money)	→ ተበደረ	täbäddärä	borrow
አዋሰ	awasä	lend (things)	→ ተዋሰ	täwasä	borrow
መለሰ	mälläsä	give back, reply	→ ተመለሰ	tämälläsä	return, go back*
አጠበ	at't'äbä	wash something	→ ታጠበ	tat't'äbä	wash oneself

*as well as 'be given back'

Lastly, remember that not all verbs that begin in ተ **tä** are **tä-** stem derivatives; the **t** may be the first consonant of the basic root, as in the words below:

ተኛ	tänña	lie down, sleep	[2-lit¹ B]
ተከለ	täkkälä	plant	[3-lit A]
ተረተ	tärrätä	tell a story	[3 lit B]
ተኰሰ	täkkwäsä	iron (clothes); fire, shoot (a gun)	[3-lit B]
ተረጐመ	täräggwämä	translate	[4-lit]

The inflexion of tä- stem derivatives

	3-lit A		3-lit B	
s. past	ተሰበረ	täsäbbärä	ተፈለገ	täfällägä
s. impf.	ይሰበር	yïssäbbär	ይፈለግ	yïffälläg
c. impf.	ይሰበራል	yïssäbbäral	ይፈለጋል	yïffällägal
juss.	ይሰበር	yïssäbär	ይፈለግ	yïffäläg
imp.	ተሰበር	täsäbär	ተፈለግ	täfäläg

	3-lit A		3-lit B	
ger.	ተሰብሮ	täsäbro	ተፈልጎ	täfälligo
c. ger.	ተሰብኳል	täsäbrwal	ተፈልጓል	täfälligwal
inf.	መሰበር	mässäbär	መፈለግ	mäffäläg
inst.	መሰበሪያ	mässäbäriya	መፈለጊያ	mäffälägiya
ag.	ተሰጋሪ	täsäbari	ተፈላጊ	täfällagi

ተሰበረ täsäbbärä 'be broken'; ተፈለገ täfällägä 'be wanted'.

Points to note

1 The tä- prefix *only* appears in tenses and forms that are formed without a prefix; in those parts that are formed with a prefix [simple and compound imperfect, jussive, infinitive and instrument noun] the tä- prefix is 'absorbed' and replaced by the doubling, or 'gemination', of the first consonant of the root. So, in the case of ተሰበረ this is s, and in ተፈለገ it is f. Note that this is different with the tä- stem of verbs whose roots begin with a (see below).

2 A and B types have different patterns only in the gerundive (and hence the compound gerundive) and the agent noun. Otherwise they are inflected identically.

3 In terms of the written form, those parts where the tä- prefix is 'absorbed' differ from the corresponding simple stem forms only in one letter. In pronunciation, of course, there is the additional difference of 'gemination'. So:

ይሰብራል	he breaks	→	ይሰብራል	it will be broken
yïsäbral			yïssäbbäral	
መሰበር	to break	→	መሰበር	to be broken
mäsbär			mässäbär	
ይጨምር	let him add	→	ይጨመር	let it be added
yïč'ämmïr			yïč'č'ämär	

The inflexion of the tä- stem of verbs in a

	3-lit A		3-lit B	
s. past	ታገለ	taggälä	ታደሰ	taddäsä
s. impf.	ይታገል	yïttaggäl	ይታደስ	yïttaddäs
c. impf.	ይታገላል	yïttaggälal	ይታደሳል	yïttaddäsal
jussive	ይታገል	yïttagäl	ይታደስ	yïttadäs

	3-lit A		3-lit B	
imp.	ታገል	tagäl	ታደስ	tadäs
ger.	ታግሎ	taglo	ታድሶ	taddïso
c. ger.	ታግሏል	taglwal	ታድሷል	taddïswal
inf.	መታገል	mättagäl	መታደስ	mättadäs
inst.	መታገያ	mättagäya	መታደሻ	mättadäša
ag.	ታጋይ	tagay	ታዳሽ	taddaš

ታገል **taggälä** 'struggle'; ታደስ **taddäsä** 'be renewed'

Point to note

1 The **t** of the prefix remains throughout and 'geminated' in the
tenses and other parts that are formed by means of a prefix and
operates like the initial consonant of the root.

Other stem types

	2-lit¹ A		2-lit¹ B	
s. past	ተበላ	täbälla	ተጠጣ	tät'ät't'a
s. impf.	ይበላ	yïbbälla	ይጠጣ	yït't'ät't'a
c. impf.	ይበላል	yïbbällal	ይጠጣል	yït't'ät't'al
juss.	ይበላ	yïbbäla	ይጠጣ	yït't'ät'a
imp.	ተበላ	täbäla	ተጠጣ	tät'ät'a
ger.	ተበልቶ	täbälto	ተጠጥቶ	tät'ät't'ïto
c. ger.	ተበልቷል	täbältwal	ተጠጥቷል	tät'ät't'ïtwal
inf.	መበላት	mäbbälat	መጠጣት	mät't'ät'at
inst.	መበያ	mäbbäya	መጠጫ	mät't'äč'a
ag.	ተበይ	täbäy	ተጠጪ	tät'äč'č'i

	2-lit² A		2-lit² B	
s. past	ተሰጠ	täsät't'ä	ተለየ	täläyyä
s. impf.	ይሰጥ	yïssät't'	ይለይ	yïlläyy
c. impf.	ይሰጣል	yïssät't'al	ይለያል	yïlläyyal
juss.	ይሰጥ	yïssät'	ይለይ	yïlläy
imp.	ተሰጥ	täsät'	ተለይ	täläy
ger.	ተሰጥቶ	täsät'to	ተለይቶ	täläyyïto
c. ger.	ተሰጥቷል	täsät'twal	ተለይቷል	täläyyïtwal
inf.	መሰጠት	mässät'ät	መለየት	mälläyät

	2-lit² A		2-lit² B	
inst.	መሰጪ	mässäč'a	መለያ	mälläya
ag.	ተሰጪ	täsäč'i	ተለዪ	täläyyi

ተበላ 'be eaten', ተጠጣ 'be drunk', ተሰጠ 'be given', ተለየ 'be separated, different'

Point to note

1 The imperfect (simple and compound) of the tä- stems of these classes of verbs is identical in its written form to the imperfect of the corresponding simple stems. In pronunciation only the position of 'gemination' differentiates the two stems:

ይሰጣል   he gives   → ይሰጣል   he is being given
yïsät'al   yïssät't'al

The same applies to the infinitive of B-type verbs:

መለየት   to separate   → መለየት   to be separated, etc.
mäläyyät   mälläyät

This is a good illustration of how important consonant doubling or 'gemination' is in Amharic!

	2-lit³		2-lit⁴		2-lit⁵	
s. past	ተማረ	tämarä	ተሼጠ	täšet'ä	ተሾመ	täšomä
s. impf.	ይማር	yïmmar	ይሼጥ	yïššet'	ይሾም	yïššom
c. impf.	ይማራል	yïmmaral	ይሼጣል	yïššet'al	ይሾማል	yïššomal
juss.	ይማር	yïmmar	ይሼጥ	yïššet'	ይሾም	yïššom
imp.	ተማር	tämar	ተሼጥ	täšet'	ተሾም	täšom
ger.	ተምሮ	tämïro	ተሼጦ	täšet'o	ተሾሞ	täšomo
c. ger.	ተምፉል	tämïrwal	ተሼጣል	täšet'wal	ተሾማል	täšomwal
inf.	መማር	mämmar	መሼጥ	mäššet'	መሾም	mäššom
inst.	መማሪያ	mämmariya	መሼጪ	mäššeč'a	መሾሚያ	mäššomiya
ag.	ተማሪ	tämari	ተሻጪ	täšač'i	ተሿሚ	täšwami

ተማረ 'learn'; ተሼጠ, ተሸጠ * 'be sold'; ተሾመ 'be appointed'

*Remember that ሼ še can and usually does become ሸ šä in the verb ሼጠ, ተሼጠ.

	4-lit		3-lit X	
s. past	ተሰበሰበ	täsäbässäbä	ተዘረጋ	täzärägga
s. impf.	ይሰበስብ	yïssäbässäb	ይዘረጋ	yïzzärägga
c. impf.	ይሰበስባል	yïssäbässäbal	ይዘረጋል	yïzzäräggal
juss.	ይሰብስብ	yïssäbsäb	ይዘርጋ	yïzzärga
imp.	ተሰብሰብ	täsäbsäb	ተዘርጋ	täzärga
ger.	ተሰብሶ	täsäbsïbo	ተዘርጊቶ	täzärgito
c. ger.	ተሰብሷል	täsäbsïbwal	ተዘርጊቷል	täzärgïtwal
inf.	መሰብሰብ	mässäbsäb	መዘርጋት	mäzzärgat
inst.	መሰብሰቢያ	mässäbsäbiya	መዘርጊያ	mäzzärgiya
ag.	ተሰብሳቢ	täsäbsabi	ተዘርጊ	täzärgi

	3-lit Y	
s. past	ተጉበኘ	tägwäbäññä
s. impf.	ይጉበኝ	yïggwäbäññ
c. impf.	ይጉበኛል	yïggwäbäññal
juss.	ይጉበኝ	yïggwäbäñ
imp.	ተጉበኝ	tägwäbä
ger.	ተጉብኚቶ	tägwäbñïto
c. ger.	ተጉብኚቷል	tägwäbñïtwal
inf.	መጉብኛት	mäggwäbäñät
inst.	መጉብኛ	mäggwäbäña
ag.	ተጉብኚ	tägwäbñi

ተሰበሰበ 'be assembled, gathered'; ተዘረጋ 'be stretched out'; ተጉበኘ 'be visited'.

The irregular verb አለ alä 'say' has the 'passive' form ተባለ täbalä 'be said, called', which inflects as a regular 2-lit 3 derived stem in tä-.

s. past	ተባለ	täbalä	ger.	ተብሎ	täbïlo, täblo
s. impf.	ይባል	yïbbal	c. ger.	ተብሏል	täbïlwal, täblwal
c. impf.	ይባላል	yïbbalal	inf.	መባል	mäbbal
juss.	ይባል	yïbbal	inst.	መባያ	mäbbaya
imp.	ተባል	täbal	ag.	ተባይ	täbay

The tä- + C-type derived stem

The derivative prefixes a- and tä- can also combine with internal changes inside the verb stem to form yet more derived stems, several of which you have already in fact met in the dialogues. One of the commonest of these combinational derived stems is formed by the addition of the prefix tä- *plus* the insertion of the vowel a inside the verb stem. Because the a vowel is reminiscent of the C-type pattern this derived stem may conveniently be called the tä- + C-type pattern. The first example of this derived stem that we met was ተናገረ tänaggärä 'talk' from the simple stem ነገረ näg-gärä 'speak'.

The usual meaning of the tä- + C-type derived stem is to express an action that is carried on between more than one person, that is done 'to one another'. This can be called a 'reciprocal' action. For example, ነገረ means simply to 'speak' or 'pronounce words', whilst ተናገረ implies that the speaking involves others and goes both ways, that is to 'talk (together)'. Whereas in English we might use the word 'together' or the phrase 'one another', this idea is contained within the 'reciprocal' verb in Amharic. Of course, there are ways in Amharic to say 'together' or 'one another', but you do not need to use them with this kind of verb. Below are some other examples to illustrate this idea.

ወደደ	wäddädä	love	→	ተዋደደ täwaddädä	love one another
መከረ	mäkkärä	advise	→	ተማከረ tämakkärä	advise one another, consult
መታ	mätta	hit	→	ተማታ tämatta	hit one another
ወጋ	wägga	stab	→	ተዋጋ täwagga	stab one another, fight

As with other derived stems, sometimes the tä- + C-type pattern does not always mean what you might expect, but has some figurative or special meaning, or is even used to express the basic meaning of a verb. Consider the examples that follow.

ነደደ	näddädä	catch fire	→	ተናደደ tänaddädä	get angry
ቀረበ	k'ärräbä	approach	→	ተቃረበ täk'arräbä	approach
ሰነበተ	sänäbbätä	spend a while	→	ተሰናበተ täsänabbätä	say goodbye
ገባ	gäbba	enter	→	ተጋባ tägabba	get married

ተሻገረ	täšaggärä	cross	*but no*	*ሻገረ
ተቃጠለ	täk'at't'älä	be on fire	*but no*	*ቀጠለ (ቀጠለ 'follow' is unrelated)
ተጫወተ	täč'awwätä	play	*but no*	*ጨወተ

The inflexion of the tä- + C-type stems

You can see that the patterns of inflexion follow the normal tä-stem types except that the vowel **a** is always present inside the stem.

	3-lit		*2-lit¹*	
s. past	ተሻገረ	täšaggärä	ተጋባ	tägabba
s. impf.	ይሻገር	yïššaggär	ይጋባ	yïggabba
c. impf.	ይሻገራል	yïššaggäral	ይጋባል	yïggabbal
juss.	ይሻገር	yïššagär	ይጋባ	yïggaba
imp.	ተሻገር	täšagär	ተጋባ	tägaba
ger.	ተሻግሮ	täšagro	ተጋብቶ	tägabto
c. ger.	ተሻግሯል	täšagrwal	ተጋብቷል	tägabtwal
inf.	መሻገር	mäššagär	መጋባት	mäggabat
inst.	መሻገሪያ	mäššagäriya	መጋቢያ	mäggabiya
ag.	ተሻጋሪ	täšagari	ተጋቢ	tägabi

	4-lit	
s. past	ተሰናበተ	täsänabbätä
s. impf.	ይሰናበት	yïssänabbät
c. impf.	ይሰናበታል	yïssänabbätal
juss.	ይሰናበት	yïssänabät
imp.	ተሰናበት	täsänabät
ger.	ተሰናብቶ	täsänabto
c. ger.	ተሰናብቷል	täsänabtwal
inf.	መሰናበት	mässänabät
inst.	መሰናበቻ	mässänabäča
ag.	ተሰናባች	täsänabač

ተሻገረ 'cross'; ተጋባ 'get married'; ተሰናበተ 'say goodbye'.

Exercises

1 Rewrite the following sentences as passives. Be sure to keep the same tense as in the original

> *Example:* ሊጋውን ይዟል ➜ ሊጋው ተይዟል

1 ደብዳቤውን ጻፈች።
2 ሲኒውን ትሰብራለህ።
3 ስብስባውን ይጀምሩ።
4 ጋዜጣውን አነበብኩ።
5 በሩን ዝጋ።

6 ገንዘቡን አግኝታለች።
7 ጻዮውን ይብላ።
8 ቴሌቪዥኑን ልክፈት።
9 መጽሐፉህን መልሻለሁ።
10 ልጅዋን ትወጻለች።

2 Convert the following passive sentences into active ones using the word in brackets as subject

> *Example:* መጽሐፉ ተገኘ። (አልማዝ _____) ➜
> አልማዝ መጽሐፉን አገኘች።

1 ከበደ እውነቱን እንደተናገረ ይታወቃል። (እኔ _____)
2 እንግዶቹ እስከ 4 ሰዓት ይጠበቃሉ። (እኛ _____)
3 ትምሕርቱ ተጀምፉል (አስተማሪው _____)
4 ቤቱ ታድጓል። (አባቴ _____)
5 ያዋስከኝ መጽሐፍ ገገ ይመለሳል። (እኔ _____)
6 መስኮቱ ተከፍቷል እንዴ? (ተማሪዎቹ _____)
7 መኪናዬ መቼ ይሽጣል? (አሻሻጡ _____)

3 Complete the answers to the following questions

1 ይህ ቦታ ተይዝዋል? የለም፤ _____
2 በታክሲ ብንሄድ ይሻላል? የለም፤ _____
3 አቶ ዘውዴ ከኢትዮጵያ ተመልሰዋል? አይ፤ ገና ነው። ገገ _____
4 በዬት አገር ነው የተወለዱበት? እኔ _____
5 በባቡር ትንዛለህ ወይስ በመኪና? እንጃ፤ ምናልባት በባቡር _____
6 ተማሪዎቹ ጠንክረው ይማራሉ? አይ፤ ያሳዝንኛል። ጠንከረው _____

4 *Read and translate the following weather report taken from a newspaper. Then, following the report as a model and using the vocabulary supplied below, write a report on the weather wherever you are*

የሰሞኑ አየር ሁኔታ

በሚቀጥሉት አምስት ቀናት ውስጥ በምዕራብና
በደቡብ ምዕራብ ከፍታማ ቦታዎች ደመናማ
የሚሆን ሲሆን ባንጻንድ ቦታዎች
ላይ ነጉድጓዳማ ዝናብ ይዘንባል ፡፡
በሰሜን በሚገኙ ደጋማ ቦታዎች ላይ
ደገሞ በከፊል ደመናማ ሆኖ መጠነኛ
ዝናብ ይዘንባል ፡፡ በሌሎች ቄላማ
ቦታዎች ላይ ግን ኃይለኛ ፀሐይ
ይሆናል በማለት በብሔራዊ ሜትርሎጂ
አገልግሎት ድርጅት የአየር ሁኔታ
ትንበያ ክፍል ትናንትና አስታውቋል ፡፡

Here is some vocabulary to help you

ቀናት	k'änat	= ቀኖች
ከፍታማ	käffitamma	= ከፍተኛ
ደመናማ	dämmänamma	cloudy (*cf.* ደመና dämmäna cloud)
ነጉድጓዳማ	nägwädgwadamma	thundery (*cf.* ነጉድጓድ nägwädgwad thunder)
ደጋማ	dägamma	highland (*from* ደጋ däga highlands)
ቄላማ	k'wällamma	lowland (*from* ቄላ k'wälla lowlands)
ከፊል	käfil	part, portion
መጠነኛ	mät'änäñña	normal, moderate
ትንበያ	tïnbäya	forecasting

Weather vocabulary

ካፊያ	kaffiyya	drizzle
ጉም	gum	mist, fog
በረዶ	bärädo	hail, ice
በረዶ ሆነ	bärädo honä	be icy, freeze
በረዶ ጣለ	bärädo t'älä	hail (*lit.* 'throw hail')
በረቀ	bärräk'ä	thunder, lighten [3-lit A]

መብረቅ	mäbräk'	lightning
ድርቅ	dïrk'	drought
ሙቅ	muk'	hot
ፀሐይ	s'ähay	sun
ወጀብ	wäjäb	storm, gale
ነፋስ	näfas	wind
ደረቅ	däräk'	dry
እርጥብ	ïrt'ïb	wet, damp
ጉርፍ	gwärf	flood
ብርድ	bïrd	cold
ቀዝቃዛ	k'äzk'azza	cool
ፀሐያማ	s'ähayamma	sunny

The seasons in Ethiopia

ክረምት	kïrämt, krämt	the rainy season (end of June to early September)
በጋ	bäga	the dry season (mid September to end of April)
ፀደይ	s'äday	the sowing season (early May to end of June)

The period of April and May may also contain the 'little rains' which are known in Amharic as በልግ **bälg.**

The Amharic terms ደጋ and ቆላ (or ቆላ) refer to different climatic and ecological zones: ደጋ is the land above about 8,000' (the altitude of Addis Ababa) which has a temperate climate. Land below 6,000' is called ቆላ and has a hot dry or tropical climate. According to Amhara custom the best zone for traditional agriculture is called ወይና ደጋ **wäyna däga,** which falls between the two other zones at 6,000' to 8,000'.

Grammar

Adverbial expressions

In Amharic there is no one particular way of forming adverbs such as we can do in English by adding '-*ly*' to an adjective. In the dialogue in this lesson a number of adverbial expressions do occur, however, that are formed by means of the preposition በ- **bä-.**

በጉጉት	bäguggut	eagerly	በግል	bägïll	privately
በስፋት	bäsïfat	widely	በቀላሉ	bäk'ällalu	easily
በሰፊው	bäsäffiw	widely	በቅርቡ	bäk'ïrbu	shortly
በቀጥታ	bäk'ät't'ïta	directly	በአብዛኛው	bäabzaññaw	mostly
በጥሞና	bät'ïmmona	carefully			

You can see that these fall into two groups:

(a) በ- + abstract noun (በጉጉት, በስፋት, በቀጥታ, በጥሞና, *etc.*)
(b) በ- + adjective + definite article (በሰፊው, በቅርቡ, በቀላሉ, *etc.*)

Here are some more that you might find useful to add to your vocabulary

በትክክል	bätïkïkkïl	equally	በድንገት	bädïngät	suddenly
በከንቱ	bäkäntu	in vain	በደስታ	bädässïta	happily
በፍጥነት	bäfit'nät	hurriedly	በኃይል	bähayl	greatly
በደንብ	bädänb	properly	በሙሉ ልብ	bämulu lïbb	wholeheartedly

Note also: ከልብ kälïbb 'sincerely, willingly' with the preposition ከ-.

There are other ways in which Amharic can express the equivalent of English adverbs. One of the commonest is to use the gerundive of an appropriate verb. Sometimes gerundives used as adverbs remain 'fixed' in the third person masculine singular form, at other times they agree with the person of the verb they accompany. Below are a few examples that have occurred in the dialogues to date.

ቀደም ብሎ	k'ädämm bïlo	previously	ቶሎ ብሎ	tolo bïlo	quickly
ቀስ ብሎ	k'äss bïlo	slowly	ቀጥሎ	k'ät't'ïlo	subsequently
አጥብቆ	at'bïk'o	strictly, keenly	ጨርሶ	č'ärrïso	completely
ዝም ብሎ	zïmm bïlo	silently, simply	አብሮ	abro	together

Often the gerundive of አደረገ adärägä 'do' is used to 'support' an adverb as in ደህና አድርጎ ሠርቶታል dähna adrïgo särtotal 'he's done it well'.

Gerundive 'adverbs' that remain 'fixed'

These include the following:

ደግሞ	dägmo	also, then (*lit.* 'repeating')
ቀድሞ	k'ädmo	firstly, formerly, previously
ከቶ	kätto	fully, not at all, never (*with a negative verb*)

| ፈጽሞ | fäs's'imo | totally, not at all (*with a negative verb*) |
| አውቆ | awk'o | knowingly, wittingly, on purpose |

Exercises

5 Fill in the gaps in the following sentences with the appropriate adverb from the list given below

1 _____ ያለ ምንም ስህተት ለማንበብ ትችያለሽ።
2 ገረዲቱ ብርጭቆውን _____ ሰበረች እንዴ?
3 ያንተ አጻብ _____ ያስደነቃል።
4 አማኝ ኦርቶዶክሳዊ በጾም ሥጋ _____ አይበላም።
5 _____ ከበደንና ዘውዴን ባቡር ጣቢያ ላይ አገኘኋቸው።
6 መኪና ባቆምኩ ጊዜ እንደ ልጅ _____ ደርሶ ልጠብቅልም አለኝ።
7 ቡና ትፈልጋለህ? አዎ ፥ _____ ቡና አጠጣለሁ።

ባጋጣሚ, አውቆ, በእውነት, በፍጥነት, በቅርቡ, በደስታ, ከቶ

Grammar

The verb 'to be'

In the first lesson we met two parts of the verb 'to be': ነው **näw** and ሁን **hun**. From this, and from what you have subsequently learned in the ensuing lessons, it is apparent that 'to be' in Amharic is a particularly irregular verb. It will be useful to summarize all these irregularities at this juncture.

| present affirmative | ነው | näw | አለ | allä |
| present negative | አይደለም | aydälläm | የለም | yälläm |

1 ነው has its own pattern of inflexion
2 አለ, አይደለም and የለም inflect like simple past tense verbs
3 of these only አለ can be used in subordinate clauses:

with the relative prefix የ-: ያለ **yallä** which there is
with ስ-: ሳለ **sallä** when there is
with ክ-: ካለ **kallä** since there is

with አን-:   አንዳለ indallä as there is
with አይ-:   አያለ iyyallä while there is

The negative of አለ in subordinate positions is ሌለ lellä, which also
inflects like a simple past verb: የሌለ yälellä 'which there is
not';ከሌለ kälellä 'since there is not'; አንደሌለ indälellä 'as there is
not'; አይሌለ iyyälellä 'whilst there is not'.

| past affirmative | ነበረ | näbbärä |
| past negative | አልነበረም | alnäbbäräm |

Note: ነበረ has regular inflexion. Other parts are usually drawn from
the verb ሆነ:

future/'subjunctive'	ይሆናል	yïhonal	it will be, may be
	አይሆንም	ayhonïm	it cannot be
simple imperfect	ይሆን	yïhon	(ሲሆን sihon when it is;
			ቢሆን bihon if it is, *etc.*)
jussive	ይሁን	yïhun	let it be, may it be
imperative	ሁን	hun	be!
gerundive	ሆኖ	hono	it being
infinitive	መሆን	mähon	to be

Below are some more noun derivatives óf ሆነ that are commonly
used. (Some of these you may recognize.)

መሆኛ	mähoña	means of being useful
ሕን, ሁዋን	hwañ, huwañ	someone who is useful,
		supporter
አኳኋን, አኋኋን	akkwahwan,	condition, state of affairs,
	ahwahwan	fashion, style
ሁኔታ	huneta	status, circumstance, manner,
		condition
ሁነኛ	hunäñña	reliable, dependable; *also*
		representative, principal, chief

Sometimes the verb ኖረ norä is also used to supplement the verb 'to
be'.

Reading passage

ብሔራዊ ቡድናችን ዛሬ ማታ
ከአምባሳደር ጋር ይጫወታል

ብሔራዊ የቅርጫት ኳስ ቡድናችን ዛሬ ማታ ከምሽቱ ፪ ሰዓት ጀምሮ ከአሜሪካው አምባሳደር ቡድን ጋር ደ ጋጠማል። ቦታው በቀድሞ አዲስ ፖላንድ ማረፊያ አካባቢ ባለው የአሜሪካ ኮሙኒቲ ት/ቤት ግቢ ውስጥ መሆኑን ፌዴሬሽኑ ገልጿል።

የአሜሪካ አምባሳደር ስፖርት ክለብ የተመሠረተው በ፲፱፻፳፪ ዓ·ም፡ ሲሆን፡ በዚሁ መጠሪያ ስም አንድ ሌላ ቡድን በምዕራብና በመካከለኛ አፍሪካ ሲሂዚር እዚህ የመጣው ቡድን ደግሞ ቀድሞ የደረሰው ኬንያ ነው። በዚያም ፭ ሳምንት ቆይቶ ፲፪ ግጥሚያዎች አድርጎ በሙሉ ያሸነፈ መሆኑን አሠልጣኙ ሚስተር ሐንክ ቦወን ጠቅሰው ከዚህ በኋላ ወደ ግብፅ ከዚያም ወደ ሀገሩ ነው መመለሱን ገልጸዋል።

የአሜሪካ አምባሳደር ቅርጫት ኳስ ቡድን ሀገራችን ከገባ ወዲህ ከመኩሪያ ቡድን ጋር ገጥሞ ፪ያ፪ ለ፭፻ ረትቷል። ከዚያ በኋላ ወደክማን ፪ያ፪ ለ፬፻ አሸንፏል። በመሐል ደግሞ ወደ ደብረ ዘይት ሔዶ ከአየር ኃይል ጋር ባደረገው ጫዋታ ፭፪ ለ፬፻ ረትቷል። ናዝሬት ላይ ለተማሪዎች የጫዋታውን ጥበብ አሳይቷል።

የአምባሳደር ቡድን ተጫዋቾች በሙሉ የዩኒቨርሲቲ ተማሪዎች ሲሆኑ፡ ትልቁ ፳፬፡ ወጣቱ ፲፪ ዕድሜ ያላቸው ናቸው። በቁመቱ በኩል አጭሩ ፩ ሜትር ፹ ሲሆን፡ ረጅሙ ፪ ሜትር ከስምንት ሳንቲ ሜትር ከፍታ ያለው ነው። ብዙዎቹ ግብ ሲያስቆጥሩ ከቁመታቸው መርዘም የተነሣ እጃቸውን ቅርጫቱ ውስጥ አያገቡ ነው። ከመሐላቸው ረጅሙ ጳርል ቦይድ ለአሜሪካ ብሔራዊ ኦሊምፒክ ቡድን ለመሠለፍ ተስፋ እንዳለው አሠልጣኙ ገልጸዋል።

(Abridged from አዲስ ዘመን ሐምሌ ፭ ቀን ፲፱፻፳፯ ዓ·ም፡)

Supplementary vocabulary

ቡድን	budïn	team
ቅርጫት	k'ïrč'at	kind of basket
የቅርጫት ኳስ	yäk'ïrč'at kwas	basketball
ገጠመ	gät't'ämä	join, deal with, engage (*an enemy*) [3-lit A]
ተጋጠመ	tägat't'ämä	confront, meet (*armies, teams*)

ግጥሚያ	gït'miya	match, bout, conflict
ት/ቤት	= ትምሕርት ቤት	
መሠረተ	mäsärrätä	found, establish [4-lit]
መጠሪያ ስም	mät't'äriya sïm	title, appelation, nomenclature (cf. ተጠሪ be called)
ዟዟረ	zwazwarä	wander, roam, tour [derived stem from ዞረ go round]
አሸነፈ	aššännäfä	win (a battle or a game), defeat someone [3-lit as- stem]
ጠቀሰ	t'äk'k'äsä	mention, quote, refer to something [3-lit A]
ሀገር	hagär = አገር	
ኩራ	kwärra	be proud [2-lit¹ A]
መኩሪያ	mäkuriya	prestigious
ረታ	rätta	win, beat [2-lit¹ A]
ወወከማ	Wäwäkïma	name of a basketball team
የአየር ኃይል	yäayyär hayl	Air Force
ጥበብ	t'ïbäb	skill, technique, wisdom
ቁመት	k'umät	height (cf. ቆመ stand)
ገብ	gïb	goal (cf. ገባ go in)
ቁጠረ	k'wät't'ärä	count [3-lit A]
ተነሣ	tänässa	get up, set off, arise [2-lit¹ A tä- stem]
ከ- - የተነሣ	kä- - yätänässa	as a result of (lit. 'which arose from')
ሠለፈ	sälläfä	be in line, parade [3-lit B]

14 እንዳንድ የመጽሔት መጣጥፎች
andand yämäs'het mät'at'ïfoč

Some magazine articles

By the end of this lesson you should:

- be aware of some other derived stem types of verbs
- be aware of some abstract noun patterns

Newspaper and magazine articles

In this lesson you will read a couple of short articles and some adverts taken from recent Amharic magazines or newspapers. At first you may find them difficult, but with the help of the vocabulary, you should try to read and understand them. You will find an English translation in the key to exercises at the end of the book, but only look at this after you have attempted to understand the passages.

Passage 1

ትምሕርት
በፖስታ

ሥራዎን እየሠሩ በትርፍ ጊዜዎ በጥቂት ገንዘብ
ከፍተኛ ዕውቀት ይገብዩ ።
ከ12ኛ ክፍል ፈተና (ጂ.ሲ.ኢ) እናዘጋጃዎታለን ።
አጅገን ቀላል በሆነ ክፍያ በቤ የተምህርት

መሣሪያዎች በመሰጠት ራስዎን በራስዎ እንዲያሩ
የሚያደርግ ዘዴም አለን ፡፡
የጀመሩትን ትምህርት አቋርጠው ከሆነም
ትምህርትዎን የሚቀጥሉበት መንገድ አዘጋጅተናል ፡፡
የመምሪያችን መጽሐፍ በነጻ ለማግኘት ስምና
አድራሻዎን ይላኩልን ፡፡

የፋና ቴቶሪያል ኮሌጅ

ፖ ፡ ሣ ፡ ቁ 10602   ስልክ 245669
አዲስ አበባ

Vocabulary

ፈተና	fätäna	test, examination
ክፍያ	kïfiyya	payment, share (cf. ከፈለ käffälä pay, divide)
ፋና	fana	torch (not electric, which is ባትሪ batri)

Verbs

ገበየ	gäbäyyä	go shopping, purchase [3-lit Y]
አቋረጠ	ak'k'warrät'ä	interrupt [3-lit at- + C-type stem]. (See grammar section); cf. ቀረጠ k'wärrät'ä cut
መራ	märra	lead, guide [2-lit¹ A]
መምሪያ	mämriya	guide (book)
ላከ	lakä	send [2-lit³]

Particles, phrases

ራስዎ	raswo	yourself [ራስ + possessive pronoun suffix]
በነጻ	bänäs'a	for free, gratis

Passage 2

የማያርፈው ሞተር

ያንድ ሰው የልብ ትርታ በደቂቃ ከ60 እስከ 80 ይደርሳል፡፡
በዓመት 40 ሚሊዮን ያህል ጊዜ ይመታል ማለት ነው፡፡
በያንዳንዱ ትርታ ወቅት 1/4 ሊተር ደም ወደ ልብ ይገባል
ማለት ነው፡፡ ልብ በአንድ ቀን ውሎው 2200 ጋሎን ያህል
ደም ይረጫል፡፡ በሌላ አነጋገር 56 ሚሊዮን ጋሎን ያህል
ደም በአማካኝ የሕይወት ዘመን ውስጥ ይረጫል ማለት ነው፡፡
ምንም እድሳት ሳያስፈልገው የልብን ያህል ሥራ
የሚያከናውን ሰው ሠራሽ መሣሪያ ይኖር ይሆን?! ልብን
እንደ ማምረቻ መሣሪያ እንጠቀምበት ብንል ሁለት ኪሎ
የሚመዝን ዕቃ ሁለት ጫማ ርዝማኔ ድረስ ለማንጠልጠል
ለአንዲት ትርታ በሚያደርገው የእንቅስቃሴ ፍጆታ ይበቃዋል፡፡
እንድ ስፖርተኛ እጅግ አስቸጋሪ ስፖርታዊ እንቅስቃሴዎች
በሚያደርግበት ጊዜ 20 ሊተር የሚገመት ደም ይገፋል፡፡
ወደ አንጎል የሚንዣዘው ደም አንጎል ደርሶ ወደ ልብ
ለመመለስ 8 ሴኮንድ ይፈጅበታል፡፡ ወደ እግር ጣቶች
የወረደው ደም ወደ አንጎል ለመመለስ የሚፈጅበት ጊዜ 18
ሴኮንድ መሆኑ ተረጋግጧል፡፡

Vocabulary

ትርታ	tïrrïta	beating, pounding (cf. ትር አለ tïrr alä beat (of heart))
የልብ ትርታ	yälïbb tïrrïta	heartbeat, pulse
ወቅት	wäk't	time
ደም	däm	blood
ውሎ	wïlo	full day, a day's rest, a day's duration (cf. ዋለ walä spend the day)
አነጋገር	annägagär	way of speaking (cf. ነገረ näggärä speak)
አማካኝ	ammakañ	average
እድሳት	iddïsat	repair, restoration (cf. አደሰ addäsä be new)
ሰው ሠራሽ	säw särraš	man made
ጫማ	č'amma	shoe, foot (measurement)
ርዝማኔ	rïzmane	length, height (cf. ረዘመ räzzämä be long)
ፍጆታ	fïjota	expenditure, destruction (cf. ፈጀ fäjjä use up, destroy)
አንጎል	angol	brain

ጣት	t'at	finger
የእግር ጣት	yäigir t'at	toe (*lit.* 'finger of the foot')

Verbs

ረጪ	räč'č'ä	spray, splash, pump [2-lit² A]
አከናወነ	akkänawwänä	accomplish, complete, carry something out [4-lit at- + C-type stem]. (*See grammar section*)
አመረተ	amärrätä	produce [3-lit A a- stem]
ማምረቻ	mamräča	means of production [instrument noun]
አንጠለጠለ	ant'älät't'älä	hang up, suspend, hold up, carry something in one's hand [4-lit **an-** stem]. (*See grammar section*)
በቃ	bäk'k'a	be enough, sufficient [2-lit¹ A]
በዚህ ይበቃዋል	bäzzih yïbäk'awal	he/it will have enough of this
ተገመተ	tägämmätä	be estimated, calculated [3-lit A tä- stem]
ተገፋ	tägäffa	be pushed [2-lit¹ A tä- stem]
ተረጋገጠ	tärägaggät'ä	be confirmed [3-lit reduplicating stem in **tä-**]. (*See grammar section*)

Passage 3

ጨረታ

በአዲስ አበባ ዩኒቨርሲቲ የአዋሳ እርሻ ኮሌጅ ከመስከረም 10/83 ጀምሮ ለአንድ ዓመት ልዩ ልዩ የምግብ ሸቀጣ ሸቀጦችን በጨረታ ለመግዛት ይፈልጋል ፡፡

በጨረታው ለመሳተፍ የሚፈልግ ማንኛውም ተጫራች ይህ ማስታወቂያ ከወጣበት ዕለት ጀምሮ ዘወትር በሥራ ሰዓት

ከኮሌጅ አስተዳደር ቢሮ የመጫረቻ ሰነዶችን ብር 10
በመግዛት፤ ጨረታቸውን የሚያቀርቡበትን ዋጋ በታሸገ
ኤንቬሎፕ አስክ መስከረም 7/83 10 ሰዓት ድረስ በፖስታው
ላይ በመጻፍ ለጨረታ በተዘጋጀው ሣጥን ውስጥ መክተት
ይቻላል ። ጨረታውም መስከረም 8/83 ልክ በሃስት ሰዓት
ተጫራቾች ወይም ሕጋዊ ወኪሎቻቸው በሚገኙበት በኮሌጅ
ዲን የሚከፈት መሆኑን እንገልጸለን ።
ተጫራቾች ለሚያቀርጓቸው ሁሉ ሕጋዊ የንግድ ፈቃድ
እንዲኖራቸውና የሚገባቸውን የንብር ገዴታ ያሟሉ መሆን
ይኖርባቸዋል ።
ተጫራቾች የጨረታ ማስከበሪያ ዋስትና ብር 3,000 በጥሬ
ገንዘብ ማስያዝ ይኖርባቸዋል ።
ኮሌጁ ለሥራው አፈጻጸም የተሻለ ዘዴ ካገኘ በጨረታው
አይገደድም ።

የአዋሳ እርሻ ኮሌጅ

Vocabulary

ጨረታ	č'äräta	bid, tender (cf. ተጫረተ täč'arrätä in the verb list below)
ሸቀጥ	šäk'ät'	goods, merchandise
ሸቀጣ ሸቀጥ	šäk'ät'a šäk'ät'	merchandise, goods of various kinds
ማስታወቂያ	mastawäk'iya	notice, announcement (cf. አስታወቀ astawwäk'ä inform)
አስተዳደር	astädadär	administration
ሰነድ	sänäd	document, draft, bill, form
ሕግ	higg	law
ሕጋዊ	higgawi	legal
ወኪል	wäkkil	agent, representative
ዲን	din	dean
ንግድ	nigd	trade, commerce
ፈቃድ	fäk'ad	permission, permit, license
ግብር	gibir	tax
ገዴታ	giddeta	requirement, obligation, condition (cf. ገደደ gäddädä in the verb list below)
ዋስትና	wastinna	guarantee, insurance
ጥሬ	t'ire	raw
ጥሬ ገንዘብ	t'ire gänzäb	cash (lit. 'raw money' – i.e. not a cheque)
አፈጻጸም	affäs'as'äm	manner of fulfilling (cf. ፈጸመ fäs's'ämä fulfil, complete [3-lit B])

Verbs

ተሳተፈ	täsattäfä	participate, take part in something [3-lit tä- + C-type stem]
ተጫረተ	täč'arrätä	bid [3-lit tä- + C-type stem]
አሸገ	aššägä	seal [3-lit B]
አማላ	ammwalla	fulfill, meet (*requirements*), make complete [2-lit[1] A at- + C-type stem] (*cf.* ሞላ molla be full)
አስያዘ	asyazä	leave something in someone's care, deposit, impound, mortgage, *also* have someone arrested [2-lit[3] as- stem] from ያዘ yazä hold
ገደደ	gäddädä	oblige, force, compel [3-lit A]

Particles, phrases

ዘወትር	zäwätir	usually, regularly, as a rule, normally

Passage 4

የፀሐይ ብርሃን ውሃን ለማጥራት

በማደግ ላይ ባሉም ሆነ እድገታቸው በጫጩ ወይም በተገታ እንደ ኢትዮጵያ ባሉ አገርኮ ከተተኗው የሕዝቦች ጤና ችግር የተቆራኘው ከንጹሕ የመጠጥ ውሀ እጦትና ከውሀ ወለድ በሽታዎች ጋር ነው። በየዕለቱ ከሚመዘገበት በርካታ ሙታን በተለይም ሕጻናቶች አብዛኛዎቹ የንጹሕ መጠጥ ውሀ እጦት ሰለባዎች ናቸው። የሕክምና ባለሙያዎች ችግሩን ለቀርፍ የሚችል አዲስ ዘዴ አገኝተዋል። ከጥቂት ወራት በፊት ገነበብን «ላጎሬት» የእንግሊዛውያን የሕክምና መጽሔት ላይ እንደወጣው ውሀን በቀላሉ በፀሐይ ብርሃን ለማጥራት የተቻለ በመሆኑ ይህ አዲስ ግኝት ለአገራችን የገጠር ነዋሪ ለሰጥ የሚችለው ጥቅም ከፍተኛ ይሆናል።

Vocabulary

ብርሃን	bïrhan	light
እድገት	ïdgät	growth, progress, development (*cf.* አደገ addägä grow [3-lit A])

ተጋታ	täggïta	pause, halt (cf. ተግ አለ tägg alä stop suddenly, halt, pause [አለ verb])
አሞት	ït'ot	lack, need, shortage (cf. አጣ at't'a lack, not have [2-lit¹ A])
ወላድ	wälläd	something which arises or originates from something else – hence interest (financial); offspring, issue (cf. ወለደ wällädä have a child, bear, beget [3-lit A])
ውሀ ወላድ	wïha wälläd	water-borne (cf. አየር ወላድ ayyär wälläd air-borne)
በርካታ	bärkatta	numerous, plentiful (cf. ተበራከተ täbärakkätä be abundant [4-lit tä- + C-type stem])
ሙት	mut	dead, deceased (pl. ሙታን, ሙታኖች mutan, mutanoč (cf. ሞተ motä die [2-lit⁵]))
ሕፃን	hïs'an	small child, baby (pl. ሕፃኖች, ሕፃናት, ሕፃናቶች hïs'anoč, hïs'anat, hïs'anatoč)
ሰለባ	säläba	victim; also means trophy, booty
ባለሙያ	balämuya	expert, skilled person
ግኝት	giññït	finding, achievement (cf. አገኘ agäññä find)
ገጠር	gät'är	countryside, open country, rural area
ነዋሪ	näwari	inhabitant, dweller [agent noun of ኖረ]

Verbs

አጠራ	at'ärra	purify [2-lit¹ A a- stem]
ጨጨ	č'ač'č'ä	be stunted [2-lit³]
ተቀራኘ	täk'wäraññä	be tied, related, connected [3-lit X tä- + C-type stem]
ተመዘገበ	tämäzäggäbä	be recorded, registered [4-lit tä- stem]
ቀረፈ	k'ärräfä	shake off, remove, peel [3-lit A]

Particles, phrases

| በተለይ | bätäläyy | in particular, especially (cf. ተለየ täläyyä be separate, different) |

Passage 5

ማስታወቂያ

ሙሐመድ ቃሲም

ምርጥ የሱፍ ጨርቅ በውድ ዋጋ ገዝተው ሰፊ ሳይመርጡ
ያሰፋሉ:: ነገር ግን እንተተመችተ: እንጻሰቡት ሳይሆን
ያልፈለጉት ሆኖ: ከሰውነትም ጋር ሳይስማማ ቢቀር ምን
ያህል እንደሚያዝኑ የታወቀ ነው!! ችግሩ ከሰውነትም አቋም
ያለመስተካከል ሳይሆን ከስፌቱ ላይ ነው::

በዘመናዊ ሞድ ማሰፋት ቢፈልጉ ቀጠር በማከበር ስፊት
በማሳመር ከተመሰከረለት ሙሐመድ ቃሲምን ይጠይቁ::
ልብስዎን የሚያሳምረው ሰፊው እሱ ነው!

እድራሻችን: አሜሪካን ግቢ መሀል
ስልክ ቁጥር 65 47 21
ፖስታ ሣ. ቁ. 25029

Vocabulary

ምርጥ	mïrt'	choice, select, superior (*cf.* መረጠ märrät'ä choose [3-lit A])
ሱፍ	suf	wool
ጨርቅ	č'ärk'	cloth
ሰፊ	säfi	tailor [agent noun from ሰፋ säffa 2-lit[1] A sew]. *Note: do not confuse this with* ሰፊ säffi wide
ስፌት	sïfet	sewing, tailoring
ሰውነት	säwïnnät	body, build, figure
አቋም	ak'wam	structure, shape (*cf.* ቆመ k'omä stand)
ሞድ	mod	fashion, style (*mode*)
ቀጠር	k'ät'äro	appointment
ቀጠር አከበረ	k'ät'äro akäbbärä	keep an appointment (አከበረ [3-lit A a- stem])

Verbs

ሰፋ	säffa	sew [2-lit[1] A]
አሰፋ	assäffa	have something sewn, have clothes made by a tailor [2-lit[1] as- stem]

ተስማማ	täsmamma	agree, correspond, match [2-lit¹ reduplicating stem in tä-] from ሰማ sämma hear
ተስተካከለ	tästäkakkälä	be even, regular; be adjusted to something [3-lit reduplicating stem in tästä-] from አከለ akkälä be equal
አሳመረ	asammärä	make beautiful, embellish, improve [3-lit as- stem], the 'causative' of አመረ amarä be beautiful, look good [irregular]*
መሰከረ	mäsäkkärä	testify [4-lit]
ከተመሰከረለት	kätämäsäkkärällät	since he is renowned (*lit.* 'since it is testified in his favour')

Particles, phrases

| ሳይሆን | sayhon | not only, to say nothing of (*lit.* 'without it being') |

*

s. past	አመረ	amarä	ger.	አምሮ	amro
s. impf.	ያምር	yamïr	c. ger.	አምሯል	amrwal
c. impf.	ያምራል	yamïral	inf.	ማማር	mamar
juss.	ይመር	yïmär	inst.	ማማሪያ	mamariya
imp.	አመር	ïmär	ag.	አማሪ	amari

Grammar

More derived stems

The passages in this lesson contain a variety of derived stem types which have not been discussed in the preceding lessons. As you will now realize, there are a large number of different derived stem patterns in Amharic, more in fact that can be properly covered in an introductory textbook of this kind.

You will need to be able to recognize the different derived stem patterns, because in most dictionaries all derived stems are listed under the root, or basic stem shape.

You should note how the various patterns inflect as you make your way through the book.

The new patterns, then, that you have encountered in this lesson are the following:

1 at- + C-type stems

The examples of this stem you met in this lesson are:

አጿረጠ	ak'k'warrät'ä interrupt *from* ቍረጠ k'wärrät'ä cut
አከናወነ	akkänawwänä accomplish *from root* *ከነወነ (*not used*)
አሟላ	ammwalla fulfill *from* ሞላ molla be full

The **at-** + C-type stems are often the 'transitive' or 'causative' counterparts of **tä-** + C-type stems. Consider the pairs of verbs below:

ተናገረ	tänaggärä	talk	→ አናገረ	annaggärä	engage in conversation
ተሻገረ	täšaggärä	cross	→ አሻገረ	aššaggärä	take across
ተቃረበ	täk'arräbä	approach	→ አቃረበ	ak'k'arräbä	bring something close
ተጫወተ	täč'awwätä	play, chat	→ አጫወተ	ač'č'awwätä	entertain
ተዳመጠ	tädammät'ä	agree	→ አዳመጠ	addammät'ä	listen to something
ተቃጠለ	täk'at't'älä	be on fire	→ አቃጠለ	ak'k'at't'älä	set fire to something

Therefore also:

ተከናወነ	täkänawwänä	be accomplished	→ አከናወነ akkänawwänä accomplish
ተቋረጠ	täk'warrät'ä	be interrupted, cease	→ አቋረጠ ak'k'warrät'ä interrupt

You can see that the distinctive features of the shape of this derived stem are:

1 prefix **a-**
2 gemination of the first consonant of the root
3 vowel **a** inside the stem

2 astä- **and** tästä- **stems**

There are not a great number of these derived stem patterns, but there are a few useful and important verbs which belong to these patterns. Below are a few examples, some of which you have already met.

አስተማሪ	astämarä	teach
አስታወቀ	astawwäk'ä	inform
አስታመመ	astammämä	nurse
አስተዋለ	astäwalä	observe, pay attention
አስታወሰ	astawwäsä	recall, remember

The prefix **astä-** forms transitive verbs, whilst **tästä-** forms the intransitive equivalent. The **tästä-** prefix is found on reduplicating stems (see below). In one of the passages above you met the following example of this type:

| ተስተካከለ | tästäkakkälä | be even, adjusted to which the corresponding transitive is: |
| አስተካከለ | astäkakkälä | make even, adjust, arrange. Do you remember the Amharic for 'hairdresser'? ፀጉር አስተካካይ s'ägur astäkakay, – *lit.* 'hair arranger'! |

3 an- and tän- stems

Again, verbs with these prefixes are not very common. Most verbs with these prefixes describe noises or particular ways of movement. Like **astä-** and **tästä-**, the **an-** prefix is found on transitive verbs, whilst **tän-** forms the corresponding intransitive verb. Below are a few examples by way of illustration.

አንቀሳቀሰ	ank'äsak'k'äsä	move something	[trans.]
ተንቀሳቀሰ	tänk'äsak'k'äsä	be moved, move	[intrans.]
አንጠለጠለ	ant'älät't'älä	hang something up	[trans.]
ተንጠለጠለ	tänt'älät't'älä	be hung up	[intrans.]

4 Reduplicating stems

Another common pattern of stem derivation involves the repetition or 'reduplication' of one of the consonants of the basic stem or root followed by the vowel **a**. In addition, the reduplicating pattern is often combined with one or other of the derivative prefixes that you have met so far. One of the commonest patterns is **tä-** + reduplicating stem. Below are some examples that have occurred in the dialogues to date.

ተዋወቀ	täwawwäk'ä	know one another	from ኣወቀ awwäk'ä know
ተስማማ	täsmamma	agree	from ሰማ sämma hear
ተረጋገጠ	tärägaggät'ä	be confirmed	from *ረገጠ, cf. ኣርግጥ ïrgït' sure
ተነጋገረ	tänägaggärä	talk together	from ነገረ näggärä speak
ተከታተለ	täkätattälä	follow after	from *ከተለ, cf. ተከተለ täkättälä follow
ተለያየ	täläyayyä	be different from one another	from ለየ läyyä be different
ተገናኘ	tägänaññä	meet	from *ገኘ, cf. ኣገኘ agäññä find

Corresponding to the first of the above, you have also met:

ኣስተዋወቀ astäwawwäk'ä introduce (*lit.* 'cause to know another')

Abstract nouns

The passages in this lesson and several of the more recent dialogues have contained quite a number of abstract nouns. Like English, Amharic has a large number of ways of forming abstract nouns from other nouns, as well as from verbs.

Below are some of the commoner abstract noun patterns illustrated by examples, many of which you have encountered in the lessons so far.

1 Suffixes in 't': -ta, -ot, -ota, -et, -eta, -ït, -ät, -at

ትርታ	tïrrïta	beat, pulse	from ትር ኣለ tïrr alä beat
ደስታ	dässïta	happiness	from ደስ ኣለ däss alä be happy
ከፍታ	käffïta	height	from ከፍ ኣለ käff alä be high
ዝምታ	zïmmïta	silence	from ዝም ኣለ zïmm alä be quiet
ሁነታ	huneta	condition	from ሆነ honä be, become
ኣርዳታ	ïrdata	help	from ረዳ rädda help
ይቅርታ	yïk'ïrta	forgiveness	from ይቅር yïk'ïr let it be omitted (ቀረ)
ይሉኝታ	yïluñta	propriety	from ይሉኝ yïluñ they say of me (ኣለ)
ግዴታ	gïddeta	obligation	from ገዴደ gäddädä be forced
ጥቅሜታ	t'äk'ämeta	use, usefulness	from ጠቀመ t'äk'k'ämä be useful
ፍጆታ	fïjota	destruction	from ፈጀ fäjjä destroy

ስጦታ	sït'ota	gift	from ሰጠ sät't'ä give
ችሎታ	čïlota	skill, ability	from ቻለ čalä be able
ዝግጅት	zïgïjjït	preparation	from አዘጋጀ azzägajjä prepare
ድርጅት	dïrïjjït	organization	from ደረጀ däräjjä be organized, developed
ትምህርት	tïmhïrt	study	from ተማረ tämarä study, learn
ጉጉት	guggut	longing	from ጓጓ gwaggwa long for
እድገት	ïdgät	growth	from አደገ addägä grow
ልደት	lïdät	birth	from ወለደ wällädä bear, have children
ቁመት	k'umät	height, stature	from ቆመ k'omä stand
ውበት	wïbät	beauty	from ተዋበ täwabä be beautiful
ሂደት	hidät	progress	from ሄደ hedä go
እድሳት	ïddïsat	repair	from አደሰ addäsä be new
ምክንያት	mïkïnyat	reason	from አመካኘ amäkaññä make an excuse
ስፋት	sïfat	width	from ሰፋ säffa be wide
ብዛት	bïzat	quantity	from በዛ bäzza be many
ፍራት	fïrat	fear	from ፈራ färra be afraid
ውጤት	wït't'et	result	from ወጣ wät't'a emerge
ስፌት	sïfet	sewing	from ሰፋ säffa sew
ምኞት	mïññot	wish, desire	from ተመኘ tämäññä desire
እጦት	ït'ot	lack	from አጣ at't'a be lacking
አገልግሎት	agälgïlot	service	from አገለገለ agäläggälä serve
ፍላጎት	fïllagot	need, want	from ፈለገ fällägä want

2 -nna

ሕክምና	hïkmïnna	medicine	from ሐኪም hakim doctor
ቁንጅና	k'wïnjïnna	prettiness	from ቆንጆ k'onjo pretty
ንጽህና	nïs'ïhïnna	purity	from ንጹህ nïs'uh pure
ትሕትና	tïhïtïnna	humility	from ትሑት tïhut humble
ግብርና	gïbïrïnna	agriculture	from ገበሬ gäbäre farmer

3 -nnät – *this is an especially common suffix that can be added to almost any noun or adjective, rather like the English suffixes '-ness'; '-hood'; or '-ship'.*

ሰውነት	säwïnnät	person, body	from ሰው säw man
ጓደኛነት	gwaddäññannät	companionship	from ጓደኛ gwaddäñña companion

ልጅነት	lïjjïnnät	childhood	from ልጅ lïjj child
ልዩነት	lïyyunnät	difference	from ልዩ lïyyu different
ክፉነት	kïfunnät	wickedness	from ክፉ kïfu bad, wicked
ጌትነት	getïnnät	lordship	from ጌታ geta lord, master
እብድነት	ïbdïnnät	madness	from እብድ ïbd mad
አንድነት	andïnnät	unity	from አንድ and one
ከንቱነት	käntunnät	uselessness	from ከንቱ käntu vain, useless
አስፈላጊነት	asfällaginnät	necessity	from አስፈላጊ asfällagi necessary
ኃላፊነት	halafïnnät	responsibility	from ኃላፊ halafi responsible, in charge

The suffix -nnät can also be added to any agent noun or other occupation noun to form a noun describing occupation, or in more general terms, 'the job of a', or 'being a'.

አሳላፊነት	asallafïnnät	the job of waiter
ተማሪነት	tämarïnnät	being a student
ጋዜጠኛነት	gazet'äññannät	journalism, being a journalist
ሐኪምነት	hakimïnnät	the job of a doctor, medical profession
አስተማሪነት	astämarïnnät	the job of a teacher, teaching profession
ሚስትነት	mistïnnät	being a wife

4 Abstract nouns may also be formed by a variety of prefixes. You will need to be able to identify when a prefix is involved because such words will be listed in most dictionaries under the first letter of the root, and not under the prefix

ተግባር	tägbar	action, task, deed	from a root *ገበረ (*not used*)
ትእዛዝ	tïïzaz	command, order	from አዘዘ azzäzä order
ምላጭ	mïlač'	razor	from ላጨ lač'č'ä shave
ምግባር	mïgbar	behaviour, conduct	from *ገበረ (not used)

Lastly, here's an Amharic proverb you should remember when things don't seem to be going too well:

ቀስ በቀስ እንቁላል በእግሩ ይሄዳል
Little by little the egg walks on its own feet

Key to exercises

This key does not provide answers to those exercises which require the learner to reuse material or to open exercises.

Introduction

1

gomma, gamo, mamo, mido, meda, muya, märra, maru, rarra, saro, särra, siso, sara, säwa, wawe, č'äwa, gari, gara, garo, furo, färra, gätta, geta, gatä, nägä, nägga, t'ena, wäne, wašša, get'ä, täñña, tära, tuta, wazema, alama, asama, mukära, billawa, gumare, sälasa, hisabu, hudade, abäjju, gudayyu

Lesson 1

1

1 (I), 2 (I), 3 (P), 4 (P), 5 (I or P), 6 (I), 7 (I).

2

1 ነው 2 ኖት 3 ነኝ 4 ናቸው 5 ናቸው 6 ነህ – ነኝ

3

1 እርስዎ 2 እኔ 3 እርሳቸው/እነርሱ 4 አንቺ 5 አናንተስ

5

Addis Abäba, Ityop'p'ïya, Haylä Sïllase, program, Mey Dey, lojik, posta, tiyatïr, pasta, ikonomiks, bisiklet

Lesson 2

1

1 እንዚህ ሌቶች የኔ አጋቶች ናቸው። 2 እኛ ተማሪዎች ነን። 3 እነርሱ አስተማሪዎች ናቸው። 4 እነርሱ አስተማሪዎች ናቸው። 5 እናንተ ቆንጃ ልጆረደች ናችሁ። 6 የኔ አስተማሪዎች ኢትዮጵያውያን ናቸው።

2

1 አዎ፤ መላኩ ተማሪ ነው። 2 የእንግሊዝኛ ቋንቋ በጣም አስቸጋሪ ነው። 3 አይደለችም፤ የትምሕርት ቤቱ ጸሐፊ ናት። 4 አዎ፤ የምሳ ሰዓት ነው። 5 አዎ፤ የአልማዝ ጓደኛ ናት። 6 አይደሉም፤ አስተማሪ ናቸው።

3

1 በዚህ/በዚያ 2 ይቺ/ያች 3 እዚህ/እዚያ 4 እነዚህ/እነዚያ 5 ከዚህ/ከዚያ

4

1 ያች ቤት ወይዘር ሕይወት አይደለችም? 2 እነዚህ ተማሪዎች እንግሊዛውያን አይደሉም። 3 ወንድሜ እትምህርት ቤት የለም። 4 እሱ የተረፈ አባት አይደለም? 5 አሁን ጊዜ የለም። 6 እቢኒጋ ቤት የለንም።

5

1 አይደለም 2 እሉ 3 ናቸሁ 4 አይደለም 5 እሉ 6 እሉ 7 ነሽ – ነኝ 8 አይደለንም 9 የሉም 10 አይደለሁም

6

ጥሩ – መጥፎ
ትልቅ – ትንሽ
አዲስ – አርጌ
አስቸጋሪ – ቀላል
ቅርብ – ሩቅ

7

1 በጠረጴዛ ላይ ነው። 2 እዚህ ታች ጥሩ ምግብ ቤት አለ።
3 አይደለም፣ ከከተማ ሩቅ ነው። 4 አይደለም፣ ከማዘጋጃ ቤት
በስተቀኝ ነው። 5 አዎ፣ ከቴያትር ፊት ለፊት ባንክ አለ።
6 እትምህርት ቤት ናቸው። 7 እቤት ውስጥ ነው። 8 እቤት ናቸው።

8

ወደ – ሰኞ – ሕዝብ – አዞ – አሳብ – መልሶ – ቀጥሎ – ቁጣ – በር – ዘር –
ግማሽ – ዋና – እገኝ – እሳት – ጋዜጣ – መቶ – ገና – ገና –
ዱጻ – ረጻ – ሰጥታ – እትም – እያሌ – ትንሽ – ጥንት – ትርፍ – ተረፈ –
ጋብቻ – ጠቅላላ – ሌላ – ሕጉ – ትጉ

Lesson 3

1

1 አለኝ 2 አለን 3 አለቻት 4 አለው 5 አሉህ 6 አሉዋቸው 7 አለሽ –
አለኝ

2

(a) 1 ... የለኝም።
   2 ... የለንም።
   3 ... የለትም።
   4 ... የለውም?
   5 ... የሉህም?
   6 ... የሉዋቸውም።
   7 ... የለሽም? አይደለም ... የለኝም።

(b) ... ነበረኝ።
   ... ነበረንም።
   ... ነበረቻት።
   ... ነበረው።
   ... ነበሩህ።
   ... ነበሩዋቸው።
   ... ነበረሽ? አዎ፣
   ... ነበረኝ።

3

1 አስፋና ጊሩት አራት ልጆች አሉዋቸው። 2 ብዙ ገንዘብ የለንም።
3 ያቶ ሙሉጌታ ሚስት ቀይ መኪና አላቸው/አላት። 4 ትናንትና ብዙ
ትምሕርት (ክፍሎች) ነበረኝ/ነበሩኝ። 5 ወደዞር ፀሐይ ቆንጆ ምግብ
ቤት ነበራት/ነበራቸው። 6 አስተማሪው መጽሐፍ አለነበራቸውም/
አልነበረውም። 7 ብዙ ውንድሞች አሉህ/አሉሽ/አሉዎ? አይ፣ ወንድም
የለኝም።

4

አድስ መኪና	(a) አለኝ	(b) የለኝም ፡፡
ሦስት ሚ.ስቶች	(a) አሉኝ	(b) የሉኝም ፡፡
ሁለት ወንድሞችና እንዲት እህት	(a) አሉኝ	(b) የሉኝም ፡፡
ጥሩ መንገሥት	(a) አለኝ	(b) የለኝም ፡፡
ብዙ ኢትዮጵያውያንን አስተማሪዎች	(a) አሉኝ	(b) የሉኝም ፡፡

5

1 አልፈለገችም 2 ሄድን 3 አላቸው – የላቸውም 4 በላህ – በላሁ 5 በሉ
– ጠጡ 6 ገዛች 7 ደረሳችሁ – ደረስን 8 ሼጡ

6

1 ምሳ ለመብላት አልፈለግሁም ፡፡ 2 አልማዝና ከበደ አዲስ መኪና
ገዙ ፡፡ 3 ወደዚ ዓሐይ ወደ ፖስታ ቤት ሐደች ፡፡ 4 ቡና ጠጣህ/
ጠጣሽ/ጠጡ? 5 ተማሪዎቹ ወደት ሐዱ? 6 እቶ መሐመድ ሒሳቡን
አልከፈሉም ፡፡ 7 አልማዝ፡ ፈልሙን መቼ አየሽ? 8 እናቴ በሩን
ከፈተች ፡፡

7

1 አባቴ አስተማሪ ናቸው ፡፡ My father is a teacher. 2 ይቺ መኪናሽ
ነች? Is this your car? 3 ትልቁ ወንድሙ ከአዲስ አበባ ደረሰ ፡፡ His
big brother arrived in Addis Ababa. 4 ተማሪዎችዎ ትጉ ናቸው?
Are your students hard working? አዎ፡ ተማሪዎቼ በጣም ትጉ
ናቸው ፡፡ Yes, my students are very hard working. 5 እናቴ ወዴት
ሄደች? Where did my mother go? ወደእህትዋ ቤት ሄደች ፡፡ She went
to her sister's house. 6 ጓደኛቸው ብዙ ገንዘብ አለው ፡፡ Their friend
has a lot of money. 7 ስምህ ማን ነው? ስሜ ዳዊት ነው ፡፡ What
is your name? My name is Dawit. 8 መላኩ ከወንድሙ ጋር ወደ
ሲኒማ ቤት ሐደ ፡፡ Melaku went with his brother to the cinema.

8

(Note: other answers may be possible.)

1 ቀዩ መኪናዬ	my red car	6 ሀብታሙ ጓደኛችን	our rich friend
2 አዲሱ ጃኬትህ	your new jacket	7 ትንሹ ከተማው	his little town

3 ትልቁ ወንድማችን our big brother   8 ድሃው አገሬ   my poor country

4 ጥቁሩ ልብስዋ   her black dress   9 ትልቁ ክፍላቸው   their big room/class

5 አርጌው ቤታችሁ   your old house   10 ትንሿዋ እኅቱ   his little sister

9

(Note: other answers may be possible.)
1 ሰራተኛ 2 አለም 3 ፀጌረዳ 4 ውሃ/ውሀ 5 መሐንዲስ 6 ሐይለኛ/ ሃይለኛ 7 ሚሃ 8 ጸሃፊ 9 ገለፀ 10 ሥራ 11 ስነ ጽሁፍ 12 ሠንደቅ ዓላማ 13 መሥሪያ ቤት 14 ሕንጻ/ጎንጻ 15 ህዝብ

Translation of reading passage

Terrefe's father was a government worker. His mother was a secretary in a large office. They both worked in town. His mother and father were very kind people. One day his father came in from work and gave his son a large book. He still has this book today. In this book there are many beautiful pictures. Terrefe is therefore very fond of the book. It was his first book.

Lesson 4

1

1 ሁለት ኪሎ ቡና ገዛች። 2 አስተማሪው መጽሐፍችን ወሰደ። 3 አገቱ ይህን ገንዘብ ሁሉ ለልጁ ሰጠ። 4 አልማዝ ቀዩን መጽሐፊ አገኘች። 5 ወዘሮ ፀሐይ እነዚህን ደብዳቤዎች ጻፉ። 6 እት ተረፈን አምስታ ቤት ውስጥ አየሁ። 7 ጋለፈው ሳምንት ጥሩ ፊልም እሲኒማ ቤት አየን።

3

1 ሃያ ሦስት ብር 2 አምስት ኪሎ 3 አሥራ ስምንት ሰዓት 4 መቶ ስልሳ ቀን 5 ሁለት መቶ ሠላሳ ሰባት ኪሎሜትር 6 አርባ ብር ከሐምሳ ሳንቲም 7 አራት ሺህ አምስት መቶ ዓመት 8 ሠላሳ ሶስት ደቂቃ 9 አሥራ ዘጠኝ መቶ ኃምሳ ስድስት 10 አሥራ ስምንት መቶ ሰማንያ ዘጠኝ 11 ስድስት መቶ አሥራ ሰባት 12 ዘጠና ዘጠኝ 13 አርባ አምስት 14 አስራ ዘጠኝ መቶ ሰባ እንድ 15 አስራ ሰባት መቶ ዘጠና ሶስት

4

1 ሃያ አንድ ዘጠኝ ሲደመር ሠላሳ ነው ። 2 ሃያ አምስት አምስት
ሲቀነስ ሃያ ነው ። 3 አሥራ ሁለት አሥራ ሁለት ሲደመር ሃያ አራት
ነው ። 4 መቶ ሃያ ሠላሳ ሲደመር መቶ አምሳ ነው ። 5 አርባ አምሳ
ሲደመር ዘጠና ነው ። 6 አሥራ አምስት አራት ሲደመር አሥራ ዘጠኝ
ነው ። 7 አሥራ ሰባት ሰባት ሲቀነስ አሥር ነው ። 8 ስልሳ አሥራ
ስድስት ሲደመር ሰባ ስድስት ነው ። 9 አምስት መቶ አምስት መቶ
ሲደመር አንድ ሺ ነው ። 10 ሰማንያ ስምንት አሥራ አንድ ሲቀነስ
ሰባ ሰባት ነው ።

5

1 እባክህ ሦስት ኪሎ ስኳር ስጠኝ ። 2 እባክህ አራት ፓኬት ሻይ
ስጠኝ ። 3 እባክህ ሁለት መቶ ግራም ቅቤ ስጠኝ ። 4 እባክህ ስድስት
ጠርሙዝ አምቦ ውሃ ስጠኝ ። 5 እባክህ አስር ፓኬት ከብሪት
ስጠኝ ። 6 እባክህ ግማሽ ኪሎ ጥሩ ዱቄት ስጠኝ ። 7 እባክህ
አምስት ጠርሙዝ ሜታ ቢራ ስጠኝ ። 8 እባክህ ሁለት ፓኬት ሲጃራ
ስጠኝ ። 9 እባክህ አንድ ቆርቆር ሥጋ ስጠኝ ። 10 እባክህ ጥሩ
ዓይነት ሻይ ስጠኝ ።

6

1 ከዚህ በኋላ	after this	9 ፈለጉዋቸው	they wanted them
2 ጎረቤት	neighbour	10 ብዋምብዋ	tap
3 ልጆቿ	her children	11 ቆረጥኩ	I cut
4 መቁረጥ	to cut	12 አብዋራ	dust
5 ስኳር	sugar	13 የጎንደር ከተማ	the town of Gondar
6 ያማርኛ ቅዋንቅዋ	Amharic language	14 የእግር ኳስ	football
7 ቆንጆ	beautiful	15 ሂደዋል	he has gone
8 ጎደለ	it is missing		

Translation of reading passage

*Today Mrs Dinqinesh went to the market. Kebbede and Taytu went
with her. Kebbede is a little boy. He is ten years old. Taytu is Mrs
Dinqinesh's maid. Mrs Dinqinesh wanted to buy many different
things from the shop – rice and flour, tea and butter, and in addition,
oranges, papayas, tomatoes, onions and potatoes. So today Taytu has
come as well. First they went into a grocer's shop. There they bought*

flour, rice, tea and butter. But there were no fruit and vegetables. The green grocer's is not near the store, it's very far away. So they could not go on foot, and so they went by bus. Mrs Dinqinesh was very pleased with the shopping she had done and so she bought Kebbede some sweets.

Lesson 5

1

1 እንሒጻለን	6 ትጨርሻለሽ	11 ትቀዋለች	16 አያለሁ
2 አወስጻለሁ	7 እናውቃለን	12 እጽፋለሁ	17 ይስማሉ
3 ትመጣላቸሁ	8 እንደውላለን	13 ይሼጣል	18 ትጀምራለህ
4 ይሰማል	9 ይርራሉ	14 ትገዛለች	19 ታልፋለች
5 ይተኛሉ	10 ትከፍያለሽ	15 ትመርጣላቸሁ	20 ታስቢያለሽ

2

1 ገለፈው ሳምንት ተማሪዎቹ መጽሐፋቸውን ገዙ። 2 ነገ ከበደ አዲሱን መኪናውን ይሼጣል። 3 ሥራህን መቼ ትጨርሳለህ? ትሉ እጨርሳለሁ። 4 ትናንትና አዲስ ጃኬት መረጥሽ። 5 አሁን መብላት እንፈልጋለን።

3

1 አልማዝ፡ አሁን ምሳ መብላት ትፈልጊያለሽ? 2 ሕይወት፡ ትምሕርትሽን መቼ ትጨርሻለሽ? 3 ከሃስት ሰዓት በኋላ ጂማ እንደርሳለን። 4 አስተማሪው ትምሕርትን አሁን ይጀምራል። 5 ሒሳቡን ማን ይከፍላል? ጊሩት፡ እንቺ ትከፍያለሽ?

4

1 **ጩኽ** ('shout') The children are shouting. 2 **ሩጠ** ('run') Where are you running to? 3 **ሳመ** ('kiss') Kebbede is kissing Hirut. 4 **ተረተ** ('tell') We're telling this story. 5 **ፈጠነ** ('hurry') Why are you hurrying?

5

1 ከቀኑ አራት ሰዓት ተኩል 2 ከምሽቱ አሥራ ሁለት ሰዓት ከሩብ 3 ወደ ዘጠኝ ሰዓት 4 ልክ ስምንት ሰዓት ከአሥር ደቂቃ 5 ከምሽቱ

አሥራ ሁለት ሰዓት ሩብ ጉዳይ 6 ከጥዋቱ ባሥራ ሁለት ሰዓት ከሃያ አምስት ደቂቃ 7 ወደ አሥራ አንድ ሰዓት ካምስት 8 ልክ እኩለ ቀን 9 አሥር ሰዓት ከሃያ 10 ይቅርታ፣ ሰዓት የለኝም!

Translation of reading passage

My wife and I arrived in Addis Ababa this morning. We came by Ethiopian Airlines. Our plane landed at Bole Airport at precisely half-past six. We went into the arrivals hall together with the other passengers and completed everything concerning our passports and visas. Then we went to the customs hall. Now many people are waiting for the arrivals, and our friends are waiting for us, too. Our son and his wife are there together. They say welcome to us. Then after we've loaded our baggage into the car, we go into town. Their home is not far from the centre of town. So after a few minutes, at about a quarter-past eight we arrive home.

Lesson 6

1

1 ፒተር ነገ አስመራ አይሄድም፡፡ Peter isn't going to Asmara tomorrow. 2 እንግሊዝኛ አልችልም፡፡ I can't speak English. 3 ወይዘር አያልነሽ ቅቤና ወተት ለናቲ አትገዛም፡፡ Mrs Ayyalnesh is not buying butter and milk for her mother. 4 አቶ ፴ጥሮስ ደብዳቤ አይጽፍም፡፡ Mr Petros is not writing a letter. 5 አሁን ለመብላት እንፈልግም፡፡ We don't want to eat now. 6 ዛሬ ሠራተኞቹ ሥራቸውን አይጨርሱም፡፡ The workers won't finish their work today. 7 ገንዘቡን ሁሉ ለሠራተኞቹ ለምን አትሰጡም? Why don't you give all the money to the workers?

2

1 (a) አስተማሪያችን መጽሐፍ አልጻፈችም፡፡ (b) አስተማሪያችን መጽሐፍ አትጽፍም፡፡ 2 (a) ላባቴ በስልክ አልደወልኩም፡፡ (b) ላባቴ በስልክ አልደውልም፡፡ 3 (a) በመንገድ ላይ ብዙዎች መንገደኞች አላየንም፡፡ (b) በመንገድ ላይ ብዙዎች መንገደኞች አናይም፡፡ 4 (a) ሊኒማ በሦስት ሰዓት ተኩል አልጀመረም፡፡ (b) ሊኒማ በሦስት ሰዓት ተኩል አይጀምርም፡፡ 5 (a) በየቀኑ ልክ ባሥራ አንድ ሰዓት ጸሐፊዎች ሥራ አልጨረሱም፡፡ (b) በየቀኑ ልክ ባሥራ አንድ ሰዓት ጸሐፊዎች ሥራ አይጨርሱም፡፡ 6 (a) ከኛ ጋር ለምን አልመጣችሁም? (b) ከኛ ጋር ለምን አትመጡም?

3

1 ቡና አልጠጣም። 2 ነገ አይደውልም። 3 እሁን አንፈልገም። 4 ጥሩ ልብስ አይሼጥም። 5 ደብዳቤዎቹን አትልክም። 6 ቲኬት አይገዙም።

4

1 ለመገዛት (a), መሔድ (b) 2 ለማንበብ (b), መገዛት (b) 3 መብላት (c), መጠጣት (c) 4 ለመሄድ (b), ለመሠራት (b)

5

1 ጋዜጣ መግዛት/ለመግዛት እፈልጋለሁ። 2 ባስራ አንድ ሰዓት ለባሌ/ ለሚስቴ መደወል/ለመደወል እፈልጋለሁ። 3 ጥያቄ መጠየቅ/ለመጠየቅ እፈልጋለሁ። 4 ከአቶ አክሊሉ ጋር መነጋገር/ለመነጋገር እፈልጋለሁ። 5 አዲስ ጃኬት መምረጥ/ለመምረጥ እፈልጋለሁ። 6 ራዲዮን መስማት/ለመስማት እፈልጋለሁ። 7 መኪናዬን መሼጥና/ለመሼጥና አዲስ መኪና መግዛት/ለመግዛት እፈልጋለሁ። 8 ለጓደኞቼ አንዳንድ ደብዳቤዎች መጻፍ/ለመጻፍ እፈልጋለሁ። 9 አልማዝንና ተረፈን መጠየቅ/ለመጠየቅ እፈልጋለሁ።

6

ጸሐፊ በቢሮ ትሠራለች። መካኒክ በጋራዥ ይሠራል። የታክሲ ሾፈር በከተማ መንገድ ላይ ይሠራል። ጠበቃ በፍርድ ቤት የሠራል። ቄስ በቤት ክርስቲያን ይሠራል። ሐኪም በሆስፒታል ይሠራል። ባለሱቅ በሱቁ ውስጥ ይሠራል። አስተማሪ በትምህርት ቤት ይሠራል። አትክልት ሽያጭ በገበያ ይሠራል። ፖሊስ በፖሊስ ጣቢያ ይሠራል። ተዋናይ በቲያትር ይሠራል። ለማኝ በከተማ መንገድ ላይ ይሠራል። ገበሬ በማሳ ይሠራል።

7

1 እውነት አይደለም። ጋዜጠኛ በትምህርት ቤት አይሠራም። በገዜጣ መሥሪያ ቤት ይሠራል። 2 እውነት አይደለም። ዳኛ በመደብር አይሠራም። በፍርድ ቤት ውስጥ ይሠራል። 3 እውነት አይደለም። ተማሪዎች በፖሊስ ጣቢያ አይሠሩም። በትምህርት ቤት ይሠራሉ። 4 እውነት አይደለም። ያትክልት ሽያጭ በቢሮ አይሠራም። በመደብር ወይም በገበያ ይሠራል። 5 እውነት አይደለም። ጸሐፊ በመንገድ ላይ አትሠራም። በቢሮ ትሠራለች። 6 እውነት አይደለም። ፖሊስ በጸጉር ጌስተካካይ አይሠራም። በፖሊስ ጣቢያ ይሠራል።

Translation of reading passage

Ethiopia is located in the northeastern part of the continent of Africa. This region is called the Horn of Africa. The neighbouring countries of Ethiopia are Eritrea to the north, Sudan to the west, Kenya in the south, and Somalia in the southeast and east. In addition, to the east, she has a border with Jibuti which is located between Eritrea and Somalia.

In 1993 Eritrea gained her freedom. The capital city of Eritrea is Asmara. For over thirty years the people of Eritrea fought for their freedom. Before, though, Eritrea was one of the provinces of Ethiopia.

Lesson 7

1

1 በሲኒማ ቤት አገኘኋዋቸው:: 2 ጊሩት ስለ ትምሕርቲ ጠየቀቻዖ:: 3 ወደድሽኝ? 4 አቶ ሙሉጌታ ፈለጉዋት:: 5 ተማሪዎቹ ሁሉ አሁን ገዙት? 6 አላወቅነውም:: 7 ከዬት አገኘሽዉ? 8 በትምሕርቱ አልረዳሻዉም እንዴ? 9 አልሰሙንም?

2

1 ጋለፈዉ ዓመት አንድ ሊጋ መኪናዩን ሠረቀ:: 2 አቶ ሙሉጌታ አምስት ብር ለኔ ሰጡ:: 3 ተማሪዎቹን በክፍላቸዉ ዉስጥ አገኘን:: 4 ትናንትና ማታ ራዲዮን አልሰማሁም:: 5 ጋለፈዉ ሳምንት ወደዘር አልማዝን ሲኒማ ቤት አየሁ:: 6 እኔን ስለምን መረጥህ? 7 ተማሪዉን በትምህርቱ ረዳሁ:: 8 እኔን ስለምን ጠየቅሽኝ? መልሱን አላወቅሁ::

4

1 በሲኒማ ቤት አገኛቸዋለሁ:: 2 ጊሩት ስለ ትምሕርቲ ተጠይቀዋለች:: 3 ተወጂናለሽ? 4 አቶ ሙሉጌታ ይፈልጉዋታል:: 5 ተማሪዎቹ ሁሉ አሁን ይገዙታል? 6 እናዉቀዉም:: 7 ከዬት ታገኘዋለህ? 8 በትምሕርቱ አትረጂዉም እንዴ? 9 አይሰሙንም?

5

(Note: other answers may be possible.)

1 የታክሲ ሾፈር ወይዘሮ አልማዝን ፖስታ ቤት አጠገብ ይጠብቃል። The taxi driver is waiting for Mrs Almaz next to the post office.
2 ነገ የፈተናውን መልስ እናንተን አሳያለሁ። I'll show you the examination answers tomorrow. 3 ከበደና ሒሩት ፒተርን ያማርኛ ቋንቋ ያስተምራሉ። Kebbede and Hirut are teaching Peter the Amharic language. 4 እማማ፣ እኛን ወደ ገበያ መቼ ትወስጃለሽ? Mummy, when are you taking us to the market? 5 እናቴ እህቷን በጣም ብዙ ትወዳለች። My mother loves her sister very much.
6 ከሳምንቱ መጨረሻ በፊት ገንዘቡን ለናንተ እልካለሁ። I'll send the money to you before the end of the week.

6 (a)

1 -bb- 3 -ll- 5 -bb- 7 -bb- 2 -bb- 4 -bb- 6 -bb- 8 -bb-

6 (b)

1 ገንዘቤ ሁሉ ጠፋብኝ። 2 ልጁን መታበት። 3 አገቴ አጋደሰልኝ። 4 ምን ከፉ ዕድል ደረሰብናል! 5 ዷኛው አስረኛውን ፈረደበት። 6 ፒተር ይቀመጥበታል። 7 ነገ ላንተ እነግርባቸዋለሁ። 8 ዬት ጠፋብህ?

7

1 ብዙ ስተት ይገኝበታል። 2 ደብጻቤውን እመረምርልሃለሁ። 3 አልማዝ ሁለት ኪሎ ብርቱካን ገዛቸልኝ። 4 በቤቱ ውስጥ ምን ያደርጋሉ? ዝም ብለው ይቀመጡበታል። 5 የኔ ብዕር ዬት ነው? ሐዲስ ይጽፍበታል። 6 ነገ ከሰዓት በኋላ እንደውልላቸዋለን።

Translation of reading passage

This is our village. Nearby there's a wide valley. There are ten houses in our village. In the middle of the village there's a field. The boys like to play football in the field. The girls, however, fetch water every morning for their mothers from the spring. The spring isn't far from the village, so it isn't any trouble to them. Every day from eight o'clock in the morning all the children of the village go to school and study. The school is close by. The children like their teacher very

*much; they say he's a kind man. There's a large shop in our village.
From the shop we buy coffee, salt and sugar. In addition, we have a
police station and a little clinic. At present, however, we don't have
electric light. In a few weeks' time, though, we hope that they'll be
bringing us [electric] light.*

Lesson 8

1

1 የምንሰማው ወሬ the news that we hear/are hearing/shall hear
2 የምትጠይቁኝ ጥያቄ the question that you're asking me
3 የምትጽፈው ደብዳቤ the letter that she's writing 4 የምደውልለት
ጓደኛዬ my friend whom I'm phoning 5 ዓሣ የሚወደው ሰውዬ the
man who likes fish 6 መንገድ ላይ የሚቆመው መኪና the car that'll
be standing on the road 7 የሚገዙት ዳቦ the bread that they're buying 8 የምትጀምሩት ሥራ the job that you're starting 9 የምታደርግልኝ
ጥሪ the call that you're making to me 10 የሚጠጡ ቡና the coffee
that they're drinking

2

1 አልማዝ የለበሰችው ልብስ ቀይ ነው ቡናማ? (... የምትለብሰው)
2 ሠራተኞቹ ትናንትና የጀመሩት ሥራ መቼ ይጨርሳሉ? 3 ሚስተህ
የገዛቸው ቀሚስ ቀለሙ ምን ዓይነት ነው? (... የምትገዛው)
4 ከአሥመራ የሚደርሰው አይሮፕላን መቼ ያርፋል? 5 እናንተ
የቀጠራችሁት ሰውዬ አሁን መጣ? 6 ከበደ ዕቃውን የወሰደበት መኪና
የማን ነው? (... የሚወስድበት) 7 አሁን አንተ ከመንገዱ ወደ ግራ
የምታየው ቤት ፖሊስ ጣቢያ ነው።

3

1 ባለፈው ዓመት ዩኒቨርሲቲ የገባችው አማረች ናት። 2 ሲኒማ ቤት
በየቀኑ የምሄደው እኔ ነኝ። 3 አስተማሪ ለመሆን የሚፈልገው
አየለ ነው። 4 ፎቶግራፍ አንሺ ለመሆን የሚፈልጉት ማሞና ከበደ
ናቸው። 5 የሞተው ሰውዬ የሙሉጌታ አባት ነው። 6 ሻይ በወተት
የምንጠጣ እኛ ነን። 7 ሙሉ ቀን አገበያ የዋለችው ወይዘሮ አበበች
ናት።

4

1 ያማርኛ ቋንቋ ነው የምንማረው/የምንማረው ያማርኛ ቋንቋ ነው። 2 ሁሉም የሚወደው መጽሐፍ ማንበብ ነው። 3 ስንት ነው ከበደ ለመኪናው የከፈለው? 4 ስለምን ነው ፒተር የሚጽፈው? 5 ትናንትና የመጡት ማን ናቸው? 6 ስለዚህ ነው ያቶ ሙሉጌታን አጓል የማልወደው። 7 መቼ ነበር በሩን የዘጋኸው? 8 ስለምን ነው ይህን ወረ ያላራሽኝ? 9 ተማርቼ ሥራቸውን የሚጀምሩት ሰኞ ነው። 10 አልማዝ ኖት ቡና ያፈላችው።

5

1 ሙሉ ቀን ምንም ያልበላው ሰው በጣም ራበው። 2 ብዙ ሥራ የሠራው ሰው እጥብቅ ደከመው። 3 መቶ ብር በድንገት የሚያገኘው ሰው ደስ ይለዋል። 4 ማንበብ ያወቀ ሰው ጥሩ ሥራ ለመሥራት ይቻለዋል። 5 ትናንትና ከሆስፒታል የገባው ልጅ ራሱን አመመው። 6 ከጥዋት ጀምር ልጁ ስላልጠጣ አሁን ጠማው።

6

(Other answers are possible.)

1 ተማሪዎች የሚያስተምረው ሰው አስተማሪ ይባላል። 2 መኪና የሚያሳድሰው ሰው መካኒክ ይባላል። 3 በሆስፒታል የሚሠራው ሰው ሐኪም ይባላል። 4 ዕቃ የሚሠርቀው ሰው ሌባ ይባላል። 5 ብዙ የሚያውቀው ሰው አዋቂ ይባላል። 6 ፎቶግራፍ የሚያነሣው ሰው ፎቶ አንሺ ይባላል። 7 ቲኬት የሚቆርጠው ሰው ቲኬት ቆራጭ ይባላል። 8 በምግብ ቤት የሚሠራው ሰው አሳላፊ ይባላል። 9 ታክሲ የሚነዳው ሰው የታክሲ ሾፌር ይባላል። 10 ተማሪዎች የሚሠሩበት ቦታ ትምህርት ቤት ይባላል። 11 አስረኛ የሚታሰርበት ቦታ እስር ቤት ይባላል። 12 አይሮፕላን የሚያርፍበት ቦታ አይሮፕላን ማረፊያ ይባላል።

7

1 (a) ... መሔድ አለብኝ። (b) ... መሔድ ያስፈልገኛል። 2 (a) ... መደወል አለብህ። (b) ... መደወል ያስፈልግሃል። 3 (a) ... መግዛት ነበረብን። (b) ... መግዛት አስፈለገን። 4 (a) ... መምረጥ ነበረባት። (b) ... መምረጥ አስፈለጋት። 5 (a) ... ማሳየት አለባቸው። (b) ... ማሳየት ያስፈልጋቸዋል። 6 (a) ... መክፈል ነበረባት። (b) ... መክፈል አስፈለጋት። 7 (a) ... መስጠት አልነበረባችሁም? (b) ... መስጠት አላስፈለጋችሁም?

Translation of reading passage

Ethiopia is located in the north-eastern part of the African continent. Ethiopia's neighbouring countries are Eritrea to the north, Sudan to the west, Kenya to the south, and Somalia and Jibuti to the southeast and east.

Ethiopia is a very beautiful country. Natural resources of all kinds can be found in the country. For instance, Ethiopia is mostly a mountainous country. Ethiopia's highest mountain is called Ras Dashen. It is to be found in the north. There, that is to say, towards the north and in the centre of the country, there are deep valleys and gorges. The region towards the south and east, however, is a sandy plain that is desert.

Whilst the country is divided by the great Rift Valley, there are many lakes there. The largest and most well-known amongst Ethiopia's lakes, however, is T'ana. It is to be found in the north. Amongst Ethiopia's rivers, the Blue Nile (Abbay), the Awash, the Wabi Shebele and the Omo, are well known.

Lesson 9

1

1 gerundive 2 -ና 3 -ና 4 gerundive 5 gerundive 6 gerundive

2

1 ጨርሳ 2 ገብቶ 3 ይዤ 4 አድርገህ 5 ጨርሼ 6 አይታችሁ 7 ጠርተን
8 ጨርሼ በልቼ

3

1 አይሽ ገበያ ሄዳ የሚያስፈልጋትን ትገዛለች። 2 አቶ ሙሉጌታ ዝም
ብለው ተቀመጡ። 3 ከነገ ወዲያ ገንዘቡን ይዤ እመጣለሁ።
4 አስተማሪው አጥብቆ ከለከላቸው። 5 እናንተ ልጆች፣ ሮርሳውን
ይዛችሁ ወዴት ነው የምትሄዱ? 6 ትናንትና ጸሐፊዋ ዘጠኝ ደብዳቤ
ጽፋ ላከች። 7 ትንሽ ቆይ፣ አፖስታ ቤት ገብቼ ቴምር አገዛለሁ።
8 ምሳ በልተን ከበደን ለመጠየቅ እንሂድ!

5

1 ሙሉ ቀን እዚህ ቈይተናል። 2 ወደ አሥመራ ሔደዋል። 3 ተማሪዎቹ በጊዜ ደርሰዋል? 4 እናቷን ለመጠየቅ ሄዳለች። 5 ባቡሩ ተነሥቷል። 6 ወረውን ሰምታችኋል? 7 ኧረ፡ ወተት አልቋል! 8 አማረች ረጅም ደብዳቤ ጽፋለች።

6

1 ከትናንትና ወዲያ እናታችን ጥሩ ምሳ ሠራችልን። 2 ዛሬ ከሰዓት በፊት ጸሐፊዋ አምስት ደብዳቤዎች ትጽፋለች። 3 ባለፈው ሳምንት ጥላሽን አገኙልሽ? 4 ነገ ከበደ መኪናውን ይሼጣል። 5 ካንድ ሰዓት በፊት ልጆቹ ተኙ።/. . . ይተኛሉ። 6 ተነገ ወዲያ ስልሳ ብር እሰጣታለሁ። 7 ዛሬ ማታ ሐኪሙ ወረውን ይነግሩኛል። 8 ከጥቂት ቀን በኋላ በሽተኞቹ አዲስ ሆስፒታል ይሄዳሉ።

7

1 . . . ለሚመጡት 2 . . . ከደረሰው 3 . . . በሚመጣው 4 . . . በምትልኪው 5 . . . ስለምንማረው 6 . . . ስለደረስንበት

8

1 ትናንትና ዝናብ ስለዘነበ ከቤት ውጭ አልወጣሁም። 2 ምሳህን እየበላህ መናገር አይገባም! 3 ትምህርትህን ደህና አድርገህ ከተማርክ በቀር ዩኒቨርሲቲ አትገባም። 4 ጥዋት ከተነሣሁ በፊት ራዲዮ እከፍታለሁ። 5 ጊሩት ገበያ ከሄደች ቁጥር ቡና ትገዛለች። 6 ነገ ከበደ አብሮዋችሁ ስለሚመጣ እኔ አልሄድም። 7 አሁን እንደሚመስለኝ ይህ ያንተ አሳብ ጥሩ አይደለም። 8 ደብዳቤ በጻፍኩ ጊዜ ሰላምታዬን እልክለታለሁ።

Translation of reading passage

Mr Nigusu's family very much like to gather round the television every evening and watch until the end of the programmes. Mr Nigusu, however, has no desire either to watch the television or listen to the radio. So, this evening when his children turned the televison on as usual, he quickly went to his study and started to read a book or a magazine.

Mr Nigusu is a wealthy businessman. He has a large hotel. He is sad that both his father and he have remained businessmen. He is, however, very pleased that his son has had a legal education and is

intending to become a High-Court judge. As he himself says, "I'd like it if I could give up all the wealth I have and become an ordinary person! It's true, an education is better than worldly wealth and money."

Lesson 10

1

1 እንተ ደብጻቤ ስትጽፍ ብዙ ጊዜ ይፈጃል:: 2 ተረፈ ወደ ጂማ ሲሔድ በርበሬ ይዞ መጣ:: 3 ገረዲቱ ቤቱን ስትጠርግ ከወምበር በታች ሃያ ብር አገኘች:: 4 እኛ ባሜሪካን አገር ስንሔድ ጊዜ ግራንድ ካንዮን ለማየት ፈለግን:: 5 እነዚህ ተማሪዎች ጥያቄ ሲጠይቁ ሌሎች ይስቃሉ:: 6 ድንቅነሽ ሙዚቃ ስትሰማ ልትዘፍን ትፈልጋለች:: 7 አውቶቡስ ሲመጣ ሁሉም ባንድ ላይ ለመውጣት ሞከሩ::

2

1 እርስዎ አዲስ መኪና ለመግዛት/ልገዙ ይፈልጋሉ? 2 ቲያትር ለማየት/ልናይ ነው የመጣነው:: 3 ሙዚቃ ለመስማት/ልትሰሚ ትወጃለሽ? 4 ወደ ትምሕርት ቤት ለመሄድ/ልሄድ አልፈልግም:: 5 ልጁን ለመርዳት/ልትረዱት የማታስቡ ስለምን ነው? 6 ሊባው እንጀራ ለመግዛት/ልገዛ ገንዘቡን ሠረቀ::

3

1 ዛሬ ባይዘንብ ካባትና እናቴ ጋር ወደ መናፈሻ ቦታ አብረን እንሄዳለን:: If it doesn't rain today we'll go to the park with my mother and father. 2 ይህን ለማድረግ ባትፈልግ ፈቃድ ያስፈልጋል:: You'll need permission if you don't want to do this. 3 ይህን የመሰለ ነገር እንዳይደርስብህ ተስፋ አደርጋለሁ:: I hope that a thing like this doesn't happen to you. 4 ጋዜጣ ሳያነብ እንቅልፍ ወሰደው:: He fell asleep without reading/before he read the newspaper. 5 ወደ ውጭ አገር እንዳልሄድ ተፈቅዶልኛል:: I've been given permission not to go abroad.

4

1 ነገ ከሰዓት በኋላ አቶ ለማ ፋብሪካ ይጎብኙ ይሆናል:: Mr Lemma might visit the factory tomorrow afternoon. 2 የተማሪዎች

ቄጥር እየተጨመረ ይሄድ ይሆናል። The student numbers may go
on increasing. 3 እዚህ ሆቴል ውስጥ በጣም ጥሩ ሙዚቃ እንሰማ
ይሆናል። We might hear some very good music in this hotel.
4 ጉንፋን ስለያዘኝ ቤቴ ውስጥ አቆይ ይሆናል። As I've caught a
cold I might stay in the house.

1 ገረዲቱ እጅዋን ትታጠብ ጀመር። The maid started to wash her
hands. 2 አሳላፊው ሳሕኑን በጨረቅ ይጠርግ ጀመር። The waiter
started to wipe the plate with a cloth. 3 ትናንትና ቤቱን እቀባ
ጀመር። Yesterday I started to paint the house. 4 ልጆቹ የገዛ
አልጋቸውን ይዘረጉ ጀመር። The children started to make their own
beds.

1 ለዮሐንስ ደብዳቤ እጽፍ ነበር። I was writing a letter to
Yohannis. 2 አቶ አብዱልመጂድ የቤቱን ኪራይ ይከፍሉ ነበር። Mr
Abdulmejid used to pay the (house) rent. 3 አልማዝ መኪና ቶሎ
ቶሎ ትነዳ ነበር። Almaz used to drive the car very fast. 4 ተረፈ
ሲገባ እኛ ሬዲዮን እንሰማ ነበር። When Terrefe came in we were
listening to the radio.

5

1 ሳታይ – አየ: Oh ox, you saw the grass without seeing the cliff.
2 ሲወድቅ – ወደቀ: Whilst a rich man falls from a balcony, a poor
man falls on the ground. 3 ብትል – አለ : If you act [*lit.* say] for
another man you'll be lost, if you act for God you'll prosper.
4 ሳይማሩ – ተማረ : ሳይበሉ – በላ: Reading without learning (is like)
being satisfied without eating. 5 ሲሰበሰብ – ተሰበሰበ: When the flies
gather don't open the lid. 6 ሊሰላ – በላ: A woman (becomes) a thief
so that a man may eat. 7 ብለምነው – ለመነ: If I ask (God) for a fish
(I get) a python; if I ask for rain (I get) hail.

6

1 ሰው በመቀመጫ ይቀመጣል: ለምሳሌ ወንበር መቀመጫ ነው።
2 ሰው በመሄጃ ይሄዳል: ለምሳሌ መንገድ መሄጃ ነው። 3 ሰው
በመጠጫ ይጠጣል: ለምሳሌ ብርጭቆ መጠጫ ነው። 4 ሰው
በማንበቢያ ያነባል: ለምሳሌ መጽሐፍ ማንበቢያ ነው። 5 ሰው
በመተኛ ይተኛል: ለምሳሌ አልጋ መተኛ ነው። 6 ሰው በመጻፊያ
ይጽፋል: ለምሳሌ እርሳስ መጻፊያ ነው። 7 ሰው በመስፊያ
ይሰፋል: ለምሳሌ መርፌ መስፊያ ነው። 8 ሰው በዕቃ መግዣ
ዕቃ ይገዛል: ለምሳሌ ገንዘብ የዕቃ መግዣ ነው። 9 ሰው በበዓት
መቁጠሪያ ሰዓት ይቆጥራል: ለምሳሌ የእጅ ሰዓት የሰዓት

መቁጠሪያ ነው።፡ 10 ሰው በመከፈቻ እንድ ነገር ይከፍታል፡ ለምሳሌ ቁልፍ መከፈቻ ነው።፡ 11 ሰው በመኖሪያ ይኖራል፡ ለምሳሌ ቤት መኖሪያ ነው።፡ 12 ሰው በመለኪያ እንድ ነገር ይለካል፡ ለምሳሌ ሜትር መለኪያ ነው።፡

7

Often when someone catches a cold they sneeze a lot and their throat hurts. In addition, they may have a temperature. When some people catch a cold they stay off work and go to bed and sleep. Also, someone who's caught a cold must cover their mouth and nose with a handkerchief when they cough and sneeze. Otherwise, their sickness may be passed on to another person.

1 ብዙ ያነጥስና ጉሮሮውን ያመዋል።፡ 2 አፍ፡ በጣም ተላላፊ ነው።፡ 3 በሽታው ወደ ሌላ ሰው እንዳይተላለፍ ነው።፡ 4 ቢስልና ቢያነጥስ አፉንና አፍንጫውን በመሐረብ መሸፈን ያስፈልገዋል።፡

Translation of reading passage

Is the human body a mineral mine?

It has been ascertained that whereas the human body is 60% water, 39% physical matter and 1% mineral salts, there is also to be found in the body of a person weighing 70 kilogrammes the following minerals:

45.5 kg oxygen
12.6 kg carbon
7 kg hydrogen
2.1 kg nitrogen (azote)
1 kg calcium
0.7 kg phosphorus
0.214 kg potassium
3 g iron
3 g magnesium
2 g zinc and other minerals (we find).

If it is (the case) as a German expert has established, it has been recognized that it would be possible to make various things out of the minerals that are found in the human body.

For example   5 kilogrammes of candles
65 dozen pencils
7 nails

820,000 matchsticks
20 tea or salt spoons
50 lumps of sugar
42 litres of water

Lesson 11

1

1 እንቺ በሩን ክፈች/ዘጊ! 2 እናንተ ልጆች መጽሐፎቻችሁን ይዛችሁ ኑ! 3 እኔ ዛሬ ማታ ስልክ ልደውል (ልህ/ልሽ)፡፡ 4 አሁን ለጤናችን እንጠጣ! 5 ነገ ገረዲቱ እንደራ በወጥ ትሥራ/ታዘጋጅ! 6 አቶ ዓለማየሁ እባክዎ ክፍል ውስጥ ይግቡ! 7 ገንዘቡን ክፈለኝ/ስጠኝ ብዬ አዘዝኩት፡፡ 8 እንዴ ጠብቂኝ ብሎ ተናገራት፡፡

2

1 ነገ ስልክ አትደውዩልኝ! 2 መስኮቱን አትዝጋ! 3 እስቲ ሰዓቱን አትንገሪኝ! 4 አባባ ኪራይን አይክፈሉልኝ! 5 በቀኝ በኩል አትውጡ! 6 የቤት ሥራቸውን አትጨርሱ! 7 የሱን ስልክ ቁጥር አትስጪኝ! 8 እንጨቱን እዚህ አይትከሉ!

3 (a)

1 መኪናውን አጠብ/አጠበው! 2 ስልኩን መልስ/መልሰው! 3 እራትህን በልተህ ጨርስ/ጨርሰው! 4 በሩን ዝጋ/ዝጋው! 5 ሱቁ ሂደህ እንድ ጠርሙዝ አምቦ ውሀ ግዛ! 6 እንዴ ጠብቅ! 7 ጠረጲዛውን ጥረግ/ጥረገው! 8 ዝም በል!

3 (b)

1 መኪናውን አጠቢ/አጠቢው! 2 ስልኩን መልሺ/መልሺው! 3 እራትሽን በልተሽ ጨርሺ/ጨርሺው! 4 በሩን ዝጊ/ዝጊው! 5 ሱቁ ሂደሽ እንድ ጠርሙዝ አምቦ ውሀ ግዢ! 6 እንዴ ጠብቂ! 7 ጠረጲዛውን ጥረጊ/ጥረጊው! 8 ዝም በዪ/በይ!

Translation of reading passage (1)

Concerning musical instruments

Do you like to play musical instruments? The indigenous instruments that you will most often hear in Ethiopia are of three kinds: masinko, krar *and drum. The one called a* krar *is the largest of the three instruments and has six strings made of sinew. The one called a* masinko *has one horse-hair string and one plays it with a bow. Many people sing whilst they are playing these stringed instruments. There is another instrument called a* washint *(or flute). As one plays the* washint, *though, by means of the breath, it is not easy to play. A lot of studying is needed before one should try to play it. Otherwise it does not produce a nice sound. The one called a* kebero *(or drum), however, is of the same kind as other drums.*

4

1 ማስንቆ ስድስት ገመድ አለው:: 2 ዋሽንት መጫወት አስቸጋሪ ነው ይላሉ:: 3 አም: እንደ ሌሎቹ ከበርቶ ነው:: 4 በክራርና በማስንቆ ሲጫወቱ ነው የሚዘፍኑ:: 5 በጣት ነው የሚጫወቱት::

5

1 ነገ ስጦታ ይዤ እመጣለሁ ብላ አልማዝ ነገረችኝ:: 2 በፍጹም አላውቅም ብዬ መለስኩላት:: 3 ሰዓቱ ስንት ነው ብሎ ጠየቀኝ:: 4 በስንት ሰዓት ነው ላንጋና የምንደርሰው ብዬ ልጠይቀው:: 5 በሚመጣው ሳምንት አዋሳ እንሂድ ብለን አስበናል:: 6 ዛሬ ማታ ግንድ ሰዓት አደዋላለሁ ብሎ ነገረኝ::

6

1 ባማርኛ ስልክ ማለት በንግሊዝኛ telephone ማለት ነው:: 2 ደመራ የተባለው ከንጨት የተሠራ: በመስቀል በዓል የሚያቃጥሉት ነው:: በንግሊዝኛ bonfire ይባላል:: 3 በንግሊዝኛ wood ማለት ባማርኛ እንጨት ማለት ነው:: 4 ስሜ ... ይባላል::/... እባላለሁ:: 5 ሰውሲራበው ለመብላት ነው የሚፈልገው:: 6 የኢትዮጵያ ዋና ከተማ ስም አዲስ አበባ ነው::

Translation of reading passage (2)

Yusef and Markos

There were two friends. They were called Markos and Yusef. They were very fond of one another. They used to go into the forest to hunt both small and large animals. One day they went hunting and failed to find anything [lit. 'stayed without finding anything']. Giving up

*hope, when they were on the point of returning home, Markos found
a small pot at the foot of a tree. When Yusef opened the pot and had
a look he found that it was filled with gold. Instead of sharing it out
they both forgot their friendship and started a tussle saying, 'It's mine,
it's mine.' Markos said, 'Because it was me who found the pot first the
gold's mine,' and then he made ready to box. Yusef was no better
than Markos. "It was me who first touched the pot and opened it and
had a look, so I deserve it," he said. They argued a lot. If Markos
hadn't invented a plan they'd have been on the point of thrashing one
another with their fists [lit. 'by boxing'] in a sudden quarrel.*

[*To be continued.*]

Lesson 12

1

1 አሳላፊው ሻይ አቀረበ። አሳላፊው ሻይ ያቀርጋል። 2 ኩሊ
ዕቃውን አወረደ። ኩሊ ዕቃውን ያወርዳል። 3 የድርጅቱ ጎላፊ
ሠራተኞቹን አሰለጠኑ። የድርጅቱ ጎላፊ ሠራተኞቹን ያሰለጥናሉ።
4 መኪና በቀይ መብራት አቆምኩ። መኪና በቀይ መብራት
አቆማለሁ። 5 አሽከርቹ ፈረስ አጠጡ። አሽከርቹ ፈረስ ያጠጣሉ።
6 ክፍሉን አጨለምክ። ክፍሉን ታጨልማለህ። 7 ሐኪሙ ቁስሉን
አዳነለት። ሐኪሙ ቁስሉን ያድንለታል። 8 ገላገርቹ የሊጋውን ቤት
አፈረሱ። ገላገርቹ የሊጋውን ቤት ያፈርጋሉ።

2

1 አስተማሪው ተማሪዎቹን ፈተናውን አሳለፋቸው። 2 ከበደን በሩን
አስከፍተዋለሁ። 3 አቶ ሙሉጌታ አልማዝን የቤት ኪራይ
አስከፍለውታል። 4 ዘበኛውን ድንኳኑን እናስተክለዋለን። 5 አልማዝ
ተረፈን ጠርሙዙን አስከፍታዋለች። 6 ጌቶች ሶስት ሰዓት ላይ ሥራ
አስጨረሱኝ። 7 እኑቱ አስታማሚዋን ልጅዋን አስመርጋታለች።
8 ፀሐይ ብሔራዊ ሙዚዬምን አሳየችህ?

3

1 አሊ ገለፈው ሳምንት ያነሣቸውን ፎቶዎች አሳየኝ። 2 በገብዛው
ብዙ አበሉንና አጠጡን። 3 አምና የፋብሪካው ጎላፊ ምርት ከፍ
አደረገ። 4 ማታ ሙዚቃ መስማት በጣም ደስ ያደርጋል/ያሰኛል።
5 እነዚህን እንግዶች ለማሳደር ትችላለህ?

5

Last week my elder brother came to pay us a visit. He works in a large factory. The factory is a shoe factory [lit. 'whilst the factory is a shoe factory'] and the biggest of the organizations in the town. My brother has three small children. Though the smallest, who is called Tirunesh, is younger (in age) than her brothers, she is more able than them [lit. 'she is greater in ability']. She is the cleverest of the three children. For instance, every evening when she returns home from school she reads a book or writes an essay. Her brothers, though, only watch television without doing their homework.

1 አይ ፡ ቴሊቪዥን ለማየት አትወድም ። 2 ጥሩነሽ የምተገለው ታናሺቱ ናት ። 3 አይ ፡ የሚሠራበት ፋብሪካ በከተማው ውስጥ ከሚገኙት ፋብሪካዎች ትልቁ ነው ። 4 አይደለም ፡ የቤት ሥራቸውን አይሠሩም ። 5 ከርሷ ብላህ አይደለም ።

6

Translation of the advert

Tsedey Auto and Real Estate Company
Sees to everything!
Get to know Tsedey

*Tsedey Auto and Real Estate Company is famous and foremost both in kind and in content;

*When you want to buy, sell or rent domestic, freight or transport vehicles which are in good condition and will serve you by utilizing your time properly and without giving any bother;

*When you want to buy, sell or rent property for accommodation, business or office use;

Ask Tsedey

Address
You'll find Tsedey on the Debre Zeit Road, along the road which leads to St. Kirkos' Church, a little below the Ministry of Agriculture.
Phone   75 63 23
Fax   251-1-626556
P.O.B.   22608

1 መኪናዎችና ቤቶች በያይነቱ ነው የሚሸጡ። 2 በርገጥ፣ በጣም
ቀላል ነው ይላሉ። 3 እኔ፣ መኪና ለመከራየት ይቻላል።
4 አይደለም፣ በደብረ ዘይት መንገድ ከገብርና ሚኒስቴር አጠገብ
ነው የሚገኘው። 5 አዲስ የሆነ ይመስላል።

Translation of reading passage (2)

Yusef and Markos

(*Continued from lesson eleven*)

The idea that Markos suggested is this: 'My friend, we must consider one another. If we mean to take the gold away there's no use in fighting. Let's take it home and share it out. A good bag will be needed, though, for something to take it in. Go to the town and buy a bag, and bring some food. We'll need to eat something in order to carry this heavy thing,' he said. Yusef hesitated. If he goes and leaves Markos with the gold he might disappear with it; but after he had weighed it up he agreed to his idea. Yusef went into town. Markos had another idea. When Yusef returned with the bag and the food he would attack him and kill him! And the gold would be his alone. So he got his dagger ready. Yusef, in turn, was thinking in what way he might kill Markos! 'Yes! I'll go back with the bag and the food. But I'll add poison to the food and Markos will eat the food and die. I shall take the gold for myself alone,' he said to himself.

Markos waited for Yusef hiding in the forest. Because Yusef was late, he was angry thinking that he wasn't coming [lit. 'he had stayed away']. Yusef came along with a bag in one hand and some food in the other. Yusef was looking for Markos. But Markos leapt out from the place where he was hiding and pounced on him from behind and killed him. Markos put the gold, along with the pot, into the bag. But because he was hungry he got ready to eat the food that Yusef had brought and before going home. He tasted the food and thought [lit. 'said'] that it was very tasty. When he had finished eating, his stomach was gripped with a sharp pain. Within a few minutes he stretched out by the side of Yusef's body and died. The gold in the pot remained inside the bag. Neither of them got the gold.

Lesson 13

1

1 ደብጻቤው ተጻፈ ። 2 ሲኒው ይሰበራል ። 3 ስብሰባው ይጀመር ። 4 ጋዜጣው ተነበበ ። 5 በሩ ተዘጋ ። 6 ገንዘቡ ተገኘቷል ። 7 ጻሮው ይበላ ። 8 ቴሌቪዥን ይከፈት ። 9 መጽሐቱህ ተመልጓል ። 10 ልጅዋ ይወደጻል ።

2

1 ከበደ እውነቱን እንደተናገረ (እኔ) አውቃለሁ ። 2 እንገዳቸን አስከ 4 ሰዓት እንጠብቃለን ። 3 አስተማሪው ትምሕርቱን ጀምፉል/ጀምረዋል ። 4 አባቴ ቤቱን አሳድሶታል/አሳድሰውታል ። 5 ያዋስኩትን መጽሐፍ ነገ እመልሳለሁ ። 6 ተማሪዎቹ መስኮቱን ከፍተዋል እንዲ? 7 አሻጣ߿ መኪናዮን መቼ ይሸጣል?

3

1 የላም ፡ አልተያዘም ። 2 የላም ፡ አይሻልም ። 3 አይ ፡ ገና ነው ። ነገ ይመለሳሉ ። 4 እኔ በ...... አገር ተወለድኩ ። 5 እንጃ ፡ ምናልባት በገቡር እንዛለሁ ። 6 አይ ፡ ያሳዝነኛል ። ጠንክረው አይማሩም ።

4

This week's weather

Whilst during the next five days it will be cloudy in highland areas in the west and southwest, in some places there will be thundery rain. In highland areas situated in the north it will be partly cloudy and there will be light rain. In other lowland areas, however, there will be bright [lit. 'strong'] sun, the Weather Forecasting Department of the National Meteorological Organization announced yesterday.

5

1 በቅርቡ ያለ ምንም ስህተት ለማንበብ ትችያለሽ ። 2 ገረዲቱ ብርጭቆውን እውቆ ሰበረች እንዲ? 3 ያንተ አሳብ በእውነት ያስደነቃል ። 4 አማኝ ኦርቶዶክሳዊ በጾም ሥጋ ከቶ አይበላም ። 5 ገጋጣሚ ከበደንና ዘውዴን ባቡር ጣቢያ ላይ አገኘኋቸው ። 6 መኪና ባቆምኩ ጊዜ እንድ ልጅ በቅጥነት ደርሶ ልጠብቅልዎ አለኝ ። 7 ቡና ትፈልጋለህ? አዎ ፡ በደስታ ቡና እጠጣለሁ ።

Translation of reading passage

Our national team plays against the Ambassadors
this evening

Our national basketball team meets the American Ambassadors team this evening from 7 p.m. onwards. The location will be in the American Community School compound in the vicinity of the Old Airport, the Federation has announced.

Whereas the American Ambassadors Sports Club was founded in 1962 [or 1969/70], and another team is touring in West and Central Africa under the same title, the team that has come here was previously in Kenya. Their coach, Mr Hank Bowen, mentioned that during those 3 weeks they had had 18 matches and had won throughout, and then disclosed that after this they would be going on to Egypt and then returning home [to their country].

Upon coming to our country, the American Ambassadors basketball team met the Mekuriya team and won 107 to 63. Then they beat WWKM 108 to 75. In the meantime they went to Debre Zeit and in the game they played with the Air Force, won 74 to 38. In Nazret they showed their game skills to students.

Whilst the players of the Ambassadors team are all university students, the eldest is 24 and the youngest 18. As to their height, whilst the shortest is 1 metre 80, the tallest is 2 metres 8 centimetres tall. When many of them score a goal because of their height [lit. 'as a result of the tallness of their height'] they place their hand into the basket. The tallest of them, Daryl Boyd, hopes to be placed with the American National Olympic Team, their coach disclosed.

(*Abridged from* Addis Zemen, *Hamle 8th 1967*)

Lesson 14

Translation of passage 1

Study
By Post

Acquire advanced knowledge while you work,
in your spare time and for a little money.
We prepare you for 12th grade examinations (GCE).
We also have a scheme which lets you teach yourself
with sufficient study aids at very easy payments.

*And if you have interrupted the studies you began we have
prepared a way in which you can continue your studies.
To obtain our free guidebook send us your name and
address.*

The 'Torch' Tutorial College
POB 10602   Telephone 245669
Addis Ababa

Translation of passage 2

The motor that doesn't rest

*The human heartbeat reaches from 60 to 80 a minute. That means, it
beats about 40 million times a year, which means, at the time of each
beat ¼ litre of blood enters the heart. The heart pumps about 2,200
gallons of blood in the duration of one day. In another manner of
speaking, that means it pumps about 56 million gallons of blood in
an average life time.*

*Can there possibly be a man-made machine which accomplishes as
much work as the heart without needing any repairs?! If we say, let's
apply the heart like a working machine, in order to hold up an object
weighing two kilos to the height of two feet the expenditure of energy
will be equivalent to that used for one heartbeat [lit. 'it will have
enough of what it does for one beat']. When an athlete does any
very difficult sporting activities approximately 20 litres of blood are
pushed round.*

*Once the blood travelling to the brain has reached the brain it takes
8 seconds to return to the heart. It has been confirmed that blood that
has descended to the toes takes 18 seconds to return to the heart.*

Translation of passage 3

Tender

*At Addis Ababa University, Awasa Agricultural College wishes to
purchase by tender various items of foodstuffs for one year as of 10th
Meskerem 1983 [20th September 1990].*

*Any bidder wishing to participate in the tender can do so by pur-
chasing the tender forms for 10 birr from the College Administration
Office, normally during working hours from the date of the publication of this notice, or by writing (by post) the price at which they are
offering their bid in a sealed envelope before 10 o'clock on 7th
Meskerem 1983 [4.00 p.m. 17th September 1990], or may place his*

bid in the box that has been prepared for the tender. We declare that the bids will be opened in the College Dean's Office on 8th Meskerem 1983 [18th September 1990] at exactly three o'clock [9.00] in the presence of the bidders or their legal representatives.

Bidders will have to have a legal trade licence for everything that they offer and will have to meet the tax obligations which are due against them.

Bidders will have to deposit 3,000 birr in cash as a guarantee securing the bid.

If the College obtains a better means of fulfilling the job it will not be bound by the tender.

Awasa Agricultural College

Translation of passage 4

Purifying water by sunlight

In countries which are in the process of developing, or in countries whose development is arrested or halted, like Ethiopia, the biggest public health problem is linked with the lack of pure drinking water and with water-borne diseases. Of the numerous deaths that are recorded daily, and in particular [those of] children, the majority are victims of the lack of pure drinking water. Medical experts have found a new method which can remove the problem. According to what was published [lit. 'came out'] in the English medical journal Lancet *which we read a few months ago, in so far as it is possible to purify water easily by sunlight, the benefit which this new finding will be able to give to the rural inhabitants of our country will be great.*

Translation of passage 5

Advertisement

Muhammad Kasim

You have bought some superior woollen cloth at great expense and are going to have it made up, but haven't chosen a tailor [lit. 'without choosing a tailor']. But it's not what you wanted, to say nothing of as you wished it or intended it, and aside from the fact that it doesn't fit your figure, it's obvious how much you're upset! The problem is with the tailoring, and not just that it isn't adjusted to the shape of your body.

If you want to have it made up in a modern style visit Muhammad Kasim as he is renowned for keeping appointments and improving tailoring. He is the tailor who will improve your clothes!

Our Address: at the Centre of the American Compound

Telephone number 65 47 21

Post Box No. 25029

Amharic–English glossary

Words are entered in the glossary following the order of letters in the Ethiopian script, or ፊደል, with the exception that the homophonous letters ሰ and ሠ, አ and ዐ, ጸ and ፀ, and ሀ, ሐ, ኀ and ኸ are grouped together. Similarly, the letters ጀ and ዠ are also grouped together as they are interchangeable at the beginning of a word. This follows the practice of the better European-language dictionaries of Amharic.

The order of letters is therefore:

ሀ/ሐ/ኀ/ኸ ለ መ ረ ሰ/ሠ ሸ ቀ በ ተ ቸ ነ ኘ አ/ዐ ከ ወ
ዘ የ ደ ጀ/ዠ ገ ጠ ጨ ጸ ጸ/ፀ ፈ ፐ.

Within each letter-section words are then entered 'alphabetically' according to the sequence of consonants, and not regarding the vowels. Where entries occur that have the same consonant pattern, however, then they are listed following the sequence of the seven vowel orders: so ቤት before ቦታ; አባት before አቤት; ሰማ before ሰመ;and so on.

Finally, entries are mostly made under roots, where these occur in this book. So, you will find ሥራ listed under the root (which is usually a verb) ሠራ . The exceptions are as follows:

1 where the root does not occur in this book, or in the case of verbs where the root or simple stem is not used, you will find the entry under the simplest or most basic form. So, አገኘ is listed under አ and not ገ from the underlying root *ገኘ, and similarly ተቀመጠ is listed under ተ and not ቀ.

2 derivatives formed by a prefix (usually መ- but also occasionally ት-) whose relationship to the underlying root might not be immediately obvious are listed in the first place under the initial letter as well as under the root.

Verbs are given in the third person masculine of the simple past, and are identified by their class.

ህ/ሐ/ነ/ኸ – H		ለመሆኑ	(at the beginning of a phrase) by the way
ሀሎ	hello (when speaking on the telephone)	ቢሆን	(following a noun) even, as for
ሁሉ	all, every	ቢሆንም	(at the beginning of a phrase) however, still
ሁሉም	everybody, everything		
ሁልጊዜ	always	እንደሆነ	(following a simple impf. or gerundive) if
ኋላ	behind, back, later, afterwards		
በኋላ	later, afterwards, then; behind, at the back	የሆነ ሆኖ	nevertheless
		ይሁን እንጂ	nevertheless
ከ- በኋላ	behind, after (place or time)	ሁኔታ	condition, situation, attitude, position
ሐለመ	dream [3-lit A]; see also አለመ		
		ሁነኛ	reliable
ሕልም	dream	ሕንጻ	building
ሁለት	two	ሐኪም	doctor
ሁለቱም	both	ሕክምና	medicine, medical treatment
ሁለተኛ	second		
ኃላፊ	boss, curator, head, (person) responsible	ሕዝብ	people
		ሕዝባዊ	public, civic
		ሃያ	twenty
ሐምሌ	Hamle (eleventh month of the year: 8 July–6 August)	ኃይል	power, might, force
		በኃይል	by force; strongly, very much
ሕመም	sickness, disease		
ሐሙስ	Thursday (see also እሑስ)	ኃይለኛ	strong, powerful
		ሃይማኖት	faith, religion
ሃምሳ	fifty (also አምሳ)	ሐይቅ	lake
ሒሳብ	bill, check, account	ሕይወት	life
		ሄደ	go [2-lit⁴]
ሆስፒታል	hospital	አስኬደ	lead (road), make or let s.o. go
ኅብረት	union, harmony		
ኅብረተ ሰብ	society	ሂደት	progress
ሀብት	wealth	መሂጃ	means or place of going; sidewalk
ሀብታም	rich		
ሆቴል	hotel	ሆድ	stomach
ሆነ	become, be	ሕዳር	Hidar (third month of the year:
ሆነ	(between nouns) or, as well as		

	10 November–9 December)	ለበሰ	wear (*clothes*), get dressed [3-lit A]
ሕግ	law	አለበሰ	dress s.o. [a- stem]
ሕጋዊ	legal, lawful	ልብስ	clothes, dress
ሕፃን	infant, small child	ሊትር, ሊተር	litre
		ለካ	measure, gauge [2-lit¹ B]
ለ – L			
ለ-	to, for	ልክ	measurement; exact, correct; precisely, exactly
-ሊለ	is not (*in subordinate clauses*)		
ሌላ	other, another	ላከ	send [2-lit³]
ሎሌ	servant	ለወጠ	change, alter sth. [3-lit B]
ሊሊት	night		
ለማ	prosper, thrive [2-lit¹ A]	ለየ	distinguish, separate [2-lit² B]
ላም	cow	ልዩ	different, separate
ሎሚ	lime (*fruit*)	ልዩ ልዩ	various
ለምለም	fertile, green	ላይ	on, upon, on top
ለመነ	beg [3-lit B]	በ- ላይ	on top of, above, in addition to
ለማኝ	beggar		
ለምን	why? (ለ- & ምን)	ላይኛ	upper
ለመደ	get used to sth. [3-lit A]	ልደት	birth, Christmas
		የልደት በዓል	birthday
ልማድ	habit, custom, convention	ልጅ	child (*boy, girl, son, daughter*)
ለስላሳ	soft, smooth, mild	ሴት ልጅ	girl
ሊቅ	expert, scholar (pl. ሊቃውንት)	ወንድ ልጅ	boy
		የልጅ ልጅ	grandchild
ለቀመ	pick up, gather, collect [3-lit A]	ልጅነት	childhood
		ልጃገረድ	girl
ለቀቀ	abandon, give up [3-lit A]	ላጨ	shave s.o. [2-lit³]
		ተላጨ	shave oneself [tä- stem]
ሌባ	thief		
ልብ	heart	ምላጭ	razor
ልብ አለ	pay attention, take note of [አለ verb]		
		መ – M	
		-ማ	but, as for
ልብ አደረገ	encourage, draw s.o.'s attention	-ም	and, even, also, too
ልብ ወለድ	fiction	መሃል	middle, centre
ከልብ	heartily, sincerely, warmly	መሃል ከተማ	city centre
		መሐረብ	handkerchief

ም<u></u>ሕረት	mercy	መሪ	guide, leader
ዓመተ ምሕረት	Year of Mercy	ማር	honey
	(year of the	መረመረ	examine, investigate [4-lit]
	Christian era		
	according to the	ምርመራ	investigation, analysis, inquiry
	Ethiopian		
	calendar)	መረት	earth, ground
ማኅበር	association, society	ምርት	product, production, produce
መሕንዲስ	engineer		(see also አመረተ)
መላ	all, whole, the whole of (see also ሙሉ)	ማረከ	capture; attract, appeal [3-lit C]
ሙሉ	whole, full (see also ሙሉ)	ምርኮኛ	prisoner, captive
ሞላ	fill, be full [2-lit¹ A]	ማርካ	trademark
ተማላ	be complete [tä- & C-type stem]	መርከብ	ship, boat
		መርካቶ	the Mercato
ሙሉ	whole, complete		(central market of Addis Ababa)
በሙሉ	wholly, completely	መረዘ	poison, pollute [3-lit B]
መለሰ	give back, return sth., reply [3-lit B]	መርዝ	poison
		መርዛኛ	poisonous, toxic, pestilent
ተመለሰ	return, go or come back [tä- stem]	መረጃ	proof, evidence (see also ረጃ)
መልስ	answer, reply; change (in money)	መረጠ	choose, select [3-lit A]
ምላስ	tongue	ምርጥ	select, best, superior
ማለት	that is to say, it means (see አለ₂)	የምርጫ ድምፅ	vote [lit. 'voice of election']
መልክ	form, looks, appearance	መርፌ	needle, syringe; injection
መልካም	beautiful, nice	ማሰ	dig, work the soil [2-lit³]
መልክት	message	ማሳ	farm, field
ማለደ	get up early in the morning [3-lit C]	ምሳ	lunch
ማለዳ	early (in the morning)	መሰለ	be like, resemble, seem [3-lit A]
ማለፊያ	excellent, fine (see also አለፈ)	መሰለው	he thought, supposed [impers.]
መራ	lead, guide [2-lit¹ A]		

መሳይ	similar, alike	መስጊድ	mosque
ምሳሌ	example; proverb, saying	ምስጢር	secret, mystery
		በምስጢር	confidentially
መሰለ₂	fashion, portray, sketch [3-lit B]	ምስጢራዊ	confidential, secret
ምስል	likeness, image, model	መሸ	become evening [2-lit² A]
መሠላል	ladder	አመሸ	spend the evening; be late in the evening, be too late for sth. [a- stem]
ሙስሊም	Muslim		
መሥመር	line		
ማሥመሪያ	ruler (for drawing lines)		
		ምሽት	evening
ምስማር, ሚስማር	nail, spike	ሞቀ	be hot, warm [2-lit⁵]
ምሳር	axe	ሙቅ	hot, warm
ምስር	lentils	ሙቀት	heat, warmth, temperature
ምስር₂	Egypt		
ምሥራቅ	east	መቆሚያ	stop, stopping place (see ቆመ)
መሣሪያ	tool, instrument, weapon		
		መቀመጫ	seat (see ተቀመጠ)
መስቀያ	hanger, hook (see ሰቀለ)	መቀስ	scissors
		ምቀኛ	jealous, envious (see also ተመቃኘ)
መሶብ	small round basketware table with lid on which **injera** and sauces are served		
		ምቀኝነት	jealousy, envy
		መብል	food (see also በላ)
		መብረቅ	lightning
		መብራት	lamp, light, electricity
ሚስት	wife		
ማስታወቂያ	notice, announcement, advert (see also አወቀ)	መታ	hit, beat, strike [2-lit¹ A]
		ተማታ	come to blows, fight [tä- & C type]
መስታወት	mirror		
ማስንቆ	one-stringed violin	ምታት	blow, kick
መሰከረ	testify, give evidence [4-lit]	የራስ ምታት	headache
		መሞቻ	mallet, stick; bow for playing the **masinko**
ምስክር	witness		
መስከረም	Meskerem (first month of the year: 11 September– 10 October)		
		መቶ	hundred
		ማታ	evening
		ሞተ	die [2-lit⁵]
መስኮብ	Russia, Moscow		
መስኮት	window	ሙት	dead

ሞት	death	ምን ነው, ምነው	why? what's the matter?
ግች	moribund, deceased, late (*dead*)	ምን አለ	why not? why shouldn't I?
ሜትር	metre (*measurement*)	ምን አለበት	what does it matter! I don't care!
ሞተር	motor, engine		
መታሰቢያ	memento, memorial, souvenir (*see also* አስበ)	ምን ያህል	how much? how big!
		ምን ጊዜ	at what time? when?
መቸ, መቼ	when	ምን ጊዜም	always, all along, at any time
መቸም, መቼም	(*at beginning of phrase*) after all, at any rate, anyway; (*with a neg. verb*) never	ለምን	why? (*lit.* 'for what?')
		ስለምን	why? (*lit.* 'because of what?')
		እንደምን	how? (*lit.* 'like what?')
መቸስ	well! after all		
መቼውንም	in any event	ምንም	anything, something; (*with a neg. verb*) nothing, none
ለመቼውም	for ever, always		
ከመቼውም	more than ever		
ሞቹ	suitable, appropriate; convenient (*see also* ተመቸ)	ምንም ቢሆን	in any case, no matter what
		ምናምን	something, anything at all
ማን	who?	ምንድን	what?
ማንም	anyone, anybody (*also* ማንም ሰው) (*with a neg. verb*) no one, nobody	ምናልባት	perhaps, maybe
		ሚኒስቴር	ministry
		ሚኒስትር	minister
		መነኮሴ	monk [var. መናክሴ]
ማናቸውም	everyone; someone; any, anybody, anything; whoever, whatever	ማንኪያ	spoon
		መነዘረ	change money, cash (*a cheque*); scatter, disperse [4-lit]
ማንኛውም	each, every; any, anyone		
ማንነት	identity, individuality	ምንዛሬ	change, exchange (*also* የገንዘብ ምንዛሬ)
ምን	what?		
ምን ማድረግ	what's to be done?	መንደር	village

ምንድን	what? (see also ምን)	ሙከራ	test, experiment, attempt
መንግሥት	government, state, kingdom	ማክሰኞ	Tuesday
መንገድ	road, way; means, manner (way)	መኪና	car, automobile, truck; machine
አውራ መንገድ	main road, highway	የቤት መኪና	private car
የአየር መንገድ	airlines	የጽሕፈት መኪና	typewriter
የእግር መንገድ	footpath, pavement, sidewalk	የጭነት መኪና	truck, lorry
		መካኒክ	mechanic
መንገደኛ	traveller, passenger	ምክንያት	reason, cause
ምንገደኛ	carefree, happy-go-lucky (see ገደደ)	መካከል	middle, centre (see also መሃል)
		መክፈቻ	opener, key (see also ከፈተ)
መነጥር, መነጸር	spectacles; field glasses, telescope	መውጫ	exit (see also ወጣ)
		ሙዝ	banana
ምንጣፍ	carpet, rug	ሙዚቃ	music
መናፈሻ	park (also መናፈሻ ቦታ)	ሙዚቀኛ	musician
		መዘነ	weigh something; estimate, calculate [3-lit B]
መኝታ	bedroom (also መኝታ ቤት; see also ተኛ)		
		ሚዛን	balance, scales; ratio
ምኞት	desire, wish (see also ተመኘ)	ሙዚየም	museum
		መዘገበ	keep a record, enrol, catalogue [4-lit]
ምዕራብ	west		
ማእዘን	corner		
ማእዘነ ዓለም	the four cardinal directions	መዝገብ	roster, ledger
		መዝገበ ቃላት	dictionary
መከረ	advise, exhort [3-lit A]	መዝገብኛ	bookkeeper, accountant
ተማከረ	consult one another [tä- & C type] = ተመካከረ [tä- & redupl.]	መመዝገቢያ ክፍል	registration room/office
		መዝጊያ	door (see also ዝጋ)
		ሙያ	skill, craft, profession
ምክር	advice	ሚያዝያ	Miyazya (the eighth month of the year: 9 April–8 May)
ምክር ቤት	parliament, Congress		
ሞከረ	try, try on, try out [3-lit B]	ማዶ	the other side

በ- ማዶ	on the other side of, across from	ከመጠን በላይ	too much, excessively, unusually
ሜዳ	field, plain, level ground	መጠነኛ	moderate, normal, reasonable
መድኃኒት	medicine	ምጣድ	griddle (*metal plate on which* **injera** *is cooked*)
ምድር	earth, ground; the Earth		
ምድረ በዳ	desert	መጠጥ	drink, liquor, strong drink (*see* መጣ)
መደብ	stall (*market*); brick *or* stone bench; category, rank, class		
		መጥፎ	bad, ugly, wicked, evil (*see* ጠፋ)
መደበኛ	basic, standard, fundamental, principal	መጽሔት	magazine, journal
		መጽሐፍ	book
መደብር	store, bazaar	መጸዳጃ	lavatory
ማድቤት	kitchen (*also* ማድ ቤት)	መፍቻ	key, solution (*see* ፈታ)
መጋረጃ	curtain	ረ – R	
ማግሥት	the next day	ረሳ	forget [2-lit[1] A]
መገበ	nourish, feed, nurture [3-lit B]	ራስ	head
ምግብ	food, meal	ራሴ	myself, *etc.* (ራስ& possessive pronoun: ራስህ, ራሱ, etc.)
ምግብ ቤት	restaurant		
ምግባር	practice, conduct, behaviour		
መጋቢት	Meggabit (the seventh month of the year: 10 March– 8 April)	የራሴ	my own, *etc.* (የራስህ, የራሱ, *etc.*)
		ሬሳ	dead body, corpse
		ራቀ	be far [2-lit[3]]
		አራቀ	remove, take sth. far away, set sth. apart [a- stem]
መጣ	come [2-lit[1] A]		
አመጣ	bring [a- stem]		
አስመጣ	have sth. brought [as- stem]	ሩቅ	far, distant
		ራቁት	naked, bare (*also* እራቁት)
መጥረቢያ	axe, hatchet		
መጠን	amount, measure, proportion	ሩብ	quarter
		ከሩብ	a quarter past
በ- መጠን	according to, to the extent that	ሩብ ጉዳይ	a quarter to
		ራበ	be hungry [2-lit[3] impers.]; ራበው he is hungry, *etc.*
በመጠኑ	moderately, to a certain extent		

ተራበ	be starving, hungry [tä- stem]	ርጎ	soft cheese, curds (*also* እርጎ)
ራብ, ረሃብ	famine, hunger	ሮጠ	run [2-lit⁵]
ረቡ	Wednesday	ተፍፈጠ	run around, run all over the place [tä- & redupl.]
ረታ	win (*an argument, bet or game*) [2-lit¹ A]		
		ሩጫ	race
ተረታ	lose (*an argument, bet or game*) [tä- stem]	ረጠበ	be wet, damp [3-lit A]
		አረጠበ	dampen, moisten [a- stem]
ርካሽ	cheap (*also* እርካሽ)	ርጡብ	wet, damp (*also* እርጡብ)
ሪዝ	beard, whiskers		
ረዘመ	be long, tall [3-lit A]	ረፈደ	be late morning [3-lit A]
አረዘመ	lengthen, prolong [a- stem]	አረፈደ	be late for sth. [a- stem]
አራዘመ	prolong, extend [at- & C type]	ሰ, w – S	
ረጅም	long, tall	-ስ	what about? (*also indicates contrast or mild surprise; also* -ሽ)
ርዝመት	length, height		
ረዳ	help, assist [2-lit¹ A]		
ተረዳ	be helped; be persuaded, convinced [tä- stem]; *also* as an impers. verb (ተረዳ ው) realize, under- stand	ሳህን	plate, dish
		ስህተት	mistake, error (*see also* ሳት)
		ሣለ	paint [2-lit³]
		ሠዓሊ	painter
		ሥዕል, ሥል	painting, picture
		ሳለ₂	cough [2-lit³]
		ሳል	cough, pneumonia
አረዳ	announce a death, offer one's condolences [a- stem]	ስለ	because of, for the sake of (*with relative verb*) because, since, as
አስረዳ	convince, explain, demonstrate [as- stem]	ስለሆነም	therefore
		ስለምን	why?
		ስለዚህ	therefore
ርዳታ	help, aid (*also* እርዳታ)	ሰላም	peace (*also used as a greeting*)
መረጃ	proof, evidence	ሰላምታ	greetings, respects; salute
ራዲዮ, ራዲዮን	radio (*also* ሬዲዮ)		

ሠላሳ	thirty	ሠራ	do, make, work, build [2-lit¹ A]
ሥልሳ	sixty	ሥራ	work, job; deed, action
ስልት	method, manner, style		
ሰለቸ	be boring, tiring [3-lit Y]	ሠራተኛ	worker, employee
ሰለቸው	he is bored, tired [impers. verb]	መሣሪያ	tool, instrument, weapon
አሰለቸ	bore, tire [a- stem]	መሥሪያ	work place (also መሥሪያ ቤት office)
ስልክ	telephone	ሱሪ	trousers
ሰላጣ	salad, lettuce	ሣር	grass
ሠለጠነ	be skilled, trained; be sophisticated [4-lit]	ሥር	vein, artery, nerve; root
አሠለጠነ	train, coach [a- stem]	የደም ሥር	blood vessel, pulse
		ከ- ሥር	at the foot of, at the bottom of
ሥልጣኔ	civilization, urban life	ሰረቀ	steal, rob [3-lit A]
ሥልጣን	power, authority	ሢሶ	third (fraction)
ሰማ	hear, listen to [2-lit¹ A]	ሦስት	three
		ሦስተኛ	third
ተሰማ	be heard [tä- stem]	ሱቅ	shop, store
ተሰማው	feel, sense [tä- stem impers.]	ሳቀ	laugh [2-lit³]
		ሰባ	seventy
ተሰማማ	agree, consent [tä- & redupl.]	ሳበ	pull, draw; attract, appeal [2-lit³]
ስሜት	feeling, emotion	ሰበረ	break [3-lit A]
ሰም	wax, candle	ሰበሰበ	assemble, collect, gather (trans.) [4-lit]
ሳመ	kiss [2-lit³]		
ስም	name	ተሰበሰበ	be assembled; assemble (intrans.) [tä- stem]
ስመ ጥሩ	famous, renowned		
ሰሜን	north		
ሳሙና	soap	ስብሰባ	gathering, meeting
ሳምንት	week	ሰባት	seven
ስምንት	eight	ሰባተኛ	seventh
ስምንተኛ	eighth	ሳተ	be mistaken; miss [2-lit³]
ሰማንያ	eighty		
ሰማይ	sky, heaven	ተሳተ	be wrong, mistaken [tä- stem]
ሰማያዊ	blue [lit. 'heavenly]		
ስምጥ ሸለቆ	the Rift Valley		

ሰተት, ስሕተት	mistake, error	ሥውር	hidden, secret
ሴት	woman; female	በሥውር	secretly, surreptitiously
ሴት ልጅ	girl, daughter		
ሰኔ	Senie (the tenth month of the year: 8 June–7 July)	ስድስት	six
		ስድስተኛ	sixth
ሲኒ	small china cup	ሰደበ	insult, abuse, call s.o. names [3-lit A]
ሲኒማ	cinema, movies		
ሰነበተ	spend a while, several days [4-lit]	ስድብ	insult
		ሰደደ	send, send away, banish [3-lit A]
ተሰናበተ	be dismissed, say goodbye [tä- & C type]	ስደት	emigration, exile
		ስደተኛ	refugee
አሰናበተ	dismiss, fire [at- & C type]	ሥጋ	meat, flesh
		ሥጋ ሻጭ/ሻያጭ	butcher
ሰንበት	Sabbath, Sunday	ሰጠ	give [2-lit² A]
ስንት	how much? how many?	ስጦታ	gift
		ሣጥን	box, chest
ሳንቲም	cent	ቁም ሣጥን	cupboard
ሳንቲ ሜትር	centimetre	ሰፋ	be wide, broad, extend (intrans.) [2-lit¹ A]
ሰንደቅ ዓላማ	flag		
ሰነፍ	lazy	አሰፋ	widen, expand, extend (trans.); [a- stem]
ሰኞ	Monday		
ሥዕል	painting, picture (see ሣለ)	ሰፊ	wide, broad, large
		በሰፊው	broadly, extensively
ሰዓት	hour, time, o'clock; watch, clock	ሰፋ₂	sew [2-lit¹ A]
		ሰፊ	tailor
ስኳር	sugar (also ሱካር)	ሱፍ	wool
ሰው	man, person	ሰፈር	neighbourhood, section of town
የሰው ልጅ	mankind, humanity, human being		
		ስፍራ	place, position, site
ሁሉ ሰው	everybody		
ሰውነት	(human) body	ስፖርት	sport (also እስፖርት)
ሰውዬ	(individual) man, person		
ወወረ	hide, conceal (trans.); [3-lit B]	ሸ – Š	
		ሺ	thousand (also ሺህ)
ተወወረ	be hidden; hide (intrans.); [tä- stem]	ሸለቆ	valley, gorge

ሸማ	shamma (*toga-like traditional dress of the Ethiopian Highlands*)	ቀላደኛ	joker, jokester
		ቁልፈ	lock [3-lit B]
		ቁልፍ	key; button (*also* ቱልፍ)
ሸምብራ	chickpea	ቆመ	stand, be upright; come to a stop, stand still [2-lit⁵]
ሸሚዝ	shirt, blouse		
ሸምግሌ	old man, elder		
ሹራብ	sweater	ተቃወመ	oppose, object to sth. [tä- & C type]
ሾርባ	soup, broth		
ሸሸ	run away, flee [2-lit² A]; (irreg. inf. መሸሽ)	አቆመ	erect, set up; stop sth. [a- stem]
ሽሽት	flight, escape	ተፋፋመ	struggle against, defy; be established [tä- & redupl.]
ሸሸገ	hide sth. (trans.); [3-lit B]		
ሽንኩርት	onion		
ነጭ ሽንኩርት	garlic	አፋፋመ	establish, found, organize [a- & redupl.]
ሻንጣ	suitcase		
ሹካ	fork		
ሻይ	tea	ቁም	sincere, important
ሺጠ, ሸጠ	sell [2-lit⁴]	ቁም ነገር	something important, essentials or basics
ሻጭ	vendor, clerk (*in a store*); (*also* ሸያጭ)		
አሻሻጭ	salesclerk, salesman, dealer	ቁመት	size, height, length, stature
ሾፌር	driver	መቆሚያ	stopping place, stop, parking place
ቀ – K'			
ቃል	word	ቀመም	spice(s)
ቆላ	lowlands (*usually below 2,000'*)	ቀመሰ	taste, take a taste of sth. [3-lit A]
ቀላል	light (*weight*), easy, low (*price*)	ቀሚስ	(*woman's*) dress
		ቁመት	height (*see* ቆመ)
በቀላሉ	easily	ቀረ	remain (behind), stay (away); be absent, missing; cease to be [2-lit² A]
ቀለም	ink, paint; colour		
ቀላቀለ	mix, blend, combine [4-lit C type]		
ቀለደ	joke, tease [3-lit B]	ሳይሆን ቀረ	it failed to happen (ሳ- & neg. impf. & ቀረ)
ቀልድ	joke, wit, humour		

ቢቀር	let alone	አቋረጠ	interrupt; cut across [at- & C type]
ሳይቀር	including, not forgetting		
ይቅር	forget it! never mind!	ቋርጥ	fixed, decided, firm
ይቅር አለ	forgive, pardon	ቋራጭ	in ቲኬት ቋራጭ ticket collector
ይቅርታ	forgiveness, apology; sorry!	ቀስ	slowly! carefully!
ቀርቶ	not only, not even	ቀስ በቀስ	little by little, slowly, gradually
h- በቀር	except for, other than, aside from		
h- በስተቀር	besides, except, apart from	ቀስ አለ	speak slowly, do sth. slowly [አለ verb]
አስቀረ	leave, leave out, keep out, keep back; deprive, prevent [as- stem]	ቄስ	priest
		ቆሻሻ	rubbish, trash, filth, litter
ቁርስ	breakfast	ቅቤ	butter
ቅርስ	remains; assets	ቀበሌ	locality, district, precinct; residents' association
ቀረቀረ	found (a town, etc.) [4-lit]		
ቆርቆር	tin, tin can; corrugated iron		
		ቀበረ	bury [3-lit A]
ቀረበ	approach, come close; be near [3-lit A]	መቃብር	grave, tomb
		ቀበሮ	jackal
		ቀበቶ	belt
ተቃረበ	draw near [tä- & C type]	ቀትር	noon, midday
		ቀና	be straight, straightforward [2-lit¹ A]
አቀረበ	offer, supply, propose; serve (food) [a- stem]		
		ተቃና	succeed, be successful, turn out well [tä- & C type]
አቃረበ	bring near [at- & C type]		
ቅርብ	near, close	አቀና	straighten [a- stem]
በቅርቡ	soon; recently		
አቀራቢያ	neighbourhood, vicinity	ቀና	straight, upright, honest
ቀረጠ	cut; decide [3-lit A]	ቅን	straightforward, sincere
ተቋረጠ	be interrupted, discontinued [tä- & C type]	ቀን	day, daytime
		በየቀኑ	every day, daily

ቀነሰ	decrease, reduce, diminish (trans.) [3-lit B]	ቀጠረ	hire, employ (*a worker*); make an appointment [3-lit A]
ቋንቋ	language		
ቀንድ	horn	ቀጠር	appointment
የአፍሪካ ቀንድ	the Horn of Africa	ቈጠረ	count; reckon, consider as [3-lit A]
ቆንጆ	beautiful, pretty		
ቀኝ	right (hand)	ቍጥር, ቊጥር	number
ቀዘቀዘ	be cold, cool; cool off [4-lit]	በ- ቍጥር	(*with a verb*) as often as, whenever
ቀዝቃዛ	cold, cool		
ቅዝቃዜ	cold, coolness, chill	አቈጣጠር	computing, reckoning, calculation
ቀይ	red		
ቈየ	wait, remain, stay (put) [2-lit² B]	እንደ አውሮፓ አቈጣጠር	(*date*) according to the European calendar (*abbreviated to* እ.አ.አ.)
አቈየ	keep s.o. waiting [a- stem]		
ቆዳ	skin, hide, leather		
ቀደመ	be in front, be first [3-lit A]	እንደ ኢትዮጵያ አቈጣጠር	(*date*) according to the Ethiopian calendar (*abbreviated to* እ.አ.አ.)
አስቀደመ	put sth. in front, do sth. first [as- stem]		
ቀደም	before, first(ly)	ቀጥታ	straight, direct
በቀደም	previously	በቀጥታ	directly, straight
ከዚህ ቀደም	before this, earlier	ቁጭ አለ	sit down [አለ verb]
ቀደም ብሎ	earlier, previously	ቀጭን	thin, narrow, lean (*sound*)
ቀድሞ	beforehand, earlier, first of all		
ቅዳሜ	Saturday	በ – B	
ቁጣ, ቊጣ	anger (*see* ተቈጣ)	በ-	in, on, at, with, by, through
ቀጠለ	continue, follow [3-lit B]	ባህል	culture, tradition, custom
ቀጥሎ	next, afterwards, then	ባሕር	sea, lake
ተቀጣጠለ	be attached to one another, be linked [tä- & redupl.]	ባሕር ዛፍ	eucalyptus
		ብሔር	nation
		ብሔረሰብ	nationality
		ብሔራዊ	national

በላ	eat, consume [2-lit¹ A]	ይበልጥ	more than (ከ-ይበልጥ)
አበላ	feed, give to eat [a- stem]	በለጠገ	be rich [4-lit] (see also በለጸገ)
በል	say! [imperative of አለ₂]	በለጨ	shine, glitter, flash [3-lit Y]
ገላ-	forms compound nouns denoting the person associated with the second element in the compound. (See lesson six)	በለጸገ	be rich, grow rich [4-lit]
		ገበለጸጋ	rich (also ገላጠጋ)
		ብልጸግና	wealth
		ቧምቧ	tap, water pipe, faucet
ገላሙያ	skilled person, expert	በራ	shine, be lit; become light [2-lit¹ A]
ገላቢት	owner, proprietor; husband, wife	አበራ	turn on the light, light up [a- stem]
ገልጋዥራ	companion	አገራ	clear up (weather) [a- & C type]
ገላዘ	rude, uncouth	ብርሃን	light
ገላገር	countryside; peasant	መብራት	lamp, light
ገላጸጋ	rich, rich person	በሬ	ox, bull
ገል	husband	በር	gate, door(way)
ብልህ	clever, smart	ቢራ	(European) beer
ብላሽ	damaged, spoiled, worthless (see also ተብላሽ)	ቢሮ	office, bureau
		ብር	silver, money, Ethiopian Dollar
ገላቢት	owner, proprietor; husband, wife	በረሃ	desert, wilderness, bush
ቢላዋ	knife	ብርሃን	light (see also በራ)
በልግ	small rainy season (April–May)	በረረ	fly [3-lit A]
ገላዘ	rude, uncouth, ill-mannered	አበረረ	chase away [at- & C type]
ገላገር	countryside; countryman, peasant	በረራ	flight
		ቦርሳ	wallet; briefcase
		በረቀ	lighten, thunder [3-lit A]
		መብረቅ	lightning
በለጠ	be more, excel, be better [3-lit A]	በርበሬ	Ethiopian red pepper spice
የበለጠ	more than; best; increasingly	በረታ	be strong, strict; try hard [3-lit X]

አበረታ	strengthen [a- stem]	ብቅ አለ	come into view, appear, pop in [አለ verb]
አበረታታ	encourage [at- & redupl.]	በቅሎ	mule
ብርቱ	strong, powerful, strict	በቆሎ	corn, maize
ብርታት	strength, severity	በቀር	except (see ቀሪ)
ብረት	iron, metal	ባቡር	train, locomotive
ብርቱካን	orange	የባቡር ጣቢያ	railway station
ባረከ	bless [3-lit C]	ቤት	house, home; room
በረከተ	be abundant, plentiful [4-lit]	ቤት ለንግዳ	welcome!
አበረከተ	increase; offer as a gift [a- stem]	ቤት መጻሕፍት	library
በረከት	blessing, gift, plenty	ቤት ሰብ	family, household (also ቤተሰብ)
በርካታ	numerous, copious, plentiful	ቤተ ክርስቲያን	church
		ቦታ	place
በረደ	cool down, grow cold [3-lit A]	በየቦታው	everywhere
		ባትሪ	flashlight, torch
በረዶ	hail, ice	ብች	only, merely; but
ብርድ	cold	ብቻውን	he alone, by himself [ብቻ & possessive pronoun & ን]
ብርድ ልብስ	blanket		
ብርጭቆ	(drinking) glass	ለብቻ	in private
በራፍ	doorway (see also በር)	ለብቻው	he alone, on his own, by himself [ለ- & ብቻ & possessive pronoun]
በስተ-	towards, in the direction of		
በሽታ	sickness, illness	ብቻኝ	alone, solitary, lonely
በሽተኛ	sick person, invalid, patient	ብቻኝነት	loneliness
በቃ	be enough, suffice; be capable, competent [2-lit¹ A]	ቡና	coffee
		ቡናማ	brown
		ባንክ	bank
በቃኝ	I've had enough	ቤንዚን	petrol, gasoline
አበቃ	make capable; bring to an end [a- stem]	ባኞ	bath, bathtub
		ባኞ ቤት	bathroom
		በዓል	holiday, festival (also pronounced ባል)
በቂ	sufficient, ample, enough		
		ብዕር	pen

በኩል	(*not used alone*) direction; respect	በግ	sheep
በ- በኩል	with regard to, as for; in the direction of	በጣም	very, very much, a lot
		ቢጫ	yellow
በበኩሉ	on his part, as for him [በበኩል & possessive pronoun]	**ተ – T**	
		ታሕሣስ	Tahsas (fourth month of the year: 10 December– 8 January)
በውነት	really, truly (*see* አውነት)		
በዛ	be (too) much, many; be numerous [2-lit¹ A]	ቶሎ	quickly, soon
		ቶሎ ቶሎ	fast, (very) quickly
		ትልቅ	big, great, large, grown up, senior
ቢበዛ	at the most		
አበዛ	increase, multiply (trans.); [a- stem]	ታላቅ	big, older, elder
		ትምሕርት	education, study, lesson (*see also* ተማረ)
ብዙ	much, many		
ብዙውን ጊዜ	most of the time, commonly		
		ተመለከተ	look, look at; consider, notice [4-lit tä- stem]
በብዙ	a lot, greatly, a great deal		
ብዛት	quantity, amount, large number	አመለከተ	show, indicate, observe [a- stem]
		ምልክት	indication, sign
አብዛኛ	bigger part, majority	ተማረ	study, learn [2-lit³ tä- stem]
አብዛኛው	especially, mostly	አስተማረ	teach [astä- stem]
አብዛኛውን ጊዜ	most of the time	ተማሪ	student, pupil
ባዶ	empty, bare, vacant, blank	ትምሕርት	education, study, lesson
ባዶ ቡና	black coffee	ትምሕርት ቤት	school
ብድር	loan (*see also* ተበደረ)	አስተማሪ	teacher
		ትምባሆ	tobacco
ቡድን	team, group	ቴምብር	postage stamp
ብድግ አለ	stand up (suddenly); rise [አለ verb]	ቲማቲም	tomato
		ተመቸ	be convenient, suitable [2-lit² B tä- stem]
በጁ	alright! OK!		
በጋ	dry season (*late September to early April*)	አመቸ	be comfortable, handy, opportune [a- stem]

አስመቸ	arrange, adjust; make sth. ready [as- stem]
ተመኘ	desire, wish, long for [2-lit² A tä-stem]
ምኞት	wish, desire
ተራ	turn, order, queue
ተራ ሰው	ordinary, common man
ተራ ነገር	routine matter
በተራ	in turn, in order
ተራራ	mountain
ትራስ	pillow, cushion
ቱሪስት	tourist
ተረተ	tell a story [3-lit B]
ተረት	story, fable
ታሪክ	history
ታሪካዊ	historical
ተረጐመ	translate, interpret [4-lit]
ተርጓሚ	translator, interpreter
ትርጓሜ	translation
ተረፈ	be left over, be extra, in excess [3-lit A]
በተረፈ	moreover
ከ- በተረፈ	besides, apart from, except for
አተረፈ	make a profit; preserve, save [a- stem]
ትርፍ	profit, gain, surplus
ትርፍ ጊዜ	spare time, leisure
ትራፊክ	traffic, traffic police
ተሰናዳ	be prepared, ready [3-lit X tä- & C type]
አሰናዳ	prepare, make ready [at- & C type]
ተስፋ	hope
ተስፋ አለው	hope [lit. 'have hope']
ተስፋ አደረገ	hope, promise [lit. 'make hope']
ተሻለ	get better, improve; be better, preferable [2-lit3 tä- stem]
ተሻለው	get better; prefer [impers.]
ተሻሻለ	be improved, improve (intrans.); [tä- & redupl.]
አሻሻለ	improve, make better [at- & redupl.]
ተሸከመ	carry [3-lit B tä-stem]
ሸክም	load, burden
ተሻገረ	cross, cross over [3-lit C tä- stem]
አሻገረ	take across [as- stem]
ባሻገር	beyond, across, on the other side of (ከ- ባሻገር)
ተቀመጠ	sit, sit down; settle, stay for a while [3-lit B tä- stem]
አስቀመጠ	have s.o. sit down; put down, put away [as- stem]
መቀመጫ	seat
ተቀበለ	receive, accept, welcome [3-lit B tä- stem]

አቀበለ	hand over, pass on [a- stem]	አስተኛ	put to bed, send to sleep [as- stem]
አስቀበለ	give back [as- stem]	መኝታ, መኜታ	bed, sleeping place
መቀበያ	reception (place)	መኜታ ቤት	bedroom
የስልክ መቀበያ	telephone receiver	ትእዛዝ	order, command
ተቈጣ	be angry [2-lit¹ A tä- stem]		(see also አዘዘ)
አስቈጣ	make angry [as- stem]	ተከለ	plant; pitch (a tent), fix in the ground [3-lit A]
ቍ·ጣ, ቍጣ	anger	አታክልት	garden, garden produce, vegetables
ተቃጠለ	burn, be on fire [3-lit C tä- stem]		
አቃጠለ	burn (trans.), set fire to [at- & C type]	አትክልት	vegetables
		ተኩል	and a half (in expressions of time or sums of money)
ተባለ	be said, called (see አለ₂)		
ተበላሸ	spoil, go bad, go wrong [3-lit Y tä- & C type]	ተከራየ	rent (take on hire), lease, hire (3-lit Y tä- & C type]
አበላሸ	spoil, ruin, damage [at- & C type]	አከራየ	rent out, let (at- & C type)
ተበደረ	borrow (money); [3-lit B tä- stem]	ኪራይ	rent, lease
		ተኰሰ	iron, press clothes; fire a gun; scorch [3-lit B]
አበደረ	lend (money); [a- stem]		
ብድር	loan, credit	ትኵስ, ትኩስ	hot, fresh (food, news)
ታች	below, lower part		
ከ- ታች	below, under	ትኵሳት	temperature, fever
ከ- በታች	below, under		
ታችኛ	lower	የትኵሳት ለመለኪያ	thermometer
ትንሽ	little, small	ትከሻ	shoulder
ታናሽ	younger	ቲኬት	ticket
ትንቢያ	forecasting	ተከተለ	follow [3-lit B tä- stem]
ትናንትና	yesterday		
ተናፈስ	go for a walk, take the air [3-lit C tä- stem]	ተከታተለ	pursue, follow in succession [tä- & redupl.]
		አስከተለ	give rise to, result in [as- stem]
ትንፋሽ	breath		
ተኛ	sleep, go to sleep; go to bed, lie down [2-lit¹ B]	ትክክል	straight, equal, accurate, correct

ተወ	leave, leave off, give up, stop [irreg. verb]	አስደሳች	pleasing, pleasant, enjoyable
ተዋሰ	borrow (an object, not money) [2-lit³ tä- stem]	ታዲያ	so then! well now!
		ታገለ	struggle, fight, wrestle [3-lit C]
አዋሰ	lend (an object, not money) [a- stem]	ትግል	struggle, effort, conflict
ተዋበ	be beautiful [2-lit³ tä- stem]	ተጓዘ	travel, go on a journey [2-lit³ tä- stem]
ውብ	beautiful, scenic	ጉዞ	journey, trip, voyage
ውበት	beauty, splendour	ተጫወተ	play; chat, converse [3-lit tä- & C type]
ትዝ አለው	remember, recall [አለ impers. verb]	አጫወተ	converse, keep s.o. company, amuse s.o. [at- & C type]
ትዝታ	remembrance memory, memoirs		
ተዝናና	relax, be carefree [2-lit¹ tä- & redupl.]	ጨዋታ	game, conversation
		ተጫዋች	player, performer
ተዘጋጀ	be ready, prepared [3-lit Y tä- & C type]	አጫዋች	entertainer; referee
አዘጋጀ	make ready, put in order [at- & C type]	ተፈጥሮ	natural state, nature (see ፈጠረ)
ዝግጁ	ready, prepared	ች – Č	
ዝግጅት	preparation, arrangement	ቻለ	be able, can; be able to speak a language [2-lit³]
ማዘጋጃቤት	municipality, city hall		
		ተቻለ	be possible [tä- stem]
ቲያትር	theatre, play, drama	አስቻለ	enable, make possible [as- stem]
ተደሰተ	enjoy o.s.; be glad [3-lit B tä- stem]		
አስደሰተ	make happy, please, amuse [as- stem]	ችሎታ	ability, skill
		ችር	good, generous, magnanimous
ደስታ	happiness, joy (see also ደስ አለው)	ችርታ	charity, generosity

ቸኩለ	hurry, be in a hurry, rush [3-lit B]	ኑር	life, livelihood (*see also* ኗሬ)
አስቸኩለ	hurry (trans.) [as- stem]	ነዋሪ, ኗሪ	inhabitant, resident
ቸኩላ	hurry, haste	ነርስ	nurse
በቸኩላ	in a hurry, hastily	ነሣ	take away, take [2-lit¹ A]
አስቸኳይ	urgent	እጅ ነሣ	greet, pay one's respects
ቸገረ	be in difficulty, in need [3-lit B]	ተነሣ	get up, rise; leave, set out, set off [tä- stem]
ቸገረው	be in trouble [impers.]	ከ- የተነሣ	as a result of
ተቸገረ	be in trouble, be bothered [tä- stem]	አነሣ	raise, lift up; remove, take away [a- stem]
አስቸገረ	cause trouble [as- stem]	ፎቶ አነሣ	take a photo
ቸግር	difficulty, problem, need, trouble	መነሻ	departure (*place or time*)
ቸገረኛ	needy, poor, afflicted	ነቃ	wake up, be awake [2-lit¹ A]
አስቸጋሪ	difficult	አነቃ	wake up (trans.) [a- stem]
ነ – N		ንቁ	awake, alert
ና	come! (irreg. imperative of መጣ)	ንቃት	vigilance, alertness
-ና	and (*also as an independent word እና, especially at the beginning of a sentence*)	ነበረ	was [simple past of አለ and of ነው]
		ንብረት	possessions, belongings
		ነካ	touch; harm [2-lit¹ A]
		ነከሰ	bite (*a person or a thing, but not food*), sting [3-lit A]
ነሐሴ	Nehasie (the twelfth month of the year: 6 August– 5 September)	ነው	is [irreg. verb]
		ነዳ	drive [2-lit¹ A]
		ነጅ, ነጇ	driver
ኗሬ	live, exist, dwell, be [2-lit⁵]	ነደደ	burn, catch fire [3-lit A]
አኗሬ	put, place, put aside [a- stem]	ተናደደ	get angry, mad [tä- & C type]

አናደደ	anger, irritate [**at-** & C type]
ንዴት	anger, fury
ነገ	tomorrow
ነጋ	dawn, become day [2-lit^1 A]
ንጋት	dawn, daybreak
ነገረ	tell, speak [3-lit A]
ተናገረ	speak, talk, converse [**tä-** & C type]
ተነጋገረ	speak to one another, discuss [**tä-** & redupl.]
አናገረ	address, talk to s.o. [**at-** & C type]
ነገር	word, thing, matter
ነገር ግን	but
ለነገሩ	by the way
ንግግር	speech, lecture
ነገደ	trade, do business [3-lit B]
ነጋዴ	merchant, businessman
ንግድ	business, commerce
ነጐድጓድ	thunder
ነጭ	white
ነጻ	be clean, pure [2-lit^1 A]
ንጹ	clean, pure, tidy
ነፃ	free, independent
ነፃ ወጣ	be free, freed, liberated
ነፃነት	freedom, liberation
ነፈሰ	blow (*wind*) [3-lit A]
ተናፈሰ	take the air (*see under* **ተ**)
ንፋስ, ነፋስ	wind
መንፈስ	spirit
መናፈሻ	park, place for taking the air
ናፍታ	diesel fuel

አ, ዐ – [vowel]

አ	in, on, at, to
አህ	eh?
እህል	grain, cereal(s)
እኅት	sister
አሁን	now
እሑድ	Sunday
አህጉር	continent
አለ	is, there is [irreg. verb]
አለው	he has [**አለ** & object pronoun]
አለ$_2$	say, tell [irreg. verb] (*see also lesson eleven*)
ተባለ	be said, called [2-lit^3 **tä-** stem]
ማለት	that is to say, namely, it means
አለ$_3$	without
አለዚያም	otherwise
አለመ	dream [3-lit A]
ሕልም, ሕልም	dream
ዓላማ	aim, objective, intent; flag
ሰንደቅ ዓላማ	flag
ዓለም	world
አለቀ	end, finish, be finished [3-lit A]
አለቃ	boss, superior
አለቀሰ	weep, cry [3-lit A **a-** stem]
ዕለት	day
አለዚያም	otherwise (*see also* **አለ**$_3$)

አልጋ	bed, couch (*the traditional Ethiopian type of bed*)	አማረው	feel like (doing sth.) [impers.]
		አምር	well, good
አልጫ	a stew made without *barbare* spice	አሳመረ	make beautiful, adorn [3-lit as- stem]
አለፈ	pass, pass by [3-lit A]	አምስት	five
ተላለፈ	be transmitted, passed on [tä- & redupl.]	አምስተኛ	fifth
		አመሰገነ	thank, praise [4-lit a- stem]
		ተመሰገነ	be praised, thanked [tä- stem]
አሳለፈ	let through; serve food [as- stem]	ምስጋና	praise, thanks, gratitude
አስተላለፈ	transmit, transfer, communicate [astä- & redupl.]		
		አምቢ አለ	refuse, say no [አለ verb]
አላፊ	transient; someone in charge (*see also* ጎላፊ)	ዓመት	year
		አሚቴ	Madam!
		አመነ	believe, trust [3-lit A]
አሳላፊ	waiter		
ማለፊያ	good, fine	ታመነ	be faithful, trustworthy [tä- stem]
አልፍ	ten thousand		
አምላክ	God		
አመለጠ	escape [3-lit A a- stem]	አሳመነ	persuade, convince [as- stem]
አመመ	hurt, be sore, ache [3-lit A]	እምነት	faith, belief, trust
		ታማኝ	faithful, loyal, trustworthy
አመመው	be ill, feel pain [impers.]		
ታመመ	fall ill, feel ill, be sick [tä- stem]	አምና	last year
		አመነታ	hesitate, [3-lit X a- stem]
አሳመመ	make ill, cause pain [as- stem]		
		አምፑል	light bulb
አስታመመ	nurse, take care of a sick person [astä- stem]	ኧረ	oh! really! why!
		አረሰ	plough, till the soil [3-lit A]
አመም, ሕመም	sickness		
እማማ	Mum! Mummy!	አርሻ	farm, farmland, farming
አማረ	look beautiful; be pleasant [irreg. verb]		
		አርሱ	he (*also* እሱ)
		አርሷ	she (*also* እሷ)
		አርሳስ	pencil

እርሳቸው	he, she (*respectful*) (*also* እሳቸው)	እስላም	Muslim (*also* ሙስሊም)
እርስዎ	you (*respectful*) (*also* እሳዎ)	እስላምና	Islam
		እስረ	tie, bind, imprison [3-lit A]
እርባ	forty		
ዓርብ	Friday	እስር ቤት	prison, jail
እራት	four	እስረኛ	prisoner
እራተኛ	fourth	እሥር	ten
እራት	supper, evening meal	እሥረኛ	tenth
		እሥራ	(*forms numbers 11 to 19:* እሥራ አንድ
ኤርትራ	Eritrea		11, *etc.*)
እረንዓዴ	green		
እራዊት	wild animal(s)	እሰብ	think, think of, reckon, plan, imagine [3-lit B]
እረጀ	grow old, wear out [3-lit Y]		
		እሳሰብ	remind, suggest [as- stem]
እርጅና	old age		
እርጊ	old; old man	እሳብ	thought, idea, plan
እርጊት	old woman	መታሰቢያ	souvenir, memorial
እርጎ	yogurt (*see also* ረጎ)		
		እሰት	lie, falsehood
እርግጥ	certain, sure, definite	እሰተኛ	liar
		እሳት	fire
በርግጥ	for certain, for sure, certainly	እስቲ	please!
		እስተርጓሚ	translator (*see* ተረጉመ)
እርግጠኛ	certain, sure, reliable		
		እስተዋለ	pay attention, observe [2-lit³ astä- stem]
እርጥብ	damp, wet (*see also* ረጠበ)		
		እስተዋይ	observant, attentive, prudent
እረፈ	rest, settle, land; die [3-lit A]		
እሳረፈ	bring to rest, land (trans.) [as- stem]	እስታወሰ	recall, remind [3-lit astä- stem]
ዕረፍት	rest, repose, vacation	ማስታወሻ	memorandum, note
ማረፊያ	place or time for resting	እስታወቀ	inform, announce (*see also* አወቀ)
ማረፊያ ቤት	waiting room		
የአይሮፕላን ማረፊያ	airport	እስተያየት	opinion, view (*see* also* አየ)
ዓሣ	fish		
እሱ, እሷ, እሳቸው	(*see* እርሱ, እርሷ, እርሳቸው)	እስተዳደር	administration, management

አስቸኳይ	urgent (see also ቸኩል)	አባይ₂	Blue Nile
		አብዮት	revolution
አስቸጋሪ	difficult (see also ቸገረ)	አብድ	mad, crazy
		አቶ	Mister
አሰኘ	name, designate; also forms the causative of አለ verbs [2-lit² as- stem]	አታክልት	garden (see also ተከለ)
		ኢትዮጵያ	Ethiopia
		ኢትዮጵያዊ	Ethiopian
		እኔ	I
አስከ	until, up to, as far as	አነሰ	be less, diminish; be too short [3-lit A]
አሺ	OK!		
አሸዋ	sand	አሳነሰ	reduce (trans.) [as- stem]
ዕቃ	thing(s), goods, baggage, furniture	አነስተኛ	little, unimportant, minimum
ዕቃ ቤት	storehouse, warehouse	አንሶላ	bed sheet
		እንስሳ	animal (usually domestic)
አበረ	join up, ally with [3-lit B]	እንቁላል	egg
አብሮ	together with	እንቅልፍ	sleep
ተጋበረ	be joined togther, be united [tä- & redupl.]	እንባ	tear(s)
		አንበሳ	lion
		አነበበ	read, recite [3-lit A a- stem]
አስተጋበረ	unite, combine [astä- & redupl.]	ተነበበ	be read, recited [tä- stem]
አበባ	flower		
አባባ	Dad! Daddy!	አንተ	you (masc. sg.)
አባት	father	እናት	mother
አቤት	response when one is called; also used when one asks for sth. to be repeated, rather like 'pardon?'	አንቺ	you (fem. sg.)
		እናንተ	you (plur.)
		እንካ	take it! here!
		እንኳ, እንኳን	even, not only . . . but also
		እነዚህ	these
አባክህ	please (masc.) (also አባክሽ, አባካችሁ, አባክም [አባክ- & 2nd pers. object pronoun]	እነዚያ	those
		አንድ	one
		አንድ ላይ	together
		አንድ አንድ	one by one, singly, one at a time
አባይ	liar, fake	አንዱ	one of them, somebody

አንዴ	once	አንግዳ	guest, stranger, visitor; strange
አንዲት	one (fem.)		
አንድነት	unity, unison	አንግዳቤት	living room
አንጻነድ	some, several	አንግዲህ	well then, in any case
አንጻነዴ	sometimes		
አንደኛ	first (one), one of	አንጨት	wood, timber; piece of wood
አንደ	as, like, according to, as, while, when; just as (on a verb)	እኛ	we
		እኮ	indeed, in fact, actually
አንደ	what! (exclamation of surprise)	አኳኋን	condition, state, style (see also ሁን)
አንዲህ	such, thus, so, like this		
		አከለ	be equal, be worth, amount to [3-lit A]
አንዲሁም	likewise		
አንደሆነ,አንደሆን	as for; if (following) – if not literally አንደ & ሁን	ተካከለ	be equal, equivalent, uniform, even [tä- & redupl.]
አንደምን	how?		
አንደምንም	somehow, anyhow	አስተካከለ	equalize, make uniform, straighten; cut hair [astä- & redupl.]
አንደበት	tongue		
አንዲታ	of course!		
አንዴት	how?		
አንዲያው	for no reason, for nothing, just, merely	አኩል	equal, even, uniform; half
		አኩል ቀን	noon
አንዲያውም	as a matter of fact, for that matter	አኩል ሌሊት	midnight
		በኩል	(see under በ)
አንደገና	again	ተኩል	(see under ተ)
አንጂ	but, on the contrary, rather; (emphasizes a preceding command)	አኩሊታ	half, equal part
		ትክክል	straight, even, accurate
		አካል	body
አንጃ	I don't know!	አከመ	treat (medically) [3-lit B]
አንጀራ	Ethiopian flat bread		
		አካባቢ	surrounding area, environs, outskirts (see also ከበበ)
አንግሊዝ	English (person)		
አንግሊዝኛ	English (language)		
አንግሊዛዊ	Englishman		
አንገት	neck	በ- አካባቢ	around

አዎ	yes	አሳዘነ	sadden, depress
አወራ	tell, report; gossip		[as- stem]
	[2-lit 1 A a- stem]	አዘን	sadness, sorrow
ወሬ	news, rumour,	አዘዘ	order, command
	talk, gossip		[3-lit A]
አውራ	male (of animals);	ታዛዥ	obedient, dutiful
	main, chief	ትዛዝ, ትእዛዝ	order, command
አውራ መንገድ	main road,	አዚያ	there
	highway	አየ	see, look at
አውሬ	wild animal		[2-lit² A]
አውርፓ,	Europe	ታየ	be seen, be visible;
አውርጳ			appear, seem
አወቀ	know, realize		[tä- stem]
	[3-lit A]	አሳየ	show [as- stem]
ተዋወቀ	be acquainted with	አስተያየት	view, opinion
	one another, be	አይ	oh! (exclamation
	friends [tä- &		of surprise,
	redupl.]		sadness); no!
አስታወቀ	inform, announce		(exclamation of
	[astä- stem]		contradiction –
አስተዋወቀ	introduce		also in this sense
	(people)		አይ)
	[astä- & redupl.]	አይ-	whilst (on verbs)
አዋቂ	intelligent,		each, every (on
	knowledgeable;		nouns)
	adult	አየር	air, climate,
አውቀት	knowledge		weather
ማስታወቂያ	notice,	የአየር ሁኔታ	weather conditions
	advertisement,	የአየር መልእክት	airmail, air letter
	information	የአየር መንገድ	airlines
አውቶቡስ	bus	አይሮፕላን	aircraft, aeroplane
አውነት	truth	አይብ	a kind of soft
አውነቱን ነው	he's right [አውነት		cheese, curd
	& possessive		cheese
	pronoun & -ን	ዓይን	eye
	& ነው]	ዓይነት	kind, sort, type
በአውነት,	truly, really	በያይነቱ	of various kinds,
በውነት			all-sorts
አውነተኛ	genuine, true	ዓይነተኛ	typical; important,
አዚህ	here		special
አዘነ	be sad, grieve	አይደለም	is not [irreg. verb;
	[3-lit A]		neg. of ነው]

ዕዳ	debt	አሳደግ	raise, rear, bring up [as- stem]
ዕድል	luck, fortune		
ዕድለኛ	lucky, fortunate	እድገት	growth, development, progress
ዕድሜ	age, life, lifetime		
አዳመጠ	listen to [3-lit at- & C type]	አደጋ	accident, danger
		አደገኛ	dangerous, unsafe
አደረ	spend the night, stay overnight; stay [3-lit A]	እጅ	hand, arm
		እጅ ነሣ	greet, pay one's respects
አሳደረ	put up for the night [as- stem]	የእጅ ሰዓት	wrist watch
		የእጅ ጓሪብ	glove
አስተዳደረ	administer, manage [astä- & redupl.]	የእጅ ቦርሳ	handbag
		እጅግ	sleeve
አያደር	gradually, bit by bit	እጅግ	very, much
		አገለገለ	serve, be in use, support [4-lit a- stem]
አዳራሽ	hall, auditorium (see also ደረሰ)		
		አገልግሎት	service, benefit
አድራሻ	address	አገልጋይ	servant, attendant
አደረገ	do, make, act; put on (shoes, glasses, hat, etc.) [3-lit A a- stem]; forms the causative of አለ verbs	አገር	country, district, land, region
		አገር ቤት	countryside
		እግር	foot, leg
		እግር ኳስ	football, soccer (also የእግር ኳስ)
ተደረገ	be done, made; happen [tä- stem]	የእግር ጣት	toe
		አገረኛ	pedestrian
አድርጎ	often used to carry an adverbial expression; can also mean as, like [gerundive]	አገኘ	find, acquire, get; meet [2-lit 2 A a- stem]
		ተገኘ	be found; be located; be present [tä- stem]
ድርጊት	action, event, happening, incident	ተገናኘ	meet one another [tä- & redupl.]
		አገናኘ	introduce people [at- & redupl.]
አደሰ	renew, renovate, repair [3-lit B]		
		አስገኘ	produce, result in [as- stem]
አዲስ	new		
አደባባይ	public place, square	መገናኛ	junction; rendezvous, meeting place
አደነ	hunting, hunt (intrans.) [3-lit A]		

እግዜር	God (see also እግዚአብሔር)	ግን ጻ ፍታ	in no time, instantly, at a stroke [i.e. ግንድ አፍታ]
እግዚአብሔር	God		
አጋጣሚ	chance, coincidence, opportunity	አፍንጫ	nose
በአጋጣሚ	by chance	ክ – K	
አጣ	lack; miss; not have [2-lit' A]	ከ-	from, out of; at, to (with verbs of going); than, rather than if, since (with simple past verb) unless (with neg. simple past verb)
አሳጣ	deprive [as- stem]		
እጦት	lack, want, need, shortage		
አጠረ	be short, too short [3-lit A]		
አጠረው	be short of sth. [impers.]	ኪሎ	kilo(gram)
		ኪሎ ሜትር	kilometre
አሳጠረ	shorten, cut short [as- stem]	ክሊኒክ	clinic
		ከለከለ	prevent, prohibit, forbid [4-lit]
አጭር	short		
አጠበ	wash, bathe (trans.) [3-lit A]	ክልክል	forbidden, prohibited
ታጠበ	be washed, get washed, wash o.s. [tä- stem]	ኮሌጅ	college
		ካሜራ	camera
		ክምር	heap, pile
መታጠቢያ	sink, bathtub	ኮራ	be proud, haughty; show off [2-lit' A]
መታጠቢያ ቤት	bathroom		
አጠገብ	near, beside		
በ- አጠገብ	near, beside, next to	ኩሩ, ኩሩ	proud, vain, haughty
አጭር	short (see also አጠረ)	ኩራት, ኩራት	pride, vanity
		ኩራተኛ	proud, vain, conceited
ባጭሩ	in short, briefly, to sum up	ከረሜላ	sweets, candy
አፍ	mouth; opening, edge	ከረምት	rainy season (late June–early September)
አፈር	earth, dirt, soil		
አፋር	shy, bashful, timid	ክራር	krar (Ethiopian six-stringed lyre or harp)
አፍረት	shame, disgrace, shyness		
አፍታ	moment	ክርስትና	Christianity; baptism

ክርስቲያን	Christian	ክብደት	weight, seriousness
ቤተ ክርስቲያን	church	ከፍ	fully, completely, absolutely never, not at all (*with neg. verb*)
ካርታ	map; playing card(s)		
ክርክር	argument, quarrel		
ኪራይ	rent, rental, lease (*see also* ተከራየ)	ከተውንም	on the contrary
		ከተማ	town, city
ካርድ	postcard, (identity) card	ክትፎ	*finely chopped raw meat with butter and spices*
ኪስ	pocket		
ኳስ	ball		
ከበረ	be well-to-do; be honoured [3-lit A]	ከን-	including, along with, together with
ተከበረ	be respected; be celebrated (*holiday*) [tä- stem]	ከንቱ	vain, futile, useless
		በከንቱ	in vain, to no avail, uselessly
አከበረ	respect; celebrate (*holiday*) [a- stem]	ኪኒን	pill
		ክንድ	arm, forearm
ክቡር	respected; Your Honour; dear (*in formal letter style*)	ከንፈር	lip
		ኮከብ	star
		ከፋ	be bad, wicked [2-lit¹ A]
ክቡራትና ክቡራን	ladies and gentlemen	ተከፋ	be sad, unhappy, discontent [tä- stem]
ከበሮ	drum		
ካፖርት	coat, overcoat	አከፋ	defame; worsen [a- stem]
ክብሪት	matches		
ከበበ	surround, crowd round [3-lit A]	አስከፋ	displease, offend [as- stem]
አካባቢ	surrounding area, environs	ክፉ	bad, evil, wicked, mean
ኩባያ	enamel mug	ክፉተኛ	troublemaker
ከበደ	be heavy; be respected; be serious [3-lit A]	ከፍ አለ	be high, lofty; be important [አለ verb]
ከበደው	it's hard for him [impers.]	ከፍ አደረገ	raise, elevate, lift
ከባድ	difficult, heavy, serious	ከፍታ	height, elevation
		ከፍተኛ	high, elevated, maximum

ከፈለ	divide, part; pay, pay out, repay [3-lit A]
ተካፈለ	share, participate [tä- & C type]
አካፈለ	distribute, share sth. out [at- & C type]
ከፋል	portion, share
(በከፋል	in part, partially)
ክፍል	part, room, class(room), division, section
ክፍለ ሀገር	region
ክፍለ ዘመን	century
ክፍያ	payment
ከፈተ	open, turn on (*light, radio, TV, etc.*) [3-lit A]
ክፍት	open
መክፈቻ	key, opener
ከፍታ	height, elevation (*see also* ከፍ አለ)
ወ – W	
ውሀ	water
ዋለ	spend the day [2-lit³]
አስተዋለ	pay attention (astä- stem) (*see also under* አ)
ወለቀ	be taken off, removed (*clothes*) [3-lit A]
አወለቀ	take off, remove (*clothes*) [a- stem]
ወለደ	have children [3-lit A]
ተወለደ	be born [tä- stem]
ወለድ	offspring, issue
ብር ወለድ	interest (*money*)
ውሀ ወለድ	waterborne
ወላጅ	parent
ልደት	birth, birthday (*see also under* ለ)
ልጅ	(*see also under* ለ)
ወምበር	chair, seat (*also* ወንበር)
ወሬ	news, talk (*see also* አወራ)
ወር	month
ወራት	season
ወራተኛ	seasonal
ወርቅ	gold
ወርቃማ	golden, gilded
ወረቀት	paper, document
ወረወረ	throw, hurl, fling [4-lit]
ወረደ	go down, come down, get off [3-lit A]
ተዋረደ	be humiliated [tä- & C type]
አወረደ	put down, take down, set down [a- stem]
አዋረደ	humiliate [at- & C type]
ውርደት	humiliation
ውርጭ	frost
ወሰነ	delimit, define; decide [3-lit B]
ወሰን	border, boundary, limit
ውሳኔ	decision
ወሰደ	take, take away [3-lit A]
ውስጥ	inside, interior
በ- ውስጥ	inside, within (*also* እ- ውስጥ, ውስጥ alone, *etc.*)
ዋሸ	tell a lie, lie [2-lit² C]

ውሸት	lie	ውድ	dear, expensive
ውሸታኛ	liar		(see also መደደ)
ውሻ	dog	መዲህ	hither, (to) here
መቅት	time, occasion	ከ- መዲህ	ever since
ውብ	beautiful (see also ተዋበ)	መደቀ	fall, fall down, fall off [3-lit A]
ውበት	beauty	መዴት	where? where to?
መተት	milk		(see also ዬት)
መታደC	soldier	መዲያ	there, shoo! scram!
ዋና	chief, main, principal	መዲያና መዲህ	hither and thither
ዋና መንገድ	main road, highway	መዲያው	suddenly, right away
ዋና ከተማ	capital city	መደደ	love, like [3-lit A]
ዋና	swimming (see ዋኝ)	መደ	willingly, deliberately [gerundive]
መንዝ	river, stream	ውድ	expensive, dear
መንድ	male, man, boy	መዳጅ	(close) friend, lover
መንድ ልጅ	boy, son		
መንድም	brother	መዳጅነት	friendship
መንጀል	crime	ተመዳጅ	beloved, popular, likeable
መንጀለኛ	criminal		
ዋኝ	swim [2-lit² C]	መጅብ	storm, rainstorm, gale
ዋና	swimming		
ዋናተኛ	swimmer	መጋ	stab, pierce, prick [2-lit¹ A]
መኪል	agent, representative	ተዋጋ	fight [tä- & C type]
ውክልና	agency	ውጋት	(sharp) pain
ዋዛ	joke (see also ተዋዛ)	ውጊያ	battle, attack
ዋዜማ	eve of a holiday	ዋጋ	price, cost, value
መይ	oh dear! (exclamation of sorrow)	መገን	side, team, family, race
መይም	or (also መይንም)	መገደ	quit, go away [3-lit B]
መይስ	or (in a question) (also መይንስ)	ተመገደ	avoid, refrain from [tä- stem]
መይን	grape, raisin	አስመገደ	eliminate, get rid of [as- stem]
መይን ጠጅ	wine		
መይዘሮ	Mrs		
መይዘሪት	Miss		
መደ	towards, to, into; approximately		

ወጣ	go out, come out, leave; go up; be published [2-lit[1] A]	ዝም አለ	be quiet, keep quiet, be silent [አለ verb]
ተወጣ	overcome (*difficulties*) [tä- stem]	ዝም ብሎ	quietly; just so, simply, for no reason
አወጣ	take out, bring out; spend (*money*); publish [a- stem]	ዝምታ	silence
		ዘመረ	sing [3-lit B]
		አዝማሪ	minstrel, singer
		ዝምብ	fly (*insect*)
ወጭ	costs, expense; output	ዘመን	time, period, date, era
ውጣ ውረድ	haggling, bargain; fuss, bother	ዘመናዊ	contemporary, modern
ወጣት	youth, young person	ዘመድ	relative; family; friend (*Addis Ababa slang*)
ውጤት	result, outcome	ዛሬ	today
ውጭ	outside, exterior (*see also under* ወጭ)	ዜሮ	zero
		ዞረ	go round, turn round [2-lit[5]] (*see also* ዘወረ)
መውጪ	exit, way out		
ወጥ	stew or sauce made with **barbare** spice	ተዞረ	be surrounded [tä- stem]
		አዞረ	turn (trans.) [a- stem]
ወጥ ቤት	kitchen, cook	ዙሪያ	surrounding area, environs
ዋጠ	swallow [2-lit[3]]		
ወጣት	youth, young person (*see also* ወጣ)	በ- ዙሪያ	around
		ዘረዘረ	list, itemize, explain [4-lit]
ውጤት	result, outcome (*see also* ወጣ)	ዝርዝር	list; small change
ወፍ	bird	በዝርዝር	one by one, in detail, thoroughly
ወፍራም	fat, thick		
		ዘረጋ	spread, spread out, stretch out [3-lit X]
ዘ – Z			
ዘለለ	jump, leap, skip [3-lit A]	ዝቅ አለ	be low, inferior; decline [አለ verb]
ዘላለም	forever (*also* ዘለዓለም)	ዝቅታ	lowering, decline
ለዘላለም, በዘላለም	forever, always	ዘብ	guard, sentry

ዘበኛ	guard, watchman, custodian	አዘገየ	delay, detain, postpone [a- stem]
ዜና	news, fame		
ዘነበ	rain [3-lit A]	ዝግጁ	ready (see also
ዝናብ	rain		ተዘጋጀ)
ዘንድ	near, beside (following a noun)	ዝግጅት	preparation, arrangement
	so that (following a simple impf. verb)	ዘጠና	ninety
		ዘጠኝ	nine
		ዘጠነኛ	ninth
		ዛፍ	tree
ዘንድር	this year	ዘፈነ	sing, dance and sing [3-lit A]
ዘነጋ	forget [3-lit X]		
ዘወረ	twist, turn, wind up (trans.) [3-lit B]	ዘፈን	song, dance
		ዘፋኝ	singer, dancer
ተዘዋወረ	move around; travel [tä- & redupl.]	የ – Y	
		የ-	of (possessive); who, what, which (relative prefix with past tense verbs)
ዘወር አለ	move away, keep out of the way [አለ verb]		
ዘወትር	normally, usually	የ	that (-ዪያ after prepositions)
ዘይት	oil		
ዘዴ	plan, method, scheme, trick	ያንን	= ያን (that & direct object suffix)
ዘጋ	shut, close [2-lit¹ A]	ያኛው	that one, that there
ዝግ	closed, shut	ያው	the same
መዝጊያ	door	ይህ	this (-ዪህ after prepositions)
ዜጋ	national, subject, citizen		
ዜግነት	nationality, citizenship (also ዜጋነት)	ይህንን	= ይሁን (this & direct object suffix)
		ይኽኛው	this one, this here
ዝግ አለ	be slow, slow down [አለ verb]	ይኽው	here you are!
		ይኽውም	namely, and so then
ዝግታ	slowness	ይኽውና	here it is!
በዝግታ	slowly	ያለ	without
ዘገየ	be late, delayed [3-lit Y]	የለም	there is not [irreg.]
		ይልቅ	more (see ላቀ)

የት, ዬት	where?
የትም	anywhere, any place, somewhere, wherever
የትኛው	which one?
ወዴት	where? where to? (= ወደ & የት)
የካቲት	Yekkatit (the sixth month of the year: 8 February–9 March)
ያዘ	hold, seize, catch, take; contain; arrest, capture; possess [2-lit³]
ይዞ	with, including, along with [gerundive]
ተያዘ	be taken, caught, occupied [tä- stem]
ተያያዘ	be linked, attached [tä- & redupl.]
አያያዘ	join together, attach, connect [at- & redupl.]
አስያዘ	have s.o. caught, arrested [as- stem]
ይዘት	content (of a book, etc.)
ይዞታ	content(s); control, dealings, business, occupation
ደ – D	
ድሃ	poor, poor person
ድህነት	poverty
ደኅና	well, good, safe, fine, alright
ደለደለ	level, even out, flatten, smooth [4-lit]
ደልዳላ	smooth, level, flat; well-off
ድልድይ	bridge
ደም	blood
የደም ሥር	vein, artery, blood vessel
ደመረ	add up (trans.); make a *demera* bonfire [3-lit B]
ተደመረ	be piled, added together [tä- & C type]
ደመራ	Meskel bonfire
ደመቀ	liven up; be crowded; be bright, attractive [3-lit A]
ደማቅ	bright, lively
ደምብ	rule, principle, procedure (*also* ደንብ)
በደምብ	properly, thoroughly, perfectly
ደምበኛ	regular, correct; customer
ደምበር	border, frontier, boundary
ድመት	cat
ደመና	cloud
ደመናማ	cloudy
ደሞዝ	salary, wages
ደሞዘኛ	salaried worker, wage earner
ድምፅ	voice, sound
ዱር	forest, wood
ቀድሞ	formerly, previously, long ago

በጹር ዘመን	in olden times	ተደረቀ	be dried, dried out [tä- stem]
ጹርውንም	all along, already		
ዳረ	give in marriage, marry (trans.) [2-lit³]	አደረቀ	dry (trans.) [a- stem]
ተዳረ	be married off [tä- stem]	ደረቅ	dry, stiff; plain, simple
ተዳC	marriage, married life	ድርቅ	drought
		ድርቀት	drought, dryness
ተዳC ያዘ	get married	ደረት	chest, bosom
ዳC	edge, shore, (river) bank	ዳርቻ	end, limit, edge
		ደርዘን	dozen
ዳCዳሩን	all along the edge, on all sides	ደረጀ	be organized; be well-off [3-lit Y]
በ-ዳC	on the edge of		
ዶC	chicken, hen	ተደረጀ	be ready, organized [tä- stem]
ደረሰ	arrive, reach; happen to, befall [3-lit A]		
		አደረጀ	build up, amass [a- stem]
አደረሰ	deliver, bring; result in [a- stem]	አደራጀ	arrange, put in order; make ready, equip [at- & C type]
አዳረሰ	spread (news); distribute, provide [at- & C type]		
		ድርጅ	ready, equipped; solid, firm
ደርሶ	unexpectedly, suddenly [gerundive]	ድርጅት	organization, firm, institute
ደርሶ መጣ	he arrived (somewhere) and came back, he's back (from where he went to)	ደረጃ	stairs, step(s)
		በ- ደረጃ	on the level of
		የኑሮ ደረጃ	standard of living
		ደርግ	committee, council; the central governing committee of the Marxist regime – 'the Dergue'
ድረስ	until, as far as [usually with prep. እስከ : እስከ – ድረስ]		
ደረሰኝ	receipt	ደስ አለው	be happy, pleased [አለ verb, impers.] (see also ተደሰተ)
አዳራሽ	hall, auditorium, reception room		
ደረቀ	dry (intrans.), be dry [3-lit A]	ደስ አሰኝ	please, gladden
		ደስታ	happiness, joy

በደስታ	happily, gladly, willingly	ደነቀ	be wonderful; astonish, surprise [3-lit A]
ደሴት	island		
ዱቄት	flour, powder		
ዳቦ	raised bread, *European-style* bread	ተደነቀ	be impressed, surprised [tä- stem]
ደባለቀ	mix (trans.); confuse [4-lit C type]	አደነቀ	admire [a- stem]
		አስደነቀ	astonish, amaze [as- stem]
ተደባለቀ	mix (intrans.) [tä- stem]	ድንቅ	something amazing; marvel, wonder
ተደበላለቀ	be intermingled, confused [tä- & redupl.]		
		አስደናቂ	amazing, wonderful
አደባለቀ	mix (trans.) [at- & C type]	ደንቆሮ	deaf, ignorant, stupid
ድብልቅ	mixture, compound	ድንች	potato
		ድንኳን	tent, marquee
ድብልቅልቅ	confusion, muddle, chaos	ድንገት	sudden; unforeseen, unexpected
ደብር	large church, main church	ለድንገት	accidentally
		በድንገት	suddenly, unexpectedly
ደቡብ	south		
ደብዳቤ	letter	ድንገተኛ	sudden, adrupt, unexpected
ዳነ	be saved, cured; heal (intrans.) [2-lit³]	ድንጋይ	rock, stone; battery
አዳነ	save, rescue; cure, heal (trans.) [a- stem]	ደነገጠ	be startled, alarmed, terrified [4-lit]
መድን	immunity, recovery (*also* መድኅን)	ተደናገጠ	be surprised; be scared [tä- & C type]
መዳኒት	medicine, drug (*also* መድኃኒት)	አደናገጠ	surprise, startle [at- & C type]
መድኃኒት ቤት	pharmacy, drugstore	አስደነገጠ	scare, frighten [as- stem]
ደነሰ	dance (European style) [3-lit B]	ድንጋጤ	fright, alarm, shock
ጨነሰ	dance	ዳኛ	judge

ደከመ	be tired, weak, feeble; endeavour [3-lit A]
ደከመው	he is tired, exhausted [impers.]
ተደከመ	be tired, exhausted [tä- stem]
አደከመ	tire, exhaust, weaken [a- stem]
ደካማ	tired, weary, exhausted; weak, frail
ድካም	weakness, tiredness; toil, effort
ዶክተር	doctor
ደወለ	ring, strike (clock); ring s.o. up, call [3-lit B]
ደወለለት	he rang him [& -ll- pronoun suffix]
ደወል	bell
ደጅ	(front) door, doorway; out of doors
ደጃፍ	doorway
ደጋ	highlands (land above 8000')
ደጋማ	highland
ደግ	good, kind
ደግነት	goodness, kindness
ደገመ	repeat, do again [3-lit A]
ደጋገመ	do over again [redupl.]
ደግሞ	furthermore, again, besides, moreover, too (also ደም)

ድጋሚ	again, a second time
ደፈረ	be bold; be disrespectful [3-lit A]
ተደፈረ	be humiliated, insulted [tä- stem]
ደፋር	bold, daring, fearless; insolent, rude
ድፍረት	boldness; impudence
ጀ, ዠ – J, Ž	
ጀመረ	begin, start (trans. & intrans.) [3-lit B]
ተጀመረ	begin (intrans.), be begun [tä- stem]
ከ- ጀምሮ	ever since, starting from
መጀመሪያ	beginning, start; first
ጀሮ	ear
ጀርባ	back (of the body)
ጀራት	tail
ጅብ	hyena
ጀበና	coffee pot, kettle
ጅንጀር	baboon
ጃንጥላ	umbrella, parasol (also as ጃን ጥላ)
ጃኬት	jacket
ጀግና	brave, courageous
ገ – G	
ጎህ	dawn, daybreak
ጎህ ቀደደ	dawn, become day
ጎላ	be visible, plain, clear [2-lit¹ A]
ጉልህ, ጎልህ	visible, evident, obvious, plain

በተለሁ	clearly, plainly, obviously
ገል	private, solitary
በገል	alone, in private
በየገል	individually
የገል	one's own; personal, private
ገለሰብ	individual (*person*)
ጉልበት	knee; strength, power
ጉልበተኛ	strong, powerful
ገለጸ	reveal, explain [3-lit A] (*also* ገለጠ)
ገልጽ	visible, evident, clear
በገልጽ	openly, clearly
ጉም	mist, fog
ጎማ	tyre; anything made of rubber
ጉምሩክ	customs, customs office
ገመሰ	divide into two, cut in half [3-lit B]
ግማሽ	half
አጋማሽ	halfway, middle
በ-አጋማሽ	in mid (something)
ገመተ	estimate, guess, assess [3-lit B]
ግምት	estimate, guess, approximation
በግምት	roughly, approximately, at a guess
ገመን	cabbage, greens
ገመድ	rope
ጋር, ጋራ	with
ከ-ጋር	with, togther with, in the company of (*also* ከ-ጋራ kä- gara)
በጋራ	jointly, in common
የጋራ	common, joint, mutual
ግራ	left, lefthand
ገረመ	be wonderful, amazing, extraordinary [3-lit A]
ገረመው	he is surprised [impers.]
ተገረመ	be surprised, astonished [tä- stem]
አስገረመ	surprise, astonish, amaze [as- stem]
ግሩም	amazing, marvellous, wonderful
ጉሮሮ	throat
ጉርሻ	tip, bonus; morsel
ጉረቤት, ጎረቤት	neighbour, neighbourhood
ገረድ	maid, female servant
ጉርፍ, ጎርፍ	flood, torrent, torrential rain
ጋሻ	shield
ጋሻዬ, ጋሺ	term of address to an older man
ጎሽ	bravo! well done!
ገባ	enter, go in, come in, arrive (*at a place*) [2-lit¹ A]
ገባው	he understands [impers.]
ተገባ	be proper, appropriate; ought to [tä- stem]
በሚገባ	rightly, appropriately

ተጋባ	get married, marry one another; transfer [tä- & C type]
ተግባባ	reach an agreement, understand one another [tä- & redupl.]
አገባ	bring in, put in; marry (trans.) [a- stem]
አግባባ	influence, talk s.o. into sth., persuade [a- & redupl.]
አስገባ	admit, let in; insert, introduce [as- stem]
ገቢ	income, import(s), receipts
ገብ	objective, aim, goal
ጋብቻ	marriage
ተገቢ	proper, appropriate, pertinent
መግቢያ	entrance
አገባብ, አግባብ	propriety, proper behaviour; meaning
ገበሬ	farmer, peasant
ግብርና	farming, agriculture
ግብር	tax
ገበታ	kind of table
ጋብቻ	marriage (see also under ገባ)
ጉብኝ	visit, tour [3-lit Y]
ጉብኚ	visitor, tourist
ጉብኝት	visit, tour
ጉባኤ	assembly, conference, council
ጋበዘ	invite, offer hospitality [3-lit C]
ግብዣ	reception, party, invitation
ጉብዝ, ጎበዝ	young man; smart, clever, brilliant; brave, strong
ገበየ	go shopping, go to market [3-lit Y]
ገበያ	market
ገበያተኛ	market goer, shopper
ጌታ	lord, master
ጌቶች	the boss [lit. 'masters']
ጌታዬ	Sir!
ገና	still, yet
ገና ነው	not yet, it's too soon
ገና አሁን	just now
ገና₂	Christmas
ግን	but
ነገር ግን	but, however
ጎን, ጎን	side
ጎን ለጎን	side by side
ከ- ጎን	beside, alongside
ግንቦት	Ginbot (the ninth month of the year: 9 May– 7 June)
ገንዘብ	money, currency, coin
ግንድ	log, tree trunk
ጉንፋን	cold, cough, influenza
ገዛ	buy; own, possess; rule, govern [2-lit¹ A]

ተገዛ	be bought; be ruled, be obedient, obey [tä- stem]	ገደለ	kill, murder [3-lit A]
ገዢ, ገዥ	buyer, purchaser; ruler, governor	ተጋደለ	fight, kill one another [tä- & C type]
ግዛት	territory, domain	ተጋዳይ	champion, campaigner
ተገዢ, ተገዥ	obedient, subject	ተጋድሎ	campaign, crusade
ጊዜ	time, occasion	ገደል	cliff, precipice, ravine, canyon
ለጊዜው	at the moment, for the time being	ጐደለ	be missing, lacking; be short of, deficient in sth. [3-lit A]
በጊዜ	on time; early		
በየጊዜው	occasionally; regularly, constantly		
በ- ጊዜ	when	አጐደለ	diminish, lessen, decrease (trans.) [a- stem]
ያን ጊዜ	at that time		
ጊዜያዊ	temporary, provisional, interim	ጐድለት	lack, deficiency; defect, flaw
		ገዳም	monastery
ጉዞ	journey, trip, voyage (see also ተጓዘ)	ጐዳና, ጎዳና	road, avenue
		ጓደኛ	friend, companion (see ጓድ)
ጋዜጣ	newspaper		
ጋዜጠኛ	journalist	ጕዳይ	affair, matter, business; less (in time expressions: ሶስት ሰዓት ሩብ ጕዳይ 'a quarter to three')
ጉድ	strange, extraordinary, unusual		
ጉድ አደረገ	deceive, cheat, swindle		
ወይ ጉድ	how strange! oh my goodness!	ገደደ	force, compel, oblige [3-lit A]
ግድ	necessity, obligation (see ገደደ)	ግድ	obligation, necessity
		ግድ የለም	never mind! it doesn't matter! don't worry!
ጐዳ	harm, injure, hurt [2-lit' A]		
ጉዳት	harm, injury, damage	በግድ	necessarily; without fail; hardly
ጓድ	comrade; gang, team, corps	ግዴታ	obligation, duty
ጓደኛ	friend, companion, associate	ግድግ	wall
		ጐጆ	small hut, shack

ሻሻ	desire, be eager for, yearn for [2-lit¹ C]	ጠላት	enemy
		ጠላ₂	*Ethiopian beer*
		ጣለ	throw, throw away, throw down; drop; abandon [2-lit³]
ጕጕት	desire, longing		
ጋገረ	bake bread [3-lit C]		
ገጠመ	fit, join together (intrans.); meet up with [3-lit A]	ጥላ	shadow, shade; umbrella, parasol (*see also* ዥ ንጥላ)
ተጋጠመ	meet, come together [tä- & C type]	ጥልቅ	deep, profound, thorough
		ጥልቀት	depth
አጋጠመ	fit, join together (trans.); connect, combine [at- & C type]	ጠላት	enemy (*see* ጠላ)
		ጠማ	be thirsty [2-lit¹ A, impers.]; ጠማው he is thirsty
አጋጠመው	encounter, experience, run across [impers.]	ጢም	beard
		ጣመ	taste pleasant, be tasty (trans.) [2-lit³]
ግጥሚያ	conflict, clash; game, bout		
አጋጣሚ	coincidence, chance; experience, incident	ጣመው	have a liking for sth. [impers.]
		ጣሚ	tasty, savoury
		ጥምቀት	Epiphany [*lit.* baptism]; *the feast celebrating the baptism of Christ in the Jordan, held on 11th T'ir*
ገጽ	surface; page		
ገፋ	push, shove; push aside, push out of the way; oppress, do wrong [2-lit¹ A]		
ግፍ	violence, atrocity, injustice, wrong		
		ጥምና	calm, quiet, tranquillity
ገፈኛ	heartless, cruel, unjust	ጠራ	call, call out, summon, invite [2-lit¹ A]
		ጥሪ	call, summons
ጠ – T'		ጠራ₂	be pure, clean; clear up (*weather*) [2-lit¹ A]
ጠላ	hate, detest, dislike [2-lit¹ A]		
ተጣላ	hate one another, quarrel, dispute [tä- & C type]	ጥሩ	good, fine, pure, clear, perfect

ጥሬ	raw (*food*), unripe, uncooked	መቅላይ	chief, supreme, paramount
ማሬ	try hard; toil, strive [2-lit³]	መቅላላ	overall; general
ተማማሬ	strive, endeavour [tä- & redupl.]	በመቅላላው	in general, generally, all in all
ጥሬት	labour, effort	መጠም	be beneficial, be of use [3-lit A]
ማሪ	roof	ተጠጠም	use; benefit from [tä- stem]
ጥር	T'ir (the fifth month of the year: 9 January– 7 February)	መጣሚ	useful, profitable
		ጥቅም	benefit, profit, use
መርሙዝ	bottle	ጥቅምት	T'iqimt (the second month of the year: 11 October– 9 November)
ጥርስ	tooth		
መሬገ	sweep, wipe, clean [3-lit A]		
መጥረጊያ	broom, sweeper, vacuum cleaner	ጥቁር	black
መሬመሬ	suspect, doubt [4-lit]	ጥቂት	few, some, a little
ተመራመሬ	distrust, have one's doubts about sth. [tä- & C type]	ለጥቂት ጊዜ	for a little while, for a moment
		በጥቂቱ	at least
አመራመሬ	be in doubt; hesitate, be uncertain [at- & C type]	መሰሰ	roast, fry, toast [3-lit A]
		ጥብስ	roasted or fried meat; toast
መርማሪ	suspicious, sceptical	መሰቀ	be tight, firm, secure [3-lit A]
መሬዼዛ	table	አመሰቀ	fasten, tighten; do sth. with all one's might [a- stem]
ጢስ	smoke (intrans.) [2-lit4] (*see also* ወሰ)		
		አጥብቆ	very much, greatly [gerundive]
አጢስ	smoke (trans.) [a- stem]	አማሰቀ	stick, glue (trans.) [at- & C type]
ጢስ	smoke	ጥብቅ	tight, strict, harsh, austere, stern, firm
መጠለለ	wrap, wrap up; sum up [4-lit]		
		መማጠበቅ	glue, paste
አመጣለለ	complete a job, conclude; sum up [at- & C type]	መሰቀ₂	look after; wait for; preserve, protect [3-lit B]

ጠባቂ	guardian, keeper, attendant
ጥበቃ	protection, conservation
ጠበቃ	lawyer, attorney
ጠበበ	be narrow [3-lit A]
ጠቢብ	wise *or* clever person, artisan, craftsman
ጠባብ	narrow, tight
ጥበብ	wisdom, craft, skill
ጠባይ	nature, character, conduct, manners, personality
ጣቢያ	station
ጡት	breast
ጣት	finger
የእግር ጣት	toe
ጤና	health
ጤናማ	healthy ·
ጠነቀቀ	be careful, take care [4-lit]
ተጠነቀቀ	be careful, cautious; watch out, beware [tä- stem]
አስጠነቀቀ	warn, admonish [as- stem]
ጠንቃቃ	cautious, careful, precise, meticulous
ጥንቃቄ	caution, care, carefulness
ጥናት	study, survey
ጥንት	ancient times, origin; long ago
ጥንተንጉም	originally, in the beginning
ጥንታዊ	ancient, archaic
ጠነከረ	be strong, tough, hard [4-lit]
ተጠናከረ	take heart [tä- & C type]
አጠነከረ	strengthen, harden, consolidate [a- stem]
አጠናከረ	encourage [at- & C type]
ጠንካራ	strong, tough, solid, hard
ጥዋት, ጧት	morning
ጣይ	sun (*see* ፀሐይ)
ጠየቀ	ask, request; pay a visit [3-lit B]
ጥያቄ	question, request
ጠራ	be clean, neat [2-lit¹ A] (*see also* ፀዳ s'ädda)
አጠራ	clean, launder [a- stem]
ጠጅ	honey-wine, (*tejj*)
ጠጉር	hair
ጠጉር አስተካካይ	hairdresser
ጠጣ	drink [2-lit¹ B]
አጠጣ	give to drink, buy s.o. a drink [a- stem]
መጠጥ	drink; strong drink, liquor
ጥጥ	cotton
ጦጣ	monkey (*vervet monkey*)
ጠጠተ	regret, be sorry for [3-lit B, impers.]
ጸጸት	regret, sorrow, repentance
ጡጫ	fist, blow with the fist, punch
ጠፋ	be lost, go missing, disappear; be extinguished; be destroyed [2-lit¹ A]

መፈበት	he lost it [መፈ & -bb- pronoun suffix]
መፍት ሂደ	he's run away, he's missing
አመፈ	destroy, ruin, spoil; deprive s.o. of sth.; put out, turn off (*a light, a motor, a radio, etc.*) [a- stem]
ጥፋት	offence, wrong, fault, disaster
ጥፋተኛ	guilty person, offender
አጥፊ	wicked, bad, destructive
መጥፎ	bad, ugly, wicked, evil
ጻፈ	write [2-lit³]
ጤፍ	*a fine grain used for making the best injera; ('teff')*
ጥፍር	finger nail
ጣፈጠ	taste sweet, taste good [3-lit C]
ጣፋጭ	tasty, sweet, delicious
ጨ – Č'	
ጮኸ	shout, cry out [2-lit⁵]
ጩኸት	shout, cry; noise
ጨለመ	get dark, grow dark [3-lit B]
ጨለማ	darkness, shadow
ጫማ	shoe
ጨመረ	add, increase; put sth. into sth. (*salt, sugar, etc.*) [3-lit B]
ጭማር	added, addition, including, included
በጭማር	in addition
ተጨማሪ	additional, extra, more
ጭማቂ	juice, residue
ጭራ	fly whisk (*made from horsehair*)
ጨረሰ	finish, complete; use up, wear out [3-lit B]
ጭራሽ	completely, entirely; not at all (*with a neg. verb*)
በጭራሽ	not at all (*with a neg. verb*)
መጨረሻ	end, finish, conclusion
ጨረቃ	moon
ጨርቅ	cloth, fabric, material, rag
ጨርቅ ጨርቅ	fabrics, textiles
ጨረታ	bid, tender
ጨሰ	smoke (intrans.) [2-lit⁵] (*also written and pronounced as* ጨሰ)
አጨሰ, አጤሰ	smoke (trans.) [a- stem]
ጢስ, ጭስ	smoke
ጭቃ	mud
ጭቃ ቤት	*traditional-style house plastered with mud and then whitewashed*
ጭቃም	muddy
ጨቀጨቀ	argue, pester [4-lit]

ᜃ.ቅᜃ.ቃ	quarrelsome, argumentative	ጸአ	be clean [2-lit¹ A] (also ጠአ)
ᙡቅᙡቅ	argument, dispute	ፀደይ	spring (end of March – end of June)
ᜃ.በጠ	grasp, grip, lay hold of sth. [3-lit B]		
		ጸጊረጸ	rose (also ጸጊ ረጸ)
ተᜃ.በጠ	shake hands [tä- & C type]	ጸጥ አለ	be calm, still, quiet [አለ verb]
መᜃ.በᜃ.	handle	ጸጥታ	calm, quiet, tranquillity, security
ᜃ.ነ	load; put sth. on top of sth. [2-lit³]		
ᙡነት	load, burden, freight	ጸጸተ	regret [3-lit B] (see ጠጠተ)
የᙡነት መኪና	lorry, truck	ጸፈ	write [2-lit³] (also ጠፈ)
ᜃ.ካ	forest, jungle		
ᜃ.ው	salt		
ᜃ.ዋታ	game; conversation (see also ተᜃ.ወተ)	ፈ – F	
		ፈላ	boil (intrans.) [2-lit¹ A]
ᙡጋግ	fog, haze, mist	አፈላ	boil (trans.) [a- stem]
ጸ – P'		ፈልም	film, movie
ጸጉᜆን, ጳጉᜆን	P'agumen (the thirteenth month of the year: 5–10 September) (also ጳጉᜃ)	ፈለገ	want, look for, seek [3-lit B]
		አስፈለገ	be necessary [as- stem]; need [impers.]
ጸጸስ	bishop	ፍላጋ	search, quest; track, trace
ጸ, ፀ – S'		ፍላጎት	need, demand, will, wish
ፀሐይ	sun	አስፈላጊ	necessary
ፀሐያማ	sunny	ፈራ	fear, be afraid, be scared [2-lit¹ A]
ጸሐፈ	secretary, clerk		
ጽሑፍ	written document; newspaper article	አስፈራ	frighten, scare [as- stem]
ጽሕፈት ቤት	office	ፈሪ	fearful, timid, cowardly
የጽሕፈት መኪና	typewriter		
መጽሐፍ	book	ፍራት	fear
ጸመ	fast [3-lit⁵] (also ጠመ)	ፍሬ	fruit; product, result
ጾም	fast, fasting (also ጦም)	ፍሬፍሬ	(all kinds of) fruit

ፈረመ	sign (*a document*) [3-lit B]
ፊርማ	signature
ፈረሰ	be ruined, destroyed [3-lit A]
አፈረሰ	destroy, demolish; cancel [a- stem]
ፍራሽ	ruins, remains
ፈረስ	horse
ፈረሰኛ	horseman, rider
ፈረንጅ	European, Westerner, (white) foreigner
ፈረደ	judge, pass judgment [3-lit A]
ፍርድ	judgment, justice
ፍርድ ቤት	law court, courthouse, courtroom
ፈሰሰ	spill, be spilled; flow, run (*liquids*) [3-lit A]
አፈሰሰ	spill (trans.), pour, pour out [a- stem]
ፋሲካ	Easter
ፎቅ	story, floor (*of a building*); multistoried building; upstairs
ፍቅር	love
ፈቀደ	allow, permit, authorize; want, intend [3-lit A]
ፈቃድ	permission, consent; licence, permit
ፈቃደኛ	willing, obliging; volunteer
ፋብሪካ	factory

ፈታ	undo, untie; release, free; divorce; guess [2-lit¹ A]
ተፈታ	be undone, untied; break up, adjourn; be released, freed [tä- stem]
መፍቻ	key (*solution*)
ፊት	face, front, surface
ፊት ለፊት	face to face, facing, opposite
በፊት	before, in front
ከ- በፊት	in front of, before
ወደፊት	in the future, later on (*also* ወደ ፊት)
ፈተነ	test, experiment, examine [3-lit B]
ፈተና	test, exam, experiment
ፎቶግራፍ	photograph
ፈንታ	share, portion, turn
በ- ፈንታ	in place of, instead of
ፍንጃል	porcelain tea *or* coffee cup
ፍየል	goat
ፊደል	letter, character (*of the Ethiopian syllabary*)
ፈጀ	burn, sting; destroy, wipe out; take, spend (*time*); use up, eat up [2-lit² A]
ተፈጀ	end, come to an end; be wiped out [tä- stem]

ተፋጀ	burn, be hot (*spicy food*) [tä- & C type]		accomplish [3-lit B]
ፍጅት	disaster, destruction; consumption (*of food, resources, etc.*)	ፈጽም	completely, utterly, absolutely; not at all (*with a neg. verb*)
ፎጣ	towel	ፍጹም	finished, completed; perfect, complete
ፈጠረ	create, make, invent, devise [3-lit A]	በፍጹም	certainly, absolutely, completely
ፍጥረት	creation, creature	**T – P**	
ተፈጥሮ	natural state, nature	ፖሊስ	police, policeman
ፈጠነ	hasten, hurry, go fast [3-lit A]	ፖለቲካ	politics
ፈጥኖ	quickly, promptly [gerundive]	ቴርሞስ	thermos flask
		ፕሮግራም	programme
ተፋጠነ	be in a hurry; accelerate [tä- & C type]	ፖስታ	mail, post
		ፖስታ ቤት	post office
		ፖስታ ሣጥን	post office box
ፍጥነት	hurry, speed, haste	ፖስተኛ	postman, mailman
በፍጥነት	fast, hurriedly, hastily, rapidly	ፓስፖርት	passport
		ፓኬት	pack, box (*cigarettes, matches, etc.*)
ፈጸመ	finish, conclude, complete; fulfill,	ፓፓያ	papaya

Grammatical index

The numbers refer to Lesson numbers rather than page numbers.
Amharic is in **bold** type and English is in *italics*.

Amharic index